250 Poems

A Portable Anthology

250

Poems

A Portable Anthology

Third Edition

Edited by

PETER SCHAKEL

Hope College

JACK RIDL

Hope College

Bedford/St. Martin's   BOSTON • NEW YORK

For Bedford/St. Martin's

Executive Editor: Stephen A. Scipione
Developmental Editor: Deja Ruddick
Associate Developmental Editor: Regina Tavani
Senior Production Editor: Karen S. Baart
Senior Production Supervisor: Jennifer L. Peterson
Marketing Manager: Stacey Propps
Copyeditor: Mary Lou Wilshaw-Watts
Permissions Manager: Kalina K. Ingham
Senior Art Director: Anna Palchik
Text Design: Sandra Rigney and Janis Owens
Cover Design: Marine Miller
Cover Photo: businesswoman holding big bunch of balloons © Howard
   Kingsnorth/Gettyimages
Composition: Jouve
Printing and Binding: RR Donnelley and Sons

President, Bedford/St. Martin's: Denise B. Wydra
Presidents, Macmillan Higher Education: Joan E. Feinberg and
   Tom Scotty
Editor in Chief: Karen S. Henry
Director of Marketing: Karen R. Soeltz
Production Director: Susan W. Brown

Manufactured in the United States of America.

8 7 6 5
f e d c

For information, write: Bedford/St. Martin's, 75 Arlington Street, Boston, MA 02116   (617-399-4000)

ISBN 978–1–4576–3692–9

Acknowledgments

Acknowledgments and copyrights are continued at the back of the book on pages 410–20, which constitute an extension of the copyright page. It is a violation of the law to reproduce these selections by any means whatsoever without the written permission of the copyright holder.

Preface for Instructors

250 Poems: A Portable Anthology is a compact, inexpensive collection of poems—classic and contemporary—that is rewarding to teach and enjoyable to read. In preparing this volume, we sought to include many canonical poets along with poets of the past fifty years who have received considerable critical attention. We also present some poets who deserve such attention but who have been by and large undervalued, as well as recent poets we think will receive critical recognition in the future. We recognize, of course, that prognostication in any art is hazardous and realize that we have, reluctantly but necessarily, left out many poets worthy of inclusion. We tried to represent a wide variety of poetic strategies and forms in order to illustrate the diversity of approaches to the art. And we chose a range of poems that reveals the impact of ethnic diversity on poetry written in English.

The poems are arranged chronologically by birth date of the authors, to guide readers toward a sense of the historical development of poetry in English and the influence of earlier poets and poems on later ones. The dates given below the poems indicate earliest publication in a book, preceded in some cases by the probable date of composition, in *italics*, where that information seems useful. We have kept the apparatus in the book to a minimum. Glosses are provided for vocabulary that cannot be found readily in a current dictionary. Annotation is added to clarify lines that draw on ideas requiring specialized knowledge or practices not readily familiar in our time or outside a specific culture. We include a brief introduction to reading poetry and, following the anthology, a guide to writing about poetry, biographical sketches for every poet in the book, a selective index of poems by form and type, groupings of poems by topic and theme, and a glossary of poetic terms.

NEW TO THE THIRD EDITION

A survey of instructors who taught with earlier editions of *250 Poems* revealed that the book has been assigned in introductory literature or poetry classes and in creative writing courses. Accordingly, we have tried to make the third edition more useful for students in both types of courses. For introductory courses we have increased the number of poems by certain canonical authors (including Emily Dickinson, Robert Frost, Langston Hughes, Sylvia Plath, and Seamus Heaney) to encourage a study of their work in some depth. For creative writing courses we have increased the number of poems by very contemporary writers, among them Atsuro Riley, Natasha Trethewey, Thom Satterlee, A. E. Stallings, Kevin Young, and Aracelis Girmay. We hope that our new essay "How to Write about a Poem—and Why" will be helpful to students in literature courses and that the introduction on how to read a poem and the appendices providing selective groupings of poems in the anthology will be helpful to students and instructors in both types of courses.

ACKNOWLEDGMENTS

For assistance in selecting and annotating poets presented in earlier editions of this anthology, we are indebted to Susan Atefat Peckham, Charles Huttar, Marla Lunderberg, Jesus Montaño, and William Pannapacker. For help with the third edition, we are grateful to Susanna Childress, Rhoda Janzen, Robert Kenagy, Jesus Montaño, Pablo Peschiera, and Heather Sellers. Sarah Baar, office manager for the Department of English at Hope College, helped us in numerous ways, with her usual graciousness, patience, and competence.

The following instructors offered helpful insight and suggestions in their reviews of the second edition: Kim Ballerini, Nassau Community College; Maryam Barrie, Washtenaw Community College; Earl Braggs, University of Tennessee at Chattanooga; Mary Bush, California State University, Los Angeles; Michael Calabrese, California State University, Los Angeles; Theresa Carilli, Purdue University Calumet; Jo Cochran, Klamath Community College; Moira Egan, John Cabot University; Sydney Elliott, Tillamook Bay Community College; James Esch, Widener University; Don Foran, The Evergreen State College; Laura Garrett, California State University, Los Angeles; John Gery, University of New Orleans; Elizabeth Grubgeld, Oklahoma State University; Stefan Haag, Langara College; Erich Hintze, College of Southern Maryland; Karen Holmberg, Oregon State University; Ronald Janssen, Hofstra University; Timothy Jones, University of St. Thomas; Damien Kortum, Laramie County Community College; Daniel Martinez, New Mexico Highlands University; Cate Marvin, College of Staten Island, CUNY; Ami Massengill, Nashville State Community College–Cookeville Campus; Adam McKible, John Jay College of Criminal Justice; Brent Newsom, Texas Tech University; Laurel Peterson, Norwalk Community College; Larry Poe, Fisher

College; Jill Rosser, Ohio University; Greg Schwipps, DePauw University; Edward Taylor, Buffalo State College; Cynthia VanSickle, McHenry County College; Adam Vines, The University of Alabama at Birmingham; and Josh Weinstein, Virginia Wesleyan College.

We would also like to thank the reviewers of the first edition for their helpful suggestions: Jessica Baldanzi, Indiana University; Earl S. Braggs, University of Tennessee, Chattanooga; Julie A. Chappell, Tarleton State University; Heather Comfort, James Madison University; Alex Dick, University of British Columbia; Paul T. Gallagher, Red Rocks Community College; John Meredith Hill, University of Scranton; Margaret E. Johnson, Idaho State University; Roberta Kramer, Nassau Community College; Jessica Lang, George Mason University; Cate Marvin, College of Staten Island, CUNY; Adam McKible, John Jay College of Criminal Justice; Erin O'Neal, Asheville-Buncombe Tech; Mary Soliday, City College of New York; Tom Zimmerman, Washtenaw Community College; and Aliesa Zoecklein, Santa Fe Community College.

We also want to express our appreciation to those at Bedford/St. Martin's who helped make the third edition possible, including Joan Feinberg, Denise Wydra, and Karen Henry. Steve Scipione offered wise counsel on how to shape the revision, and Deja Earley and Regina Tavani provided keen editorial insight as they helped to make that revision a reality. We thank Karen Baart for smoothly overseeing the production of the book, Mary Lou Wilshaw-Watts for her deft copyediting, and Margaret Gorenstein for clearing permissions.

Peter Schakel
Hope College
Jack Ridl
Hope College

ADDITIONAL RESOURCES

Visit *Re:Writing for Literature*   bedfordstmartins.com/rewritinglit

Supplement your print text with our free and open resources for literature (no codes required) and flexible premium content.

Get free online help for your students.

Re:Writing for Literature provides close reading help, reference materials, and support for working with sources.

- *VirtuaLit* tutorials for close reading (fiction, poetry, and drama)
- *AuthorLinks* and biographies for 800 authors

- Quizzes on poetic elements and hundreds of literary works
- Glossary of literary terms
- MLA-style student papers
- A sampler of author videos and additional literature
- Help for finding and citing sources, including access to Diana Hacker's *Research and Documentation* online

Get teaching ideas you can use today.

Are you looking for professional resources for teaching literature and writing? How about some help with planning classroom activities?

Teaching Central. We've gathered all of our print and online professional resources in one place. You'll find landmark reference works, sourcebooks on pedagogical issues, award-winning collections, and practical advice for the classroom—all free for instructors and available at **bedfordstmartins.com/teachingcentral**.

LitBits Blog: Ideas for Teaching Literature and Creative Writing. Our *LitBits* blog—hosted by a growing team of instructors, poets, novelists, and scholars—offers a fresh, regularly updated collection of ideas and assignments. You'll find simple ways to teach with new media, excite your students with activities, and join an ongoing conversation about teaching. Go to **bedfordstmartins.com/litbits/catalog** and **bedfordstmartins.com /litbits**.

Contents

250 Poems

A Portable Anthology

How to Read
a Poem—and Why

WHAT IS POETRY? We can usually tell someone what a novel, a play, or an essay is, but a poem can be baffling to explain. It can't be defined as writing that has meter: A lot of poetry, especially modern poetry, is non-metrical. It's not confined to writing that rhymes, for many poems do not use rhyme. And though most poetry is written in lines, prose poems don't have line divisions. Much poetry uses figurative language and is intense and emotionally complex—but the same is true of powerful prose. Whatever characteristics one tries to apply are neither typical of all poetry nor exclusive to poetry. So, what can we say that poetry is?

Those who we'd think ought to know—poets themselves—usually offer subjective responses: E. E. Cummings said that poetry is "dancing on your own grave." Ezra Pound purportedly stated it is "what poets write." Emily Dickinson describes poetry by its effect: "If I read a book [and] it makes my whole body so cold no fire ever can warm me, I know **THAT** is poetry. If I feel physically as if the top of my head were taken off, I know THAT is poetry. These are the only ways I know it. Is there any other way?"

Poetry arises when some deep impulse needs expression, and a poem is the most effective way to express it. The poem comes from a sense of urgency; it feels it must be "let out," shared, given, offered up. Poet Lucille Clifton once imagined, "Poetry began when somebody walked off a savanna or out of a cave and looked up at the sky with wonder and said, 'Ah-h-h!' *That* was the first poem. The urge toward 'Ah-h-h' is very human, it's in everybody." Every day, each of us feels that impulse, and we go "Ah-h-h!" or "Wow!" or "Oh no!" or simply sigh.

WHAT DOES POETRY DO? Maybe a better question than "What is poetry?" is "What does poetry do?" Poetry can do a lot of things.

• *Poetry makes connections.* We are all citizens in the culture of joy, pain, anger, love, fear, despair, and hope. Every one of us carries the same emotions as everyone else. Our situations, stories, and conflicts

1

may differ, but the news from the heart comes to each of us. And though we can't claim, "I know just how you feel," we can say with confidence, "I, too, have known that feeling."

• *Poetry gives voice.* In our day-to-day lives, voices come at us — from the Internet, news media, sales pitches, cell phones, movies — creating information overload. It often seems our own voices are not heard. Poetry offers a chance to speak, and to speak from the deepest part of our selves. Whether we write it or read it, poetry lets us feel liberated and in touch with our selves, and with others. The words are our words; the rhythms are our rhythms; the phrasings are ours; the sounds, tones, even the attempts to be artful are ours.

• *Poetry tells stories.* We read poems as we do other stories, to discover what happened and why. We read them to feel part of a larger world, where we encounter experiences we might otherwise never have and where we may discover that our experiences are shared by others.

• *Poetry describes.* Poems may describe a person, a relationship, a city street, a scene in nature, or almost anything else — using vivid, precise language that enables readers to conjure up clear images. Descriptive poetry enables us to see the world more precisely, more vividly. More often than not, a poem, like most great art, will give us new perceptions, fresh ways of seeing what is around us.

• *Poetry reflects.* Poetry sometimes puts readers right into a poet's head and heart, allowing us to share the poet's thoughts and feelings. Lyric poems often convey meditations triggered by an object, an idea, a person, a place, or an event. Such a poem can lead you to reconnect with something from your own life, moving you deeply and stimulating your own reflections.

• *Poetry remembers.* Poet William Butler Yeats called memory the wellspring of all poetry. In one sense, a poem can come from nowhere else but the past. Poems can be acts of preservation, saving forever what has gone by, what will never happen in quite the same way again.

• *Poetry expresses, embodies, and kindles emotions.* In reading poetry, you may find a companion, someone who also has felt what you have felt. Poems can touch you and connect you to what is best in you, whether it be outrage at injustice, sorrow for another's loss, or joy for another's good fortune.

• *Poetry celebrates language.* Poets live in language. Words are as real to them as a cup of coffee. They use language to draw us *past* the words themselves and into the mystery of experience. Yet poets also draw our attention *to* language by uncommon uses of words and phrases. Poets recognize that we spend much of our adult lives in what poet William

Stafford called "language events"—talking, reading, listening, writing things down, sending and receiving e-mail messages, and so on. Poets seek to create works that enrich and invigorate our experiences in and with language.

The essence of poetry—both what it is and what it does—is elusive. There is no one way to pin it down. Though that elusiveness may challenge and perplex us, it is also part of the appeal, part of the seductiveness, of poetry. We enter the world of a poem not really knowing what to expect. And whenever we enter something new—whether an unfamiliar city or a new job or a new relationship—we tend to feel uncertain. We have to look around. We have to be attentive. We have to be open and flexible. So it is with approaching poems. We simply have to take the plunge and start reading.

HOW DO YOU START? What is the best way to approach a poem? Here are some practical tips:

• *Look at the poem.* Start by simply looking at the poem, at its shape and the way it appears on the page. Poems can have a visual effect in addition to the effects created by language, sounds, and ideas. Poets use lines and stanzas but also the white space around and throughout a poem to invite a reader to enter. Linger for a moment to absorb the poem visually.

• *Read straight through.* Go straight through a poem the first time you read it. Just wander through, stopping for a bit along the way to wonder about or savor a word or a line. Then keep going. Get a feel for the poem without worrying about what you don't know or understand.

• *Pay attention to the title.* The title is usually not just the "name" of the poem. Rather, it often establishes the context for the poem's subject. It is often significant and revealing, though its significance may not be evident during the first reading. As you reread, it's worth reflecting on possible ways the title serves as an integral part of the poem, a role worth considering thoughtfully.

• *Slow down and reread.* Slow down as you reread so you can really hear the poem. Slow reading is a genuine pleasure. You shouldn't speed-read a poem any more than you would speed up your favorite song. Reread poems you like until the poem becomes a part of you. Focus on something different each time you read it.

• *Read aloud.* Most poems are meant to be heard as well as read silently. They need to be read aloud for their sounds and rhythms to be experienced fully. So, read the poem out loud at least once, or listen to someone else read it. Find a private place if you are worried that some-one will laugh at you.

• *Hear the "music."* Poems work with the musicality of language, blending the sounds and rhythms of words and word connections. Think of song lyrics set to music; in poetry, the poem makes its own music through the sounds and rhythms of language.

• *Open yourself to the poem.* Reading a poem differs from reading a newspaper or an e-mail message or a textbook. You usually read those to glean information or ideas, without entering the work imaginatively or emotionally. Though many poems also impart information and ideas, they usually do other things, too: They can lead us to feel intensely, to experience deeply, to perceive freshly, to understand experiences differ-ent from our own, and to affirm our own ideas, feelings, and experiences.

• *Focus on what catches your attention.* You might be drawn to a particular image that alters your usual perception of something. Maybe you like the sounds of the language or the way the rhythm shifts or re-mains regular in every line. Maybe the poem is funny or poignant or both. You don't have to have a masterly grasp of the whole poem to be able to notice things within it or to wonder about it or to begin talking about it. Paying passionate attention to what is actually in a poem is a wise start-ing place.

• *Watch the words.* At some point, start paying attention to the words—not what all the words of the poem taken together *mean*, but what the words *say*. Don't be overly eager to figure out a poem's "mean-ing." When you walk through the woods, you don't keep asking, "What does that tree mean?" or "What does that stone represent?" You accept them for what they are. So it should be with poetry: Look at the words, listen for what they say, and understand them as best you can. And if at first you don't understand all that much, don't worry—there are many things in a poem that you can experience even before you "get" it.

• *Follow the sentences.* The sentences in the poem may be broken up into lines, but they are still sentences. Get their sense correct. If the order of words in a sentence is inverted, it's important to pay attention to cues that identify what is subject and what is object. If a poet uses incom-plete sentences, or "fragments," try to figure out their purpose. After working out where sentences start and stop, focus on the lines: Begin noticing what the line divisions and line breaks add to the experience of the sentence.

• *Ask questions.* You can, of course, ask what a poem means, but you don't need to start with that question. Instead, try asking questions such as, What is happening in this poem? What is this poem doing? Why am

I drawn to that phrase or line? What is the poem connecting me with or challenging me about? How is the poem shifting my usual way of seeing things and leading me to reconsider the ways I've thought and felt?

• *Let the poem be itself.* You may have heard people talk about "interpreting a poem" or finding its "hidden meaning." But poetry isn't a foreign language that needs to be translated. Poets do not hide or bury meanings so that readers need special abilities or insights to get at them. So, begin by trusting the literal. If a poem says it's about stopping by the woods on a snowy evening, trust what it says. Some readers may argue that it's also about something more, and that may be true. A poem often has a number of implications, but remember that it can't mean just anything. If you enjoy it primarily as a richly descriptive poem whose beauty enhances your life, that in itself is a valuable way to read a poem.*

Former poet laureate Rita Dove has stated, "[I want] to help people see that poetry is not something above them or somehow distant; it's part of their very lives. I would like to remind people that we *have* an interior life—even if we don't talk about it because it's not expedient, because it's not cool, because it's potentially embarrassing—and without that interior life, we are shells, we are nothing." Approaching poems that way, as a part of ourselves, paradoxically opens us to a wider life. Critic and poet C. S. Lewis once wrote that when we read, we become a thousand others, and we are never more ourselves than when we do. Read poems to feel connected to the things that you are pulled away from, things you cherish and need in your life. Read them to recover what you have lost or to hold on to what you have. Read to be challenged. Read to be shaken. Read for fun. Read to see new things or to see things in new ways. Read to be comforted or understood.

Poems can be friends, best friends, honest and trustworthy friends. As critic Helen Vendler has put it, "The strangest experience in reading poetry, as in writing it, is to find yourself in it, to be yourself in it. . . . We sometimes speak of this as finding a 'favorite poet.' . . . The important thing is to feel companioned, as you go through life, by a host of poems." We hope that you find many such friends in this anthology and that it will lead you to feel at home in the vast world of poems that lies outside it.

---

*You can find additional ideas about and examples of how to read poems closely and attentively in "How to Write about a Poem—and Why" on pages 304–18.

. . .

GEOFFREY CHAUCER   [c. 1343–1400]

From The Canterbury Tales:
The General Prologue

Here biginneth the Book of the Tales of Caunterbury.

Whan° that Aprille with his shoures sote°	*When/its showers sweet*
The droghte°of Marche hath perced° to the rote,°	*drought/pierced/root*
And bathed every veyne° in swich licour,°	
Of which vertu engendred is the flour;°	
Whan Zephirus° eek° with his swete breeth	*also* 5
Inspired hath° in every holt° and heeth°	
The tendre croppes,° and the yonge sonne	*plants*
Hath in the Ram his halfe cours y-ronne,°	
And smale fowles° maken melodye,	*birds*
That slepen al the night with open yë,°	*eyes* 10
(So priketh hem nature° in hir corages°):	*their hearts*
Than longen folk to goon° on pilgrimages	*go*
(And palmers° for to seken straunge strondes°)	*pilgrims/shores*
To ferne halwes,° couthe° in sondry londes;°	*well-known/other lands*
And specially, from every shires ende	15
Of Engelond, to Caunterbury they wende,°	
The holy blisful martir° for to seke,°	*seek*
That hem° hath holpen,° whan that they were seke.°	*them/helped/sick*

[c. 1390]

3. **veyne . . . licour:** Vein (of plants) in such moisture.
4. **Of . . . flour:** By which power the flower is conceived.
5. **Zephirus:** Zepherus, the west wind, associated with spring.
6. **Inspired . . . heath:** Hath breathed upon every grove and field.
7–8. **yonge . . . y-ronne:** The sun is young because it has just started on its annual journey, having passed the vernal equinox (the beginning of the year) and progressed halfway through Aries (the Ram), the first of the twelve zodiac signs.
11. **So . . . nature:** So Nature impels them.
14. **ferne halwes:** distant shrines.
16. **wende:** Journey, make their way.
17. **holy blisful martir:** The holy blessed martyr is Thomas à Becket, an archbishop who was murdered in Canterbury Cathedral in 1170 and canonized three years later. Canterbury had always been on the medieval pilgrimage route to Rome, but after Becket's death the cathedral itself became a destination for Christian pilgrims.

ANONYMOUS

Western Wind

Westron wynde° when wyll thow blow   *Zepherus, the spring wind*
the smalle° rayne downe can rayne   *fine, misty*
Chryst yf my love wer in my armys
and I yn my bed agayne

[*c. 1500*]

Western wind, when will thou blow,
The small rain down can rain?
Christ! if my love were in my arms,
And I in my bed again!

[modern spelling]

ANONYMOUS

Lord Randal

1

"O where ha' you been, Lord Randal, my son?
And where ha' you been, my handsome young man?"
"I ha' been at the greenwood; mother, mak my bed soon,
For I'm wearied wi' huntin', and fain wad° lie down."   *gladly would*

2

"And wha° met ye there, Lord Randal, my son?   *who*   5
And wha met you there, my handsome young man?"
"O I met wi' my true-love; mother, mak my bed soon,
For I'm wearied wi' huntin', and fain wad lie down."

3

"And what did she give you, Lord Randal, my son?
And what did she give you, my handsome young man?"   10
"Eels fried in a pan; mother, mak my bed soon,
For I'm wearied wi' huntin', and fain wad lie down."

4

"And wha gat your leavin's, Lord Randal, my son?
And wha gat your leavin's, my handsome young man?"
"My hawks and my hounds; mother, mak my bed soon,   15
For I'm wearied wi' huntin', and fain wad lie down."

5

"And what becam of them, Lord Randal, my son?
And what becam of them, my handsome young man?"
"They stretched their legs out and died; mother, mak my bed soon,
For I'm wearied wi' huntin', and fain wad lie down."   20

6

"O I fear you are poisoned, Lord Randal, my son!
I fear you are poisoned, my handsome young man!"
"O yes, I am poisoned; mother, mak my bed soon,
For I'm sick at the heart, and I fain wad lie down."

7

"What d' ye leave to your mother, Lord Randal, my son?   25
What d' ye leave to your mother, my handsome young man?"
"Four and twenty milk kye;° mother, mak my bed soon,   *cows*
For I'm sick at the heart, and I fain wad lie down."

8

"What d' ye leave to your sister, Lord Randal, my son?
What d' ye leave to your sister, my handsome young man?"   30
"My gold and my silver; mother, mak my bed soon,
For I'm sick at the heart, and I fain wad lie down."

9

"What d' ye leave to your brother, Lord Randal, my son?
What d' ye leave to your brother, my handsome young man?"
"My houses and my lands; mother, mak my bed soon,   35
For I'm sick at the heart, and I fain wad lie down."

10

"What d' ye leave to your true-love, Lord Randal, my son?
What d' ye leave to your true-love, my handsome young man?"
"I leave her hell and fire; mother, mak my bed soon,
For I'm sick at the heart, and I fain wad lie down."   40

[traditional ballad, pub. 1803]

SIR THOMAS WYATT   [1503–1542]

They flee from me

They flee from me, that sometime did me seek,
With naked foot stalking in my chamber.
I have seen them, gentle, tame, and meek,
That now are wild, and do not remember
That sometime they put themselves in danger   5
To take bread at my hand; and now they range,
Busily seeking with a continual change.

Thankèd be fortune it hath been otherwise,
Twenty times better; but once in special,
In thin array, after a pleasant guise,°   *manner of dress* 10
When her loose gown from her shoulders did fall,
And she me caught in her arms long and small,°   *slender*
Therewithall sweetly did me kiss
And softly said, "Dear heart,° how like you this?"

It was no dream, I lay broad waking.   15
But all is turned, thorough° my gentleness,   *through*
Into a strange fashion of forsaking;
And I have leave to go, of° her goodness,   *out of (motivated by)*
And she also to use newfangleness.
But since that I so kindly° am served,   20
I fain would know what she hath deserved.

[from an undated manuscript]

14. Dear heart (pun): Heart, and hart (deer).
20. kindly (pun): Graciously (ironic), and "in kind"; i.e., in a way typical of female nature.

QUEEN ELIZABETH I   [1533–1603]

When I was fair and young

When I was fair and young, and favor graced me,
Of many was I sought, their mistress for to be;
But I did scorn them all, and answered them therefore,
    "Go, go, go seek some otherwhere,
        Importune me no more!"   5

How many weeping eyes I made to pine with woe,
How many sighing hearts, I have no skill to show;
Yet I the prouder grew, and answered them therefore,
      "Go, go, go seek some otherwhere,
            Importune me no more!"   10

Then spake fair Venus' son,° that proud victorious boy,   *Cupid*
And said: "Fine dame, since that you be so coy,
I will so pluck your plumes that you shall say no more,
      'Go, go, go seek some otherwhere,
            Importune me no more!'"   15

When he had spake these words, such change grew in my breast
That neither night nor day since that, I could take any rest.
Then lo! I did repent that I had said before,
      "Go, go, go seek some otherwhere,
            Importune me no more!"   20

                                          [c. 1580s]

EDMUND SPENSER   [1552–1599]

One day I wrote her name upon the strand

One day I wrote her name upon the strand,
But came the waves and washèd it away:
Again I wrote it with a second hand,
But came the tide, and made my pains his prey.   5
"Vain man," said she, "that dost in vain assay,
A mortal thing so to immortalize,
For I myself shall like to this decay,
And eek° my name be wipèd out likewise."   *also*
"Not so," quod° I, "let baser things devise,   *quoth (said)*
To die in dust, but you shall live by fame: 10
My verse your virtues rare shall eternize,
And in the heavens write your glorious name.
Where whenas death shall all the world subdue,
Our love shall live, and later life renew."

                                          [1595]

SIR PHILIP SIDNEY   [1554–1586]

Loving in truth, and fain in verse
my love to show

Loving in truth, and fain° in verse my love to show,   *eager*
That the dear she might take some pleasure of my pain,
Pleasure might cause her read, reading might make her know,
Knowledge might pity win, and pity grace obtain,
   I sought fit words to paint the blackest face of woe: 5
Studying inventions fine, her wits to entertain,
Oft turning others' leaves, to see if thence would flow
Some fresh and fruitful showers upon my sunburned brain.
   But words came halting forth, wanting° Invention's stay;°
Invention, Nature's child, fled step-dame Study's blows,   10
And others' feet still seemed but strangers in my way.
Thus great with child to speak, and helpless in my throes,
   Biting my truant pen, beating myself for spite,
   "Fool," said my Muse to me, "look in thy heart and write."

[1582]

9. **wanting:** Lacking; **stay:** Support.

MICHAEL DRAYTON   [1563–1631]

Since there's no help,
come let us kiss and part

Since there's no help, come let us kiss and part;
Nay, I have done, you get no more of me,
And I am glad, yea glad with all my heart
That thus so cleanly I myself can free;
Shake hands forever, cancel all our vows,   5
And when we meet at any time again,
Be it not seen in either of our brows
That we one jot of former love retain.
Now at the last gasp of love's latest breath,
When, his pulse failing, passion speechless lies,   10

When faith is kneeling by his bed of death,
And innocence is closing up his eyes,
   Now if thou wouldst, when all have given him over,
   From death to life thou mightst him yet recover.

[1619]

CHRISTOPHER MARLOWE   [1564–1593]

The Passionate Shepherd to His Love

Come live with me and be my love,
And we will all the pleasures prove
That valleys, groves, hills, and fields,
Woods, or steepy mountain yields.

And we will sit upon the rocks,   5
Seeing the shepherds feed their flocks,
By shallow rivers, to whose falls
Melodious birds sing madrigals.

And I will make thee beds of roses
And a thousand fragrant posies,   10
A cap of flowers, and a kirtle
Embroidered all with leaves of myrtle.

A gown made of the finest wool
Which from our pretty lambs we pull,
Fair lined slippers for the cold,   15
With buckles of the purest gold.

A belt of straw and ivy buds,
With coral clasps and amber studs,
And if these pleasures may thee move,
Come live with me, and be my love.   20

The shepherd swains shall dance and sing
For thy delight each May morning.
If these delights thy mind may move,
Then live with me and be my love.

[1599]

WILLIAM SHAKESPEARE   [1564–1616]

Sonnet 18

Shall I compare thee to a summer's day?
Thou art more lovely and more temperate:
Rough winds do shake the darling buds of May,
And summer's lease° hath all too short a date;°   *allotted time/duration*
Sometimes too hot the eye of heaven shines,   5
And often is his gold complexion dimmed;
And every fair° from fair° sometimes declines,   *beautiful thing/beauty*
By chance or nature's changing course untrimmed;°   *stripped of its beauty*
But thy eternal summer shall not fade,
Nor lose possession of that fair thou ow'st;°   *beauty you own* 10
Nor shall death brag thou wand'rest in his shade,
When in eternal lines° to time thou grow'st:°
   So long as men can breathe, or eyes can see,
   So long lives this,° and this gives life to thee.   *this sonnet*

[1609]

12. **lines:** (Of poetry); **grow'st:** You are grafted to time.

WILLIAM SHAKESPEARE   [1564–1616]

Sonnet 73

That time of year thou mayst in me behold
When yellow leaves, or none, or few, do hang
Upon those boughs which shake against the cold,
Bare ruined choirs,° where late° the sweet birds sang.   *choir stalls/lately*
In me thou seest the twilight of such day   5
As after sunset fadeth in the west,
Which by and by black night doth take away,
Death's second self, that seals up all in rest.
In me thou seest the glowing of such fire
That on the ashes of his youth doth lie,   10
As the deathbed whereon it must expire,
Consumed with that which it was nourished by.
   This thou perceiv'st, which makes thy love more strong,
   To love that well which thou must leave ere long.

[1609]

WILLIAM SHAKESPEARE   [1564–1616]

Sonnet 116

Let me not to the marriage of true minds
Admit impediments. Love is not love
Which alters when it alteration finds,
Or bends with the remover to remove.
O, no, it is an ever-fixèd mark   5
That looks on tempests and is never shaken;
It is the star to every wandering bark,
Whose worth's unknown, although his height be taken.°   *is measured*
Love's not time's fool, though rosy lips and cheeks
Within his bending sickle's compass come;   10
Love alters not with his brief hours and weeks,
But bears it out even to the edge of doom.°   *Judgment Day*
    If this be error and upon me proved,
    I never writ, nor no man ever loved.

[1609]

WILLIAM SHAKESPEARE   [1564–1616]

Sonnet 130

My mistress' eyes are nothing like the sun;
Coral is far more red than her lips' red;
If snow be white, why then her breasts are dun;°   *dull grayish brown*
If hairs be wires, black wires grow on her head.
I have seen roses damasked,° red and white,   *variegated*   5
But no such roses see I in her cheeks;
And in some perfumes is there more delight
Than in the breath that from my mistress reeks.
I love to hear her speak, yet well I know
That music hath a far more pleasing sound.   10
I grant I never saw a goddess go;°   *walk*
My mistress, when she walks, treads on the ground.
    And yet, by heaven, I think my love as rare
    As any she° belied° with false compare.   *woman/misrepresented*

[1609]

JOHN DONNE   [1572–1631]

A Valediction: Forbidding Mourning

As virtuous men pass mildly away,
  And whisper to their souls to go,
Whilst some of their sad friends do say
  The breath goes now, and some say, No;

So let us melt, and make no noise,   5
  No tear-floods, nor sigh-tempests move;
'Twere profanation of our joys
  To tell the laity our love.

Moving of th' earth brings harms and fears,
  Men reckon what it did and meant;   10
But trepidation of the spheres,
  Though greater far, is innocent.°

Dull sublunary° lovers' love   *under the moon; hence, inconstant*
  (Whose soul is sense) cannot admit
Absence, because it doth remove   15
  Those things which elemented° it.   *composed*

But we, by a love so much refined
  That our selves know not what it is,
Inter-assurèd of the mind,
  Care less, eyes, lips, and hands to miss.   20

Our two souls therefore, which are one,
  Though I must go, endure not yet
A breach, but an expansion,
  Like gold to airy thinness beat.

If they be two, they are two so   25
  As stiff twin compasses° are two;   *drawing compasses*
Thy soul, the fixed foot, makes no show
  To move, but doth, if th' other do.

And though it in the center sit,
  Yet when the other far doth roam,   30
It leans and hearkens after it,
  And grows erect, as that comes home.

9–12. Moving . . . innocent: Earthquakes cause damage and were taken as portending further changes or dangers. Trepidation (an oscillating motion of the eighth or ninth sphere, in the Ptolemaic cosmological system) is greater than an earthquake, but not harmful or ominous.

Such wilt thou be to me, who must,
  Like th' other foot, obliquely run;
Thy firmness makes my circle just,   35
  And makes me end where I begun.

[1633]

JOHN DONNE   [1572–1631]

The Flea°

Mark but this flea, and mark in this,
How little that which thou deny'st me is;
Me it sucked first, and now sucks thee,
And in this flea, our two bloods mingled be;°
Confess it, this cannot be said°   *called* 5
A sin, or shame, or loss of maidenhead,°   *virginity*
  Yet this enjoys before it woo,°
  And pampered swells with one blood made of two,°
  And this, alas, is more than we would do.

Oh stay,° three lives in one flea spare,   10
Where we almost, nay more than married are.
This flea is you and I, and this
Our marriage bed, and marriage temple is;
Though parents grudge, and you, we are met,
And cloistered in these living walls of jet.°   15

The Flea: Fleas were used frequently in European erotic poems during the Renaissance, as a lover envies the liberties the insect takes with his lady.
4. two bloods mingled be: Renaissance medical theory held that blood was mingled during intercourse, the "little" act the lady is denying the speaker (l. 2).
7. enjoys before it woo: Takes liberties without wooing the lady.
8. swells with one blood made of two: The flea's swelling suggests pregnancy.
10. stay: Stop; refrain from killing the flea. "Die" and "kill" were Renaissance slang terms for orgasm (the sexual act was believed to reduce the length of a man's life).
15. jet: Black marble (describing the flea's body).

Though use° make you apt to kill me,   *habit*
Let not to this, self murder added be,
And sacrilege, three sins° in killing three.

Cruel and sudden, hast thou since
Purpled thy nail, in blood of innocence?   20
In what could this flea guilty be,
Except in that drop which it sucked from thee?
Yet thou triumph'st, and say'st that thou
Find'st not thyself, nor me the weaker now;
'Tis true, then learn how false, fears be;   25
Just so much honour, when thou yield'st to me,
Will waste, as this flea's death took life from thee.

[1633]

18. **three sins:** Murder (by denying him sexual gratification—l. 16), suicide, and sacrilege (destroying a "marriage temple").

JOHN DONNE   [1572–1631]

Death, be not proud

Death, be not proud, though some have callèd thee
Mighty and dreadful, for thou art not so;
For those whom thou think'st thou dost overthrow
Die not, poor Death, nor yet canst thou kill me.
From rest and sleep, which but thy pictures be,   5
Much pleasure; then from thee much more must flow,
And soonest our best men with thee do go,
Rest of their bones, and soul's delivery.
Thou art slave to fate, chance, kings, and desperate men,
And dost with poison, war, and sickness dwell,   10
And poppy° or charms can make us sleep as well   *opium*
And better than thy stroke; why swell'st° thou then?   *(with pride)*
One short sleep past, we wake eternally
And death shall be no more; Death, thou shalt die.

[1633]

BEN JONSON   [1572–1637]

On My First Son

Farewell, thou child of my right hand,° and joy;
My sin was too much hope of thee, loved boy:
Seven years thou'wert lent to me, and I thee pay,
Exacted by thy fate, on the just day.
O could I lose all father now! for why   5
Will man lament the state he should envy,
To have so soon 'scaped world's and flesh's rage,
And, if no other misery, yet age?
Rest in soft peace, and asked, say, "Here doth lie
Ben Jonson his best piece of poetry."   10
For whose sake henceforth all his° vows be such   *(the father's)*
As what he loves may never like° too much.

[1616]

1. **child . . . hand:** A literal translation of the Hebrew name "Benjamin." The boy, named for his father, was born in 1596 and died on his birthday ("the [exact] day"—that on which the loan came due) in 1603.
12. **like:** Archaic meaning "please."

LADY MARY WROTH   [c. 1587–c. 1651]

Love like a juggler comes to play his prize

Love° like a juggler comes to play his prize,°   *(Cupid)/perform well*
  And all minds draw his wonders to admire,
  To see how cunningly he, wanting eyes,°   *being blind*
  Can yet deceive the best sight of desire.
The wanton° child how he can feign° his fire   *naughty/fake*   5
  So prettily, as none sees his disguise!

How finely° do his tricks; while we fools hire   *skillfully*
  The badge and office of his tyrannies.°
For in the end such juggling he doth make,
  As he our hearts instead of eyes doth take;   10
  For men can only by their sleights abuse
The sight with nimble and delightful skill;
  But if he play, his gain is our lost will.
  Yet child-like we cannot his sports refuse.

[1621]

7–8. while . . . tyrannies: While we foolishly "buy" these external emblems and
ceremonies of tyrannical love.

ROBERT HERRICK   [1591–1674]

To the Virgins, to Make Much
of Time

Gather ye rosebuds while ye may,
  Old time is still a-flying;
And this same flower that smiles today
  Tomorrow will be dying.

The glorious lamp of heaven, the sun,   5
  The higher he's a-getting,
The sooner will his race be run,
  And nearer he's to setting.

That age is best which is the first,
  When youth and blood are warmer;   10
But being spent, the worse, and worst
  Times still succeed the former.

Then be not coy, but use your time,
  And while ye may, go marry;
For having lost but once your prime,   15
  You may forever tarry.

[1648]

GEORGE HERBERT   [1593–1633]

Easter-wings°

Lord, who createdst man in wealth and store,°
Though foolishly he lost the same,°
Decaying more and more
Till   he   became
Most   poor: 5
With   thee
O   let   me   rise
As   larks,   harmoniously,
And sing this day thy victories:
Then shall the fall further the flight in me.   10

My   tender   age   in   sorrow   did   begin:
And still with sicknesses and shame
Thou didst so punish sin,
That   I   became
Most   thin.   15
With   thee
Let   me   combine,
And   feel   thy   victory;
For, if I imp° my wing on thine,
Affliction shall advance the flight in me.   20

[1633]

Easter-wings: Originally the stanzas were printed sideways on facing pages, lines
1–10 on the left page, to be read first, then lines 11–20 on the right page.
1. store: Abundance.
2. lost the same: Through the Fall in the Garden of Eden. Early editions include
the words "this day" in line 18 (perhaps repeated by mistake from line 9); they do
not appear in the only surviving manuscript and are not required for the meter.
19. imp: A term from falconry—to graft additional feathers onto the wings of a
hawk to improve its flight.

GEORGE HERBERT   [1593–1633]

Redemption°

Having been tenant long to a rich lord,
  Not thriving, I resolvèd to be bold,
   And make a suit unto him, to afford°   *grant*
A new small-rented lease, and cancel th' old.

  In heaven at his manor I him sought;   5
   They told me there that he was lately gone
   About some land, which he had dearly bought
Long since on earth, to take possessiòn.

I straight returned, and knowing his great birth,
  Sought him accordingly in great resorts;°   10
   In cities, theaters, gardens, parks, and courts;
At length I heard a ragged° noise and mirth   *rough or discordant*

  Of thieves and murderers; there I him espied,
  Who straight, *Your suit is granted*, said, and died.

[1633]

Redemption: Herbert's allegorical sonnet retells the Christian story of the Incarnation and death of Jesus as the way of redemption, or salvation. The speaker in the poem is a tenant who requests that the landlord (God) redeem, or buy back, his old lease (his old, sinful life, from which he cannot save himself through adherence to the laws of the Old Testament) and replace it with a new lease (one in which salvation is granted through Jesus's redemptive death and God's grace and mercy, as emphasized in the New Testament).
10. resorts: Places much frequented or visited.

JOHN MILTON   [1608–1674]

When I consider how my light is spent

When I consider how my light is spent°
  Ere half my days, in this dark world and wide,
  And that one talent which is death to hide
Lodged with me useless, though my soul more bent

1. When . . . spent: Milton went blind in 1652. Lines 1–2 allude to Matthew 25:1–13; line 3, to Matthew 25:14–30; and line 11, to Matthew 11:30.

To serve therewith my Maker, and present   5
   My true account, lest he returning chide.
   "Doth God exact day-labor, light denied?"
   I fondly ask; but patience to prevent
That murmur, soon replies, "God doth not need
   Either man's work or his own gifts; who best   10
   Bear his mild yoke, they serve him best. His state
Is kingly. Thousands at his bidding speed
   And post o'er land and ocean without rest:
   They also serve who only stand and wait."

                                                    [*c. 1652;* 1673]

ANNE BRADSTREET   [c. 1612–1672]

Before the Birth of One of Her Children

All things within this fading world hath end,
Adversity doth still our joys attend;
No ties so strong, no friends so dear and sweet,
But with death's parting blow is sure to meet.
The sentence° past is most irrevocable,   5
A common thing, yet oh inevitable;
How soon, my dear,° death may my steps attend,
How soon't may be thy lot to lose thy friend;
We both are ignorant, yet love bids me
These farewell lines to recommend to thee,   10
That when that knot's untied° that made us one,
I may seem thine, who in effect am none.
And if I see not half my days that's due,°
What nature would, God grant to yours and you;
The many faults that well you know I have,   15
Let be interr'd in my oblivion's grave;°

5. sentence: According to Genesis 3, humankind incurred a death sentence because of the sin of Adam and Eve.
7. my dear: The poem is addressed to the poet's husband, as her "last words" in case she dies of complications in childbirth. Such deaths were common at that time.
11. knot's untied: The "marriage knot," untied by death.
13. half . . . due: If she should die before age thirty-five, half of the seventy years traditionally thought of as the allotted human life span (see Psalm 90.10).
15–16: faults . . . grave: That is, let her faults be forgotten, buried with her.

If any worth or virtue were in me,
Let that live freshly in thy memory,
And when thou feel'st no grief, as I no harms,
Yet love thy dead, who long lay in thine arms: 20
And when thy loss shall be repaid with gains,
Look to my little babes, my dear remains.
And if thou love thy self, or loved'st me,
These O protect from step-dame's injury.°
And if chance to thine eyes shall bring this verse,   25
With some sad sighs honor my absent Hearse;°   *corpse*
And kiss this paper for thy love's dear sake,
Who with salt tears this last farewell did take.

[1678]

24. **step-dame's injury:** Mistreatment of stepchildren was common.

ANDREW MARVELL   [1621–1678]

To His Coy Mistress°

   Had we but world enough, and time,
This coyness, lady, were no crime.
We would sit down, and think which way
To walk, and pass our long love's day.
Thou by the Indian Ganges' side   5
Shouldst rubies find; I by the tide
Of Humber would complain.° I would
Love you ten years before the Flood,
And you should, if you please, refuse
Till the conversion of the Jews.°   10
My vegetable° love should grow   *living and growing*
Vaster than empires, and more slow;

Coy: In the seventeenth century, "coy" could carry its older meaning, "shy," or the modern sense of "coquettish." "Mistress" then could still mean "a woman loved and courted by a man; a female sweetheart."
5–7. Indian Ganges', Humber: The Ganges River in India, with its distant, romantic associations, contrasts with the Humber River, running through Hull in northeast England, Marvell's hometown.
10. conversion . . . Jews: An occurrence foretold, in some traditions, as one of the concluding events of human history.

An hundred years should go to praise
Thine eyes, and on thy forehead gaze;
Two hundred to adore each breast,   15
But thirty thousand to the rest;
An age at least to every part,
And the last age should show your heart.
For, lady, you deserve this state,°   *dignity*
Nor would I love at lower rate.   20
   But at my back I always hear
Time's wingèd chariot hurrying near;
And yonder all before us lie
Deserts of vast eternity.
Thy beauty shall no more be found,   25
Nor, in thy marble vault, shall sound
My echoing song; then worms shall try
That long-preserved virginity,
And your quaint honor turn to dust,
And into ashes all my lust: 30
The grave's a fine and private place,
But none, I think, do there embrace.
   Now therefore, while the youthful hue
Sits on thy skin like morning dew,
And while thy willing soul transpires°   *breathes forth* 35
At every pore with instant fires,°   *urgent passion*
Now let us sport us while we may,
And now, like amorous birds of prey,
Rather at once our time devour
Than languish in his slow-chapped° power.   40
Let us roll all our strength and all
Our sweetness up into one ball,
And tear our pleasures with rough strife
Thorough° the iron gates of life;   *through*
Thus, though we cannot make our sun   45
Stand still,° yet we will make him run.

                                       [*c. 1650;* 1681]

---

40. slow-chapped: Slow-jawed, devouring slowly.
45–46. make our sun/Stand still: An allusion to Joshua 10:12. In answer to
Joshua's prayer, God made the sun stand still, to prolong the day and give the
Israelites more time to defeat the Amorites.

EDWARD TAYLOR   [c. 1642–1729]

Housewifery

Make me, O Lord, thy spinning wheel complete.°
Thy holy word my distaff make for me.
Make mine affections thy swift flyers neat,
   And make my soul thy holy spool to be.
   My conversation make to be thy reel,   5
   And reel the yarn thereon spun on thy wheel.

Make me thy loom then, knit therein this twine;
   And make thy holy spirit, Lord, wind quills.°   *the spools of a loom*
Then weave the web thyself. The yarn is fine.
   Thine ordinances make my fulling mills.   10
   Then dye the same in heavenly colors choice,
   All pinked° with varnished° flowers of paradise.   *ornamented/lustrous*

Then clothe therewith mine understanding, will,
   Affections, judgment, conscience, memory,
My words, and actions, that their shine may fill   15
   My ways with glory and thee glorify.
   Then mine apparel shall display before ye
   That I am clothed in holy robes for glory.

[*1682–1683;* 1939]

1. **spinning wheel complete:** In a spinning wheel, the distaff holds the raw wool or flax to be spun; the flyers twist and guide the thread; the thread is wound onto the spool as it is spun; and the reel receives the finished thread.

JONATHAN SWIFT   [1667–1745]

A Description of a City Shower°

   Careful observers may foretell the hour
(By sure prognostics°) when to dread a shower:

A Description of a City Shower: One of the earliest examples of the short-lived "town eclogue," a minor genre that humorously applies imagery and characteristics of pastoral poetry to urban settings. Swift later called the poem an imitation of Virgil's *Georgics*, poems describing rural life in Roman times.
2. **prognostics:** Omens or portents, forewarning events to come. The poem's frequent use of elevated diction to describe commonplace things is a feature of the mock-pastoral form.

While rain depends,° the pensive cat gives o'er   *impends*
Her frolics, and pursues her tail no more.
Returning home at night, you'll find the sink°   *sewer* 5
Strike your offended sense with double stink.
If you be wise, then go not far to dine;
You'll spend in coach hire more than save in wine.
A coming shower your shooting corns presage,
Old achès throb, your hollow tooth will rage.   10
Sauntering in coffeehouse is Dulman° seen;   *dull man*
He damns the climate and complains of spleen.°   *melancholy*
    Meanwhile the South,° rising with dabbled° wings,   *spattered*
A sable° cloud athwart° the welkin° flings,   *black/across/sky*
That swilled more liquor than it could contain,   15
And, like a drunkard, gives it up again.
Brisk Susan whips her linen from the rope,°   *clothesline*
While the first drizzling shower is borne aslope:°   *aslant*
Such is that sprinkling which some careless quean°   *hussy*
Flirts° on you from her mop, but not so clean: *flicks* 20
You fly, invoke the gods°; then turning, stop
To rail; she singing, still whirls on her mop.
Not yet the dust had shunned the unequal strife,°   *battle*
But, aided by the wind, fought still for life,
And wafted with its foe by violent gust,   25
'Twas doubtful which was rain and which was dust.
Ah! where must needy poet seek for aid,
When dust and rain at once his coat invade?
Sole coat, where dust cemented by the rain
Erects the nap,° and leaves a mingled stain.   30
    Now in contiguous° drops the flood comes down,   *nearly touching*
Threatening with deluge this devoted° town.   *doomed*
To shops in crowds the daggled° females fly,   *besmattered*
Pretend to cheapen° goods, but nothing buy.   *bargain for*

13. **South:** South wind.
21. **invoke the gods:** Call upon, or call to, the gods (here probably cursing rather
than praying).
30. **Erects the nap:** Causes the fibers to stand up and stiffen.

The Templar spruce,° while every spout's abroach,°   *law student/awash* 35
Stays till 'tis fair, yet seems to call a coach.
The tucked-up sempstress° walks with hasty strides,   *seamstress*
While streams run down her oiled umbrella's sides.
Here various kinds, by various fortunes led,
Commence acquaintance underneath a shed.   40
Triumphant Tories and desponding Whigs°
Forget their feuds, and join to save their wigs.
Boxed in a chair° the beau° impatient sits,   *sedan chair/fop or dandy*
While spouts run clattering o'er the roof by fits,
And ever and anon with frightful din   45
The leather sounds;° he trembles from within.
So when Troy chairmen bore the wooden steed,
Pregnant with Greeks impatient to be freed
(Those bully° Greeks, who, as the moderns do,   *rowdy*
Instead of paying chairmen, run them through),   50
Laocoön struck the outside with his spear,
And each imprisoned hero quaked for fear.°
    Now from all parts the swelling kennels° flow,   *gutters*
And bear their trophies with them as they go:
Filth of all hues and odors seem to tell   55
What street they sailed from, by their sight and smell.
They, as each torrent drives with rapid force,
From Smithfield or St. Pulchre's shape their course,
And in huge confluence joined at Snow Hill ridge,
Fall from the conduit prone° to Holborn Bridge.°   *down* 60

41. Triumphant . . . Whigs: Swift's political party, the Tories, defeated the Whigs
in a national election shortly before the poem was written.
46. leather sounds: The noise of the rain pelting the leather roof of the sedan chair.
47–52. So when . . . for fear: Swift humorously compares the huge Trojan horse,
filled with Greek soldiers being smuggled into Troy, to a sedan chair. The Trojan
priest Laocoön, who warned that the horse was a trick, struck the horse, frightening the soldiers hiding within it (Virgil, *Aeneid* 2.40–56).
55–60. Filth . . . Bridge: Swift describes quite accurately the course of London's
open sewage system, with rainwater carrying waste material of all kinds from
Smithfield Market and St. Sepulchre's Church to Fleet Ditch, which was further
polluted by garbage carried along a stream from Snow Hill. Holborn Bridge
spanned Fleet Ditch at Holborn Street.

Sweepings from butchers' stalls, dung, guts, and blood,
Drowned puppies, stinking sprats,° all drenched in mud,   *small sea fish*
Dead cats, and turnip tops, come tumbling down the flood.°

[1710]

61–63. Sweepings . . . flood: In addition to creating an effective ending, the concluding triplet and final alexandrine satirize the use of both by poets too lazy or careless to maintain regular heroic couplets.

ALEXANDER POPE   [1688–1744]

From An Essay on Criticism, Part 2°

But most by numbers° judge a poet's song,   *versification*
And smooth or rough, with them, is right or wrong.
In the bright Muse though thousand charms conspire,
Her voice is all these tuneful fools admire,   340
Who haunt Parnassus but to please their ear,
Not mend their minds; as some to church repair,
Not for the doctrine, but the music there.
These equal syllables° alone require,
Though oft the ear the open vowels tire,   345
While expletives° their feeble aid do join,
And ten low words oft creep in one dull line:
While they ring round the same unvaried chimes,
With sure returns of still expected rhymes;
Where'er you find "the cooling western breeze,"   350
In the next line, it "whispers through the trees";
If crystal streams "with pleasing murmurs creep,"
The reader's threatened (not in vain) with "sleep";

An Essay on Criticism: An Essay on Criticism is a verse epistle addressed to literary critics. In it Pope satirizes the pedantic judgments of inferior literary critics (as he does in lines 337–61, on critics who care only about the way a poem sounds and thus praise poets who produce rhyme and meter mechanically); he points out the characteristics of excellent poetry (ll. 362–83); and he offers advice to critics on how to critique literature sensibly and helpfully (ll. 384–93).
344–57. These . . . along: In alternating lines Pope describes, then illustrates satirically, the kinds of metrics or diction these critics advocate ("these . . . require"); **equal syllables:** Mechanically regular accents.
346. expletives: Unnecessary words added to give a line the number of syllables its meter requires, like *do* in this line.

Then, at the last and only couplet fraught
With some unmeaning thing they call a thought,   355
A needless Alexandrine° ends the song,
That, like a wounded snake, drags its slow length along.
Leave such to tune their own dull rhymes, and know
What's roundly smooth or languishingly slow;
And praise the easy vigor of a line   360
Where Denham's strength and Waller's sweetness join.°
True ease in writing comes from art, not chance,
As those move easiest who have learned to dance.
'Tis not enough no harshness gives offense,
The sound must seem an echo to the sense.°   365
Soft is the strain when Zephyr° gently blows,   *the West Wind*
And the smooth stream in smoother numbers flows;
But when loud surges lash the sounding shore,
The hoarse, rough verse should like the torrent roar.
When Ajax° strives some rock's vast weight to throw,   370
The line too labors, and the words move slow;
Not so, when swift Camilla° scours the plain,
Flies o'er the unbending corn, and skims along the main.
Hear how Timotheus'° varied lays surprise,
And bid alternate passions fall and rise!   375
While at each change the son of Libyan Jove°
Now burns with glory, and then melts with love;
Now his fierce eyes with sparkling fury glow,
Now sighs steal out, and tears begin to flow:
Persians and Greeks like turns of nature° found   380
And the world's victor stood subdued by sound!

356. **Alexandrine:** A metrical line with six iambic feet, illustrated in the following line.
361. **Denham's . . . join:** Combine the qualities attributed to two important shapers of the late-seventeenth-century heroic couplet: the "strength" (conciseness and emphasis on content) of Sir John Denham (1615–1669) and the "sweetness" (smoothness and musical qualities) of Edmund Waller (1606–1687).
365. **sound . . . sense:** Lines 366–83 provide examples of the precept that sound should echo sense in poetry.
370. **Ajax:** The rough hero in Homer's *Iliad* (12.378–86).
372. **Camilla:** The female warrior in Virgil's *Aeneid* (see especially 7.808ff).
374. **Timotheus':** A Theban musician in the court of Alexander the Great, whose music had powerful emotional effects. Lines 374–83 sum up the story told in John Dryden's ode "Alexander's Feast" (1697).
376. **Libyan Jove:** Alexander the Great.
380. **like turns of nature:** Similar alternations of feelings.

The power of music all our hearts allow,
And what Timotheus was, is Dryden° now.
  Avoid extremes; and shun the fault of such
Who still° are pleased too little or too much.   *always*   385
At every trifle scorn to take offense:
That always shows great pride, or little sense.
Those heads, as stomachs, are not sure the best,
Which nauseate all, and nothing can digest.
Yet let not each gay turn° thy rapture move;   390
For fools admire,° but men of sense approve:°
As things seem large which we through mists descry,
Dullness is ever apt to magnify.

[1711]

383. Dryden: John Dryden (1631–1700) was the dominant poet in England from
1660 until his death.
390. gay turn: Apt and pleasing turn of phrase.
391. admire: Marvel; **approve:** Commend thoughtfully as good.

THOMAS GRAY   [1716–1771]

Elegy Written in a Country Churchyard

The curfew° tolls the knell of parting day,   *evening bell*
  The lowing herd wind slowly o'er the lea,
The plowman homeward plods his weary way,
  And leaves the world to darkness and to me.

Now fades the glimmering landscape on the sight,   5
  And all the air a solemn stillness holds,
Save where the beetle wheels his droning flight,
  And drowsy tinklings lull the distant folds;

Save that from yonder ivy-mantled tower
  The moping owl does to the moon complain   10
Of such, as wandering near her secret bower,
  Molest her ancient solitary reign.

Beneath those rugged elms, that yew tree's shade,
  Where heaves the turf in many a moldering heap,
Each in his narrow cell forever laid,   15
  The rude forefathers° of the hamlet sleep.   *humble ancestors*

The breezy call of incense-breathing morn,
   The swallow twittering from the straw-built shed,
The cock's shrill clarion, or the echoing horn,°   *(of a hunter)*
   No more shall rouse them from their lowly bed.   20

For them no more the blazing hearth shall burn,
   Or busy housewife ply her evening care;
No children run to lisp their sire's return,
   Or climb his knees the envied kiss to share.

Oft did the harvest to their sickle yield,   25
   Their furrow oft the stubborn glebe° has broke;   *soil*
How jocund did they drive their team afield!
   How bowed the woods beneath their sturdy stroke!

Let not Ambition mock their useful toil,
   Their homely joys, and destiny obscure;   30
Nor Grandeur hear with a disdainful smile
   The short and simple annals of the poor.

The boast of heraldry,° the pomp of power,   *noble ancestry*
   And all that beauty, all that wealth e'er gave,
Awaits alike the inevitable hour.   35
   The paths of glory lead but to the grave.

Nor you, ye proud, impute to these the fault,
   If memory o'er their tomb no trophies° raise,   *memorials*
Where through the long-drawn aisle and fretted° vault   *ornamented*
   The pealing anthem swells the note of praise.   40

Can storied° urn or animated° bust   *decorated/lifelike*
   Back to its mansion call the fleeting breath?
Can Honor's voice provoke° the silent dust,   *call forth*
   Or Flattery soothe the dull cold ear of Death?

Perhaps in this neglected spot is laid   45
   Some heart once pregnant with celestial fire;
Hands that the rod of empire might have swayed,
   Or waked to ecstasy the living lyre.

But Knowledge to their eyes her ample page
   Rich with the spoils of time did ne'er unroll;   50
Chill Penury repressed their noble rage,
   And froze the genial current of the soul.

Full many a gem of purest ray serene,
   The dark unfathomed caves of ocean bear:
Full many a flower is born to blush unseen,   55
   And waste its sweetness on the desert air.

Some village Hampden,° that with dauntless breast
  The little tyrant of his fields withstood;
Some mute inglorious Milton here may rest,
  Some Cromwell° guiltless of his country's blood.   60

The applause of listening senates to command,
  The threats of pain and ruin to despise,
To scatter plenty o'er a smiling land,
  And read their history in a nation's eyes,

Their lot forbade: nor° circumscribed alone   *not* 65
  Their growing virtues, but their crimes confined;
Forbade to wade through slaughter to a throne,
  And shut the gates of mercy on mankind,

The struggling pangs of conscious truth to hide,
  To quench the blushes of ingenuous shame,   70
Or heap the shrine of Luxury and Pride
  With incense kindled at the Muse's flame.

Far from the madding crowd's ignoble strife,
  Their sober wishes never learned to stray;
Along the cool sequestered vale of life   75
  They kept the noiseless tenor of their way.

Yet even these bones from insult to protect
  Some frail memorial° still erected nigh,   *(simple tombstone)*
With uncouth rhymes and shapeless sculpture decked,
  Implores the passing tribute of a sigh.   80

Their name, their years, spelt by the unlettered Muse,
  The place of fame and elegy supply:
And many a holy text around she strews,
  That teach the rustic moralist to die.

For who to dumb Forgetfulness a prey,   85
  This pleasing anxious being e'er resigned,
Left the warm precincts of the cheerful day,
  Nor cast one longing lingering look behind?

On some fond breast the parting soul relies,
  Some pious drops° the closing eye requires;   *tears* 90
Even from the tomb the voice of Nature cries,
  Even in our ashes live their wonted fires.

57–60. Hampden, Cromwell: John Hampden (1594–1643) refused to pay a special tax imposed in 1636 and led a defense of the people's rights in Parliament. Oliver Cromwell (1599–1658) was a rebel leader in the English Civil War.

For thee,° who mindful of the unhonored dead   *(the poet himself)*
  Dost in these lines their artless tale relate;
If chance, by lonely contemplation led,   95
  Some kindred spirit shall inquire thy fate,

Haply° some hoary-headed swain° may say,   *perhaps/elderly shepherd*
  "Oft have we seen him° at the peep of dawn   *the poet*
Brushing with hasty steps the dews away
  To meet the sun upon the upland lawn.   100

"There at the foot of yonder nodding beech
  That wreathes its old fantastic roots so high,
His listless length at noontide would he stretch,
  And pore upon the brook that babbles by.

"Hard by yon wood, now smiling as in scorn,   105
  Muttering his wayward fancies he would rove,
Now drooping, woeful wan, like one forlorn,
  Or crazed with care, or crossed in hopeless love.

"One morn I missed him on the customed hill,
  Along the heath and near his favorite tree;
Another° came; nor yet beside the rill,   110
  Nor up the lawn, nor at the wood was he;   *(another day)*

"The next with dirges due in sad array
  Slow through the churchway path we saw him borne.
Approach and read (for thou canst read) the lay,   115
  Graved on the stone beneath yon aged thorn."

THE EPITAPH

Here rests his head upon the lap of Earth
  A youth to fortune and to Fame unknown.
Fair Science° frowned not on his humble birth,   *learning*
  And Melancholy marked him for her own.   120

Large was his bounty, and his soul sincere,
  Heaven did a recompense as largely send:
He gave to Misery all he had, a tear,
  He gained from Heaven ('twas all he wished) a friend.

No farther seek his merits to disclose,   125
  Or draw his frailties from their dread abode
(There they alike in trembling hope repose),
  The bosom of his Father and his God.

[1751]

CHRISTOPHER SMART   [1722–1771]

From Jubilate Agno°

For I will consider my Cat Jeoffry.
For he is the servant of the Living God, duly and daily serving him.
For at the first glance of the glory of God in the East he worships in
   his way.
For is this done by wreathing his body seven times round with elegant
   quickness.
For then he leaps up to catch the musk, which is the blessing of God
   upon his prayer.   5
For he rolls upon prank° to work it in.   *prankishly*
For having done duty and received blessing he begins to
   consider himself.
For this he performs in ten degrees.
For first he looks upon his forepaws to see if they are clean.
For secondly he kicks up behind to clear away there.   10
For thirdly he works it upon stretch with the forepaws extended.
For fourthly he sharpens his paws by wood.
For fifthly he washes himself.
For sixthly he rolls upon wash.
For seventhly he fleas himself, that he may not be interrupted upon
   the beat.°   15
For eighthly he rubs himself against a post.
For ninthly he looks up for his instructions.
For tenthly he goes in quest of food.
For having considered God and himself he will consider his neighbor.
For if he meets another cat he will kiss her in kindness.   20
For when he takes his prey he plays with it to give it a chance.
For one mouse in seven escapes by his dallying.
For when his day's work is done his business more properly begins.
For he keeps the Lord's watch in the night against the adversary.
For he counteracts the powers of darkness by his electrical skin and
   glaring eyes.   25
For he counteracts the Devil, who is death, by brisking about the life.

Jubilate Agno: "Rejoice in the Lamb" (Latin); i.e., in Jesus, the Lamb of God. The poem was written while Smart was confined for madness from 1759 to 1763. It is influenced by the form of Hebrew poetry, particularly the biblical psalms. The best-known section is that concerning his cat Jeoffry, his companion during his confinement.
15. that . . . beat: Not need to stop to scratch while on his daily rounds of hunting.

For in his morning orisons° he loves the sun and the sun loves him.
For he is of the tribe of Tiger.
For the Cherub Cat is a term of the Angel Tiger.°
For he has the subtlety and hissing of a serpent, which in goodness he
    suppresses.   30
For he will not do destruction if he is well-fed, neither will he spit
    without provocation.
For he purrs in thankfulness when God tells him he's a good Cat.
For he is an instrument for the children to learn benevolence upon.
For every house is incomplete without him, and a blessing is lacking
    in the spirit.
For the Lord commanded Moses concerning the cats at the departure
    of the Children of Israel from Egypt.   35
For every family had one cat at least in the bag.°
For the English Cats are the best in Europe.
For he is the cleanest in the use of his forepaws of any quadruped.
For the dexterity of his defense is an instance of the love of God to him
    exceedingly.
For he is the quickest to his mark of any creature.   40
For he is tenacious of his point.
For he is a mixture of gravity and waggery.
For he knows that God is his Savior.
For there is nothing sweeter than his peace when at rest.
For there is nothing brisker than his life when in motion.   45
For he is of the Lord's poor, and so indeed is he called by benevolence
    perpetually—Poor Jeoffry! poor Jeoffry! the rat has bit thy throat.
For I bless the name of the Lord Jesus that Jeoffry is better.
For the divine spirit comes about his body to sustain it in complete cat.
For his tongue is exceeding pure so that it has in purity what it
    wants° in music.   *lacks*
For he is docile and can learn certain things.   50
For he can sit up with gravity, which is patience upon approbation.
For he can fetch and carry, which is patience in employment.
For he can jump over a stick, which is patience upon proof positive.
For he can spraggle upon waggle° at the word of command.
For he can jump from an eminence into his master's bosom.   55

27. orisons: Prayers.
29. Cherub . . . Tiger: As a cherub is a small angel, so a cat is like a small tiger.
36. cat . . . bag: No cats are mentioned in the biblical account of the Exodus, but
Smart may have been aware that images of cats were among the Egyptian gods
and may be speculating that cats were among the jewelry of silver and gold the
Egyptians gave the Israelites as they left (Exodus 12:35–36).
54. spraggle upon waggle: Sprawl when his master waggles a finger.

For he can catch the cork and toss it again.
For he is hated by the hypocrite and miser.
For the former is afraid of detection.
For the latter refuses the charge.
For he camels his back to bear the first notion of business.   60
For he is good to think on, if a man would express himself neatly.
For he made a great figure in Egypt for his signal services.
For he killed the Ichneumon° rat, very pernicious by land.
For his ears are so acute that they sting again.
For from this proceeds the passing quickness of his attention.   65
For by stroking of him I have found out electricity.
For I perceived God's light about him both wax and fire.
For the electrical fire is the spiritual substance which God sends from
     heaven to sustain the bodies both of man and beast.
For God has blessed him in the variety of his movements.
For, though he cannot fly, he is an excellent clamberer.   70
For his motions upon the face of the earth are more than any other
     quadruped.
For he can tread to all the measures upon the music.
For he can swim for life.
For he can creep.

[c. 1760; 1939]

63. Ichneumon: Egyptian species of mongoose that somewhat resembles a large
rat. It is, however, regarded as beneficial and was domesticated by the ancient
Egyptians.

WILLIAM BLAKE   [1757–1827]

The Lamb

Little Lamb, who made thee?
  Dost thou know who made thee?
Gave thee life & bid thee feed,
By the stream & o'er the mead;
Gave thee clothing of delight,   5
Softest clothing wooly bright;
Gave thee such a tender voice,
Making all the vales rejoice!
  Little Lamb who made thee?
  Dost thou know who made thee?   10

Little Lamb I'll tell thee,
Little Lamb I'll tell thee!
He is callèd by thy name,
For he calls himself a Lamb:
He is meek & he is mild,   15
He became a little child:
I a child & thou a lamb,
We are callèd by his name.
   Little Lamb God bless thee.
   Little Lamb God bless thee.   20

[1789]

WILLIAM BLAKE   [1757–1827]

The Tyger

Tyger, Tyger, burning bright
In the forests of the night,
What immortal hand or eye
Could frame thy fearful symmetry?

In what distant deeps or skies   5
Burnt the fire of thine eyes?
On what wings dare he aspire?
What the hand, dare seize the fire?

And what shoulder, & what art,
Could twist the sinews of thy heart?   10
And when thy heart began to beat,
What dread hand? & what dread feet?

What the hammer? what the chain?
In what furnace was thy brain?
What the anvil? what dread grasp   15
Dare its deadly terrors clasp?

When the stars threw down their spears
And water'd heaven with their tears,
Did he smile his work to see?
Did he who made the Lamb make thee?   20

Tyger, Tyger, burning bright
In the forests of the night,
What immortal hand or eye
Dare frame thy fearful symmetry?

[1794]

WILLIAM BLAKE   [1757–1827]

A Poison Tree

I was angry with my friend:
I told my wrath, my wrath did end.
I was angry with my foe:
I told it not, my wrath did grow.

And I water'd it in fears,   5
Night & morning with my tears:
And I sunnéd it with smiles,
And with soft deceitful wiles.

And it grew both day and night,
Till it bore an apple bright.   10
And my foe beheld it shine,
And he knew that it was mine,

And into my garden stole,
When the night had veil'd the pole;°   *sky*
In the morning glad I see   15
My foe outstretched beneath the tree.

[1794]

ROBERT BURNS   [1759–1796]

A Red, Red Rose

O my luve's like a red, red rose,
    That's newly sprung in June;
O my luve's like the melodie
    That's sweetly played in tune.

As fair art thou, my bonnie lass,   5
   So deep in luve am I;
And I will luve thee still, my dear,
   Till a' the seas gang dry.

Till a' the seas gang dry, my dear,
   And the rocks melt wi' the sun: 10
O I will love thee still, my dear,
   While the sands o' life shall run.

And fare thee weel, my only luve,
   And fare thee weel awhile!
And I will come again, my luve,   15
   Though it were ten thousand mile.

[1796]

WILLIAM WORDSWORTH   [1770–1850]

Lines

Composed a Few Miles above Tintern Abbey°
on Revisiting the Banks of the Wye
During a Tour. July 13, 1798

Five years have passed; five summers, with the length
Of five long winters! and again I hear
These waters, rolling from their mountain-springs
With a soft inland murmur. Once again
Do I behold these steep and lofty cliffs,   5
That on a wild secluded scene impress
Thoughts of more deep seclusion; and connect
The landscape with the quiet of the sky.
The day is come when I again repose
Here, under this dark sycamore, and view   10
These plots of cottage ground, these orchard tufts,
Which at this season, with their unripe fruits,

Tintern Abbey: The ruins of a medieval abbey that Wordsworth had visited in
August 1793. Wordsworth says that he composed the poem in his head in four or
five hours as he walked from Tintern to Bristol in 1798, and then wrote it down
without revisions.

Are clad in one green hue, and lose themselves
'Mid groves and copses. Once again I see
These hedgerows, hardly hedgerows, little lines   15
Of sportive wood run wild; these pastoral farms,
Green to the very door; and wreaths of smoke
Sent up, in silence, from among the trees!
With some uncertain notice, as might seem
Of vagrant dwellers in the houseless woods,   20
Or of some Hermit's cave, where by his fire
The Hermit sits alone.

                        These beauteous forms,
Through a long absence, have not been to me
As is a landscape to a blind man's eye;
But oft, in lonely rooms, and 'mid the din   25
Of towns and cities, I have owed to them,
In hours of weariness, sensations sweet,
Felt in the blood, and felt along the heart;
And passing even into my purer mind,
With tranquil restoration—feelings too   30
Of unremembered pleasure; such, perhaps,
As have no slight or trivial influence
On that best portion of a good man's life,
His little, nameless, unremembered, acts
Of kindness and of love. Nor less, I trust,   35
To them I may have owed another gift,
Of aspect more sublime; that blessed mood,
In which the burthen of the mystery,
In which the heavy and the weary weight
Of all this unintelligible world,   40
Is lightened—that serene and blessed mood,
In which the affections gently lead us on—
Until, the breath of this corporeal frame
And even the motion of our human blood
Almost suspended, we are laid asleep   45
In body, and become a living soul;
While with an eye made quiet by the power
Of harmony, and the deep power of joy,
We see into the life of things.

                        If this
Be but a vain belief, yet, oh! how oft—   50
In darkness and amid the many shapes
Of joyless daylight; when the fretful stir

Unprofitable, and the fever of the world,
Have hung upon the beatings of my heart—
How oft, in spirit, have I turned to thee, 55
O sylvan° Wye! thou wanderer through the woods, *wooded*
How often has my spirit turned to thee!

And now, with gleams of half-extinguished thought,
With many recognitions dim and faint,
And somewhat of a sad perplexity, 60
The picture of the mind revives again;
While here I stand, not only with the sense
Of present pleasure, but with pleasing thoughts
That in this moment there is life and food
For future years. And so I dare to hope, 65
Though changed, no doubt, from what I was when first
I came among these hills; when like a roe
I bounded o'er the mountains, by the sides
Of the deep rivers, and the lonely streams,
Wherever nature led—more like a man 70
Flying from something that he dreads than one
Who sought the thing he loved. For nature then
(The coarser pleasures of my boyish days,
And their glad animal movements all gone by)
To me was all in all.—I cannot paint 75
What then I was. The sounding cataract
Haunted me like a passion; the tall rock,
The mountain, and the deep and gloomy wood,
Their colors and their forms, were then to me
An appetite; a feeling and a love, 80
That had no need of a remoter charm,
By thought supplied, nor any interest
Unborrowed from the eye.—That time is past,
And all its aching joys are now no more,
And all its dizzy raptures. Not for this 85
Faint° I, nor mourn nor murmur; other gifts *become discouraged*
Have followed; for such loss, I would believe,
Abundant recompense. For I have learned
To look on nature, not as in the hour
Of thoughtless youth; but hearing oftentimes 90
The still, sad music of humanity,
Nor harsh nor grating, though of ample power
To chasten and subdue. And I have felt
A presence that disturbs me with the joy

Of elevated thoughts; a sense sublime   95
Of something far more deeply interfused,
Whose dwelling is the light of setting suns,
And the round ocean and the living air,
And the blue sky, and in the mind of man:
A motion and a spirit, that impels   100
All thinking things, all objects of all thought,
And rolls through all things. Therefore am I still
A lover of the meadows and the woods,
And mountains; and of all that we behold
From this green earth; of all the mighty world   105
Of eye, and ear—both what they half create,
And what perceive; well pleased to recognize
In nature and the language of the sense
The anchor of my purest thoughts, the nurse,
The guide, the guardian of my heart, and soul   110
Of all my moral being.

                Nor perchance,
If I were not thus taught, should I the more
Suffer my genial spirits° to decay: *creative powers*
For thou art with me here upon the banks
Of this fair river; thou my dearest Friend,°   115
My dear, dear Friend; and in thy voice I catch
The language of my former heart, and read
My former pleasures in the shooting lights
Of thy wild eyes. Oh! yet a little while
May I behold in thee what I was once,   120
My dear, dear Sister! and this prayer I make,
Knowing that Nature never did betray
The heart that loved her; 'tis her privilege,
Through all the years of this our life, to lead
From joy to joy: for she can so inform   125
The mind that is within us, so impress
With quietness and beauty, and so feed
With lofty thoughts, that neither evil tongues,
Rash judgments, nor the sneers of selfish men,
Nor greetings where no kindness is, nor all   130
The dreary intercourse of daily life,
Shall e'er prevail against us, or disturb

115. Friend: Wordsworth's sister Dorothy, who is made to sound younger by more than the year and a half that separated them.

Our cheerful faith, that all which we behold
Is full of blessings. Therefore let the moon
Shine on thee in thy solitary walk;   135
And let the misty mountain winds be free
To blow against thee: and, in after years,
When these wild ecstasies shall be matured
Into a sober pleasure; when thy mind
Shall be a mansion for all lovely forms,   140
Thy memory be as a dwelling place
For all sweet sounds and harmonies; oh! then,
If solitude, or fear, or pain, or grief
Should be thy portion, with what healing thoughts
Of tender joy wilt thou remember me,   145
And these my exhortations! Nor, perchance—
If I should be where I no more can hear
Thy voice, nor catch from thy wild eyes these gleams
Of past existence—wilt thou then forget
That on the banks of this delightful stream   150
We stood together; and that I, so long
A worshiper of Nature, hither came
Unwearied in that service; rather say
With warmer love—oh! with far deeper zeal
Of holier love. Nor wilt thou then forget,   155
That after many wanderings, many years
Of absence, these steep woods and lofty cliffs,
And this green pastoral landscape, were to me
More dear, both for themselves and for thy sake!

[1798]

WILLIAM WORDSWORTH   [1770–1850]

I wandered lonely as a cloud

I wandered lonely as a cloud
That floats on high o'er vales and hills,
When all at once I saw a crowd,
A host, of golden daffodils;
Beside the lake, beneath the trees,   5
Fluttering and dancing in the breeze.

Continuous as the stars that shine
And twinkle on the milky way,
They stretched in never-ending line
Along the margin of a bay: 10
Ten thousand saw I at a glance,
Tossing their heads in sprightly dance.

The waves beside them danced; but they
Outdid the sparkling waves in glee:
A poet could not but be gay,   15
In such a jocund company:
I gazed—and gazed—but little thought
What wealth the show to me had brought:

For oft, when on my couch I lie
In vacant or in pensive mood,   20
They flash upon that inward eye
Which is the bliss of solitude;
And then my heart with pleasure fills,
And dances with the daffodils.

                                                        [1807]

WILLIAM WORDSWORTH   [1770–1850]

Ode

*Intimations of Immortality from Recollections
of Early Childhood*

*The Child is father of the Man;
And I could wish my days to be
Bound each to each by natural piety.°*

1

There was a time when meadow, grove, and stream,
The earth, and every common sight,
        To me did seem
        Appareled in celestial light,
The glory and the freshness of a dream.   5

Epigraph: The final lines of Wordsworth's "My Heart Leaps Up."

It is not now as it hath been of yore—
    Turn whereso'er I may,
       By night or day,
The things which I have seen I now can see no more.

2

    The Rainbow comes and goes,   10
    And lovely is the Rose,
    The Moon doth with delight
Look round her when the heavens are bare,
    Waters on a starry night
    Are beautiful and fair;   15
  The sunshine is a glorious birth;
  But yet I know, where'er I go,
That there hath passed away a glory from the earth.

3

Now, while the birds thus sing a joyous song,
  And while the young lambs bound   20
    As to the tabor's° sound,
To me alone there came a thought of grief:
A timely utterance gave that thought relief,
    And I again am strong:
The cataracts blow their trumpets from the steep;   25
No more shall grief of mine the season wrong;
I hear the Echoes through the mountains throng,
The Winds come to me from the fields of sleep,
    And all the earth is gay;
       Land and sea   30
    Give themselves up to jollity,
      And with the heart of May
    Doth every Beast keep holiday—
      Thou Child of Joy,
Shout round me, let me hear thy shouts, thou happy Shepherd-boy! 35

4

Ye blessèd Creatures, I have heard the call
  Ye to each other make; I see
The heavens laugh with you in your jubilee;
  My heart is at your festival,
    My head hath its coronal,°   40

---

21. tabor: A small drum, used chiefly as an accompaniment to the pipe or trumpet.
40. coronal: A wreath of flowers or leaves for the head; a garland.

The fullness of your bliss, I feel—I feel it all.
      Oh, evil day! if I were sullen
      While Earth herself is adorning,
         This sweet May morning,
      And the Children are culling   45
         On every side,
      In a thousand valleys far and wide,
      Fresh flowers; while the sun shines warm,
And the Babe leaps up on his Mother's arm—
      I hear, I hear, with joy I hear!   50
      —But there's a Tree, of many, one,
A single Field which I have looked upon,
Both of them speak of something that is gone:
         The Pansy at my feet
         Doth the same tale repeat: 55
Whither is fled the visionary gleam?
Where is it now, the glory and the dream?

5

Our birth is but a sleep and a forgetting:
The Soul that rises with us, our life's Star,
      Hath had elsewhere its setting,   60
         And cometh from afar:
      Not in entire forgetfulness,
      And not in utter nakedness,
But trailing clouds of glory do we come
      From God, who is our home: 65
Heaven lies about us in our infancy!
Shades of the prison-house begin to close
      Upon the growing Boy
         But he
Beholds the light, and whence it flows,   70
      He sees it in his joy;
The Youth, who daily farther from the east
      Must travel, still is Nature's Priest,
      And by the vision splendid
      Is on his way attended;   75
At length the Man perceives it die away,
And fade into the light of common day.°

77. Lines 58–77 reflect Plato's belief that human souls inhabit "a pre-existent state" (in Wordsworth's terms) before being born into this world. Though imprisoned in a physical body and the material world, the soul of the infant has recollections of and longs to return to the perfect world of ideas. As the child grows older,

6

Earth fills her lap with pleasures of her own;
Yearnings she hath in her own natural kind,
And, even with something of a Mother's mind,   80
      And no unworthy aim,
    The homely° Nurse doth all she can   *simple, kindly*
To make her foster child, her Inmate Man,
      Forget the glories he hath known,
And that imperial palace whence he came.   85

7

Behold the Child among his newborn blisses,
A six-years' Darling of a pygmy size!
See, where 'mid work of his own hand he lies,
Fretted° by sallies of his mother's kisses,   *annoyed*
With light upon him from his father's eyes!   90
See, at his feet, some little plan or chart,
Some fragment from his dream of human life,
Shaped by himself with newly-learnèd art;
      A wedding or a festival,
      A mourning or a funeral;   95
        And this hath now his heart,
      And unto this he frames his song;
        Then will he fit his tongue
To dialogues of business, love, or strife;
      But it will not be long   100
      Ere this be thrown aside,
      And with new joy and pride
The little Actor cons° another part;   *learns*
Filling from time to time his "humorous stage"°
With all the Persons,° down to palsied Age,   *dramatis personae* 105
That Life brings with her in her equipage;°
      As if his whole vocation
      Were endless imitation.

---

those memories begin to fade, though reminders of that primal glory recur (usually from experiences with things in nature). By adulthood, such glimpses become rare and the adult becomes reconciled to the material world and its values.
104. "humorous stage": Quoted from a sonnet by the Elizabethan poet Samuel Daniel: the varied temperaments (humors) of characters represented on the stage. Lines 103–05 echo Jaques's "All the world's a stage" speech in Shakespeare's *As You Like It* (2.7.138–65), with its description of the "seven ages" in the life of a person.
105–06. all . . . equipage: All that is needed for a military operation, a journey, or a domestic establishment.

8

Thou, whose exterior semblance doth belie
       Thy Soul's immensity;   110
Thou best Philosopher, who yet dost keep
Thy heritage, thou Eye among the blind,
That, deaf and silent, read'st the eternal deep,
Haunted forever by the eternal mind—
       Mighty Prophet! Seer blest!   115
       On whom those truths do rest,
Which we are toiling all our lives to find,
In darkness lost, the darkness of the grave;
Thou, over whom thy Immortality
Broods like the Day, a Master o'er a Slave,   120
A Presence which is not to be put by;
Thou little Child, yet glorious in the might
Of heaven-born freedom on thy being's height,
Why with such earnest pains dost thou provoke
The years to bring the inevitable yoke,   125
Thus blindly with thy blessedness at strife?
Full soon thy Soul shall have her earthly freight,
And custom lie upon thee with a weight,
Heavy as frost, and deep almost as life!

9

       O joy! that in our embers   130
       Is something that doth live,
       That nature yet remembers
       What was so fugitive!
The thought of our past years in me doth breed
Perpetual benediction: not indeed   135
For that which is most worthy to be blest;
Delight and liberty, the simple creed
Of Childhood, whether busy or at rest,
With new-fledged hope still fluttering in his breast—
       Not for these I raise   140
       The song of thanks and praise;
       But for those obstinate questionings
       Of sense and outward things,
       Fallings from us, vanishings;
       Blank misgivings of a Creature   145
Moving about in worlds not realized,°   *not seeming real*
High instincts before which our mortal Nature

Did tremble like a guilty Thing surprised;
    But for those first affections,
    Those shadowy recollections,   150
   Which, be they what they may,
Are yet the fountain light of all our day,
Are yet a master light of all our seeing;
    Uphold us, cherish, and have power to make
Our noisy years seem moments in the being   155
Of the eternal Silence: truths that wake,
    To perish never;
Which neither listlessness, nor mad endeavor,
    Nor Man nor Boy,
Nor all that is at enmity with joy,   160
Can utterly abolish or destroy!
    Hence in a season of calm weather
    Though inland far we be,
Our Souls have sight of that immortal sea
    Which brought us hither,   165
   Can in a moment travel thither,
And see the Children sport upon the shore,
And hear the mighty waters rolling evermore.

            10

Then sing, ye Birds, sing, sing a joyous song!
    And let the young Lambs bound   170
    As to the tabor's sound!
We in thought will join your throng,
    Ye that pipe and ye that play,
    Ye that through your hearts today
    Feel the gladness of the May!   175
What though the radiance which was once so bright
Be now forever taken from my sight,
   Though nothing can bring back the hour
Of splendor in the grass, of glory in the flower;
    We will grieve not, rather find   180
    Strength in what remains behind;
    In the primal sympathy
    Which having been must ever be;
    In the soothing thoughts that spring
    Out of human suffering;   185
    In the faith that looks through death,
In years that bring the philosophic mind.

11

And O, ye Fountains, Meadows, Hills, and Groves,
Forebode not any severing of our loves!
Yet in my heart of hearts I feel your might;   190
I only have relinquished one delight
To live beneath your more habitual sway.
I love the Brooks which down their channels fret,°   *move in agitated waves*
Even more than when I tripped lightly as they;
The innocent brightness of a newborn Day   195
　　　Is lovely yet;
The clouds that gather round the setting sun
Do take a sober coloring from an eye
That hath kept watch o'er man's mortality;
Another race hath been, and other palms° are won.   *symbols of victory* 200
Thanks to the human heart by which we live,
Thanks to its tenderness, its joys, and fears,
To me the meanest° flower that blows° can give   *most ordinary/blooms*
Thoughts that do often lie too deep for tears.

[1807]

WILLIAM WORDSWORTH   [1770–1850]

The world is too much with us

The world is too much with us; late and soon,
Getting and spending, we lay waste our powers;
Little we see in Nature that is ours;
We have given our hearts away, a sordid boon!°   *gift*
This Sea that bares her bosom to the moon,   5
The winds that will be howling at all hours,
And are up-gathered now like sleeping flowers,
For this, for everything, we are out of tune;
It moves us not.—Great God! I'd rather be
A Pagan suckled in a creed outworn;   10
So might I, standing on this pleasant lea,°   *open meadow*
Have glimpses that would make me less forlorn;

Have sight of Proteus° rising from the sea;
Or hear old Triton° blow his wreathèd° horn.

[1807]

13. Proteus: In Greek mythology, a sea god who could change his own form or appearance at will.
14. Triton: A Greek sea god with the head and upper body of a man and the tail of a fish, usually pictured as playing on a conch-shell trumpet; **wreathèd:** Curved.

SAMUEL TAYLOR COLERIDGE   [1772–1834]

Kubla Khan

Or, a Vision in a Dream. A Fragment°

In Xanadu did Kubla Khan
A stately pleasure dome decree:°
Where Alph,° the sacred river, ran
Through caverns measureless to man
    Down to a sunless sea.   5
So twice five miles of fertile ground
With walls and towers were girdled round:
And there were gardens bright with sinuous rills,
Where blossomed many an incense-bearing tree;
And here were forests ancient as the hills,   10
Enfolding sunny spots of greenery.

But oh! that deep romantic chasm which slanted
Down the green hill athwart a cedarn cover!
A savage place! as holy and enchanted
As e'er beneath a waning moon was haunted   15

Or, a Vision . . . A Fragment: Coleridge stated in a preface that this poem composed itself in his mind during "a profound sleep" (actually an opium-induced reverie); that he began writing it down immediately upon waking but was interrupted by a caller; and that when he returned to his room an hour later he could not complete it.
1–2. In . . . decree: "In Xamdu did Cublai Can build a stately Palace, encompassing sixteene miles of plaine ground with a wall" (Samuel Purchas, *Purchas his Pilgrimage* [1613]). The historical Kublai Khan (1215–1294) was the founder of the Yüan dynasty of China and overlord of the Mongol Empire.
3. Alph: Probably derived from the name of the River Alpheus in southern Greece, which according to mythology ran under the sea and emerged at Syracuse (Italy) in the fountain of Arethusa.

By woman wailing for her demon lover!
And from this chasm, with ceaseless turmoil seething,
As if this earth in fast thick pants were breathing,
A mighty fountain momently was forced:
Amid whose swift half-intermitted burst   20
Huge fragments vaulted like rebounding hail,
Or chaffy grain beneath the thresher's flail:
And 'mid these dancing rocks at once and ever
It flung up momently the sacred river.
Five miles meandering with a mazy motion   25
Through wood and dale the sacred river ran,
Then reached the caverns measureless to man,
And sank in tumult to a lifeless ocean:
And 'mid this tumult Kubla heard from far
Ancestral voices prophesying war!   30
    The shadow of the dome of pleasure
    Floated midway on the waves;
    Where was heard the mingled measure
    From the fountain and the caves.
It was a miracle of rare device,   35
A sunny pleasure dome with caves of ice!

    A damsel with a dulcimer
    In a vision once I saw:
    It was an Abyssinian maid,
    And on her dulcimer she played,   40
    Singing of Mount Abora.°
    Could I revive within me
    Her symphony and song,
    To such a deep delight 'twould win me,
That with music loud and long,   45
I would build that dome in air,
That sunny dome! those caves of ice!
And all who heard should see them there,
And all should cry, Beware! Beware!
His flashing eyes, his floating hair!   50
Weave a circle round him thrice,
And close your eyes with holy dread,
For he on honey-dew hath fed,
And drunk the milk of Paradise.

[*c. 1797–1798;* 1813]

39–41. Abyssinian . . . Abora: See *Paradise Lost* 4.280–82: "where Abassin Kings
their issue Guard, / Mount Amara, though this by some supposed / True Paradise
under the Ethiop Line."

GEORGE GORDON, LORD BYRON   [1788–1824]

She walks in beauty

1

She walks in beauty, like the night
  Of cloudless climes and starry skies;
And all that's best of dark and bright
  Meet in her aspect and her eyes:
Thus mellowed to that tender light   5
  Which heaven to gaudy day denies.

2

One shade the more, one ray the less,
  Had half impaired the nameless grace
Which waves in every raven tress,
  Or softly lightens o'er her face;   10
Where thoughts serenely sweet express
  How pure, how dear their dwelling place.

3

And on that cheek, and o'er that brow,
  So soft, so calm, yet eloquent,
The smiles that win, the tints that glow,   15
  But tell of days in goodness spent,
A mind at peace with all below,
  A heart whose love is innocent!

[1815]

PERCY BYSSHE SHELLEY   [1792–1822]

Ozymandias°

I met a traveler from an antique land
Who said: Two vast and trunkless legs of stone
Stand in the desert. Near them, on the sand,
Half sunk, a shattered visage lies, whose frown,

Ozymandias: The Greek name for Ramses II of Egypt (thirteenth century B.C.E.),
who erected the largest statue in Egypt as a memorial to himself.

And wrinkled lip, and sneer of cold command,   5
Tell that its sculptor well those passions read
Which yet survive, stamped on these lifeless things,
The hand that mocked them, and the heart that fed:
And on the pedestal these words appear:
"My name is Ozymandias, king of kings: 10
Look on my works, ye Mighty, and despair!"
Nothing beside remains. Round the decay
Of that colossal wreck, boundless and bare
The lone and level sands stretch far away.

[1818]

PERCY BYSSHE SHELLEY   [1792–1822]

Ode to the West Wind

1

O wild West Wind, thou breath° of Autumn's being,
Thou, from whose unseen presence the leaves dead
Are driven, like ghosts from an enchanter fleeing,

Yellow, and black, and pale, and hectic red,
Pestilence-stricken multitudes: O thou,   5
Who chariotest to their dark wintry bed

The wingèd seeds, where they lie cold and low,
Each like a corpse within its grave, until
Thine azure sister of the Spring shall blow

Her clarion o'er the dreaming earth, and fill   10
(Driving sweet buds like flocks to feed in air)
With living hues and odors plain and hill:

Wild Spirit, which art moving everywhere;
Destroyer and preserver; hear, oh, hear!

1. breath: In many ancient languages, the words for *breath*, *wind*, *soul*, and *inspiration* are the same or closely related: in Latin, *spiritus*. Shelley uses this word to interconnect nature and artistic inspiration (poetry) in his poem.

2

Thou on whose stream, mid the steep sky's commotion,   15
Loose clouds like earth's decaying leaves are shed,
Shook from the tangled boughs of Heaven and Ocean,

Angels of rain and lightning: there are spread
On the blue surface of thine airy surge,
Like the bright hair uplifted from the head   20

Of some fierce Maenad,° even from the dim verge
Of the horizon to the zenith's height,
The locks of the approaching storm. Thou dirge

Of the dying year, to which this closing night
Will be the dome of a vast sepulcher,   25
Vaulted with all thy congregated might

Of vapors, from whose solid atmosphere
Black rain, and fire, and hail will burst: oh, hear!

3

Thou who didst waken from his summer dreams
The blue Mediterranean, where he lay,   30
Lulled by the coil of his crystàlline streams,

Beside a pumice° isle in Baiae's bay,°
And saw in sleep old palaces° and towers
Quivering within the wave's intenser day,

All overgrown with azure moss and flowers   35
So sweet, the sense faints picturing them! Thou
For whose path the Atlantic's level powers

Cleave themselves into chasms, while far below
The sea-blooms and the oozy woods which wear
The sapless foliage of the ocean, know   40

Thy voice, and suddenly grow gray with fear,
And tremble and despoil themselves: oh, hear!

21. Maenad: A female votary of Dionysus, Greek god of wine and vegetation, who took part in the wild, orgiastic rites that characterize his worship.
32. pumice: Porous volcanic stone; **Baiae's bay:** West of Naples, Italy.
33. old palaces: Villas built by the Roman emperors.

4

If I were a dead leaf thou mightest bear;
If I were a swift cloud to fly with thee;
A wave to pant beneath thy power, and share   45

The impulse of thy strength, only less free
Than thou, O uncontrollable! If even
I were as in my boyhood, and could be

The comrade of thy wanderings over Heaven,
As then, when to outstrip thy skyey speed   50
Scarce seemed a vision; I would ne'er have striven

As thus with thee in prayer in my sore need.
Oh, lift me as a wave, a leaf, a cloud!
I fall upon the thorns of life! I bleed!

A heavy weight of hours has chained and bowed   55
One too like thee: tameless, and swift, and proud.

5

Make me thy lyre,° even as the forest is:
What if my leaves are falling like its own!
The tumult of thy mighty harmonies

Will take from both a deep, autumnal tone,   60
Sweet though in sadness. Be thou, Spirit fierce,
My spirit! Be thou me, impetuous one!

Drive my dead thoughts over the universe
Like withered leaves to quicken a new birth!
And, by the incantation of this verse,   65

Scatter, as from an unextinguished hearth
Ashes and sparks, my words among mankind!
Be through my lips to unawakened earth

The trumpet of a prophecy! O Wind,
If Winter comes, can Spring be far behind?   70

[1820]

---

57. lyre: An Aeolian harp, whose strings produce a sequence of rising and falling harmonies as air blows over them.

JOHN KEATS   [1795–1821]

When I have fears
that I may cease to be

When I have fears that I may cease to be
  Before my pen has gleaned my teeming brain,
Before high piled books, in charactry,°   *writing*
  Hold like rich garners° the full ripened grain;   *granaries*
When I behold, upon the night's starred face,   5
  Huge cloudy symbols of a high romance,
And think that I may never live to trace
  Their shadows, with the magic hand of chance;
And when I feel, fair creature of an hour,
  That I shall never look upon thee more,   10
Never have relish in the fairy power
  Of unreflecting love;—then on the shore
Of the wide world I stand alone, and think
Till love and fame to nothingness do sink.

[*1818;* 1848]

JOHN KEATS   [1795–1821]

La Belle Dame sans Merci°

O what can ail thee, Knight at arms,
  Alone and palely loitering?
The sedge° has withered from the Lake   *rushes*
  And no birds sing!

O what can ail thee, Knight at arms,   5
  So haggard, and so woebegone?
The squirrel's granary is full
  And the harvest's done.

I see a lily on thy brow
  With anguish moist and fever dew,   10

La Belle Dame sans Merci: "The beautiful lady without pity" (French). This version, first published in 1888, is earlier than the one Keats published in 1820, and is generally the preferred version.

And on thy cheeks a fading rose
  Fast withereth too.

"I met a Lady in the Meads,°   *meadows*
  Full beautiful, a faery's child,
Her hair was long, her foot was light   15
  And her eyes were wild.

"I made a Garland for her head,
  And bracelets too, and fragrant Zone;°   *girdle*
She looked at me as she did love
  And made sweet moan.   20

"I set her on my pacing steed
  And nothing else saw all day long,
For sidelong would she bend and sing
  A faery's song.

"She found me roots of relish sweet,   25
  And honey wild, and manna dew,
And sure in language strange she said
  'I love thee true.'

"She took me to her elfin grot°   *grotto, cave*
  And there she wept and sighed full sore,   30
And there I shut her wild wild eyes
  With kisses four.

"And there she lulléd me asleep,
  And there I dreamed, Ah Woe betide!
The latest° dream I ever dreamt   *last* 35
  On the cold hill side.

"I saw pale Kings, and Princes too,
  Pale warriors, death-pale were they all;
They cried, 'La belle dame sans merci
  Hath thee in thrall!'   40

"I saw their starved lips in the gloam°   *twilight*
  With horrid warning gapéd wide,
And I awoke, and found me here
  On the cold hill's side.

"And this is why I sojourn here,   45
  Alone and palely loitering;
Though the sedge is withered from the Lake
  And no birds sing."

                                      [*1819;* 1888]

JOHN KEATS   [1795–1821]

To Autumn

I

Season of mists and mellow fruitfulness,
  Close bosom-friend of the maturing sun;
Conspiring with him how to load and bless
  With fruit the vines that round the thatch-eves run;
To bend with apples the mossed cottage-trees,   5
  And fill all fruit with ripeness to the core;
    To swell the gourd, and plump the hazel shells
With a sweet kernel; to set budding more,
  And still more, later flowers for the bees,
  Until they think warm days will never cease,   10
    For Summer has o'er-brimmed their clammy cells.

II

Who hath not seen thee oft amid thy store?
  Sometimes whoever seeks abroad may find
Thee sitting careless on a granary floor,
  Thy hair soft-lifted by the winnowing wind;   15
Or on a half-reaped furrow sound asleep,
  Drowsed with the fume of poppies, while thy hook°   *scythe*
    Spares the next swath and all its twinèd flowers:
And sometimes like a gleaner thou dost keep
  Steady thy laden head across a brook;   20
  Or by a cider-press, with patient look,
    Thou watchest the last oozings hours by hours.

III

Where are the songs of Spring? Aye, where are they?
  Think not of them, thou hast thy music too,—
While barrèd clouds bloom the soft-dying day,   25
  And touch the stubble-plains with rosy hue;
Then in a wailful choir the small gnats mourn
  Among the river sallows,° borne aloft   *willows*
    Or sinking as the light wind lives or dies;
And full-grown lambs loud bleat from hilly bourn;°   *region* 30
  Hedge-crickets sing; and now with treble soft
  The red-breast whistles from a garden-croft;
    And gathering swallows twitter in the skies.

[1820]

ELIZABETH BARRETT BROWNING   [1806–1861]

How do I love thee?
Let me count the ways

How do I love thee? Let me count the ways.
I love thee to the depth and breadth and height
My soul can reach, when feeling out of sight
For the ends of Being and ideal Grace.
I love thee to the level of everyday's   5
Most quiet need, by sun and candlelight.
I love thee freely, as men strive for Right;
I love thee purely, as they turn from Praise.
I love thee with the passion put to use
In my old griefs, and with my childhood's faith.   10
I love thee with a love I seemed to lose
With my lost saints—I love thee with the breath,
Smiles, tears, of all my life!—and, if God choose,
I shall but love thee better after death.

[1850]

EDGAR ALLAN POE   [1809–1849]

The Raven

Once upon a midnight dreary, while I pondered, weak and weary,
Over many a quaint and curious volume of forgotten lore—
While I nodded, nearly napping, suddenly there came a tapping,
As of some one gently rapping, rapping at my chamber door.
"'Tis some visiter," I muttered, "tapping at my chamber door—   5
        Only this and nothing more."

Ah, distinctly I remember it was in the bleak December;
And each separate dying ember wrought its ghost upon the floor.
Eagerly I wished the morrow;—vainly I had sought to borrow
From my books surcease° of sorrow—sorrow for the lost Lenore—   10
For the rare and radiant maiden whom the angels name Lenore—
        Nameless *here* for evermore.

10. surcease: Ending.

And the silken, sad, uncertain rustling of each purple curtain
Thrilled me—filled me with fantastic terrors never felt before;
So that now, to still the beating of my heart, I stood repeating   15
"'Tis some visiter entreating entrance at my chamber door—
Some late visiter entreating entrance at my chamber door;—
                     This it is and nothing more."

Presently my soul grew stronger; hesitating then no longer,
"Sir," said I, "or Madam, truly your forgiveness I implore;   20
But the fact is I was napping, and so gently you came rapping,
And so faintly you came tapping, tapping at my chamber door,
That I scarce was sure I heard you"—here I opened wide the door;—
                     Darkness there and nothing more.

Deep into that darkness peering, long I stood there wondering, fearing,   25
Doubting, dreaming dreams no mortal ever dared to dream before;
But the silence was unbroken, and the stillness gave no token,
And the only word there spoken was the whispered word, "Lenore?"
This I whispered, and an echo murmured back the word, "Lenore!"
                     Merely this and nothing more.   30

Back into the chamber turning, all my soul within me burning,
Soon again I heard a tapping somewhat louder than before.
"Surely," said I, "surely that is something at my window lattice;
Let me see, then, what thereat is, and this mystery explore—
Let my heart be still a moment and this mystery explore;—   35
                     'Tis the wind and nothing more!"

Open here I flung the shutter, when, with many a flirt and flutter,
In there stepped a stately Raven of the saintly days of yore;
Not the least obeisance made he; not a minute stopped or stayed he;
But, with mien of lord or lady, perched above my chamber door—   40
Perched upon a bust of Pallas° just above my chamber door—
                     Perched, and sat, and nothing more.

Then this ebony bird beguiling my sad fancy into smiling,
By the grave and stern decorum of the countenance it wore,
"Though thy crest be shorn and shaven, thou," I said, "art sure no
   craven,   45
Ghastly grim and ancient Raven wandering from the Nightly shore—
Tell me what thy lordly name is on the Night's Plutonian° shore!"
                     Quoth the Raven "Nevermore."

---

41. Pallas: Athena, Greek goddess of wisdom and the arts.
47. Plutonian: Black (Pluto was the Greek god of the underworld).

Much I marveled this ungainly fowl to hear discourse so plainly,
Though its answer little meaning—little relevancy bore;   50
For we cannot help agreeing that no living human being
Ever yet was blessed with seeing bird above his chamber door—
Bird or beast upon the sculptured bust above his chamber door,
                        With such name as "Nevermore."

But the Raven, sitting lonely on the placid bust, spoke only   55
That one word, as if his soul in that one word he did outpour.
Nothing farther then he uttered—not a feather then he fluttered—
Till I scarcely more than muttered "Other friends have flown before—
On the morrow *he* will leave me, as my Hopes have flown before."
                     Then the bird said "Nevermore."   60

Startled at the stillness broken by reply so aptly spoken,
"Doubtless," said I, "what it utters is its only stock and store
Caught from some unhappy master whom unmerciful Disaster
Followed fast and followed faster till his songs one burden bore—
Till the dirges of his Hope that melancholy burden bore   65
                        Of 'Never—nevermore.'"

But the Raven still beguiling my sad fancy into smiling,
Straight I wheeled a cushioned seat in front of bird, and bust and door;
Then, upon the velvet sinking, I betook myself to linking
Fancy unto fancy, thinking what this ominous bird of yore—   70
What this grim, ungainly, ghastly, gaunt, and ominous bird of yore
                    Meant in croaking "Nevermore."

This I sat engaged in guessing, but no syllable expressing
To the fowl whose fiery eyes now burned into my bosom's core;
This and more I sat divining, with my head at ease reclining   75
On the cushion's velvet lining that the lamp-light gloated o'er,
But whose velvet-violet lining with the lamp-light gloating o'er,
                  She shall press, ah, nevermore!

Then, methought, the air grew denser, perfumed from an unseen censer
Swung by seraphim° whose foot-falls tinkled on the tufted floor.   80
"Wretch," I cried, "thy God hath lent thee—by these angels he hath
    sent thee
Respite—respite and nepenthe° from thy memories of Lenore;
Quaff, oh quaff this kind nepenthe and forget this lost Lenore!"
                Quoth the Raven "Nevermore."

---

80. **seraphim:** Angels of the highest rank.
82. **nepenthe:** A drug bringing, or supposed to bring, forgetfulness of trouble or grief.

"Prophet!" said I, "thing of evil!—prophet still, if bird or devil!—   85
Whether Tempter° sent, or whether tempest tossed thee here ashore,   *devil*
Desolate yet all undaunted, on this desert land enchanted—
On this home by Horror haunted—tell me truly, I implore—
Is there—*is* there balm in Gilead?°—tell me—tell me, I implore!"
                             Quoth the Raven "Nevermore."   90

"Prophet!" said I, "thing of evil!—prophet still, if bird or devil!
By that Heaven that bends above us—by that God we both adore—
Tell this soul with sorrow laden if, within the distant Aidenn,°
It shall clasp a sainted maiden whom the angels name Lenore—
Clasp a rare and radiant maiden whom the angels name Lenore."   95
                             Quoth the Raven "Nevermore."

"Be that word our sign of parting, bird or fiend!" I shrieked, upstarting—
"Get thee back into the tempest and the Night's Plutonian shore!
Leave no black plume as a token of that lie thy soul hath spoken!
Leave my loneliness unbroken!—quit the bust above my door!   100
Take thy beak from out my heart, and take thy form from off my door!"
                             Quoth the Raven "Nevermore."

And the Raven, never flitting, still is sitting, *still* is sitting
On the pallid bust of Pallas just above my chamber door;
And his eyes have all the seeming of a demon's that is dreaming,   105
And the lamp-light o'er him streaming throws his shadow on the floor;
And my soul from out that shadow that lies floating on the floor
                        Shall be lifted—nevermore!

                                [1845]

89. balm in Gilead: A balm is an aromatic ointment used to heal wounds and
soothe pain. The phrase alludes to Jeremiah 8:22, "Is there no balm in Gilead?"
Gilead, east of the Jordan River, was known for a balm made from the resin of the
Styrax tree.
93. Aidenn: Poe's poetic spelling of *Eden*, the biblical garden of paradise.

EDGAR ALLAN POE   [1809–1849]

Annabel Lee

It was many and many a year ago,
  In a kingdom by the sea,
That a maiden there lived whom you may know
  By the name of Annabel Lee;

And this maiden she lived with no other thought   5
   Than to love and be loved by me.

She was a child and *I* was a child,
   In this kingdom by the sea,
But we loved with a love that was more than love—
   I and my Annabel Lee—   10
With a love that the wingèd seraphs° of Heaven
   Coveted her and me.

And this was the reason that, long ago,
   In this kingdom by the sea,
A wind blew out of a cloud by night   15
   Chilling my Annabel Lee;
So that her highborn kinsmen came
   And bore her away from me,
To shut her up in a sepulchre
   In this kingdom by the sea.   20

The angels, not half so happy in Heaven,
   Went envying her and me:
Yes! that was the reason (as all men know,
   In this kingdom by the sea)
That the wind came out of the cloud, chilling   25
   And killing my Annabel Lee.

But our love it was stronger by far than the love
   Of those who were older than we—
   Of many far wiser than we—
And neither the angels in Heaven above   30
   Nor the demons down under the sea,
Can ever dissever my soul from the soul
   Of the beautiful Annabel Lee:

For the moon never beams without bringing me dreams
   Of the beautiful Annabel Lee;   35
And the stars never rise but I see the bright eyes
   Of the beautiful Annabel Lee;
And so, all the night-tide, I lie down by the side
Of my darling, my darling, my life and my bride,
   In her sepulchre there by the sea—   40
   In her tomb by the side of the sea.

[1849]

11. seraphs: Angels of the highest order.

ALFRED, LORD TENNYSON   [1809–1892]

Ulysses°

It little profits that an idle king,
By this still hearth, among these barren crags,
Matched with an agèd wife, I mete and dole
Unequal laws unto a savage race,°
That hoard, and sleep, and feed, and know not me.   5

   I cannot rest from travel; I will drink
Life to the lees. All times I have enjoyed
Greatly, have suffered greatly, both with those
That loved me, and alone; on shore, and when
Through scudding drifts° the rainy Hyades°   10
Vexed the dim sea. I am become a name;
For always roaming with a hungry heart
Much have I seen and known—cities of men
And manners, climates, councils, governments,
Myself not least, but honored of them all—   15
And drunk delight of battle with my peers,
Far on the ringing plains of windy Troy.
I am a part of all that I have met;
Yet all experience is an arch wherethrough
Gleams that untraveled world whose margin fades   20
Forever and forever when I move.
How dull it is to pause, to make an end,
To rust unburnished, not to shine in use!

Ulysses (the Roman form of *Odysseus*): The hero of Homer's epic *The Odyssey*,
which tells the story of Odysseus's adventures on his voyage back to Ithaca, the
small island of which he was king, after he and the other Greek heroes had defeated Troy. It took Odysseus ten years to reach Ithaca, where his wife (Penelope)
and son (Telemachus) had been waiting for him. Upon his return, he defeated
the suitors who had been trying to marry the faithful Penelope, and he resumed
the kingship and his old ways of life. Here Homer's story ends, but in Canto 26
of the *Inferno*, Dante extended the story: Odysseus eventually became restless and
dissatisfied with his settled life and decided to return to the sea and sail west, into
the unknown sea, and seek whatever adventures he might find there. Tennyson's
poem amplifies the speech delivered in Dante's poem as Ulysses challenges his
men to accompany him on this new voyage.
3–4. mete . . . race: Administer inadequate laws (unequal to what is needed) to a
still somewhat lawless race.
10. scudding drifts: Wind-driven spray; Hyades: Five stars in the constellation
Taurus whose rising was assumed to be followed by rain.

As though to breathe were life! Life piled on life
Were all too little, and of one to me   25
Little remains; but every hour is saved
From that eternal silence, something more,
A bringer of new things; and vile it were
For some three suns° to store and hoard myself,   *years*
And this gray spirit yearning in desire   30
To follow knowledge like a sinking star,
Beyond the utmost bound of human thought.

   This is my son, mine own Telemachus,
To whom I leave the scepter and the isle—
Well-loved of me, discerning to fulfill   35
This labor, by slow prudence to make mild
A rugged people, and through soft degrees
Subdue them to the useful and the good.
Most blameless is he, centered in the sphere
Of common duties, decent not to fail   40
In offices of tenderness, and pay
Meet adoration to my household gods,
When I am gone. He works his work, I mine.

   There lies the port; the vessel puffs her sail;
There gloom the dark, broad seas. My mariners,   45
Souls that have toiled, and wrought, and thought with me—
That ever with a frolic welcome took
The thunder and the sunshine, and opposed
Free hearts, free foreheads—you and I are old;
Old age hath yet his honor and his toil.   50
Death closes all; but something ere the end,
Some work of noble note, may yet be done,
Not unbecoming men that strove with Gods.
The lights begin to twinkle from the rocks;
The long day wanes; the slow moon climbs; the deep   55
Moans round with many voices. Come, my friends,
'Tis not too late to seek a newer world.
Push off, and sitting well in order smite
The sounding furrows; for my purpose holds
To sail beyond the sunset, and the baths°   60
Of all the western stars, until I die.
It may be that the gulfs will wash us down;

60. baths: The outer river or ocean surrounding the flat earth, in Greek cosmology, into which the stars descended upon setting.

It may be we shall touch the Happy Isles,°
And see the great Achilles,° whom we knew.
Though much is taken, much abides; and though   65
We are not now that strength which in old days
Moved earth and heaven, that which we are, we are—
One equal temper of heroic hearts,
Made weak by time and fate, but strong in will
To strive, to seek, to find, and not to yield.   70

[1833]

63. Happy Isles: The Islands of the Blessed, or Elysian Fields, in Greek myth, which lay in the western seas beyond the Strait of Gibraltar and were the abode of heroes after death.
64. Achilles: The hero of the Greeks, and Odysseus's comrade, in Homer's *Iliad*.

ALFRED, LORD TENNYSON   [1809–1892]

Crossing the Bar

Sunset and evening star,
    And one clear call for me!
And may there be no moaning of the bar,°
    When I put out to sea,

But such a tide as moving seems asleep,   5
    Too full for sound and foam,
When that which drew from out the boundless deep
    Turns again home.

Twilight and evening bell,
    And after that the dark!   10
And may there be no sadness of farewell,
    When I embark;

For though from out our bourne of Time and Place
    The flood may bear me far,
I hope to see my Pilot face to face   15
    When I have crossed the bar.

[1889]

3. moaning of the bar: The mournful sound of waves crashing against a sand bar at the mouth of a river or harbor at low tide.

ROBERT BROWNING   [1812–1889]

My Last Duchess

Ferrara°

That's my last Duchess° painted on the wall,
Looking as if she were alive. I call
That piece a wonder, now: Frà Pandolf's° hands
Worked busily a day, and there she stands.
Will't please you sit and look at her? I said   5
"Frà Pandolf" by design, for never read
Strangers like you that pictured countenance,
The depth and passion of its earnest glance,
But to myself they turned (since none puts by
The curtain I have drawn for you, but I)   10
And seemed as they would ask me, if they durst,
How such a glance came there; so, not the first
Are you to turn and ask thus. Sir, 'twas not
Her husband's presence only, called that spot
Of joy into the Duchess' cheek: perhaps   15
Frà Pandolf chanced to say "Her mantle laps
Over my lady's wrist too much," or "Paint
Must never hope to reproduce the faint
Half-flush that dies along her throat": such stuff
Was courtesy, she thought, and cause enough   20
For calling up that spot of joy. She had
A heart—how shall I say?—too soon made glad,
Too easily impressed; she liked whate'er
She looked on, and her looks went everywhere.
Sir, 'twas all one! My favor at her breast,   25
The dropping of the daylight in the West,
The bough of cherries some officious fool
Broke in the orchard for her, the white mule
She rode with round the terrace—all and each
Would draw from her alike the approving speech,   30
Or blush, at least. She thanked men,—good! but thanked
Somehow—I know not how—as if she ranked

Ferrara: The poem is based on events that occurred in the life of Alfonso II, duke
of Ferrara in Italy, in the sixteenth century.
1. last Duchess: Ferrara's first wife, Lucrezia, died in 1561 at age seventeen after
three years of marriage.
3. Frà Pandolf: Brother Pandolf, a fictional painter.

My gift of a nine-hundred-years-old name
With anybody's gift. Who'd stoop to blame
This sort of trifling? Even had you skill   35
In speech—(which I have not)—to make your will
Quite clear to such an one, and say, "Just this
Or that in you disgusts me; here you miss,
Or there exceed the mark"—and if she let
Herself be lessoned so, nor plainly set   40
Her wits to yours, forsooth, and made excuse,
—E'en then would be some stooping; and I choose
Never to stoop. Oh sir, she smiled, no doubt,
Whene'er I passed her; but who passed without
Much the same smile? This grew; I gave commands;   45
Then all smiles stopped together. There she stands
As if alive. Will't please you rise? We'll meet
The company below, then. I repeat,
The Count your master's known munificence
Is ample warrant that no just pretence   50
Of mine for dowry will be disallowed;
Though his fair daughter's self, as I avowed
At starting, is my object. Nay, we'll go
Together down, sir. Notice Neptune, though,
Taming a sea-horse, thought a rarity,   55
Which Claus of Innsbruck° cast in bronze for me!

[1842]

56. Claus of Innsbruck: A fictional sculptor.

WALT WHITMAN   [1819–1892]

From Song of Myself°

1

I celebrate myself, and sing myself,
And what I assume you shall assume,
For every atom belonging to me as good belongs to you.

Song of Myself: The poem was first published in 1855 as an untitled section of *Leaves of Grass*. It was a rough, rude, and vigorous example of antebellum American cultural politics and free verse experimentation. The version used here, from the sixth edition (1891–1892), is much longer, more carefully crafted, and more conventionally punctuated. Sections 1–3 introduce the persona and the scope and

I loafe and invite my soul,
I lean and loafe at my ease observing a spear of summer grass.   5

My tongue, every atom of my blood, form'd from this soil, this air,
Born here of parents born here from parents the same, and their
     parents the same,
I, now thirty-seven years old in perfect health begin,
Hoping to cease not till death.

Creeds and schools in abeyance,   10
Retiring back a while sufficed at what they are, but never forgotten,
I harbor for good or bad, I permit to speak at every hazard,
Nature without check with original energy.

                                        2

Houses and rooms are full of perfumes, the shelves are crowded with
     perfumes,
I breathe the fragrance myself and know it and like it,   15
The distillation would intoxicate me also, but I shall not let it.

The atmosphere is not a perfume, it has no taste of the distillation,
     it is odorless,
It is for my mouth forever, I am in love with it,
I will go to the bank by the wood and become undisguised and naked,
I am mad for it to be in contact with me.   20

The smoke of my own breath,
Echoes, ripples, buzz'd whispers, love-root, silk-thread, crotch and vine,
My respiration and inspiration, the beating of my heart, the passing of
     blood and air through my lungs,
The sniff of green leaves and dry leaves, and of the shore and
     dark-color'd sea-rocks, and of hay in the barn,
The sound of the belch'd words of my voice loos'd to the eddies of the
     wind,   25
A few light kisses, a few embraces, a reaching around of arms,
The play of shine and shade on the trees as the supple boughs wag,

---

method of the poem; section 6 explains grass as a symbol; sections 7–10, examples
of Whitman's dynamic panoramic miniatures, are also of historical significance
regarding Native and African Americans; section 14 extends the outward sweep of
7–10; section 21 develops Whitman's theme of sex and nature; section 24 extends
the handling of the poem's persona; sections 46 and 48 recapitulate the major
themes of the poem; sections 51 and 52 deal with the absorption of the poet's persona into the converted reader.

The delight alone or in the rush of the streets, or along the fields and
   hill-sides,
The feeling of health, the full-noon trill, the song of me rising from bed
   and meeting the sun.

Have you reckon'd a thousand acres much? have you reckon'd the earth
   much?   30
Have you practis'd so long to learn to read?
Have you felt so proud to get at the meaning of poems?

Stop this day and night with me and you shall possess the origin of all
   poems,
You shall possess the good of the earth and sun, (there are millions of
   suns left,)
You shall no longer take things at second or third hand, nor look
   through the eyes of the dead, nor feed on the spectres in books,   35
You shall not look through my eyes either, nor take things from me,
You shall listen to all sides and filter them from your self.

3

I have heard what the talkers were talking, the talk of the beginning
   and the end,
But I do not talk of the beginning or the end.

There was never any more inception than there is now,   40
Nor any more youth or age than there is now,
And will never be any more perfection than there is now,
Nor any more heaven or hell than there is now.
Urge and urge and urge,
Always the procreant urge of the world.   45

Out of the dimness opposite equals advance, always substance and
   increase, always sex,
Always a knit of identity, always distinction, always a breed of life.

To elaborate is no avail, learn'd and unlearn'd feel that it is so.

Sure as the most certain sure, plumb in the uprights, well entretied,°
   braced in the beams,
Stout as a horse, affectionate, haughty, electrical,   50
I and this mystery here we stand.

Clear and sweet is my soul, and clear and sweet is all that is not my soul.

---

49. entretied: Cross-braced, as between two joists in carpentry.

Lack one lacks both, and the unseen is proved by the seen,
Till that becomes unseen and receives proof in its turn.

Showing the best and dividing it from the worst age vexes age,   55
Knowing the perfect fitness and equanimity of things, while they discuss
  I am silent, and go bathe and admire myself.

Welcome is every organ and attribute of me, and of any man hearty
  and clean,
Not an inch nor a particle of an inch is vile, and none shall be less
  familiar than the rest.

I am satisfied—I see, dance, laugh, sing;
As the hugging and loving bed-fellow sleeps at my side through the
  night, and withdraws at the peep of the day with stealthy tread,   60
Leaving me baskets cover'd with white towels swelling the house with
  their plenty,
Shall I postpone my acceptation and realization and scream at my eyes,
That they turn from gazing after and down the road,
And forthwith cipher and show me to a cent,
Exactly the value of one and exactly the value of two, and which is
  ahead?   65

6

A child said *What is the grass?* fetching it to me with full hands;
How could I answer the child? I do not know what it is any more
  than he.   100

I guess it must be the flag of my disposition, out of hopeful green stuff
  woven.

Or I guess it is the handkerchief of the Lord,
A scented gift and remembrancer designedly dropt,
Bearing the owner's name someway in the corners, that we may see and
  remark, and say *Whose?*

Or I guess the grass is itself a child, the produced babe of the vegetation.   105

Or I guess it is a uniform hieroglyphic,
And it means, Sprouting alike in broad zones and narrow zones,
Growing among black folks as among white,
Kanuck,° Tuckahoe,° Congressman, Cuff,° I give them the same,
  I receive them the same.

And now it seems to me the beautiful uncut hair of graves.   110

---

109. Kanuck: A French Canadian; **Tuckahoe:** A Virginian living in the tidewater
region and eating tuckahoe, a fungus; **Cuff:** A black person.

Tenderly will I use you curling grass,
It may be you transpire from the breasts of young men,
It may be if I had known them I would have loved them,
It may be you are from old people, or from offspring taken soon out of
    their mothers' laps,
And here you are the mothers' laps.   115

This grass is very dark to be from the white heads of old mothers,
Darker than the colorless beards of old men,
Dark to come from under the faint red roofs of mouths.

O I perceive after all so many uttering tongues,
And I perceive they do not come from the roofs of mouths for nothing.   120

I wish I could translate the hints about the dead young men and women,
And the hints about old men and mothers, and the offspring taken soon
    out of their laps.
What do you think has become of the young and old men?
And what do you think has become of the women and children?

They are alive and well somewhere,   125
The smallest sprout shows there is really no death,
And if ever there was it led forward life, and does not wait at the end to
    arrest it,
And ceas'd the moment life appear'd.

All goes onward and outward, nothing collapses,
And to die is different from what any one supposed, and luckier.   130

7

Has any one supposed it lucky to be born?
I hasten to inform him or her it is just as lucky to die, and I know it.

I pass death with the dying and birth with the new-wash'd babe, and
    am not contain'd between my hat and boots,
And peruse manifold objects, no two alike and every one good,
The earth good and the stars good, and their adjuncts all good.   135

I am not an earth nor an adjunct of an earth,
I am the mate and companion of people, all just as immortal and
    fathomless as myself,
(They do not know how immortal, but I know.)

Every kind for itself and its own, for me mine male and female,
For me those that have been boys and that love women,   140
For me the man that is proud and feels how it stings to be slighted,
For me the sweet-heart and the old maid, for me mothers and the
    mothers of mothers,

For me lips that have smiled, eyes that have shed tears,
For me children and the begetters of children.

Undrape! you are not guilty to me, nor stale nor discarded,   145
I see through the broadcloth and gingham whether or no,
And am around, tenacious, acquisitive, tireless, and cannot be
    shaken away.

8

The little one sleeps in its cradle,
I lift the gauze and look a long time, and silently brush away flies with
    my hand.

The youngster and the red-faced girl turn aside up the bushy hill,   150
I peeringly view them from the top.

The suicide sprawls on the bloody floor of the bedroom,
I witness the corpse with its dabbled hair, I note where the pistol has
    fallen.

The blab of the pave, tires of carts, sluff of boot-soles, talk of the
    promenaders,
The heavy omnibus, the driver with his interrogating thumb, the clank
    of the shod horses on the granite floor,   155
The snow-sleighs, clinking, shouted jokes, pelts of snow-balls,
The hurrahs for popular favorites, the fury of rous'd mobs,
The flap of the curtain'd litter, a sick man inside borne to the hospital,
The meeting of enemies, the sudden oath, the blows and fall,
The excited crowd, the policeman with his star quickly working his
    passage to the centre of the crowd,   160
The impassive stones that receive and return so many echoes,
What groans of over-fed or half-starv'd who fall sunstruck or in fits,
What exclamations of women taken suddenly who hurry home and give
    birth to babes,
What living and buried speech is always vibrating here, what howls
    restrain'd by decorum,
Arrests of criminals, slights, adulterous offers made, acceptances,
    rejections with convex lips,   165
I mind them or the show or resonance of them—I come and I depart.

9

The big doors of the country barn stand open and ready,
The dried grass of the harvest-time loads the slow-drawn wagon,
The clear light plays on the brown gray and green intertinged,
The armfuls are pack'd to the sagging mow.   170

I am there, I help, I came stretch'd atop of the load,
I felt its soft jolts, one leg reclined on the other,
I jump from the cross-beams and seize the clover and timothy,
And roll head over heels and tangle my hair full of wisps.

10

Alone far in the wilds and mountains I hunt,   175
Wandering amazed at my own lightness and glee,
In the late afternoon choosing a safe spot to pass the night,
Kindling a fire and broiling the fresh-kill'd game,
Falling asleep on the gather'd leaves with my dog and gun by my side.

The Yankee clipper is under her sky-sails, she cuts the sparkle and
    scud,   180
My eyes settle the land, I bend at her prow or shout joyously from the
    deck.

The boatmen and clam-diggers arose early and stopt for me,
I tuck'd my trowser-ends in my boots and went and had a good time;
You should have been with us that day round the chowder-kettle.

I saw the marriage of the trapper in the open air in the far west, the
    bride was a red girl,   185
Her father and his friends sat near cross-legged and dumbly smoking,
    they had moccasins to their feet and large thick blankets hanging
    from their shoulders,
On a bank lounged the trapper, he was drest mostly in skins, his
    luxuriant beard and curls protected his neck, he held his bride by
    the hand,
She had long eyelashes, her head was bare, her coarse straight locks
    descended upon her voluptuous limbs and reach'd to her feet.

The runaway slave came to my house and stopt outside,
I heard his motions crackling the twigs of the woodpile,   190
Through the swung half-door of the kitchen I saw him limpsy and
    weak,
And went where he sat on a log and led him in and assured him,
And brought water and fill'd a tub for his sweated body and bruis'd
    feet,
And gave him a room that enter'd from my own, and gave him some
    coarse clean clothes,
And remember perfectly well his revolving eyes and his awkwardness,   195
And remember putting plasters on the galls of his neck and ankles;
He staid with me a week before he was recuperated and pass'd north,
I had him sit next me at table, my fire-lock lean'd in the corner.

14

The wild gander leads his flock through the cool night,   245
Ya-honk he says, and sounds it down to me like an invitation,
The pert may suppose it meaningless, but I listening close,
Find its purpose and place up there toward the wintry sky.

The sharp-hoof'd moose of the north, the cat on the house-sill, the
   chickadee, the prairie-dog,
The litter of the grunting sow as they tug at her teats,   250
The brood of the turkey-hen and she with her half-spread wings,
I see in them and myself the same old law.

The press of my foot to the earth springs a hundred affections,
They scorn the best I can do to relate them.

I am enamour'd of growing out-doors,   255
Of men that live among cattle or taste of the ocean or woods,
Of the builders and steerers of ships and the wielders of axes and mauls,
   and the drivers of horses,
I can eat and sleep with them week in and week out.

What is commonest, cheapest, nearest, easiest, is Me,
Me going in for my chances, spending for vast returns,   260
Adorning myself to bestow myself on the first that will take me,
Not asking the sky to come down to my good will,
Scattering it freely forever.

21

I am the poet of the Body and I am the poet of the Soul,
The pleasures of heaven are with me and the pains of hell are with me,
The first I graft and increase upon myself, the latter I translate into a
   new tongue.

I am the poet of the woman the same as the man,   425
And I say it is as great to be a woman as to be a man,
And I say there is nothing greater than the mother of men.

I chant the chant of dilation or pride,
We have had ducking and deprecating about enough,
I show that size is only development.   430

Have you outstript the rest? are you the President?
It is a trifle, they will more than arrive there every one, and still
   pass on.

I am he that walks with the tender and growing night,
I call to the earth and sea half-held by the night.

Press close bare-bosom'd night—press close magnetic nourishing night!   435
Night of south winds—night of the large few stars!
Still nodding night—mad naked summer night.

Smile O voluptuous cool-breath'd earth!
Earth of the slumbering and liquid trees!
Earth of departed sunset—earth of the mountains misty-topt!   440
Earth of the vitreous pour of the full moon just tinged with blue!
Earth of shine and dark mottling the tide of the river!
Earth of the limpid gray of clouds brighter and clearer for my sake!
Far-swooping elbow'd earth—rich apple-blossom'd earth!
Smile, for your lover comes.   445

Prodigal, you have given me love—therefore I to you give love!
O unspeakable passionate love.

24

Walt Whitman, a kosmos, of Manhattan the son,
Turbulent, fleshy, sensual, eating, drinking and breeding,
No sentimentalist, no stander above men and women or apart from them,
No more modest than immodest.   500

Unscrew the locks from the doors!
Unscrew the doors themselves from their jambs!

Whoever degrades another degrades me,
And whatever is done or said returns at last to me.

Through me the afflatus° surging and surging, through me the current
    and index.   505

I speak the pass-word primeval, I give the sign of democracy,
By God! I will accept nothing which all cannot have their counterpart
    of on the same terms.

Through me many long dumb voices,
Voices of the interminable generations of prisoners and slaves,
Voices of the diseas'd and despairing and of thieves and dwarfs,   510
Voices of cycles of preparation and accretion,
And of the threads that connect the stars, and of wombs and of the
    father-stuff,
And of the rights of them the others are down upon,
Of the deform'd, trivial, flat, foolish, despised,
Fog in the air, beetles rolling balls of dung.   515

505. **afflatus:** Inspiration (from the Latin for "to blow on").

Through me forbidden voices,
Voices of sexes and lusts, voices veil'd and I remove the veil,
Voices indecent by me clarified and transfigur'd.

I do not press my fingers across my mouth,
I keep as delicate around the bowels as around the head and heart,   520
Copulation is no more rank to me than death is.

I believe in the flesh and the appetites,
Seeing, hearing, feeling, are miracles, and each part and tag of me is a
    miracle.

Divine am I inside and out, and I make holy whatever I touch or am
    touch'd from,
The scent of these arm-pits aroma finer than prayer,   525
This head more than churches, bibles, and all the creeds.

If I worship one thing more than another it shall be the spread of my
    own body, or any part of it,
Translucent mould of me it shall be you!
Shaded ledges and rests it shall be you!
Firm masculine colter° it shall be you!   530
Whatever goes to the tilth° of me it shall be you!
You my rich blood! your milky stream pale strippings of my life!
Breast that presses against other breasts it shall be you!
My brain it shall be your occult convolutions!
Root of wash'd sweet-flag! timorous pond-snipe! nest of guarded
    duplicate eggs! it shall be you!   535
Mix'd tussled hay of head, beard, brawn, it shall be you!
Trickling sap of maple, fibre of manly wheat, it shall be you!
Sun so generous it shall be you!
Vapors lighting and shading my face it shall be you!
You sweaty brooks and dews it shall be you!   540
Winds whose soft-tickling genitals rub against me it shall be you!
Broad muscular fields, branches of live oak, loving lounger in my
    winding paths, it shall be you!
Hands I have taken, face I have kiss'd, mortal I have ever touch'd, it
    shall be you.

46

I know I have the best of time and space, and was never measured and
    never will be measured.

530. **colter:** Blade or disk on a plow for cutting the earth.
531. **tilth:** Cultivation of land.

I tramp a perpetual journey, (come listen all!)
My signs are a rain-proof coat, good shoes, and a staff cut from the
    woods,
No friend of mine takes his ease in my chair,
I have no chair, no church, no philosophy,   1205
I lead no man to a dinner-table, library, exchange,
But each man and each woman of you I lead upon a knoll,
My left hand hooking you round the waist,
My right hand pointing to landscapes of continents and the public road.

Not I, not any one else can travel that road for you,   1210
You must travel it for yourself.

It is not far, it is within reach,
Perhaps you have been on it since you were born and did not know,
Perhaps it is everywhere on water and on land.

Shoulder your duds dear son, and I will mine, and let us hasten forth,   1215
Wonderful cities and free nations we shall fetch as we go.

If you tire, give me both burdens, and rest the chuff° of your hand
    on my hip,
And in due time you shall repay the same service to me,
For after we start we never lie by again.

This day before dawn I ascended a hill and look'd at the crowded
    heaven,   1220
And I said to my spirit *When we become the enfolders of those orbs, and
    the pleasure and knowledge of every thing in them, shall we be fill'd and
    satisfied then?*
And my spirit said *No, we but level that lift to pass and continue beyond.*

You are also asking me questions and I hear you,
I answer that I cannot answer, you must find out for yourself.

Sit a while dear son,   1225
Here are biscuits to eat and here is milk to drink,
But as soon as you sleep and renew yourself in sweet clothes, I kiss you
    with a good-by kiss and open the gate for your egress hence.

Long enough have you dream'd contemptible dreams,
Now I wash the gum from your eyes,
You must habit yourself to the dazzle of the light and of every moment
    of your life.   1230

1217. **chuff:** Weight.

Long have you timidly waded holding a plank by the shore,
Now I will you to be a bold swimmer,
To jump off in the midst of the sea, rise again, nod to me, shout, and
    laughingly dash with your hair.

48

I have said that the soul is not more than the body,
And I have said that the body is not more than the soul,   1270
And nothing, not God, is greater to one than one's self is,
And whoever walks a furlong without sympathy walks to his own
    funeral drest in his shroud,
And I or you pocketless of a dime may purchase the pick of the earth,
And to glance with an eye or show a bean in its pod confounds the
    learning of all times,
And there is no trade or employment but the young man following it
    may become a hero,   1275
And there is no object so soft but it makes a hub for the wheel'd
    universe,
And I say to any man or woman, Let your soul stand cool and composed
    before a million universes.

And I say to mankind, Be not curious about God,
For I who am curious about each am not curious about God,
(No array of terms can say how much I am at peace about God and
    about death.)   1280

I hear and behold God in every object, yet understand God not in the
    least,
Nor do I understand who there can be more wonderful than myself.

Why should I wish to see God better than this day?
I see something of God each hour of the twenty-four, and each
    moment then,
In the faces of men and women I see God, and in my own face in the
    glass,   1285
I find letters from God dropt in the street, and every one is sign'd by
    God's name,
And I leave them where they are, for I know that wheresoe'er I go,
Others will punctually come for ever and ever.

51

The past and present wilt—I have fill'd them, emptied them,
And proceed to fill my next fold of the future.   1320

Listener up there! what have you to confide to me?
Look in my face while I snuff° the sidle° of evening,
(Talk honestly, no one else hears you, and I stay only a minute longer.)

Do I contradict myself?
Very well then I contradict myself,   1325
(I am large, I contain multitudes.)

I concentrate toward them that are nigh, I wait on the door-slab.

Who has done his day's work? who will soonest be through with his
    supper?
Who wishes to walk with me?

Will you speak before I am gone? will you prove already too late?   1330

52

The spotted hawk swoops by and accuses me, he complains of my gab
    and my loitering.

I too am not a bit tamed, I too am untranslatable,
I sound my barbaric yawp over the roofs of the world.

The last scud of day holds back for me,
It flings my likeness after the rest and true as any on the shadow'd
    wilds,   1335
It coaxes me to the vapor and the dusk.

I depart as air, I shake my white locks at the runaway sun,
I effuse my flesh in eddies, and drift it in lacy jags.

I bequeath myself to the dirt to grow from the grass I love,
If you want me again look for me under your boot-soles.   1340

You will hardly know who I am or what I mean,
But I shall be good health to you nevertheless,
And filter and fibre your blood.

Failing to fetch me at first keep encouraged,
Missing me one place search another,   1345
I stop somewhere waiting for you.

[1855; 1891–1892]

1322. snuff: Snuff out; sidle: Sidewise or stealthy movement.

WALT WHITMAN   [1819–1892]

When Lilacs Last in the Dooryard Bloom'd°

1

When lilacs last in the dooryard bloom'd,
And the great star early droop'd in the western sky in the night,
I mourn'd, and yet shall mourn with ever-returning spring.

Ever-returning spring, trinity sure to me you bring,
Lilac blooming perennial and drooping star in the west,   5
And thought of him I love.

2

O powerful western fallen star!
O shades of night—O moody, tearful night!
O great star disappear'd—O the black murk that hides the star!
O cruel hands that hold me powerless—O helpless soul of me!   10
O harsh surrounding cloud that will not free my soul.

3

In the dooryard fronting an old farm-house near the white-wash'd
     palings,
Stands the lilac-bush tall-growing with heart-shaped leaves of rich
     green,
With many a pointed blossom rising delicate, with the perfume strong
     I love,
With every leaf a miracle—and from this bush in the dooryard,   15
With delicate-color'd blossoms and heart-shaped leaves of rich green,
A sprig with its flower I break.

4

In the swamp in secluded recesses,
A shy and hidden bird is warbling a song.
Solitary the thrush,   20
The hermit withdrawn to himself, avoiding the settlements,
Sings by himself a song.

When Lilacs Last in the Dooryard Bloom'd: This is one of four elegies written by
Whitman on the death of President Abraham Lincoln, 14 April 1865, and first
published as an addendum to *Drum-Taps* called "Sequel to *Drum-Taps*." Whitman
later added the *Drum-Taps* volume to *Leaves of Grass*. The version used here is
from the sixth edition of *Leaves of Grass* (1891–1892).

Song of the bleeding throat,
Death's outlet song of life, (for well dear brother I know,
If thou wast not granted to sing thou would'st surely die.)   25

5

Over the breast of the spring, the land, amid cities,
Amid lanes and through old woods, where lately the violets peep'd from
    the ground, spotting the gray debris,
Amid the grass in the fields each side of the lanes, passing the endless
    grass,
Passing the yellow-spear'd wheat, every grain from its shroud in the
    dark-brown fields uprisen,
Passing the apple-tree blows of white and pink in the orchards,   30
Carrying a corpse to where it shall rest in the grave,
Night and day journeys a coffin.

6

Coffin that passes through lanes and streets,°
Through day and night with the great cloud darkening the land,
With the pomp of the inloop'd flags with the cities draped in black,   35
With the show of the States themselves as of crape-veil'd women
    standing,
With processions long and winding and the flambeaus° of the night,
With the countless torches lit, with the silent sea of faces and the
    unbared heads,
With the waiting depot, the arriving coffin, and the sombre faces,
With dirges through the night, with the thousand voices rising strong
    and solemn,   40
With all the mournful voices of the dirges pour'd around the coffin,
The dim-lit churches and the shuddering organs—where amid these
    you journey,
With the tolling tolling bells' perpetual clang,
Here, coffin that slowly passes,
I give you my sprig of lilac.   45

7

(Nor for you, for one alone,
Blossoms and branches green to coffins all I bring,

---

33. lanes and streets: President Lincoln's funeral procession traveled from
Washington to Springfield, Illinois, with stops at cities and towns to enable people
to honor their assassinated president.
37. flambeaus: Flaming torches.

For fresh as the morning, thus would I chant a song for you O sane and
  sacred death.

All over bouquets of roses,
O death, I cover you over with roses and early lilies,   50
But mostly and now the lilac that blooms the first,
Copious I break, I break the sprigs from the bushes,
With loaded arms I come, pouring for you,
For you and the coffins all of you O death.)

8

O western orb sailing the heaven,   55
Now I know what you must have meant as a month since I walk'd,
As I walk'd in silence the transparent shadowy night,
As I saw you had something to tell as you bent to me night after night,
As you droop'd from the sky low down as if to my side, (while the other
  stars all look'd on,)
As we wander'd together the solemn night, (for something I know not
  what kept me from sleep,)   60
As the night advanced, and I saw on the rim of the west how full you
  were of woe,
As I stood on the rising ground in the breeze in the cool transparent
  night,
As I watch'd where you pass'd and was lost in the netherward black of
  the night,
As my soul in its trouble dissatisfied sank, as where you sad orb,
Concluded, dropt in the night, and was gone.   65

9

Sing on there in the swamp,
O singer bashful and tender, I hear your notes, I hear your call,
I hear, I come presently, I understand you,
But a moment I linger, for the lustrous star has detain'd me,
The star my departing comrade holds and detains me.   70

10

O how shall I warble myself for the dead one there I loved?
And how shall I deck my song for the large sweet soul that has gone?
And what shall my perfume be for the grave of him I love?

Sea-winds blown from east and west,
Blown from the Eastern sea and blown from the Western sea, till there
  on the prairies meeting,   75
These and with these and the breath of my chant,
I'll perfume the grave of him I love.

11

O what shall I hang on the chamber walls?
And what shall the pictures be that I hang on the walls,
To adorn the burial-house of him I love?   80

Pictures of growing spring and farms and homes,
With the Fourth-month eve at sundown, and the gray smoke lucid and
    bright,
With floods of the yellow gold of the gorgeous, indolent, sinking sun,
    burning, expanding the air,
With the fresh sweet herbage under foot, and the pale green leaves of
    the trees prolific,
In the distance the flowing glaze, the breast of the river, with a
    wind-dapple here and there,   85
With ranging hills on the banks, with many a line against the sky, and
    shadows,
And the city at hand with dwellings so dense, and stacks of chimneys,
And all the scenes of life and the workshops, and the workmen
    homeward returning.

12

Lo, body and soul—this land,
My own Manhattan with spires, and the sparkling and hurrying tides,
    and the ships,   90
The varied and ample land, the South and the North in the light, Ohio's
    shores and flashing Missouri,
And ever the far-spreading prairies cover'd with grass and corn.

Lo, the most excellent sun so calm and haughty,
The violet and purple morn with just-felt breezes,
The gentle soft-born measureless light,   95
The miracle spreading, bathing all, the fulfill'd noon,
The coming eve delicious, the welcome night and the stars,
Over my cities shining all, enveloping man and land.

13

Sing on, sing on you gray-brown bird,
Sing from the swamps, the recesses, pour your chant from the bushes,   100
Limitless out of the dusk, out of the cedars and pines.

Sing on dearest brother, warble your reedy song,
Loud human song, with voice of uttermost woe.

O liquid and free and tender!
O wild and loose to my soul—O wondrous singer!   105

You only I hear—yet the star holds me, (but will soon depart,)
Yet the lilac with mastering odor holds me.

14

Now while I sat in the day and look'd forth,
In the close of the day with its light and the fields of spring, and the
　farmers preparing their crops,
In the large unconscious scenery of my land with its lakes and forests,　　110
In the heavenly aerial beauty, (after the perturb'd winds and the storms,)
Under the arching heavens of the afternoon swift passing, and the
　voices of children and women,
The many-moving sea-tides, and I saw the ships how they sail'd,
And the summer approaching with richness, and the fields all busy with
　labor,
And the infinite separate houses, how they all went on, each with its
　meals and minutia of daily usages,　　115
And the streets how their throbbings throbb'd, and the cities pent—lo,
　then and there.
Falling upon them all and among them all, enveloping me with the rest,
Appear'd the cloud, appear'd the long black trail,
And I knew death, its thought, and the sacred knowledge of death.

Then with the knowledge of death as walking one side of me,　　120
And the thought of death close-walking the other side of me,
And I in the middle as with companions, and as holding the hands of
　companions,
I fled forth to the hiding receiving night that talks not,
Down to the shores of the water, the path by the swamp in the dimness,
To the solemn shadowy cedars and ghostly pines so still.　　125

And the singer so shy to the rest receiv'd me,
The gray-brown bird I know receiv'd us comrades three,
And he sang the carol of death, and a verse for him I love.

From deep secluded recesses,
From the fragrant cedars and the ghostly pines so still,　　130
Came the carol of the bird.

And the charm of the carol rapt me,
As I held as if by their hands my comrades in the night,
And the voice of my spirit tallied the song of the bird.

Come lovely and soothing death,　　135
Undulate round the world, serenely arriving, arriving,
In the day, in the night, to all, to each,
Sooner or later delicate death.

Prais'd be the fathomless universe,
For life and joy, and for objects and knowledge curious,   140
And for love, sweet love—but praise! praise! praise!
For the sure-enwinding arms of cool-enfolding death.

Dark mother always gliding near with soft feet,
Have none chanted for thee a chant of fullest welcome?
Then I chant it for thee, I glorify thee above all,   145
I bring thee a song that when thou must indeed come, come unfalteringly.

Approach strong deliveress,
When it is so, when thou hast taken them I joyously sing the dead,
Lost in the loving floating ocean of thee,
Laved in the flood of thy bliss O death.   150

From me to thee glad serenades,
Dances for thee I propose saluting thee, adornments and feastings for thee,
And the sights of the open landscape and the high-spread sky are fitting,
And life and the fields, and the huge and thoughtful night.

The night in silence under many a star,   155
The ocean shore and the husky whispering wave whose voice I know,
And the soul turning to thee O vast and well-veil'd death,
And the body gratefully nestling close to thee.

Over the tree-tops I float thee a song,
Over the rising and sinking waves, over the myriad fields and the
*   prairies wide,*   160
Over the dense-pack'd cities all and the teeming wharves and ways,
I float this carol with joy, with joy to thee O death.

15

To the tally of my soul,
Loud and strong kept up the gray-brown bird,
With pure deliberate notes spreading filling the night.   165

Loud in the pines and cedars dim,
Clear in the freshness moist and the swamp-perfume,
And I with my comrades there in the night.

While my sight that was bound in my eyes unclosed,
As to long panoramas of visions.   170

And I saw askant the armies,
I saw as in noiseless dreams hundreds of battle-flags,
Borne through the smoke of the battles and pierc'd with missiles I
    saw them,

And carried hither and yon through the smoke, and torn and bloody,
And at last but a few shreds left on the staffs, (and all in silence,)   175
And the staffs all splinter'd and broken.

I saw battle-corpses, myriads of them,
And the white skeletons of young men, I saw them,
I saw the debris and debris of all the slain soldiers of the war,
But I saw they were not as was thought,   180
They themselves were fully at rest, they suffer'd not,
The living remain'd and suffer'd, the mother suffer'd,
And the wife and the child and the musing comrade suffer'd,
And the armies that remain'd suffer'd.

16

Passing the visions, passing the night,   185
Passing, unloosing the hold of my comrades' hands,
Passing the song of the hermit bird and the tallying song of my soul,
Victorious song, death's outlet song, yet varying ever-altering song,
As low and wailing, yet clear the notes, rising and falling, flooding
    the night,
Sadly sinking and fainting, as warning and warning, and yet again
    bursting with joy,   190
Covering the earth and filling the spread of the heaven,
As that powerful psalm in the night I heard from recesses,
Passing, I leave thee lilac with heart-shaped leaves,
I leave thee there in the door-yard, blooming, returning with spring.

I cease from my song for thee,   195
From my gaze on thee in the west, fronting the west, communing
    with thee,
O comrade lustrous with silver face in the night.

Yet each to keep and all, retrievements out of the night,
The song, the wondrous chant of the gray-brown bird,
And the tallying chant, the echo arous'd in my soul,   200
With the lustrous and drooping star with the countenance full of woe,
With the holders holding my hand nearing the call of the bird,
Comrades mine and I in the midst, and their memory ever to keep, for
    the dead I loved so well,
For the sweetest, wisest soul of all my days and lands—and this for his
    dear sake,
Lilac and star and bird twined with the chant of my soul,   205
There in the fragrant pines and the cedars dusk and dim.

[*1865;* 1891–1892]

WALT WHITMAN   [1819–1892]

A Noiseless Patient Spider

A noiseless patient spider,
I mark'd where on a little promontory it stood isolated,
Mark'd how to explore the vacant vast surrounding,
It launch'd forth filament, filament, filament, out of itself,
Ever unreeling them, ever tirelessly speeding them.   5

And you O my soul where you stand,
Surrounded, detached, in measureless oceans of space,
Ceaselessly musing, venturing, throwing, seeking the spheres to connect
   them,
Till the bridge you will need be form'd, till the ductile anchor hold,
Till the gossamer thread you fling catch somewhere, O my soul.   10

[*1868;* 1881]

MATTHEW ARNOLD   [1822–1888]

Dover Beach

The sea is calm tonight.
The tide is full, the moon lies fair
Upon the straits; on the French coast the light
Gleams and is gone; the cliffs of England stand,
Glimmering and vast, out in the tranquil bay.   5
Come to the window, sweet is the night-air!
Only, from the long line of spray
Where the sea meets the moon-blanched land,
Listen! you hear the grating roar
Of pebbles which the waves draw back, and fling,   10
At their return, up the high strand,
Begin, and cease, and then again begin,
With tremulous cadence slow, and bring
The eternal note of sadness in.

Sophocles long ago   15
Heard it on the Aegean, and it brought
Into his mind the turbid ebb and flow
Of human misery; we

Find also in the sound a thought,
Hearing it by this distant northern sea.   20

The Sea of Faith
Was once, too, at the full, and round earth's shore
Lay like the folds of a bright girdle furled.
But now I only hear
Its melancholy, long, withdrawing roar,   25
Retreating, to the breath
Of the night-wind, down the vast edges drear
And naked shingles° of the world.   *pebble-covered beaches*

Ah, love, let us be true
To one another! for the world, which seems   30
To lie before us like a land of dreams,
So various, so beautiful, so new,
Hath really neither joy, nor love, nor light,
Nor certitude, nor peace, nor help for pain;
And we are here as on a darkling plain   35
Swept with confused alarms of struggle and flight,
Where ignorant armies clash by night.

[*c. 1851;* 1867]

CHRISTINA ROSSETTI   [1830–1894]

Song

When I am dead, my dearest,
  Sing no sad songs for me;
Plant thou no roses at my head,
  Nor shady cypress tree:
Be the green grass above me   5
  With showers and dewdrops wet;
And if thou wilt, remember,
  And if thou wilt, forget.

I shall not see the shadows,
  I shall not feel the rain;   10
I shall not hear the nightingale
  Sing on, as if in pain:

And dreaming through the twilight
    That doth not rise nor set,
Haply I may remember,   15
    And haply may forget.

[1862]

EMILY DICKINSON   [1830–1886]

Wild Nights — Wild Nights!

Wild Nights — Wild Nights!
Were I with thee
Wild Nights should be
Our luxury!

Futile — the Winds —   5
To a Heart in port —
Done with the Compass —
Done with the Chart!

Rowing in Eden —
Ah, the Sea!   10
Might I but moor — Tonight —
In Thee!

[c. *1861;* 1891]

EMILY DICKINSON   [1830–1886]

Much Madness is divinest Sense

Much Madness is divinest Sense —
To a discerning Eye —
Much Sense — the starkest Madness —
'Tis the Majority
In this, as All, prevail —   5
Assent — and you are sane —
Demur — you're straightway dangerous —
And handled with a Chain —

[c. *1862;* 1890]

EMILY DICKINSON   [1830–1886]

I heard a Fly buzz—when I died

I heard a Fly buzz—when I died—
The Stillness in the Room
Was like the Stillness in the Air—
Between the Heaves of Storm—

The Eyes around—had wrung them dry—   5
And Breaths were gathering firm
For that last Onset—when the King
Be witnessed—in the Room—

I willed my Keepsakes—Signed away
What portion of me be   10
Assignable—and then it was
There interposed a Fly—

With Blue—uncertain stumbling Buzz—
Between the light—and me—
And then the Windows failed—and then   15
I could not see to see—

[c. 1862; 1890]

EMILY DICKINSON   [1830–1886]

I like to see it lap the Miles

I like to see it lap the Miles—
And lick the Valleys up—
And stop to feed itself at Tanks—
And then—prodigious step

Around a Pile of Mountains—   5
And supercilious peer
In Shanties—by the sides of Roads—
And then a Quarry pare

To fit its Ribs
And crawl between   10
Complaining all the while
In horrid—hooting stanza—
Then chase itself down Hill—

And neigh like Boanerges°—
Then—punctual as a Star   15
Stop—docile and omnipotent
At its own stable door—

[*c. 1862;* 1891]

14. like Boanerges: As loud as thunder. *Boanerges* is the surname given by Jesus
to James and John in Mark 3:17, translated there as "the sons of thunder."

EMILY DICKINSON   [1830–1886]

Because I could not stop for Death

Because I could not stop for Death—
He kindly stopped for me—
The Carriage held but just Ourselves—
And Immortality.

We slowly drove—He knew no haste   5
And I had put away
My labor and my leisure too,
For His Civility—

We passed the School, where Children strove
At Recess—in the Ring—   10
We passed the Fields of Gazing Grain—
We passed the Setting Sun—

Or rather—He passed Us—
The Dews drew quivering and chill—
For only Gossamer, my Gown—   15
My Tippet°—only Tulle°—   *scarf/silk net*

We paused before a House that seemed
A Swelling of the Ground—
The Roof was scarcely visible—
The Cornice—in the Ground—   20

Since then—'tis Centuries—and yet
Feels shorter than the Day
I first surmised the Horses' Heads
Were toward Eternity—

[*c. 1863;* 1890]

THOMAS HARDY   [1840–1928]

The Darkling° Thrush

I leant upon a coppice° gate
  When Frost was spectre-grey,
And Winter's dregs made desolate
  The weakening eye of day.
The tangled bine-stems° scored the sky   5
  Like strings of broken lyres,
And all mankind that haunted nigh
  Had sought their household fires.

The land's sharp features seemed to be
  The Century's corpse° outleant,   10
His crypt° the cloudy canopy,
  The wind his death-lament.
The ancient pulse° of germ° and birth
  Was shrunken hard and dry,
And every spirit upon earth   15
  Seemed fervourless as I.

At once a voice arose among
  The bleak twigs overhead
In a full-hearted evensong
  Of joy illimited;   20
An aged thrush, frail, gaunt, and small,
  In blast-beruffled plume,
Had chosen thus to fling his soul
  Upon the growing gloom.

So little cause for carolings   25
  Of such ecstatic sound
Was written on terrestrial things
  Afar or nigh around,

Darkling: In the dark.
1. coppice: A wood or thicket of brush and small trees.
5. bine-stems: Shoots or stems of a climbing plant.
10. Century's corpse: The poem was dated "December 31, 1900," the last day of the nineteenth century. Its original title was "By the Century's Deathbed."
11. crypt: Burial place beneath a church.
13. pulse: Successive beat or throb indicating vitality or energy; **germ:** Initial stage from which something may develop; source of life.

That I could think there trembled through
   His happy good-night air   30
Some blessed Hope, whereof he knew
   And I was unaware.

[1901]

GERARD MANLEY HOPKINS   [1844–1889]
God's Grandeur

The world is charged with the grándeur of God.
   It will flame out, like shining from shook foil;°   *shaken gold foil*
   It gathers to a greatness, like the ooze of oil°   *(from olives)*
Crushed. Why do men then now not reck° his rod°?   *recognize / discipline*
Génerátions have trod, have trod, have trod;   5
   And all is seared with trade; bleared, smeared, with toil;
   And wears man's smudge and shares man's smell: the soil
Is bare now, nor can foot feel, being shod.

Ánd, for° all this, náture is never spent;   *despite*
   There lives the dearest freshness deep down things;   10
And though the last lights off the black West went
   Oh, morning, at the brown brink eastward, springs—
Because the Holy Ghost óver the bent
   World broods with warm breast and with ah! bright wings.

[1877; 1918]

GERARD MANLEY HOPKINS   [1844–1889]
Pied° Beauty

Glóry be to God for dappled things—
   For skies of couple-colour as a brinded° cow;   *streaked*
      For rose-moles all in stipple upon trout that swim;

Pied: Multicolored, variegated.

Fresh-firecoal chestnut-fálls; fínches' wings;
  Lándscape plotted and pieced—fold, fallow, and plough;   5
  And áll trádes, their gear and tackle and trim.

All things counter, original, spáre, stránge;
  Whatever is fickle, freckled (who knows how?)
    With swift, slow; sweet, sour; adazzle, dim;
He fathers-forth whose beauty is pást chánge: 10
          Práise hím.

[*1877;* 1918]

GERARD MANLEY HOPKINS   [1844–1889]

Spring and Fall

to a young child

Márgarét, áre you gríeving
Over Goldengrove unleaving?
Leáves, líke the things of mán, you
With your fresh thoughts care for, can you?
Áh! ás the héart grows ólder   5
It will come to such sights colder
By and by, nor spare a sigh
Though worlds of wanwood leafmeal° lie;
And yet you *will* weep and know why.
Now no matter, child, the name: 10
Sórrow's spríngs áre the sáme.
Nor mouth had, no nor mind, expressed
What héart héard of, ghóst° guéssed: *spirit*
It ís the blíght man was bórn for,
It is Margaret you mourn for.   15

[*1880;* 1918]

8. **wanwood leafmeal:** Colorless forest with scattered leaves.

A. E. HOUSMAN   [1859–1936]

Loveliest of trees, the cherry now

Loveliest of trees, the cherry now
Is hung with bloom along the bough,
And stands about the woodland ride
Wearing white for Eastertide.

Now, of my threescore years and ten,   5
Twenty will not come again,
And take from seventy springs a score,
It only leaves me fifty more.

And since to look at things in bloom
Fifty springs are little room,   10
About the woodlands I will go
To see the cherry hung with snow.

[1896]

A. E. HOUSMAN   [1859–1936]

To an Athlete Dying Young

The time you won your town the race
We chaired you through the market-place;
Man and boy stood cheering by,
And home we brought you shoulder-high.

To-day, the road all runners come,   5
Shoulder-high we bring you home,
And set you at your threshold down,
Townsman of a stiller town.

Smart lad, to slip betimes away
From fields where glory does not stay   10
And early though the laurel grows
It withers quicker than the rose.

Eyes the shady night has shut
Cannot see the record cut,°   *broken*
And silence sounds no worse than cheers   15
After earth has stopped the ears:

Now you will not swell the rout
Of lads that wore their honours out,
Runners whom renown outran
And the name died before the man.   20

So set, before its echoes fade,
The fleet foot on the sill of shade,
And hold to the low lintel up
The still-defended challenge-cup.

And round that early-laurelled head   25
Will flock to gaze the strengthless dead,
And find unwithered on its curls
The garland briefer than a girl's.

                                                          [1896]

WILLIAM BUTLER YEATS   [1865–1939]

The Second Coming°

Turning and turning in the widening gyre
The falcon cannot hear the falconer;
Things fall apart; the centre cannot hold;
Mere anarchy is loosed upon the world,
The blood-dimmed tide is loosed, and everywhere   5
The ceremony of innocence is drowned;
The best lack all conviction, while the worst
Are full of passionate intensity.

Surely some revelation is at hand;
Surely the Second Coming is at hand.   10
The Second Coming! Hardly are those words out

The Second Coming: Alludes to Matthew 24:3–44, on the return of Christ at the
end of the present age. Yeats viewed history as a series of 2,000-year cycles
(imaged as gyres, cone-shaped motions). The birth of Christ in Bethlehem brought
to an end the cycle that ran from the Babylonians through the Greeks and
Romans. The approach of the year 2000, then, anticipated for Yeats the end of
another era (the Christian age). Yeats wrote this poem shortly after the Russian
Revolution of 1917 (lines 4–8), which may have confirmed his sense of imminent
change and of a new beginning of an unpredictable nature (Yeats expected the
new era to be violent and despotic).

When a vast image out of *Spiritus Mundi*°
Troubles my sight: somewhere in sands of the desert
A shape with lion body and the head of a man,
A gaze blank and pitiless as the sun,   15
Is moving its slow thighs, while all about it
Reel shadows of the indignant desert birds.
The darkness drops again; but now I know
That twenty centuries of stony sleep
Were vexed to nightmare by a rocking cradle,   20
And what rough beast, its hour come round at last,
Slouches towards Bethlehem to be born?

[1921]

12. *Spiritus Mundi:* Latin, "the spirit of the universe." Yeats believed in a Great
Memory, a universal storehouse of symbolic images from the past. Individuals,
drawing on it for images, are put in touch with the soul of the universe.

WILLIAM BUTLER YEATS   [1865–1939]

Leda and the Swan°

A sudden blow: the great wings beating still
Above the staggering girl, her thighs caressed
By the dark webs, her nape caught in his bill,
He holds her helpless breast upon his breast.

How can those terrified vague fingers push   5
The feathered glory from her loosening thighs?
And how can body, laid in that white rush,
But feel the strange heart beating where it lies?

A shudder in the loins engenders there
The broken wall, the burning roof and tower   10

Leda and the Swan: In Greek mythology, Leda was seduced (or raped) by Zeus,
who approached her in the form of a swan. She gave birth to Helen, whose abduc-
tion by Paris gave rise to the Trojan War (referred to in line 10). The Greek forces
were headed by Agamemnon, who was killed (line 11) upon his return to Greece
by his wife Clytemnestra, daughter of Leda by her husband, Tyndareus. Yeats
regarded Zeus's visit as a "violent annunciation" of the founding of Greek civilization, with parallels to the annunciation to Mary (Luke 1:26–38), 2,000 years later,
of the coming of the Christian age. See the note to "The Second Coming" for
Yeats's view of historical eras (p. 98).

And Agamemnon dead.
                    Being so caught up,
So mastered by the brute blood of the air,
Did she put on his knowledge with his power
Before the indifferent beak could let her drop?   15

[1928]

EDWIN ARLINGTON ROBINSON   [1869–1935]

Richard Cory

Whenever Richard Cory went down town,
We people on the pavement looked at him:
He was a gentleman from sole to crown,
Clean favored, and imperially slim.

And he was always quietly arrayed,   5
And he was always human when he talked;
But still he fluttered pulses when he said,
"Good-morning," and he glittered when he walked.

And he was rich—yes, richer than a king—
And admirably schooled in every grace: 10
In fine, we thought that he was everything
To make us wish that we were in his place.

So on we worked, and waited for the light,
And went without the meat, and cursed the bread;
And Richard Cory, one calm summer night,   15
Went home and put a bullet through his head.

[1897]

PAUL LAURENCE DUNBAR   [1872–1906]

We Wear the Mask

We wear the mask that grins and lies,
It hides our cheeks and shades our eyes,—
This debt we pay to human guile;

With torn and bleeding hearts we smile,
And mouth with myriad subtleties.   5

Why should the world be over-wise,
In counting all our tears and sighs?
Nay, let them only see us, while
   We wear the mask.

We smile, but, O great Christ, our cries   10
To thee from tortured souls arise.
We sing, but oh the clay is vile
Beneath our feet, and long the mile;
But let the world dream otherwise,
   We wear the mask!   15

[1896]

GERTRUDE STEIN   [1874–1946]

Susie Asado

Sweet sweet sweet sweet sweet tea.
   Susie Asado.
Sweet sweet sweet sweet sweet tea.
   Susie Asado.
Susie Asado which is a told tray sure.   5
A lean on the shoe this means slips slips hers.
When the ancient light grey is clean it is yellow, it is a silver seller.
This is a please this is a please there are the saids to jelly. These are
the wets these say the sets to leave a crown to Incy.
Incy is short for incubus.
A pot. A pot is a beginning of a rare bit of trees. Trees tremble, the old
vats are in bobbles, bobbles which shade and shove and render clean,
render clean must.   10
   Drink pups.
Drink pups drink pups lease a sash hold, see it shine and a bobolink
has pins. It shows a nail.
   What is a nail. A nail is unison.
Sweet sweet sweet sweet sweet tea.

[1913]

ROBERT FROST   [1874–1963]

After Apple-Picking

My long two-pointed ladder's sticking through a tree
Toward heaven still,
And there's a barrel that I didn't fill
Beside it, and there may be two or three
Apples I didn't pick upon some bough.   5
But I am done with apple-picking now.
Essence of winter sleep is on the night,
The scent of apples: I am drowsing off.
I cannot rub the strangeness from my sight
I got from looking through a pane of glass   10
I skimmed this morning from the drinking trough
And held against the world of hoary grass.
It melted, and I let it fall and break.
But I was well
Upon my way to sleep before it fell,   15
And I could tell
What form my dreaming was about to take.
Magnified apples appear and disappear,
Stem end and blossom end,
And every fleck of russet showing clear.   20
My instep arch not only keeps the ache,
It keeps the pressure of a ladder-round.
I feel the ladder sway as the boughs bend.
And I keep hearing from the cellar bin
The rumbling sound   25
Of load on load of apples coming in.
For I have had too much
Of apple-picking: I am overtired
Of the great harvest I myself desired.
There were ten thousand thousand fruit to touch,   30
Cherish in hand, lift down, and not let fall.
For all
That struck the earth,
No matter if not bruised or spiked with stubble,
Went surely to the cider-apple heap   35
As of no worth.
One can see what will trouble
This sleep of mine, whatever sleep it is.
Were he not gone,

The woodchuck could say whether it's like his   40
Long sleep, as I describe its coming on,
Or just some human sleep.

[1914]

ROBERT FROST   [1874–1963]

The Death of the Hired Man

Mary sat musing on the lamp-flame at the table,
Waiting for Warren. When she heard his step,
She ran on tiptoe down the darkened passage
To meet him in the doorway with the news
And put him on his guard. "Silas is back."   5
She pushed him outward with her through the door
And shut it after her. "Be kind," she said.
She took the market things from Warren's arms
And set them on the porch, then drew him down
To sit beside her on the wooden steps.   10

"When was I ever anything but kind to him?
But I'll not have the fellow back," he said.
"I told him so last haying, didn't I?
If he left then, I said, that ended it.
What good is he? Who else will harbor him   15
At his age for the little he can do?
What help he is there's no depending on.
Off he goes always when I need him most.
He thinks he ought to earn a little pay,
Enough at least to buy tobacco with,   20
So he won't have to beg and be beholden.
'All right,' I say, 'I can't afford to pay
Any fixed wages, though I wish I could.'
'Someone else can.' 'Then someone else will have to.'
I shouldn't mind his bettering himself   25
If that was what it was. You can be certain,
When he begins like that, there's someone at him
Trying to coax him off with pocket money—
In haying time, when any help is scarce.
In winter he comes back to us. I'm done."   30

"Sh! not so loud: he'll hear you," Mary said.

"I want him to: he'll have to soon or late."

"He's worn out. He's asleep beside the stove.
When I came up from Rowe's I found him here,
Huddled against the barn door fast asleep,   35
A miserable sight, and frightening, too—
You needn't smile—I didn't recognize him—
I wasn't looking for him—and he's changed.
Wait till you see."

           "Where did you say he'd been?"

"He didn't say. I dragged him to the house,   40
And gave him tea and tried to make him smoke.
I tried to make him talk about his travels.
Nothing would do: he just kept nodding off."

"What did he say? Did he say anything?"

"But little."

          "Anything? Mary, confess   45
He said he'd come to ditch the meadow for me."

"Warren!"

       "But did he? I just want to know."

"Of course he did. What would you have him say?
Surely you wouldn't grudge the poor old man
Some humble way to save his self-respect.   50
He added, if you really care to know,
He meant to clear the upper pasture, too.
That sounds like something you have heard before?
Warren, I wish you could have heard the way
He jumbled everything. I stopped to look   55
Two or three times—he made me feel so queer—
To see if he was talking in his sleep.
He ran on Harold Wilson—you remember—
The boy you had in haying four years since.
He's finished school, and teaching in his college.   60
Silas declares you'll have to get him back.
He says they two will make a team for work:
Between them they will lay this farm as smooth!
The way he mixed that in with other things.
He thinks young Wilson a likely lad, though daft   65
On education—you know how they fought

All through July under the blazing sun,
Silas up on the cart to build the load,
Harold along beside to pitch it on."

"Yes, I took care to keep well out of earshot."   70

"Well, those days trouble Silas like a dream.
You wouldn't think they would. How some things linger!
Harold's young college-boy's assurance piqued him.
After so many years he still keeps finding
Good arguments he sees he might have used.   75
I sympathize. I know just how it feels
To think of the right thing to say too late.
Harold's associated in his mind with Latin.
He asked me what I thought of Harold's saying
He studied Latin, like the violin,   80
Because he liked it—that's an argument!
He said he couldn't make the boy believe
He could find water with a hazel prong—
Which showed how much good school had ever done him.
He wanted to go over that. But most of all   85
He thinks if he could have another chance
To teach him how to build a load of hay——"

"I know, that's Silas' one accomplishment.
He bundles every forkful in its place,
And tags and numbers it for future reference,   90
So he can find and easily dislodge it
In the unloading. Silas does that well.
He takes it out in bunches like big birds' nests.
You never see him standing on the hay
He's trying to lift, straining to lift himself."   95

"He thinks if he could teach him that, he'd be
Some good perhaps to someone in the world.
He hates to see a boy the fool of books.
Poor Silas, so concerned for other folk,
And nothing to look backward to with pride,   100
And nothing to look forward to with hope,
So now and never any different."

Part of a moon was falling down the west,
Dragging the whole sky with it to the hills.
Its light poured softly in her lap. She saw it   105
And spread her apron to it. She put out her hand
Among the harplike morning-glory strings,

Taut with the dew from garden bed to eaves,
As if she played unheard some tenderness
That wrought on him beside her in the night.   110
"Warren," she said, "he has come home to die:
You needn't be afraid he'll leave you this time."

"Home," he mocked gently.

                         "Yes, what else but home?
It all depends on what you mean by home.
Of course he's nothing to us, any more   115
Than was the hound that came a stranger to us
Out of the woods, worn out upon the trail."

"Home is the place where, when you have to go there,
They have to take you in."

                         "I should have called it
Something you somehow haven't to deserve."   120

Warren leaned out and took a step or two,
Picked up a little stick, and brought it back
And broke it in his hand and tossed it by.
"Silas has better claim on us you think
Than on his brother? Thirteen little miles   125
As the road winds would bring him to his door.
Silas has walked that far no doubt today.
Why doesn't he go there? His brother's rich,
A somebody—director in the bank."

"He never told us that."

                         "We know it, though."   130

"I think his brother ought to help, of course.
I'll see to that if there is need. He ought of right
To take him in, and might be willing to—
He may be better than appearances.
But have some pity on Silas. Do you think   135
If he had any pride in claiming kin
Or anything he looked for from his brother,
He'd keep so still about him all this time?"

"I wonder what's between them."

                         "I can tell you.
Silas is what he is—we wouldn't mind him—   140
But just the kind that kinsfolk can't abide.
He never did a thing so very bad.

He don't know why he isn't quite as good
As anybody. Worthless though he is,
He won't be made ashamed to please his brother."   145

"*I* can't think Si ever hurt anyone."

"No, but he hurt my heart the way he lay
And rolled his old head on that sharp-edged chair-back.
He wouldn't let me put him on the lounge.
You must go in and see what you can do.   150
I made the bed up for him there tonight.
You'll be surprised at him—how much he's broken.
His working days are done; I'm sure of it."

"I'd not be in a hurry to say that."

"I haven't been. Go, look, see for yourself.   155
But, Warren, please remember how it is:
He's come to help you ditch the meadow.
He has a plan. You mustn't laugh at him.
He may not speak of it, and then he may.
I'll sit and see if that small sailing cloud   160
Will hit or miss the moon."

                  It hit the moon.
Then there were three there, making a dim row,
The moon, the little silver cloud, and she.

Warren returned—too soon, it seemed to her—
Slipped to her side, caught up her hand and waited.   165

"Warren?" she questioned.

                 "Dead," was all he answered.

                      [1914]

ROBERT FROST   [1874–1963]

The Road Not Taken

Two roads diverged in a yellow wood,
And sorry I could not travel both
And be one traveler, long I stood
And looked down one as far as I could
To where it bent in the undergrowth;   5

Then took the other, as just as fair,
And having perhaps the better claim,
Because it was grassy and wanted wear;
Though as for that, the passing there
Had worn them really about the same,   10

And both that morning equally lay
In leaves no step had trodden black.
Oh, I kept the first for another day!
Yet knowing how way leads on to way,
I doubted if I should ever come back.   15

I shall be telling this with a sigh
Somewhere ages and ages hence:
Two roads diverged in a wood, and I—
I took the one less traveled by,
And that has made all the difference.   20

                                        [1916]

ROBERT FROST   [1874–1963]

"Out, Out—"

The buzz saw snarled and rattled in the yard
And made dust and dropped stove-length sticks of wood,
Sweet-scented stuff when the breeze drew across it.
And from there those that lifted eyes could count
Five mountain ranges one behind the other   5
Under the sunset far into Vermont.
And the saw snarled and rattled, snarled and rattled,
As it ran light, or had to bear a load.
And nothing happened: day was all but done.
Call it a day, I wish they might have said   10
To please the boy by giving him the half hour
That a boy counts so much when saved from work.
His sister stood beside them in her apron
To tell them "Supper." At the word, the saw,
As if to prove saws knew what supper meant,   15
Leaped out at the boy's hand, or seemed to leap—
He must have given the hand. However it was,
Neither refused the meeting. But the hand!
The boy's first outcry was a rueful laugh,

As he swung toward them holding up the hand,   20
Half in appeal, but half as if to keep
The life from spilling. Then the boy saw all—
Since he was old enough to know, big boy
Doing a man's work, though a child at heart—
He saw all spoiled. "Don't let him cut my hand off—   25
The doctor, when he comes. Don't let him, sister!"
So. But the hand was gone already.
The doctor put him in the dark of ether.
He lay and puffed his lips out with his breath.
And then—the watcher at his pulse took fright.   30
No one believed. They listened at his heart.
Little—less—nothing!—and that ended it.
No more to build on there. And they, since they
Were not the one dead, turned to their affairs.

[1916]

ROBERT FROST   [1874–1963]

Stopping by Woods on a Snowy Evening

Whose woods these are I think I know.
His house is in the village, though;
He will not see me stopping here
To watch his woods fill up with snow.

My little horse must think it queer   5
To stop without a farmhouse near
Between the woods and frozen lake
The darkest evening of the year.

He gives his harness bells a shake
To ask if there is some mistake.   10
The only other sound's the sweep
Of easy wind and downy flake.

The woods are lovely, dark and deep,
But I have promises to keep,
And miles to go before I sleep,   15
And miles to go before I sleep.

[1923]

WALLACE STEVENS   [1879–1955]

Thirteen Ways of Looking at a Blackbird

I

Among twenty snowy mountains,
The only moving thing
Was the eye of the blackbird.

II

I was of three minds,
Like a tree   5
In which there are three blackbirds.

III

The blackbird whirled in the autumn winds.
It was a small part of the pantomime.

IV

A man and a woman
Are one.   10
A man and a woman and a blackbird
Are one.

V

I do not know which to prefer,
The beauty of inflections
Or the beauty of innuendoes,   15
The blackbird whistling
Or just after.

VI

Icicles filled the long window
With barbaric glass.
The shadow of the blackbird   20
Crossed it, to and fro.
The mood
Traced in the shadow
An indecipherable cause.

VII

O thin men of Haddam,°   25
Why do you imagine golden birds?
Do you not see how the blackbird
Walks around the feet
Of the women about you?

VIII

I know noble accents   30
And lucid, inescapable rhythms;
But I know, too,
That the blackbird is involved
In what I know.

IX

When the blackbird flew out of sight,   35
It marked the edge
Of one of many circles.

X

At the sight of blackbirds
Flying in a green light,
Even the bawds° of euphony   *women who run brothels* 40
Would cry out sharply.

XI

He rode over Connecticut
In a glass coach.
Once, a fear pierced him,
In that he mistook   45
The shadow of his equipage
For blackbirds.

XII

The river is moving.
The blackbird must be flying.

XIII

It was evening all afternoon.   50
It was snowing

25. Haddam: A town in Connecticut. The thin men are fictitious.

And it was going to snow.
The blackbird sat
In the cedar-limbs.

[1917]

WALLACE STEVENS   [1879–1955]

The Emperor of Ice-Cream

Call the roller of big cigars,
The muscular one, and bid him whip
In kitchen cups concupiscent curds.
Let the wenches dawdle in such dress
As they are used to wear, and let the boys   5
Bring flowers in last month's newspapers.
Let be be finale of seem.
The only emperor is the emperor of ice-cream.

Take from the dresser of deal,°
Lacking the three glass knobs, that sheet   10
On which she embroidered fantails once
And spread it so as to cover her face.
If her horny feet protrude, they come
To show how cold she is, and dumb.
Let the lamp affix its beam.   15
The only emperor is the emperor of ice-cream.

[1923]

9. deal: Fir or pine wood.

WALLACE STEVENS   [1879–1955]

Sunday Morning

I

Complacencies° of the peignoir,° and late
Coffee and oranges in a sunny chair,

1. Complacencies: Feelings of quiet pleasure or security; smugness; peignoir:
Light dressing gown or negligee.

And the green freedom of a cockatoo
Upon a rug mingle to dissipate
The holy hush of ancient sacrifice.   5
She dreams a little, and she feels the dark
Encroachment of that old catastrophe,
As a calm darkens among water-lights.
The pungent oranges and bright, green wings
Seem things in some procession of the dead,   10
Winding across wide water, without sound.
The day is like wide water, without sound,
Stilled for the passing of her dreaming feet
Over the seas, to silent Palestine,°
Dominion of the blood° and sepulchre.°   15

II

Why should she give her bounty to the dead?
What is divinity if it can come
Only in silent shadows and in dreams?
Shall she not find in comforts of the sun,
In pungent fruit and bright, green wings, or else   20
In any balm or beauty of the earth,
Things to be cherished like the thought of heaven?
Divinity must live within herself:
Passions of rain, or moods in falling snow;
Grievings in loneliness, or unsubdued   25
Elations when the forest blooms; gusty
Emotions on wet roads on autumn nights;
All pleasures and all pains, remembering
The bough of summer and the winter branch.
These are the measures destined for her soul.   30

III

Jove° in the clouds had his inhuman birth.
No mother suckled him,° no sweet land gave
Large-mannered motions to his mythy mind

---

14. Palestine: The Holy Land, ancient Israel.
15. blood: Jesus's blood, which Christians believe was shed sacrificially in his death; **sepulchre:** The tomb, or cave, in Jerusalem where Jesus's body was placed after his death.
31. Jove: Jupiter, the chief of the Roman deities, was a sky god. He was of divine, not human, birth.
32. No mother suckled him: Zeus, Jupiter's Greek equivalent, was suckled by a goat named Amalthea.

He moved among us, as a muttering king,
Magnificent, would move among his hinds,°   *farmhands* 35
Until our blood, commingling, virginal,
With heaven, brought such requital to desire
The very hinds discerned it, in a star.
Shall our blood fail? Or shall it come to be
The blood of paradise? And shall the earth   40
Seem all of paradise that we shall know?
The sky will be much friendlier then than now,
A part of labor and a part of pain,
And next in glory to enduring love,
Not this dividing and indifferent blue.   . 45

IV

She says, "I am content when wakened birds,
Before they fly, test the reality
Of misty fields, by their sweet questionings;
But when the birds are gone, and their warm fields
Return no more, where, then, is paradise?"   50
There is not any haunt of prophecy,
Nor any old chimera° of the grave,
Neither the golden underground, nor isle
Melodious, where spirits gat° them home,   *got*
Nor visionary south, nor cloudy palm   55
Remote on heaven's hill, that has endured
As April's green endures; or will endure
Like her remembrance of awakened birds,
Or her desire for June and evening, tipped
By the consummation of the swallow's wings.   60

V

She says, "But in contentment I still feel
The need of some imperishable bliss."
Death is the mother of beauty; hence from her,
Alone, shall come fulfilment to our dreams
And our desires. Although she strews the leaves   65
Of sure obliteration on our paths,
The path sick sorrow took, the many paths
Where triumph rang its brassy phrase, or love

52. **chimera:** In Greek mythology, a fire-breathing monster with a lion's head, a
goat's body, and a serpent's tail; in modern use, an unreal, imaginary creature, a
wild fancy.

Whispered a little out of tenderness,
She makes the willow shiver in the sun   70
For maidens who were wont to sit and gaze
Upon the grass, relinquished to their feet.
She causes boys to pile new plums and pears
On disregarded plate.° The maidens taste
And stray impassioned in the littering leaves.   75

VI

Is there no change of death in paradise?
Does ripe fruit never fall? Or do the boughs
Hang always heavy in that perfect sky,
Unchanging, yet so like our perishing earth,
With rivers like our own that seek for seas   80
They never find, the same receding shores
That never touch with inarticulate pang?
Why set the pear upon those river-banks
Or spice the shores with odors of the plum?
Alas, that they should wear our colors there,   85
The silken weavings of our afternoons,
And pick the strings of our insipid lutes!
Death is the mother of beauty, mystical,
Within whose burning bosom we devise
Our earthly mothers waiting, sleeplessly.   90

VII

Supple and turbulent, a ring of men
Shall chant in orgy on a summer morn
Their boisterous devotion to the sun,
Not as a god, but as a god might be,
Naked among them, like a savage source.   95
Their chant shall be a chant of paradise,
Out of their blood, returning to the sky;
And in their chant shall enter, voice by voice,
The windy lake wherein their lord delights,
The trees, like serafin,° and echoing hills,   *seraphim, angels* 100
That choir among themselves long afterward.

74. plate: "Plate is used in the sense of so-called family plate [gold or silver vessels and utensils]. Disregarded refers to the disuse into which things fall that have been possessed for a long time. I mean, therefore, that death releases and renews. What the old have come to disregard, the young inherit and make use of" (*Letters of Wallace Stevens* [New York: U of California P, 1966], 183–84).

They shall know well the heavenly fellowship
Of men that perish and of summer morn.
And whence they came and whither they shall go
The dew upon their feet shall manifest.   105

VIII

She hears, upon that water without sound,
A voice that cries, "The tomb in Palestine
Is not the porch of spirits lingering.
It is the grave of Jesus, where he lay."
We live in an old chaos of the sun,   110
Or old dependency of day and night,
Or island solitude, unsponsored, free,
Of that wide water, inescapable.
Deer walk upon our mountains, and the quail
Whistle about us their spontaneous cries;   115
Sweet berries ripen in the wilderness;
And, in the isolation of the sky,
At evening, casual flocks of pigeons make
Ambiguous undulations as they sink,
Downward to darkness, on extended wings.   120

[1923]

WILLIAM CARLOS WILLIAMS   [1883–1963]

The Red Wheelbarrow

so much depends
upon

a red wheel
barrow

glazed with rain   5
water

beside the white
chickens.

[1923]

WILLIAM CARLOS WILLIAMS   [1883–1963]

Spring and All

By the road to the contagious hospital
under the surge of the blue
mottled clouds driven from the
northeast—a cold wind. Beyond, the
waste of broad, muddy fields   5
brown with dried weeds, standing and fallen

patches of standing water
the scattering of tall trees

All along the road the reddish
purplish, forked, upstanding, twiggy   10
stuff of bushes and small trees
with dead, brown leaves under them
leafless vines—

Lifeless in appearance, sluggish
dazed spring approaches—   15

They enter the new world naked,
cold, uncertain of all
save that they enter. All about them
the cold, familiar wind—

Now the grass, tomorrow   20
the stiff curl of wildcarrot leaf

One by one objects are defined—
It quickens: clarity, outline of leaf

But now the stark dignity of
entrance—Still, the profound change   25
has come upon them: rooted, they
grip down and begin to awaken

[1923]

WILLIAM CARLOS WILLIAMS   [1883–1963]

This Is Just to Say

I have eaten
the plums
that were in
the icebox

and which   5
you were probably
saving
for breakfast

Forgive me
they were delicious   10
so sweet
and so cold

[1934]

EZRA POUND   [1885–1972]

The River-Merchant's Wife:
A Letter

While my hair was still cut straight across my forehead
I played about the front gate, pulling flowers.
You came by on bamboo stilts, playing horse,
You walked about my seat, playing with blue plums.
And we went on living in the village of Chokan: 5
Two small people, without dislike or suspicion.

At fourteen I married My Lord you.
I never laughed, being bashful.
Lowering my head, I looked at the wall.
Called to, a thousand times, I never looked back.   10

At fifteen I stopped scowling,
I desired my dust to be mingled with yours
Forever and forever and forever.
Why should I climb the look out?

At sixteen you departed,   15
You went into far Ku-to-yen, by the river of swirling eddies,
And you have been gone five months.
The monkeys make sorrowful noise overhead.

You dragged your feet when you went out.
By the gate now, the moss is grown, the different mosses,   20
Too deep to clear them away!
The leaves fall early this autumn, in wind.
The paired butterflies are already yellow with August
Over the grass in the West garden;
They hurt me. I grow older.   25
If you are coming down through the narrows of the river Kiang,
Please let me know beforehand,
And I will come out to meet you
              As far as Cho-fu-Sa.

                                                            By Rihaku°

                                                            [1915]

By Rihaku: An adaptation of a Chinese poem by the famous poet Li Po (701–762
C.E.), whose Japanese name is Rihaku.

EZRA POUND   [1885–1972]

In a Station of the Metro

The apparition of these faces in the crowd;
Petals on a wet, black bough.

                                                            [1917]

H. D. [HILDA DOOLITTLE]   [1886–1961]

Garden

I

You are clear
O rose, cut in rock,
hard as the descent of hail.

I could scrape the colour
from the petals
like spilt dye from a rock.   5

If I could break you
I could break a tree.

If I could stir
I could break a tree —   10
I could break you.

II

O wind, rend open the heat,
cut apart the heat,
rend it to tatters.

Fruit cannot drop   15
through this thick air —
fruit cannot fall into heat
that presses up and blunts
the points of pears
and rounds the grapes.   20

Cut the heat —
plough through it,
turning it on either side
of your path.

[1916]

ROBINSON JEFFERS   [1887–1962]

Hurt Hawks

I

The broken pillar of the wing jags from the clotted shoulder,
The wing trails like a banner in defeat,
No more to use the sky forever but live with famine
And pain a few days: cat nor coyote
Will shorten the week of waiting for death, there is game without
    talons.   5

He stands under the oak-bush and waits
The lame feet of salvation; at night he remembers freedom
And flies in a dream, the dawns ruin it.
He is strong and pain is worse to the strong, incapacity is worse.
The curs of the day come and torment him   10
At distance, no one but death the redeemer will humble that head,
The intrepid readiness, the terrible eyes.
The wild God of the world is sometimes merciful to those
That ask mercy, not often to the arrogant.
You do not know him, you communal people, or you have forgotten him;   15
Intemperate and savage, the hawk remembers him;
Beautiful and wild, the hawks, and men that are dying, remember him.

II

I'd sooner, except the penalties, kill a man than a hawk; but the great
    redtail
Had nothing left but unable misery
From the bone too shattered for mending, the wing that trailed under
    his talons when he moved.   20
We had fed him six weeks, I gave him freedom,
He wandered over the foreland hill and returned in the evening, asking
    for death,
Not like a beggar, still eyed with the old
Implacable arrogance. I gave him the lead gift in the twilight. What fell
    was relaxed,
Owl-downy, soft feminine feathers; but what   25
Soared: the fierce rush: the night-herons by the flooded river cried fear
    at its rising
Before it was quite unsheathed from reality.

[1928]

EDITH SITWELL   [1887–1964]

Lullaby

Though the world has slipped and gone,
Sounds my loud discordant cry
Like the steel birds' song on high:

"Still one thing is left—the Bone!"
Then out danced the Babioun.°   *baboon*   5

She sat in the hollow of the sea—
A socket whence the eye's put out—
She sang to the child a lullaby
(The steel birds' nest was thereabout).

"Do, do, do, do—   10
Thy mother's hied to the vaster race:
The Pterodactyl made its nest
And laid a steel egg in her breast—
Under the Judas-colored sun.
She'll work no more, nor dance, nor moan,   15
And I am come to take her place
Do, do.

There's nothing left but earth's low bed—
(The Pterodactyl fouls its nest):
But steel wings fan thee to thy rest,   20
And wingless truth and larvae lie
And eyeless hope and handless fear—
All these for thee as toys are spread,
Do—do—

Red is the bed of Poland, Spain,   25
And thy mother's breast, who has grown wise
In that fouled nest. If she could rise.
Give birth again,
In wolfish pelt she'd hide thy bones
To shield thee from the world's long cold,   30
And down on all fours shouldst thou crawl
For thus from no height canst thou fall—
Do, do.

She'd give no hands: there's nought to hold
And nought to make: there's dust to sift,   35
But no food for the hands to lift.
Do, do.

Heed my ragged lullaby,
Fear not living, fear not chance;
All is equal—blindness, sight,   40
There is no depth, there is no height:
Do, do.

The Judas-colored sun is gone,
And with the Ape thou art alone—
Do,   45
   Do."

[1942]

MARIANNE MOORE   [1887–1972]

Poetry

I, too, dislike it: there are things that are important beyond all this fiddle.
  Reading it, however, with a perfect contempt for it, one discovers in
  it after all, a place for the genuine.
    Hands that can grasp, eyes
    that can dilate, hair that can rise   5
      if it must, these things are important not because a

high-sounding interpretation can be put upon them but because they are
  useful. When they become so derivative as to become unintelligible,
  the same thing may be said for all of us, that we
    do not admire what   10
    we cannot understand: the bat
      holding on upside down or in quest of something to

eat, elephants pushing, a wild horse taking a roll, a tireless wolf under
  a tree, the immovable critic twitching his skin like a horse that feels a
                       flea, the base-

ball fan, the statistician—   15
    nor is it valid
      to discriminate against "business documents and

school-books"; all these phenomena are important. One must make a
                       distinction
  however: when dragged into prominence by half poets, the result is
                       not poetry,
  nor till the poets among us can be   20
    "literalists of
    the imagination"—above
      insolence and triviality and can present

for inspection, "imaginary gardens with real toads in them," shall we
                                                        have
  it. In the meantime, if you demand on the one hand,   25
  the raw material of poetry in
    all its rawness and
    that which is on the other hand
      genuine, you are interested in poetry.

[1921]

JOHN CROWE RANSOM   [1888–1974]

Bells for John Whiteside's Daughter

There was such speed in her little body,
And such lightness in her footfall,
It is no wonder her brown study°
Astonishes us all.

Her wars were bruited° in our high window.   *made famous* 5
We looked among orchard trees and beyond
Where she took arms against her shadow,
Or harried unto the pond

The lazy geese, like a snow cloud
Dripping their snow on the green grass,   10
Tricking and stopping, sleepy and proud,
Who cried in goose, Alas,

For the tireless heart within the little
Lady with rod that made them rise
From their noon apple-dreams and scuttle   15
Goose-fashion under the skies!

But now go the bells, and we are ready,
In one house we are sternly stopped
To say we are vexed at her brown study,
Lying so primly propped.   20

[1924]

3. **brown study:** Being deeply absorbed in one's thoughts; reverie.

T. S. ELIOT   [1888–1965]

The Love Song of J. Alfred Prufrock

S'io credesse che mia risposta fosse
A persona che mai tornasse al mondo,
Questa fiamma staria senza piu scosse.
Ma perciocche giammai di questo fondo
Non torno vivo alcun, s'i'odo il vero,
Senza tema d'infamia ti rispondo.°

Let us go then, you and I,
When the evening is spread out against the sky
Like a patient etherised upon a table;
Let us go, through certain half-deserted streets,
The muttering retreats   5
Of restless nights in one-night cheap hotels
And sawdust restaurants with oyster-shells:
Streets that follow like a tedious argument
Of insidious intent
To lead you to an overwhelming question . . .   10
Oh, do not ask, "What is it?"
Let us go and make our visit.

   In the room the women come and go
Talking of Michelangelo.

   The yellow fog that rubs its back upon the window-panes,   15
The yellow smoke that rubs its muzzle on the window-panes
Licked its tongue into the corners of the evening,
Lingered upon the pools that stand in drains,
Let fall upon its back the soot that falls from chimneys,
Slipped by the terrace, made a sudden leap,   20
And seeing that it was a soft October night,
Curled once about the house, and fell asleep.

Epigraph: "If I thought that my answer were being made to someone who would ever return to earth, this flame would remain without further movement; but since no one has ever returned alive from this depth, if what I hear is true, I answer you without fear of infamy" (Dante, *Inferno* 27.61–66). Dante encounters Guido de Montefeltro in the eighth circle of hell, where souls are trapped within flames (tongues of fire) as punishment for giving evil counsel. Guido tells Dante details about his evil life only because he assumes that Dante is on his way to an even deeper circle in hell and will never return to earth and be able to repeat what he has heard.

And indeed there will be time
For the yellow smoke that slides along the street,
Rubbing its back upon the window-panes;   25
There will be time, there will be time
To prepare a face to meet the faces that you meet;
There will be time to murder and create,
And time for all the works and days° of hands
That lift and drop a question on your plate;   30
Time for you and time for me,
And time yet for a hundred indecisions,
And for a hundred visions and revisions,
Before the taking of a toast and tea.

In the room the women come and go   35
Talking of Michelangelo.

And indeed there will be time
To wonder, "Do I dare?" and, "Do I dare?"
Time to turn back and descend the stair,
With a bald spot in the middle of my hair—   40
[They will say: "How his hair is growing thin!"]
My morning coat, my collar mounting firmly to the chin,
My necktie rich and modest, but asserted by a simple pin—
[They will say: "But how his arms and legs are thin!"]
Do I dare   45
Disturb the universe?
In a minute there is time
For decisions and revisions which a minute will reverse.

For I have known them all already, known them all:—
Have known the evenings, mornings, afternoons,   50
I have measured out my life with coffee spoons;
I know the voices dying with a dying fall°
Beneath the music from a farther room.
   So how should I presume?

And I have known the eyes already, known them all—   55
The eyes that fix you in a formulated phrase,
And when I am formulated, sprawling on a pin,

29. works and days: *Works and Days* is the title of a didactic poem about farming by the Greek poet Hesiod (eighth century B.C.E.) that includes instruction about doing each task at the proper time.
52. a dying fall: An allusion to Shakespeare's *Twelfth Night* (1.1.4): "That strain [of music] again! It had a dying fall" (a cadence that falls away).

When I am pinned and wriggling on the wall,
Then how should I begin
To spit out all the butt-ends of my days and ways?   60
    And how should I presume?

    And I have known the arms already, known them all—
Arms that are braceleted and white and bare
[But in the lamplight, downed with light brown hair!]
Is it perfume from a dress   65
That makes me so digress?
Arms that lie along a table, or wrap about a shawl.
    And should I then presume?
    And how should I begin?

                        .   .   .

Shall I say, I have gone at dusk through narrow streets   70
And watched the smoke that rises from the pipes
Of lonely men in shirt-sleeves, leaning out of windows? . . .

    I should have been a pair of ragged claws
Scuttling across the floors of silent seas.

                        .   .   .

And the afternoon, the evening, sleeps so peacefully!   75
Smoothed by long fingers,
Asleep . . . tired . . . or it malingers,
Stretched on the floor, here beside you and me.
Should I, after tea and cakes and ices,
Have the strength to force the moment to its crisis?   80
But though I have wept and fasted, wept and prayed,
Though I have seen my head [grown slightly bald] brought in upon a
            platter,°
I am no prophet—and here's no great matter;
I have seen the moment of my greatness flicker,
And I have seen the eternal Footman hold my coat, and snicker,   85
And in short, I was afraid.

    And would it have been worth it, after all,
After the cups, the marmalade, the tea,
Among the porcelain, among some talk of you and me,
Would it have been worth while,   90

82. head . . . platter: As a reward for dancing before King Herod, Salome, his
stepdaughter, asked for the head of John the Baptist to be presented to her on a
platter (Matt. 14:1–12; Mark 6:17–28).

To have bitten off the matter with a smile,
To have squeezed the universe into a ball
To roll it toward some overwhelming question,
To say: "I am Lazarus,° come from the dead,
Come back to tell you all, I shall tell you all"—   95
If one, settling a pillow by her head,
   Should say: "That is not what I meant at all.
   That is not it, at all."

   And would it have been worth it, after all,
Would it have been worth while,   100
After the sunsets and the dooryards and the sprinkled streets,
After the novels, after the teacups, after the skirts that trail along the
      floor—
And this, and so much more?—
It is impossible to say just what I mean!
But as if a magic lantern threw the nerves in patterns on a screen: 105
Would it have been worth while
If one, settling a pillow or throwing off a shawl,
And turning toward the window, should say:
"That is not it at all,
That is not what I meant, at all."   110

                  •   •   •

No! I am not Prince Hamlet, nor was meant to be;
Am an attendant lord, one that will do
To swell a progress,° start a scene or two,
Advise the prince; no doubt, an easy tool,
Deferential, glad to be of use,   115
Politic, cautious, and meticulous;
Full of high sentence,° but a bit obtuse;   *sententiousness*
At times, indeed, almost ridiculous—
Almost, at times, the Fool.

   I grow old . . . I grow old . . .   120
I shall wear the bottoms of my trousers rolled.

   Shall I part my hair behind? Do I dare to eat a peach?
I shall wear white flannel trousers, and walk upon the beach.
I have heard the mermaids singing, each to each.

---

94. **Lazarus:** Either the beggar Lazarus, who in Luke 16:19–31 did not return
from the dead, or Jesus's friend Lazarus, who did (John 11:1–44).
113. **progress:** Ceremonial journey made by a royal court.

I do not think that they will sing to me. 125

I have seen them riding seaward on the waves
Combing the white hair of the waves blown back
When the wind blows the water white and black.

We have lingered in the chambers of the sea
By sea-girls wreathed with seaweed red and brown 130
Till human voices wake us, and we drown.

[1917]

T. S. ELIOT   [1888–1965]

Preludes

I

The winter evening settles down
With smell of steaks in passageways.
Six o'clock.
The burnt-out ends of smoky days.
And now a gusty shower wraps 5
The grimy scraps
Of withered leaves about your feet
And newspapers from vacant lots;
The showers beat
On broken blinds and chimney-pots, 10
And at the corner of the street
A lonely cab-horse steams and stamps.
And then the lighting of the lamps.

II

The morning comes to consciousness
Of faint stale smells of beer 15
From the sawdust-trampled street
With all its muddy feet that press
To early coffee-stands.
With the other masquerades
That time resumes, 20
One thinks of all the hands
That are raising dingy shades
In a thousand furnished rooms.

III

You tossed a blanket from the bed,
You lay upon your back, and waited;   25
You dozed, and watched the night revealing
The thousand sordid images
Of which your soul was constituted;
They flickered against the ceiling.
And when all the world came back   30
And the light crept up between the shutters
And you heard the sparrows in the gutters,
You had such a vision of the street
As the street hardly understands;
Sitting along the bed's edge, where   35
You curled the papers from your hair,
Or clasped the yellow soles of feet
In the palms of both soiled hands.

IV

His soul stretched tight across the skies
That fade behind a city block,   40
Or trampled by insistent feet
At four and five and six o'clock;
And short square fingers stuffing pipes,
And evening newspapers, and eyes
Assured of certain certainties,   45
The conscience of a blackened street
Impatient to assume the world.

    I am moved by fancies that are curled
Around these images, and cling:
The notion of some infinitely gentle   50
Infinitely suffering thing.

    Wipe your hand across your mouth, and laugh;
The worlds revolve like ancient women
Gathering fuel in vacant lots.

[1917]

T. S. ELIOT   [1888–1965]

Journey of the Magi°

"A cold coming we had of it,
Just the worst time of the year
For a journey, and such a long journey:
The ways deep and the weather sharp,
The very dead of winter."°   5
And the camels galled, sore-footed, refractory,
Lying down in the melting snow.
There were times we regretted
The summer palaces on slopes, the terraces,
And the silken girls bringing sherbet.   10
Then the camel men cursing and grumbling
And running away, and wanting their liquor and women,
And the night-fires going out, and the lack of shelters,
And the cities hostile and the towns unfriendly
And the villages dirty and charging high prices: 15
A hard time we had of it.
At the end we preferred to travel all night,
Sleeping in snatches,
With the voices singing in our ears, saying
That this was all folly.   20

   Then at dawn we came down to a temperate valley,
Wet, below the snow line, smelling of vegetation;
With a running stream and a water-mill beating the darkness,
And three trees° on the low sky,
And an old white horse° galloped away in the meadow.   25
Then we came to a tavern with vine-leaves over the lintel,
Six hands at an open door dicing for pieces of silver,°

Journey of the Magi: Eliot's poem recounts Matthew 2:1–12 from the perspective of one of the wise men who traveled from the East to Bethlehem to honor the newborn king of the Jews.
1–5. "A cold . . . winter": These lines are quoted with only minor changes from a sermon by Bishop Lancelot Andrewes on Christmas Day 1622.
24. three trees: A foreshadowing of the three crosses on Calvary (Luke 23:32–33).
25. white horse: Probably an allusion to the white horse carrying the victorious Christ in the vision of St. John (Rev. 19:11–16).
27. dicing . . . silver: Foreshadowing the Roman soldiers casting lots to divide Jesus's clothing (Matt. 27:35, Mark 15:24, Luke 23:34) and the thirty pieces of silver paid to Judas for betraying Jesus (Matt. 26:14–15, Mark 14:10–11, Luke 22:3–6).

And feet kicking the empty wine-skins.
But there was no information, and so we continued
And arrived at evening, not a moment too soon   30
Finding the place; it was (you may say) satisfactory.

　All this was a long time ago, I remember,
And I would do it again, but set down
This set down
This: were we led all that way for   35
Birth or Death? There was a Birth, certainly,
We had evidence and no doubt. I had seen birth and death,
But had thought they were different; this Birth was
Hard and bitter agony for us, like Death, our death.
We returned to our places, these Kingdoms,   40
But no longer at ease here, in the old dispensation,°
With an alien people clutching their gods.
I should be glad of another death.

[1927]

41. **old dispensation:** Old (here, pre-Christian) arrangement of things.

CLAUDE McKAY   [1890–1948]

America

Although she feeds me bread of bitterness,
And sinks into my throat her tiger's tooth,
Stealing my breath of life, I will confess
I love this cultured hell that tests my youth!
Her vigor flows like tides into my blood,   5
Giving me strength erect against her hate.
Her bigness sweeps my being like a flood.
Yet as a rebel fronts a king in state,
I stand within her walls with not a shred
Of terror, malice, not a word of jeer.   10
Darkly I gaze into the days ahead,
And see her might and granite wonders there,
Beneath the touch of Time's unerring hand,
Like priceless treasures sinking in the sand.

[1922]

EDNA ST. VINCENT MILLAY   [1892–1950]

Pity me not because the light of day

Pity me not because the light of day
At close of day no longer walks the sky;
Pity me not for beauties passed away
From field and thicket as the year goes by;
Pity me not the waning of the moon,   5
Nor that the ebbing tide goes out to sea,
Nor that a man's desire is hushed so soon,
And you no longer look with love on me.
This have I known always: Love is no more
Than the wide blossom which the wind assails,   10
Than the great tide that treads the shifting shore,
Strewing fresh wreckage gathered in the gales:
Pity me that the heart is slow to learn
What the swift mind beholds at every turn.

[1923]

WILFRED OWEN   [1893–1918]

Dulce et Decorum Est

Bent double, like old beggars under sacks,
Knock-kneed, coughing like hags, we cursed through sludge,
Till on the haunting flares we turned our backs
And towards our distant rest began to trudge.
Men marched asleep. Many had lost their boots   5
But limped on, blood-shod. All went lame; all blind;
Drunk with fatigue; deaf even to the hoots
Of tired, outstripped Five-Nines° that dropped behind.

Gas! GAS! Quick, boys!—An ecstasy of fumbling,
Fitting the clumsy helmets just in time;   10
But someone still was yelling out and stumbling
And flound'ring like a man in fire or lime . . .

8. **Five-Nines:** 5.9-inch caliber shells.

Dim, through the misty panes° and thick green light,   *of a gas mask*
As under a green sea, I saw him drowning.

In all my dreams, before my helpless sight,   15
He plunges at me, guttering, choking, drowning.

If in some smothering dreams you too could pace
Behind the wagon that we flung him in,
And watch the white eyes writhing in his face,
His hanging face, like a devil's sick of sin;   20
If you could hear, at every jolt, the blood
Come gargling from the froth-corrupted lungs,
Obscene as cancer, bitter as the cud
Of vile, incurable sores on innocent tongues,—
My friend, you would not tell with such high zest   25
To children ardent for some desperate glory,
The old Lie: Dulce et decorum est
Pro patria mori.°

[1920]

27–28. Dulce . . . mori: It is sweet and fitting / to die for one's country (Horace, *Odes* 3.12.13).

E. E. CUMMINGS   [1894–1962]

in Just-

in Just-
spring   when the world is mud-
luscious the little
lame balloonman

whistles   far   and wee   5

and eddieandbill come
running from marbles and
piracies and it's
spring

when the world is puddle-wonderful   10

the queer
old balloonman whistles
far   and   wee
and bettyandisbel come dancing

from hop-scotch and jump-rope and   15

it's
spring
and
   the

      goat-footed   20

balloonMan   whistles
far
and
wee

[1923]

E. E. CUMMINGS   [1894–1962]

"next to of course god america i

"next to of course god america i
love you land of the pilgrims' and so forth oh
say can you see by the dawn's early my
country 'tis of centuries come and go
and are no more what of it we should worry   5
in every language even deafanddumb
thy sons acclaim your glorious name by gorry
by jingo by gee by gosh by gum
why talk of beauty what could be more beaut-
iful than these heroic happy dead   10
who rushed like lions to the roaring slaughter
they did not stop to think they died instead
then shall the voice of liberty be mute?"

He spoke. And drank rapidly a glass of water

[1926]

JEAN TOOMER   [1894–1967]

Face

Hair—
silver-gray,
like streams of stars,
Brows—
recurved canoes   5
quivered by the ripples blown by pain,
Her eyes—
mist of tears
condensing on the flesh below
And her channeled muscles   10
are cluster grapes of sorrow
purple in the evening sun
nearly ripe for worms.

[1923]

STERLING A. BROWN   [1901–1989]

Riverbank Blues

A man git his feet set in a sticky mudbank,
A man git dis yellow water in his blood,
No need for hopin', no need for doin',
Muddy streams keep him fixed for good.

Little Muddy, Big Muddy, Moreau and Osage,   5
Little Mary's, Big Mary's, Cedar Creek,
Flood deir muddy water roundabout a man's roots,
Keep him soaked and stranded and git him weak.

Lazy sun shinin' on a little cabin,
Lazy moon glistenin' over river trees;   10
Ole river whisperin', lappin' 'gainst de long roots:
"Plenty of rest and peace in these. . . ."

Big mules, black loam, apple and peach trees,
But seems lak de river washes us down
Past de rich farms, away from de fat lands,   15
Dumps us in some ornery riverbank town.

Went down to the river, sot me down an' listened,
Heard de water talkin' quiet, quiet lak an' slow:
"Ain' no need fo' hurry, take yo' time, take yo' time. . . ."
Heard it sayin'—"Baby, hyeahs de way life go. . . ."   20

Dat is what it tole me as I watched it slowly rollin',
But somp'n way inside me rared up an' say,
"Better be movin' . . . better be travelin' . . .
Riverbank'll git you ef you stay. . . ."

Towns are sinkin' deeper, deeper in de riverbank,   25
Takin' on de ways of deir sulky Ole Man—
Takin' on his creepy ways, takin' on his evil ways,
"Bes' git way, a long way . . . whiles you can.

"Man got his sea too lak de Mississippi
Ain't got so long for a whole lot longer way,   30
Man better move some, better not git rooted
Muddy water fool you, ef you stay. . . ."

[1932]

LANGSTON HUGHES   [1902–1967]

The Negro Speaks of Rivers

I've known rivers:
I've known rivers ancient as the world and older than the flow of human
    blood in human veins.

My soul has grown deep like the rivers.

I bathed in the Euphrates when dawns were young.
I built my hut near the Congo and it lulled me to sleep.   5
I looked upon the Nile and raised the pyramids above it.
I heard the singing of the Mississippi when Abe Lincoln went down to
    New Orleans, and I've seen its muddy bosom turn all golden in the
    sunset.

I've known rivers:
Ancient, dusky rivers.

My soul has grown deep like the rivers.   10

[1926]

LANGSTON HUGHES   [1902–1967]

Mother to Son

Well, son, I'll tell you:
Life for me ain't been no crystal stair.
It's had tacks in it,
And splinters,
And boards torn up,   5
And places with no carpet on the floor—
Bare.
But all the time,
I'se been a-climbin' on,
And reachin' landin's,   10
And turnin' corners,
And sometimes goin' in the dark
Where there ain't been no light.
So boy, don't you turn back.
Don't you set down on the steps   15
'Cause you finds it's kinder hard.
Don't you fall now—
For I'se still goin', honey,
I'se still climbin',
And life for me ain't been no crystal stair.   20

[1926]

LANGSTON HUGHES   [1902–1967]

Theme for English B

The instructor said,

> Go home and write
> a page tonight.
> And let that page come out of you—
> Then, it will be true.   5

I wonder if it's that simple?
I am twenty-two, colored, born in Winston-Salem.
I went to school there, then Durham, then here

to this college on the hill above Harlem.
I am the only colored student in my class.   10
The steps from the hill lead down into Harlem,
through a park, then I cross St. Nicholas,
Eighth Avenue, Seventh, and I come to the Y,
the Harlem Branch Y, where I take the elevator
up to my room, sit down, and write this page: 15

It's not easy to know what is true for you or me
at twenty-two, my age. But I guess I'm what
I feel and see and hear, Harlem, I hear you:
hear you, hear me—we two—you, me, talk on this page.
(I hear New York, too.) Me—who?   20
Well, I like to eat, sleep, drink, and be in love.
I like to work, read, learn, and understand life.
I like a pipe for a Christmas present,
or records—Bessie,° bop, or Bach.
I guess being colored doesn't make me *not* like   25
the same things other folks like who are other races.
So will my page be colored that I write?
Being me, it will not be white.
But it will be
a part of you, instructor.   30
You are white—
yet a part of me, as I am a part of you.
That's American.
Sometimes perhaps you don't want to be a part of me.
Nor do I often want to be a part of you.   35
But we are, that's true!
As I learn from you,
I guess you learn from me—
although you're older—and white—
and somewhat more free.   40

This is my page for English B.

[1951]

24. **Bessie:** Bessie Smith (1895–1937), American blues singer.

LANGSTON HUGHES   [1902–1967]

Harlem

What happens to a dream deferred?

Does it dry up
like a raisin in the sun?
Or fester like a sore—
And then run?   5
Does it stink like rotten meat?
Or crust and sugar over—
like a syrupy sweet?

Maybe it just sags
like a heavy load.   10

Or does it explode?

[1951]

COUNTEE CULLEN   [1903–1946]

Incident

for Eric Walrond

Once riding in old Baltimore,
    Heart-filled, head-filled with glee,
I saw a Baltimorean
    Keep looking straight at me.

Now I was eight and very small,   5
    And he was no whit bigger,
And so I smiled, but he poked out
    His tongue, and called me, "Nigger."

I saw the whole of Baltimore
    From May until December;   10
Of all the things that happened there
    That's all that I remember.

[1925]

LORINE NIEDECKER   [1903–1970]

My Life by Water

My life
  by water—
    Hear

spring's
  first frog   5
    or board

out on the cold
  ground
    giving

Muskrats   10
  gnawing
    doors

to wild green
  arts and letters
    Rabbits   15

raided
  my lettuce
    One boat

two—
  pointed toward   20
    my shore

thru birdstart
  wingdrip
    weed-drift

of the soft   25
  and serious—
    Water

[1985]

STANLEY KUNITZ   [1905–2006]

The War against the Trees

The man who sold his lawn to standard oil
Joked with his neighbors come to watch the show
While the bulldozers, drunk with gasoline,
Tested the virtue of the soil
Under the branchy sky   5
By overthrowing first the privet-row.

Forsythia-forays and hydrangea-raids
Were but preliminaries to a war
Against the great-grandfathers of the town,
So freshly lopped and maimed.   10
They struck and struck again,
And with each elm a century went down.

All day the hireling° engines charged the trees,
Subverting them by hacking underground
In grub-dominions, where dark summer's mole   15
Rampages through his halls,
Till a northern seizure shook
Those crowns, forcing the giants to their knees.

I saw the ghosts of children at their games
Racing beyond their childhood in the shade,   20
And while the green world turned its death-foxed page
And a red wagon wheeled,
I watched them disappear
Into the suburbs of their grievous age.

Ripped from the craters much too big for hearts   25
The club-roots bared their amputated coils,
Raw gorgons° matted blind, whose pocks and scars
Cried Moon! on a corner lot
One witness-moment, caught
In the rear-view mirrors of the passing cars.   30

[1958]

13. **hireling:** Serving only for hire or wages, without caring about the value of
what is accomplished.
27. **gorgons:** In Greek mythology, three sisters—Stheno, Euryale, and Medusa—
so hideous that looking at one of them turned the beholder to stone.

W. H. AUDEN   [1907–1973]

As I Walked Out One Evening

As I walked out one evening,
   Walking down Bristol Street,
The crowds upon the pavement
   Were fields of harvest wheat.

And down by the brimming river   5
   I heard a lover sing
Under an arch of the railway:
   "Love has no ending.

"I'll love you, dear, I'll love you
   Till China and Africa meet,   10
And the river jumps over the mountain
   And the salmon sing in the street,

"I'll love you till the ocean
   Is folded and hung up to dry
And the seven stars° go squawking   15
   Like geese about the sky.

The years shall run like rabbits,
   For in my arms I hold
The Flower of the Ages,
   And the first love of the world."   20

But all the clocks in the city
   Began to whirr and chime:
"O let not Time deceive you,
   You cannot conquer Time.

"In the burrows of the Nightmare   25
   Where Justice naked is,
Time watches from the shadow
   And coughs when you would kiss.

"In headaches and in worry
   Vaguely life leaks away,
And Time will have his fancy   30
   To-morrow or to-day.

15. the seven stars: An echo of the traditional counting song "Green Grow the Rushes, O": "What are your seven, O? / Seven for the seven stars in the sky."

"Into many a green valley
  Drifts the appalling snow;
Time breaks the threaded dances   35
  And the diver's brilliant bow.

"O plunge your hands in water,
  Plunge them in up to the wrist;
Stare, stare in the basin
  And wonder what you've missed.   40

"The glacier knocks in the cupboard,
  The desert sighs in the bed,
And the crack in the tea-cup opens
  A lane to the land of the dead.

"Where the beggars raffle the banknotes°   45
  And the Giant° is enchanting to Jack,
And the Lily-white Boy° is a Roarer,°
  And Jill° goes down on her back.

"O look, look in the mirror,
  O look in your distress;   50
Life remains a blessing
  Although you cannot bless.

"O stand, stand at the window
  As the tears scald and start;
You shall love your crooked neighbour   55
  With your crooked heart."°

It was late, late in the evening,
  The lovers they were gone;
The clocks had ceased their chiming,
  And the deep river ran on.   60

[1937]

45–48. "Where the beggars . . .": This stanza alludes to and—through social satire and sexual innuendo—inverts the milieu of nursery rhymes and a counting
song.
46. Giant: From the fairy tale "Jack the Giant-Killer."
47. Lily-white Boy: Echoing "Green Grow the Rushes, O": "What are your two,
O? / Two, two the lily-white boys / Clothed all in green, O"; Roarer: Hell raiser.
48. Jill: From the nursery rhyme "Jack and Jill."
55–56. "You . . . heart.": Perhaps a distorted conflation of Matthew 22:37 and
22:39: "Thou shalt love the Lord thy God with all thy heart . . . [and] thy neighbor
as thyself."

Brueghel, *Landscape with the Fall of Icarus*

W. H. AUDEN   [1907–1973]

Musée des Beaux Arts°

About suffering they were never wrong,
The Old Masters: how well they understood
Its human position; how it takes place
While someone else is eating or opening a window or just walking dully
    along;
How, when the aged are reverently, passionately waiting   5
For the miraculous birth, there always must be
Children who did not specially want it to happen, skating
On a pond at the edge of the wood:
They never forgot
That even the dreadful martyrdom must run its course   10
Anyhow in a corner, some untidy spot
Where the dogs go on with their doggy life and the torturer's horse
Scratches its innocent behind on a tree.

Musée des Beaux Arts: The painting *Landscape with the Fall of Icarus* by Pieter Brueghel the Elder, on which the poem is based, is in the Musées Royaux des Beaux-Arts in Brussels.

In Brueghel's *Icarus*, for instance: how everything turns away
Quite leisurely from the disaster; the ploughman may   15
Have heard the splash, the forsaken cry,
But for him it was not an important failure; the sun shone
As it had to on the white legs disappearing into the green
Water; and the expensive delicate ship that must have seen
Something amazing, a boy falling out of the sky,   20
Had somewhere to get to and sailed calmly on.

                                                  [1940]

GEORGE OPPEN   [1908–1984]

Myself I Sing°

Me! he says, hand on his chest.
Actually, his shirt.
                And there, perhaps,
The question.

Pioneers! But trailer people?   5
Wood box full of tools—
                The most
American. A sort of
Shrinking
                in themselves. A   10
Less than adult: old.

A pocket knife,
A tool—
                And I
Here talking to the man?   15
                The sky

That dawned along the road
And all I've been
Is not myself? I think myself
Is what I've seen and not myself   20

A man marooned
No longer looks for ships, imagines

Myself I Sing: See Walt Whitman, *Song of Myself*, page 69.

Anything on the horizon. On the beach
The ocean ends in water. Finds a dune
And on the beach sits near it. Two.   25
He finds himself by two.
                    Or more.
"Incapable of contact
Save in incidents"
                    And yet at night   30
Their weight is part of mine.
For we are all housed now, all in our apartments,
The world untended to, unwatched.
And there is nothing left out there
As night falls, but the rocks   35

                                        [1962]

THEODORE ROETHKE   [1908–1963]

My Papa's Waltz

The whiskey on your breath
Could make a small boy dizzy;
But I hung on like death:
Such waltzing was not easy.

We romped until the pans   5
Slid from the kitchen shelf;
My mother's countenance
Could not unfrown itself.

The hand that held my wrist
Was battered on one knuckle;   10
At every step you missed
My right ear scraped a buckle.

You beat time on my head
With a palm caked hard by dirt,
Then waltzed me off to bed   15
Still clinging to your shirt.

                                        [1948]

THEODORE ROETHKE   [1908–1963]

Elegy for Jane

My Student, Thrown by a Horse

I remember the neckcurls, limp and damp as tendrils;
And her quick look, a sidelong pickerel smile;
And how, once startled into talk, the light syllables leaped for her,
And she balanced in the delight of her thought,
A wren, happy, tail into the wind,   5
Her song trembling the twigs and small branches.
The shade sang with her;
The leaves, their whispers turned to kissing;
And the mold sang in the bleached valleys under the rose.

Oh, when she was sad, she cast herself down into such a pure depth,   10
Even a father could not find her:
Scraping her cheek against straw;
Stirring the clearest water.

My sparrow, you are not here,
Waiting like a fern, making a spiny shadow.   15
The sides of wet stones cannot console me,
Nor the moss, wound with the last light.

If only I could nudge you from this sleep,
My maimed darling, my skittery pigeon.
Over this damp grave I speak the words of my love: 20
I, with no rights in this matter,
Neither father nor lover.

[1953]

CHARLES OLSON   [1910–1970]

Maximus, to himself°

I have had to learn the simplest things
last. Which made for difficulties.

Maximus, to himself: From 1950 until his death, Olson worked on his magnum
opus, *The Maximus Poems*, a series of poems about Maximus (Latin for "greatest"

Even at sea I was slow, to get the hand out, or to cross
a wet deck.
        The sea was not, finally, my trade.   5
But even my trade, at it, I stood estranged
from that which was most familiar.° Was delayed,
and not content with the man's argument
that such postponement
is now the nature of   10
obedience,
        that we are all late
        in a slow time,
        that we grow up many
        And the single   15
        is not easily
        known

It could be, though the sharpness (the *achiote*°)
I note in others,
makes more sense   20
than my own distances. The agilities

        they show daily
        who do the world's
        businesses
        And who do nature's   25
        as I have no sense
        I have done either

I have made dialogues,
have discussed ancient texts,
have thrown what light I could, offered   30
what pleasures
doceat° allows

        But the known?
This, I have had to be given,

---

or "largest"), who represents both Olson (he was six feet seven inches tall) and the
second-century philosopher Maximus of Tyre; the poems are also about a place—
Gloucester, Massachusetts, which represents small-town American life generally.
6–7. estranged . . . familiar: Echoing the Greek philosopher Heracleitus (c. 540–
c. 480 B.C.E.): "We are estranged from that with which we are most familiar."
18. achiote: A tropical American shrub whose bright red fruit contains red seeds
from which is obtained a paste used as a food additive for its color and flavor.
32. doceat: Teaching (Latin; the idea that instruction is a function of poetry goes
back at least as far as the Roman poet Horace).

a life, love, and from one man   35
the world.
                    Tokens.
                    But sitting here
                    I look out as a wind
                    and water man, testing   40
                    And missing
                    some proof

I know the quarters
of the weather, where it comes from,
where it goes. But the stem of me,   45
this I took from their welcome,
or their rejection, of me

                    And my arrogance
                    was neither diminished
                    nor increased,   50
                    by the communication

2

It is undone business
I speak of, this morning,
with the sea
stretching out   55
from my feet

                                                    [1960]

ELIZABETH BISHOP   [1911–1979]

The Fish

I caught a tremendous fish
and held him beside the boat
half out of water, with my hook
fast in a corner of his mouth.
He didn't fight.   5
He hadn't fought at all.
He hung a grunting weight,
battered and venerable

and homely. Here and there
his brown skin hung in strips   10
like ancient wallpaper,
and its pattern of darker brown
was like wallpaper:
shapes like full-blown roses
stained and lost through age.   15
He was speckled with barnacles,
fine rosettes of lime,
and infested
with tiny white sea-lice,
and underneath two or three   20
rags of green weed hung down.
While his gills were breathing in
the terrible oxygen
—the frightening gills,
fresh and crisp with blood,   25
that can cut so badly—
I thought of the coarse white flesh
packed in like feathers,
the big bones and the little bones,
the dramatic reds and blacks   30
of his shiny entrails,
and the pink swim-bladder
like a big peony.
I looked into his eyes
which were far larger than mine   35
but shallower, and yellowed,
the irises backed and packed
with tarnished tinfoil
seen through the lenses
of old scratched isinglass.°   *transparent sheet of mica* 40
They shifted a little, but not
to return my stare.
—It was more like the tipping
of an object toward the light.
I admired his sullen face,   45
the mechanism of his jaw,
and then I saw
that from his lower lip
—if you could call it a lip—
grim, wet, and weaponlike,   50
hung five old pieces of fish-line,

or four and a wire leader
with the swivel still attached,
with all their five big hooks
grown firmly in his mouth.   55
A green line, frayed at the end
where he broke it, two heavier lines,
and a fine black thread
still crimped from the strain and snap
when it broke and he got away.   60
Like medals with their ribbons
frayed and wavering,
a five-haired beard of wisdom
trailing from his aching jaw.
I stared and stared   65
and victory filled up
the little rented boat,
from the pool of bilge
where oil had spread a rainbow
around the rusted engine   70
to the bailer rusted orange,
the sun-cracked thwarts,
the oarlocks on their strings,
the gunnels—until everything
was rainbow, rainbow, rainbow!   75
And I let the fish go.

                                                    [1946]

ELIZABETH BISHOP   [1911–1979]

In the Waiting Room

In Worcester, Massachusetts,
I went with Aunt Consuelo
to keep her dentist's appointment
and sat and waited for her
in the dentist's waiting room.   5
It was winter. It got dark
early. The waiting room
was full of grown-up people,

arctics and overcoats,
lamps and magazines.   10
My aunt was inside
what seemed like a long time
and while I waited I read
the *National Geographic*
(I could read) and carefully   15
studied the photographs:
the inside of a volcano,
black, and full of ashes;
then it was spilling over
in rivulets of fire.   20
Osa and Martin Johnson°
dressed in riding breeches,
laced boots, and pith helmets.
A dead man slung on a pole
—"Long Pig,"° the caption said.   25
Babies with pointed heads
wound round and round with string;
black, naked women with necks
wound round and round with wire
like the necks of light bulbs.   30
Their breasts were horrifying.
I read it right straight through.
I was too shy to stop.
And then I looked at the cover:
the yellow margins, the date.   35
Suddenly, from inside,
came an *oh!* of pain
—Aunt Consuelo's voice—
not very loud or long.
I wasn't at all surprised;   40
even then I knew she was
a foolish, timid woman.
I might have been embarrassed,
but wasn't. What took me
completely by surprise   45
was that it was *me:*
my voice, in my mouth.

21. **Osa and Martin Johnson:** Husband-and-wife explorers and naturalists.
25. **Long Pig:** Polynesian cannibals' name for a human carcass.

Without thinking at all
I was my foolish aunt,
I—we—were falling, falling,   50
our eyes glued to the cover
of the *National Geographic*,
February, 1918.

I said to myself: three days
and you'll be seven years old.   55
I was saying it to stop
the sensation of falling off
the round, turning world
into cold, blue-black space.
But I felt: you are an *I*,   60
you are an *Elizabeth*,
you are one of *them*.
Why should you be one, too?
I scarcely dared to look
to see what it was I was.   65
I gave a sidelong glance
—I couldn't look any higher—
at shadowy gray knees,
trousers and skirts and boots
and different pairs of hands   70
lying under the lamps.
I knew that nothing stranger
had ever happened, that nothing
stranger could ever happen.
Why should I be my aunt,   75
or me, or anyone?
What similarities—
boots, hands, the family voice
I felt in my throat, or even
the *National Geographic*   80
and those awful hanging breasts—
held us all together
or made us all just one?
How—I didn't know any
word for it—how "unlikely" . . .   85
How had I come to be here,
like them, and overhear
a cry of pain that could have
got loud and worse but hadn't?

The waiting room was bright   90
and too hot. It was sliding
beneath a big black wave,
another, and another.

Then I was back in it.
The War was on. Outside,   95
in Worcester, Massachusetts,
were night and slush and cold,
and it was still the fifth
of February, 1918.

[1976]

ELIZABETH BISHOP   [1911–1979]

One Art

The art of losing isn't hard to master;
so many things seem filled with the intent
to be lost that their loss is no disaster.

Lose something every day. Accept the fluster
of lost door keys, the hour badly spent.   5
The art of losing isn't hard to master.

Then practice losing farther, losing faster:
places, and names, and where it was you meant
to travel. None of these will bring disaster.

I lost my mother's watch. And look! my last, or   10
next-to-last, of three loved houses went.
The art of losing isn't hard to master.

I lost two cities, lovely ones. And, vaster,
some realms I owned, two rivers, a continent.
I miss them, but it wasn't a disaster.   15

—Even losing you (the joking voice, a gesture
I love) I shan't have lied. It's evident
the art of losing's not too hard to master
though it may look like (*Write* it!) like disaster.

[1976]

ROBERT HAYDEN   [1913–1980]

Those Winter Sundays

Sundays too my father got up early
and put his clothes on in the blueblack cold,
then with cracked hands that ached
from labor in the weekday weather made
banked fires blaze. No one ever thanked him.   5

I'd wake and hear the cold splintering, breaking.
When the rooms were warm, he'd call,
and slowly I would rise and dress,
fearing the chronic angers of that house,

Speaking indifferently to him,   10
who had driven out the cold
and polished my good shoes as well.
What did I know, what did I know
of love's austere and lonely offices?

[1962]

JOHN FREDERICK NIMS   [1913–1999]

Love Poem

My clumsiest dear, whose hands shipwreck vases,
At whose quick touch all glasses chip and ring,
Whose palms are bulls in china, burs in linen,
And have no cunning with any soft thing

Except all ill-at-ease fidgeting people: 5
The refugee uncertain at the door
You make at home; deftly you steady
The drunk clambering on his undulant floor.

Unpredictable dear, the taxi drivers' terror,
Shrinking from far headlights pale as a dime   10
Yet leaping before red apoplectic streetcars—
Misfit in any space. And never on time.

A wrench in clocks and the solar system. Only
With words and people and love you move at ease;

In traffic of wit expertly maneuver   15
And keep us, all devotion, at your knees.

Forgetting your coffee spreading on our flannel,
Your lipstick grinning on our coat,
So gaily in love's unbreakable heaven
Our souls on glory of spilt bourbon float.   20

Be with me, darling, early and late. Smash glasses—
I will study wry music for your sake.
For should your hands drop white and empty
All the toys of the world would break.

[1947]

DUDLEY RANDALL   [1914–2000]

Ballad of Birmingham
On the bombing of a church in Birmingham, Alabama, 1963

"Mother dear, may I go downtown
Instead of out to play,
And march the streets of Birmingham
In a Freedom March today?"

"No, baby, no, you may not go,   5
For the dogs are fierce and wild,
And clubs and hoses, guns and jails
Aren't good for a little child."

"But, mother, I won't be alone.
Other children will go with me,   10
And march the streets of Birmingham
To make our country free."

"No, baby, no, you may not go,
For I fear those guns will fire.
But you may go to church instead   15
And sing in the children's choir."

She has combed and brushed her night-dark hair,
And bathed rose petal sweet,
And drawn white gloves on her small brown hands,
And white shoes on her feet.   20

The mother smiled to know her child
Was in the sacred place,
But that smile was the last smile
To come upon her face.

For when she heard the explosion,   25
Her eyes grew wet and wild.
She raced through the streets of Birmingham
Calling for her child.

She clawed through bits of glass and brick,
Then lifted out a shoe.   30
"Oh, here's the shoe my baby wore,
But, baby, where are you?"

[1969]

WILLIAM STAFFORD   [1914–1995]

Traveling through the Dark

Traveling through the dark I found a deer
dead on the edge of the Wilson River road.
It is usually best to roll them into the canyon:
that road is narrow; to swerve might make more dead.

By glow of the tail-light I stumbled back of the car   5
and stood by the heap, a doe, a recent killing;
she had stiffened already, almost cold.
I dragged her off; she was large in the belly.

My fingers touching her side brought me the reason—
her side was warm; her fawn lay there waiting,   10
alive, still, never to be born.
Beside that mountain road I hesitated.

The car aimed ahead its lowered parking lights;
under the hood purred the steady engine.
I stood in the glare of the warm exhaust turning red;   15
around our group I could hear the wilderness listen.

I thought hard for us all—my only swerving—,
then pushed her over the edge into the river.

[1962]

RANDALL JARRELL   [1914–1965]

The Death of the Ball Turret Gunner°

From my mother's sleep I fell into the State,
And I hunched in its belly till my wet fur froze.
Six miles from earth, loosed from its dream of life,
I woke to black flak and the nightmare fighters.
When I died they washed me out of the turret with a hose.

[1945]

Ball Turret Gunner: "A ball turret was a plexiglass sphere set into the belly of a B-17 or B-24, and inhabited by two .50 caliber machine-guns and one man, a short small man. When this gunner tracked with his machine guns a fighter attacking his bomber from below, he revolved with the turret; hunched upside-down in his little sphere, he looked like the foetus in the womb. The fighters that attacked him were armed with cannon-firing explosive shells. The hose was a steam hose" [Jarrell's note].

JOHN BERRYMAN   [1914–1972]

Certainty before Lunch

Ninety percent of the mass of the Universe
(90%!) may be gone in collapsars,°
pulseless, lightless, forever, if they exist.
My friends are the probability man & I

& his wife the lawyer are taking a country walk   5
in the flowerless April snow in exactly two hours
and maybe won't be back. Finite & unbounded
the massive spirals absolutely fly

distinctly apart, by math *and* observation,
current math, this morning's telescopes   10
& inference. My wife is six months gone
so won't be coming. That mass must be somewhere!

2. **collapsars:** Short for *collapsed stars*, the black holes formed, according to an astronomical theory, by the gravitational collapse of massive stars.

or not? just barely possible *may not*
BE anywhere? My Lord, I'm glad we don't
on x or y depend for Your being there.   15
I know You are there. The sweat is, I am here.

[1972]

DYLAN THOMAS   [1914–1953]

Fern Hill

Now as I was young and easy under the apple boughs
About the lilting house and happy as the grass was green,
   The night above the dingle° starry,   *small wooded valley*
    Time let me hail and climb
   Golden in the heydays of his eyes,   5
And honoured among wagons I was prince of the apple towns
And once below a time I lordly had the trees and leaves
    Trail with daisies and barley
   Down the rivers of the windfall light.

And as I was green and carefree, famous among the barns   10
About the happy yard and singing as the farm was home,
   In the sun that is young once only,
    Time let me play and be
   Golden in the mercy of his means,
And green and golden I was huntsman and herdsman, the calves   15
Sang to my horn, the foxes on the hills barked clear and cold,
    And the sabbath rang slowly
   In the pebbles of the holy streams.

All the sun long it was running, it was lovely, the hay
Fields high as the house, the tunes from the chimneys, it was air   20
   And playing, lovely and watery
    And fire green as grass.
   And nightly under the simple stars
As I rode to sleep the owls were bearing the farm away,
All the moon long I heard, blessed among stables, the nightjars   25
   Flying with the ricks, and the horses
    Flashing into the dark.

And then to awake, and the farm, like a wanderer white
With the dew, come back, the cock on his shoulder: it was all

Shining, it was Adam and maiden,   30
    The sky gathered again
And the sun grew round that very day.
So it must have been after the birth of the simple light
In the first, spinning place, the spellbound horses walking warm
    Out of the whinnying green stable   35
        On to the fields of praise.

And honoured among foxes and pheasants by the gay house
Under the new made clouds and happy as the heart was long,
    In the sun born over and over,
        I ran my heedless ways,   40
    My wishes raced through the house high hay
And nothing I cared, at my sky blue trades, that time allows
In all his tuneful turning so few and such morning songs
    Before the children green and golden
        Follow him out of grace,   45

Nothing I cared, in the lamb white days, that time would take me
Up to the swallow thronged loft by the shadow of my hand,
    In the moon that is always rising,
        Nor that riding to sleep
    I should hear him fly with the high fields   50
And wake to the farm forever fled from the childless land.
Oh as I was young and easy in the mercy of his means,
    Time held me green and dying
    Though I sang in my chains like the sea.

                                                          [1946]

DYLAN THOMAS   [1914–1953]

Do not go gentle into that good night

Do not go gentle into that good night,
Old age should burn and rave at close of day;
Rage, rage against the dying of the light.

Though wise men at their end know dark is right,
Because their words had forked no lightning they   5
Do not go gentle into that good night.

Good men, the last wave by, crying how bright
Their frail deeds might have danced in a green bay,
Rage, rage against the dying of the light.

Wild men who caught and sang the sun in flight,   10
And learn, too late, they grieved it on its way,
Do not go gentle into that good night.

Grave men, near death, who see with blinding sight
Blind eyes could blaze like meteors and be gay,
Rage, rage against the dying of the light.   15

And you, my father, there on the sad height,
Curse, bless, me now with your fierce tears, I pray.
Do not go gentle into that good night.
Rage, rage against the dying of the light.

[1952]

RUTH STONE   [b. 1915]

What We Have

On the mountain
the neighbor's dog, put out in the cold,
comes to my house for the night.
He quivers with gratitude.
His short-haired small stout body   5
settles near the stove.
He snores.
Out there in the dark, snow falls.
The birch trees are wrapped in their white bandages.
Recently in the surgical theater,   10
I looked in the mirror at the doctor's hands
as he repaired my ancient frescoes.
When I was ten
we lived in a bungalow in Indianapolis.
My sister and brother, my mother and father,   15
all living then.
We were like rabbits
in the breast fur of a soft lined nest.
I know now we were desperately poor.

Bu it was spring: 20
the field, a botanist's mirage of wild flowers.
The house centered between two railroad tracks.
The tracks split at the orchard end of the street
and spread in a dangerous angle down either side.
Long lines of freight for half an hour clicking by;   25
or a passenger train,
with a small balcony at the end of the last car
where someone always stood and waved to us.
At night the wrenching scream and Doppler whistle
of the two AM express.   30
From my window I could see a fireman stoking
the open fire, the red glow reflected in the black smoke
belching from the boiler.
Once I got up and went outside.
The trees-of-heaven along the track swam in the white mist.   35
The sky arched with sickle pears.
Lilacs had just opened.
I pulled the heavy clusters to my face
and breathed them in,
suffused with a strange excitement   40
that I think, when looking back, was happiness.

                                                        [2002]

ROBERT LOWELL   [1917–1978]

Skunk Hour

for Elizabeth Bishop

Nautilus Island's hermit
heiress still lives through winter in her Spartan cottage;
her sheep still graze above the sea.
Her son's a bishop. Her farmer
is first selectman in our village;   5
she's in her dotage.

Thirsting for
the hierarchic privacy
of Queen Victoria's century,

she buys up all   10
the eyesores facing her shore,
and lets them fall.

The season's ill—
we've lost our summer millionaire,
who seemed to leap from an L. L. Bean   15
catalogue. His nine-knot yawl
was auctioned off to lobstermen.
A red fox stain covers Blue Hill.

And now our fairy
decorator brightens his shop for fall;   20
his fishnet's filled with orange cork,
orange, his cobbler's bench and awl;
there is no money in his work,
he'd rather marry.

One dark night,   25
my Tudor Ford climbed the hill's skull;
I watched for love-cars. Lights turned down,
they lay together, hull to hull,
where the graveyard shelves on the town. . . .
My mind's not right.   30

A car radio bleats,
"Love, O careless Love. . . ." I hear
my ill-spirit sob in each blood cell,
as if my hand were at its throat. . . .
I myself am hell;   35
nobody's here—

only skunks, that search
in the moonlight for a bite to eat.
They march on their soles up Main Street:
white stripes, moonstruck eyes' red fire   40
under the chalk-dry and spar spire
of the Trinitarian Church.

I stand on top
of our back steps and breathe the rich air—
a mother skunk with her column of kittens swills the garbage pail. 45
She jabs her wedge-head in a cup
of sour cream, drops her ostrich tail,
and will not scare.

                                                        [1963]

GWENDOLYN BROOKS   [1917–2000]

We Real Cool

The Pool Players.
Seven at the Golden Shovel.

We real cool. We
Left school. We

Lurk late. We
Strike straight. We

Sing sin. We   5
Thin gin. We

Jazz° June. We   *have sexual intercourse (with)*
Die soon.

[1960]

GWENDOLYN BROOKS   [1917–2000]

The Bean Eaters

They eat beans mostly, this old yellow pair.
Dinner is a casual affair.
Plain chipware on a plain and creaking wood,
Tin flatware.

Two who are Mostly Good.   5
Two who have lived their day,
But keep on putting on their clothes
and putting things away.

And remembering . . .
Remembering, with twinklings and twinges,   10
As they lean over the beans in their rented back room that
    is full of beads and receipts and dolls and cloths,
        tobacco crumbs, vases and fringes.

[1960]

CHARLES BUKOWSKI   [1920–1994]

my old man

16 years old
during the depression
I'd come home drunk
and all my clothing—
shorts, shirts, stockings—   5
suitcase, and pages of
short stories
would be thrown out on the
front lawn and about the
street.   10

my mother would be
waiting behind a tree:
"Henry, Henry, don't
go in . . . he'll
kill you, he's read   15
your stories . . ."

"I can whip his
ass . . ."

"Henry, please take
this . . . and   20
find yourself a room."

but it worried him
that I might not
finish high school
so I'd be back   25
again.

one evening he walked in
with the pages of
one of my short stories
(which I had never submitted   30
to him)
and he said, "this is
a great short story."
I said, "o.k.,"
and he handed it to me   35

and I read it.
it was a story about
a rich man
who had a fight with
his wife and had   40
gone out into the night
for a cup of coffee
and had observed
the waitress and the spoons
and forks and the   45
salt and pepper shakers
and the neon sign
in the window
and then had gone back
to his stable   50
to see and touch his
favorite horse
who then
kicked him in the head
and killed him.   55

somehow
the story held
meaning for him
though
when I had written it   60
I had no idea
of what I was
writing about.

so I told him,
"o.k., old man, you can   65
have it."
and he took it
and walked out
and closed the door.
I guess that's   70
as close
as we ever got.

[1977]

RICHARD WILBUR   [b. 1921]

Love Calls Us to the Things of This World

The eyes open to a cry of pulleys,
And spirited from sleep, the astounded soul
Hangs for a moment bodiless and simple
As false dawn.
                    Outside the open window
The morning air is all awash with angels.   5

    Some are in bed-sheets, some are in blouses,
Some are in smocks: but truly there they are.
Now they are rising together in calm swells
Of halcyon feeling, filling whatever they wear
With the deep joy of their impersonal breathing;   10

    Now they are flying in place, conveying
The terrible speed of their omnipresence, moving
And staying like white water; and now of a sudden
They swoon down into so rapt a quiet
That nobody seems to be there.
                                The soul shrinks   15

From all that it is about to remember,
From the punctual rape of every blessèd day,
And cries,
            "Oh, let there be nothing on earth but laundry,
Nothing but rosy hands in the rising steam
And clear dances done in the sight of heaven."   20

    Yet, as the sun acknowledges
With a warm look the world's hunks and colors,
The soul descends once more in bitter love
To accept the waking body, saying now
In a changed voice as the man yawns and rises,   25

    "Bring them down from their ruddy gallows;
Let there be clean linen for the backs of thieves;
Let lovers go fresh and sweet to be undone,
And the heaviest nuns walk in a pure floating
Of dark habits,
                    keeping their difficult balance."   30

                                                            [1956]

PHILIP LARKIN   [1922–1985]

High Windows

When I see a couple of kids
And guess he's fucking her and she's
Taking pills or wearing a diaphragm,
I know this is paradise

Everyone old has dreamed of all their lives —   5
Bonds and gestures pushed to one side
Like an outdated combine harvester,
And everyone young going down the long slide

To happiness, endlessly. I wonder if
Anyone looked at me, forty years back,   10
And thought, *That'll be the life;*
No God any more, or sweating in the dark

About hell and that, or having to hide
What you think of the priest. He
And his lot will all go down the long slide   15
Like free bloody birds. And immediately

Rather than words comes the thought of high windows:
The sun-comprehending glass,
And beyond it, the deep blue air, that shows
Nothing, and is nowhere, and is endless.   20

[1974]

DENISE LEVERTOV   [1923–1997]

The ache of marriage

The ache of marriage:

thigh and tongue, beloved,
are heavy with it,
it throbs in the teeth

We look for communion   5
and are turned away, beloved,
each and each

It is leviathan° and we   *a whale*
in its belly
looking for joy, some joy   10
not to be known outside it

two by two in the ark of
the ache of it.

[1964]

GERALD STERN   [b. 1925]

The Dog

What I was doing with my white teeth exposed
like that on the side of the road I don't know,
and I don't know why I lay beside the sewer
so that lover of dead things could come back
with his pencil sharpened and his piece of white paper.   5
I was there for a good two hours whistling
dirges, shrieking a little, terrifying
hearts with my whimpering cries before I died
by pulling the one leg up and stiffening.
There is a look we have with the hair of the chin   10
curled in mid-air, there is a look with the belly
stopped in the midst of its greed. The lover of dead things
stoops to feel me, his hand is shaking. I know
his mouth is open and his glasses are slipping.
I think his pencil must be jerking and the terror   15
of smell—and sight—is overtaking him;
I know he has that terrified faraway look
that death brings—he is contemplating. I want him
to touch my forehead once and rub my muzzle
before he lifts me up and throws me into   20
that little valley. I hope he doesn't use
his shoe for fear of touching me; I know,
or used to know, the grasses down there; I think
I knew a hundred smells. I hope the dog's way
doesn't overtake him, one quick push,   25
barely that, and the mind freed, something else,
some other thing, to take its place. Great heart,

great human heart, keep loving me as you lift me,
give me your tears, great loving stranger, remember
the death of dogs, forgive the yapping, forgive   30
the shitting, let there be pity, give me your pity.
How could there be enough? I have given
my life for this, emotion has ruined me, oh lover,
I have exchanged my wildness—little tricks
with the mouth and feet, with the tail, my tongue is a parrot's,   35
I am a rampant horse, I am a lion,
I wait for the cookie, I snap my teeth—
as you have taught me, oh distant and brilliant and lonely.

[1987]

MAXINE KUMIN   [b. 1925]

The Sound of Night

And now the dark comes on, all full of chitter noise.
Birds huggermugger crowd the trees,
the air thick with their vesper° cries,   *evening*
and bats, snub seven-pointed kites,
skitter across the lake, swing out,   5
squeak, chirp, dip, and skim on skates
of air, and the fat frogs wake and prink
wide-lipped, noisy as ducks, drunk
on the boozy black, gloating chink-chunk.

And now on the narrow beach we defend ourselves from dark.   10
The cooking done, we build our firework
bright and hot and less for outlook
than for magic, and lie in our blankets
while night nickers around us. Crickets
chorus hallelujahs; paws, quiet   15
and quick as raindrops, play on the stones
expertly soft, run past and are gone;
fish pulse in the lake; the frogs hoarsen.

Now every voice of the hour—the known, the supposed, the strange
the mindless, the witted, the never seen—   20
sing, thrum, impinge, and rearrange

endlessly; and debarred from sleep we wait
for the birds, importantly silent,
for the crease of first eye-licking light,
for the sun, lost long ago and sweet.   25
By the lake, locked black away and tight,
we lie, day creatures, overhearing night.

[1961]

PHILIP BOOTH   [1925–2007]

A Two Inch Wave

The sea, flat
            on a coming tide:
a two inch wave
            climbs the low sand,
drags, curls,   5
            and topples.
Over and over,
            the water toppling
gathers and
            gains on itself.   10
It tempts us,
            whoever it is
we think we are,
            to humanize
comparisons   15
            —but that belongs
to another
            century's nonsense.
Only the semi-
            palmated plovers,°   *small dark shorebirds* 20
feeding in mid-
            migration, two
strong, claim
            the advancing edge
as their own: 25
            they dip quick beaks
at something
            we cannot pretend

to see;
      inshore of ducks   30
floating calm,
          off-tide of oaks
growing tall,
        between the field
of a field   35
      and the field of the
incoming sea,
        they dip quick beaks
into a margin
          we cannot fathom;   40
they strike for
        a sustenance only
they know. We
        only partially
guess. The planet,   45
          maybe
the cosmos,
       they share with us,
or we share
        with them, is a mystery   50
not to be solved;
        what is here, now,
is *here, now*,
       beyond every knowledge
except our caring: 55
         fetched from behind
the old sun,
       in the huge blue over us still,
Arcturus° and all
        her proximate stars   60
are already bound
        to brighten and seem
to rise, as they
       even now tip to ebb,
angled into the sea   65
        on their own inviolate wavelength.

                                        [1986]

---

59. Arcturus: The brightest star in the northern celestial hemisphere; it is part of the constellation Bootes.

FRANK O'HARA   [1926–1966]

Why I Am Not a Painter

I am not a painter, I am a poet.
Why? I think I would rather be
a painter, but I am not. Well,

for instance, Mike Goldberg
is starting a painting. I drop in.   5
"Sit down and have a drink" he
says. I drink; we drink. I look
up. "You have SARDINES in it."
"Yes, it needed something there."
"Oh." I go and the days go by   10
and I drop in again. The painting
is going on, and I go, and the days
go by. I drop in. The painting is
finished. "Where's SARDINES?"
All that's left is just   15
letters, "It was too much," Mike says.

But me? One day I am thinking of
a color: orange. I write a line
about orange. Pretty soon it is a
whole page of words, not lines.   20
Then another page. There should be
so much more, not of orange, of
words, of how terrible orange is
and life. Days go by. It is even in
prose, I am a real poet. My poem   25
is finished and I haven't mentioned
orange yet. It's twelve poems, I call
it ORANGES. And one day in a gallery
I see Mike's painting, called SARDINES.

[1971]

FRANK O'HARA   [1926–1966]

The Day Lady° Died

It is 12:20 in New York a Friday
three days after Bastille day,° yes   *(July 14)*
it is 1959 and I go get a shoeshine
because I will get off the 4:19 in Easthampton
at 7:15 and then go straight to dinner   5
and I don't know the people who will feed me

I walk up the muggy street beginning to sun
and have a hamburger and a malted and buy
an ugly NEW WORLD WRITING to see what the poets
in Ghana are doing these days   10
                         I go on to the bank
and Miss Stillwagon (first name Linda I once heard)
doesn't even look up my balance for once in her life
and in the GOLDEN GRIFFIN I get a little Verlaine°   *French poet*
for Patsy with drawings by Bonnard° although I do   15
think of Hesiod,° trans. Richmond Lattimore or   *Greek poet*
Brendan Behan's° new play or *Le Balcon* or *Les Nègres*   *Irish playwright*
of Genet,° but I don't, I stick with Verlaine
after practically going to sleep with quandariness

and for Mike I just stroll into the PARK LANE   20
Liquor Store and ask for a bottle of Strega and
then I go back where I came from to 6th Avenue
and the tobacconist in the Ziegfeld Theatre and
casually ask for a carton of Gauloises° and a carton   *French cigarettes*
of Picayunes,° and a NEW YORK POST with her face on it   25

and I am sweating a lot by now and thinking of
leaning on the john door in the 5 SPOT
while she whispered a song along the keyboard
to Mal Waldron and everyone and I stopped breathing

[1964]

Lady: Jazz singer Billie Holliday.
15. Bonnard: French modernist painter.
18. Genet: French playwright and novelist.
25. Picayunes: Southern cigarettes.

ALLEN GINSBERG   [1926–1997]

A Supermarket in California

What thoughts I have of you tonight, Walt Whitman, for I walked
down the sidestreets under the trees with a headache self-conscious
looking at the full moon.

In my hungry fatigue, and shopping for images, I went into the neon
fruit supermarket, dreaming of your enumerations!

What peaches and what penumbras! Whole families shopping at
night! Aisles full of husbands! Wives in the avocados, babies in the
tomatoes!—and you, García Lorca,° what were you doing down by the
watermelons?

I saw you, Walt Whitman, childless, lonely old grubber, poking among
the meats in the refrigerator and eyeing the grocery boys.

I heard you asking questions of each: Who killed the pork chops? What
price bananas? Are you my Angel?   5

I wandered in and out of the brilliant stacks of cans following you,
and followed in my imagination by the store detective.

We strode down the open corridors together in our solitary fancy
tasting artichokes, possessing every frozen delicacy, and never passing
the cashier.

Where are we going, Walt Whitman? The doors close in an hour.
Which way does your beard point tonight?

(I touch your book and dream of our odyssey in the supermarket
and feel absurd.)

Will we walk all night through solitary streets? The trees add shade
to shade, lights out in the houses, we'll both be lonely.   10

Will we stroll dreaming of the lost America of love past blue
automobiles in driveways, home to our silent cottage?

Ah, dear father, graybeard, lonely old courage-teacher, what America
did you have when Charon° quit poling his ferry and you got out on
a smoking bank and stood watching the boat disappear on the black
waters of Lethe?°

Berkeley, 1955

[1956]

3. **García Lorca:** Spanish surrealist poet and playwright (1899–1936).
12. **Charon:** The boatman in Greek mythology who carried the dead across the
river Styx to Hades; **Lethe:** River of Forgetfulness in Hades.

ROBERT BLY   [b. 1926]

Driving to Town Late to Mail a Letter

It is a cold and snowy night. The main street is deserted.
The only things moving are swirls of snow.
As I lift the mailbox door, I feel its cold iron.
There is a privacy I love in this snowy night.
Driving around, I will waste more time.

[1962]

GALWAY KINNELL   [b. 1927]

The Bear

1

In late winter
I sometimes glimpse bits of steam
coming up from
some fault in the old snow
and bend close and see it is lung-colored   5
and put down my nose
and know
the chilly, enduring odor of bear.

2

I take a wolf's rib and whittle
it sharp at both ends   10
and coil it up
and freeze it in blubber and place it out
on the fairway of the bears.

And when it has vanished
I move out on the bear tracks,   15
roaming in circles
until I come to the first, tentative, dark
splash on the earth.

And I set out
running, following the splashes   20
of blood wandering over the world.

At the cut, gashed resting places
I stop and rest,
at the crawl-marks
where he lay out on his belly   25
to overpass some stretch of bauchy° ice   *weak, thin*
I lie out
dragging myself forward with bear-knives in my fists.

3

On the third day I begin to starve,
at nightfall I bend down as I knew I would   30
at a turd sopped in blood,
and hesitate, and pick it up,
and thrust it in my mouth, and gnash it down,
and rise
and go on running.   35

4

On the seventh day,
living by now on bear blood alone,
I can see his upturned carcass far out ahead, a scraggled,
steamy hulk,
the heavy fur riffling in the wind.   40

I come up to him
and stare at the narrow-spaced, petty eyes,
the dismayed
face laid back on the shoulder, the nostrils
flared, catching   45
perhaps the first taint of me as he
died.

I hack
a ravine in his thigh, and eat and drink,
and tear him down his whole length   50
and open him and climb in
and close him up after me, against the wind,
and sleep.

5

And dream
of lumbering flatfooted   55
over the tundra,
stabbed twice from within,

splattering a trail behind me,
splattering it out no matter which way I lurch,
no matter which parabola of bear-transcendence,   60
which dance of solitude I attempt,
which gravity-clutched leap,
which trudge, which groan.

6

Until one day I totter and fall—
fall on this   65
stomach that has tried so hard to keep up,
to digest the blood as it leaked in,
to break up
and digest the bone itself: and now the breeze
blows over me, blows off   70
the hideous belches of ill-digested bear blood
and rotted stomach
and the ordinary, wretched odor of bear,

blows across
my sore, lolled tongue a song   75
or screech, until I think I must rise up
and dance. And I lie still.

7

I awaken I think. Marshlights
reappear, geese
come trailing again up the flyway.   80
In her ravine under old snow the dam-bear
lies, licking
lumps of smeared fur
and drizzly eyes into shapes
with her tongue. And one   85
hairy-soled trudge stuck out before me,
the next groaned out,
the next,
the next,
the rest of my days I spend   90
wandering: wondering
what, anyway,
was that sticky infusion, that rank flavor of blood, that poetry, by which
    I lived?

[1967]

JOHN ASHBERY   [b. 1927]

Mixed Feelings

A pleasant smell of frying sausages
Attacks the sense, along with an old, mostly invisible
Photograph of what seems to be girls lounging around
An old fighter bomber, circa 1942 vintage.
How to explain to these girls, if indeed that's what they are,   5
These Ruths, Lindas, Pats and Sheilas
About the vast change that's taken place
In the fabric of our society, altering the texture
Of all things in it? And yet
They somehow look as if they knew, except   10
That it's so hard to see them, it's hard to figure out
Exactly what kind of expressions they're wearing.
What are your hobbies, girls? Aw nerts,
One of them might say, this guy's too much for me.
Let's go on and out, somewhere   15
Through the canyons of the garment center
To a small café and have a cup of coffee.
I am not offended that these creatures (that's the word)
Of my imagination seem to hold me in such light esteem,
Pay so little heed to me. It's part of a complicated   20
Flirtation routine, anyhow, no doubt. But this talk of
The garment center? Surely that's California sunlight
Belaboring them and the old crate on which they
Have draped themselves, fading its Donald Duck insignia
To the extreme point of legibility.   25
Maybe they were lying but more likely their
Tiny intelligences cannot retain much information.
Not even one fact, perhaps. That's why
They think they're in New York. I like the way
They look and act and feel. I wonder   30
How they got that way, but am not going to
Waste any more time thinking about them.
I have already forgotten them
Until some day in the not too distant future
When we meet possibly in the lounge of a modern airport,   35
They looking as astonishingly young and fresh as when this picture was
    made
But full of contradictory ideas, stupid ones as well as

Worthwhile ones, but all flooding the surface of our minds
As we babble about the sky and the weather and the forests of change.

[1975]

W. S. MERWIN   [b. 1927]

For the Anniversary of My Death

Every year without knowing it I have passed the day
When the last fires will wave to me
And the silence will set out
Tireless traveller
Like the beam of a lightless star   5

Then I will no longer
Find myself in life as in a strange garment
Surprised at the earth
At the love of one woman
And the shamelessness of men   10
As today writing after three days of rain
Hearing the wren sing and the falling cease
And bowing not knowing to what

[1967]

JAMES WRIGHT   [1927–1980]

A Blessing

Just off the highway to Rochester, Minnesota,
Twilight bounds softly forth on the grass.
And the eyes of those two Indian ponies
Darken with kindness.
They have come gladly out of the willows   5
To welcome my friend and me.
We step over the barbed wire into the pasture
Where they have been grazing all day, alone.

They ripple tensely, they can hardly contain their happiness
That we have come.   10
They bow shyly as wet swans. They love each other.
There is no loneliness like theirs.
At home once more,
They begin munching the young tufts of spring in the darkness.
I would like to hold the slenderer one in my arms,   15
For she has walked over to me
And nuzzled my left hand.
She is black and white,
Her mane falls wild on her forehead,
And the light breeze moves me to caress her long ear   20
That is delicate as the skin over a girl's wrist.
Suddenly I realize
That if I stepped out of my body I would break
Into blossom.

                                                              [1963]

PHILIP LEVINE   [b. 1928]

What Work Is

We stand in the rain in a long line
waiting at Ford Highland Park. For work.
You know what work is—if you're
old enough to read this you know what
work is, although you may not do it.   5
Forget you. This is about waiting,
shifting from one foot to another.
Feeling the light rain falling like mist
into your hair, blurring your vision
until you think you see your own brother   10
ahead of you, maybe ten places.
You rub your glasses with your fingers,
and of course it's someone else's brother,
narrower across the shoulders than
yours but with the same sad slouch, the grin   15
that does not hide the stubbornness,
the sad refusal to give in to

rain, to the hours wasted waiting,
to the knowledge that somewhere ahead
a man is waiting who will say, "No,   20
we're not hiring today," for any
reason he wants. You love your brother,
now suddenly you can hardly stand
the love flooding you for your brother,
who's not beside you or behind or   25
ahead because he's home trying to
sleep off a miserable night shift
at Cadillac so he can get up
before noon to study his German.
Works eight hours a night so he can sing   30
Wagner, the opera you hate most,
the worst music ever invented.
How long has it been since you told him
you loved him, held his wide shoulders,
opened your eyes wide and said those words,   35
and maybe kissed his cheek? You've never
done something so simple, so obvious,
not because you're too young or too dumb,
not because you're jealous or even mean
or incapable of crying in   40
the presence of another man, no,
just because you don't know what work is.

[1991]

ANNE SEXTON   [1928–1974]

Cinderella

You always read about it:
the plumber with twelve children
who wins the Irish Sweepstakes.
From toilets to riches.
That story.   5

Or the nursemaid,
some luscious sweet from Denmark
who captures the oldest son's heart.

From diapers to Dior.°
That story.   10

Or a milkman who serves the wealthy,
eggs, cream, butter, yogurt, milk,
the white truck like an ambulance
who goes into real estate
and makes a pile.   15
From homogenized to martinis at lunch.

Or the charwoman
who is on the bus when it cracks up
and collects enough from the insurance.
    From mops to Bonwit Teller.°   20
    That story.

Once
the wife of a rich man was on her deathbed
and she said to her daughter Cinderella:
Be devout. Be good. Then I will smile   25
down from heaven in the seam of a cloud.
The man took another wife who had
two daughters, pretty enough
but with hearts like blackjacks.
Cinderella was their maid.   30
She slept on the sooty hearth each night
and walked around looking like Al Jolson.°
Her father brought presents home from town,
jewels and gowns for the other women
but the twig of a tree for Cinderella.   35
She planted that twig on her mother's grave
and it grew to a tree where a white dove sat.
Whenever she wished for anything the dove
would drop it like an egg upon the ground.
The bird is important, my dears, so heed him.   40

Next came the ball, as you all know.
It was a marriage market.
The prince was looking for a wife.

9. **Dior:** Fashions designed by the French house of Dior, established by Christian
Dior (1905–1957).
20. **Bonwit Teller:** A fashionable and expensive department store.
32. **Al Jolson:** American entertainer (1888–1950), known particularly for singing
in blackface.

All but Cinderella were preparing
and gussying up for the big event.   45
Cinderella begged to go too.
Her stepmother threw a dish of lentils
into the cinders and said: Pick them
up in an hour and you shall go.
The white dove brought all his friends;   50
all the warm wings of the fatherland came,
and picked up the lentils in a jiffy.
No, Cinderella, said the stepmother,
you have no clothes and cannot dance.
That's the way with stepmothers.   55

Cinderella went to the tree at the grave
and cried forth like a gospel singer:
Mama! Mama! My turtledove,
send me to the prince's ball!
The bird dropped down a golden dress   60
and delicate little gold slippers.
Rather a large package for a simple bird.
So she went. Which is no surprise.
Her stepmother and sisters didn't
recognize her without her cinder face   65
and the prince took her hand on the spot
and danced with no other the whole day.

As nightfall came she thought she'd better
get home. The prince walked her home
and she disappeared into the pigeon house   70
and although the prince took an axe and broke
it open she was gone. Back to her cinders.
These events repeated themselves for three days.
However on the third day the prince
covered the palace steps with cobbler's wax   75
and Cinderella's gold shoe stuck upon it.

Now he would find whom the shoe fit
and find his strange dancing girl for keeps.
He went to their house and the two sisters
were delighted because they had lovely feet.   80
The eldest went into a room to try the slipper on
but her big toe got in the way so she simply
sliced it off and put on the slipper.
The prince rode away with her until the white dove

told him to look at the blood pouring forth.   85
That is the way with amputations.
They don't just heal up like a wish.
The other sister cut off her heel
but the blood told as blood will.
The prince was getting tired.   90
He began to feel like a shoe salesman.
But he gave it one last try.
This time Cinderella fit into the shoe
like a love letter into its envelope.

At the wedding ceremony   95
the two sisters came to curry favor
and the white dove pecked their eyes out.
Two hollow spots were left
like soup spoons.

Cinderella and the prince   100
lived, they say, happily ever after,
like two dolls in a museum case
never bothered by diapers or dust,
never arguing over the timing of an egg,
never telling the same story twice,   105
never getting a middle-aged spread,
their darling smiles pasted on for eternity.
Regular Bobbsey Twins.
That story.

[1971]

ADRIENNE RICH   [1929–2012]

Aunt Jennifer's Tigers

Aunt Jennifer's tigers prance across a screen,
Bright topaz denizens of a world of green.
They do not fear the men beneath the tree;
They pace in sleek chivalric certainty.

Aunt Jennifer's fingers fluttering through her wool   5
Find even the ivory needle hard to pull.

The massive weight of Uncle's wedding band
Sits heavily upon Aunt Jennifer's hand.

When Aunt is dead, her terrified hands will lie
Still ringed with ordeals she was mastered by.   10
The tigers in the panel that she made
Will go on prancing, proud and unafraid.

[1951]

ADRIENNE RICH   [1929–2012]

Diving into the Wreck

First having read the book of myths,
and loaded the camera,
and checked the edge of the knife-blade,
I put on
the body-armor of black rubber   5
the absurd flippers
the grave and awkward mask.
I am having to do this
not like Cousteau° with his
assiduous team   10
aboard the sun-flooded schooner
but here alone.

There is a ladder.
The ladder is always there
hanging innocently   15
close to the side of the schooner.
We know what it is for,
we who have used it.
Otherwise
it's a piece of maritime floss   20
some sundry equipment.

I go down.
Rung after rung and still

9. **Cousteau:** Jacques-Yves Cousteau (1910–1997), French underwater explorer,
photographer, and author.

the oxygen immerses me
the blue light   25
the clear atoms
of our human air.
I go down.
My flippers cripple me,
I crawl like an insect down the ladder   30
and there is no one
to tell me when the ocean
will begin.

First the air is blue and then
it is bluer and then green and then   35
black I am blacking out and yet
my mask is powerful
it pumps my blood with power
the sea is another story
the sea is not a question of power   40
I have to learn alone
to turn my body without force
in the deep element.

And now: it is easy to forget
what I came for   45
among so many who have always
lived here
swaying their crenellated° fans
between the reefs
and besides   50
you breathe differently down here.

I came to explore the wreck.
The words are purposes.
The words are maps.
I came to see the damage that was done   55
and the treasures that prevail.
I stroke the beam of my lamp
slowly along the flank
of something more permanent
than fish or weed   60

48. crenellated: Notched; *crenels* are the open spaces between the solid portions of a battlement.

the thing I came for:
the wreck and not the story of the wreck
the thing itself and not the myth
the drowned face° always staring
toward the sun   65
the evidence of damage
worn by salt and sway into this threadbare beauty
the ribs of the disaster
curving their assertion
among the tentative haunters.   70

This is the place.
And I am here, the mermaid whose dark hair
streams black, the merman in his armored body
We circle silently
about the wreck   75
we dive into the hold.
I am she: I am he

whose drowned face sleeps with open eyes
whose breasts still bear the stress
whose silver, copper, vermeil° cargo lies   80
obscurely inside barrels
half-wedged and left to rot
we are the half-destroyed instruments
that once held to a course
the water-eaten log   85
the fouled compass

We are, I am, you are
by cowardice or courage
the one who find our way
back to this scene   90
carrying a knife, a camera
a book of myths
in which
our names do not appear.

[1973]

64. **drowned face:** The ornamental female figurehead on the prow of an old sailing ship.
80. **vermeil:** Gilded silver, bronze, or copper.

DEREK WALCOTT   [b. 1930]

Sea Grapes

That sail which leans on light,
tired of islands,
a schooner beating up the Caribbean

for home, could be Odysseus,°
home-bound on the Aegean;   5
that father and husband's

longing, under gnarled sour grapes, is
like the adulterer hearing Nausicaa's name
in every gull's outcry.

This brings nobody peace. The ancient war   10
between obsession and responsibility
will never finish and has been the same

for the sea-wanderer or the one on shore
now wriggling on his sandals to walk home,
since Troy sighed its last flame,   15

and the blind giant's boulder heaved the trough
from whose groundswell the great hexameters come
to the conclusions of exhausted surf.

The classics can console. But not enough.

[1976]

4. **Odysseus:** For background, see page 65. Princess Nausicaa (line 8) fell in love
with Odysseus when he was carried by a storm to Phaiacia; he could have married
her and stayed there, but he chose to go home (responsibility) rather than to enjoy
an indulgent life with her (obsession). Odysseus blinded Polyphemus (line 16), a
giant one-eyed Cyclops, who held him prisoner; as Odysseus escaped, Polyphemus
threw great rocks in front of his boat to wash it back to shore. The *Odyssey* was
written in hexameter verse (line 17).

GARY SNYDER   [b. 1930]

Hitch Haiku

They didn't hire him
          so he ate his lunch alone:
the noon whistle

                    •   •   •

Cats shut down
        deer thread through
men all eating lunch

. . .

Frying hotcakes in a dripping shelter
        Fu Manchu°
Queets Indian Reservation in the rain

. . .

A truck went by
        three hours ago:
Smoke Creek desert

. . .

Jackrabbit eyes all night
  breakfast in Elko.

. . .

Old kanji° hid by dirt
on skidroad Jap town walls
        down the hill
to the Wobbly hall

                 Seattle

. . .

Spray drips from the cargo-booms
a fresh-chipped winch
        spotted with red lead
young fir—
        soaking in summer rain

. . .

Over the Mindanao Deep

Scrap bass
        dumpt off the fantail
falling six miles

. . .

8. Fu Manchu: Master criminal in a series of "Yellow Peril Thrillers" by Sax Rohmer (pen name of Arthur Henry Sarsfield Ward, 1883–1959) that were immensely popular in the first half of the twentieth century.
15. kanji: Japanese written characters, or ideographs, borrowed and adapted from Chinese ideographs.

[*The following two were written on classical
themes while traveling through Sappho, Washington.
The first is by Thomas L. Hoodlatch.*]

Moonlight on the burned-out temple—
            wooden horse shit.

Sunday dinner in Ithaca—
            the twang of a bowstring
                        .   .   .

After weeks of watching the roof leak
            I fixed it tonight
by moving a single board
                  .   .   .

*A freezing morning in October in the high
Sierra crossing Five Lakes Basin to the
Kaweahs with Bob Greensfelder and Claude Dalenburg*

Stray white mare
            neck rope dangling
forty miles from farms.
                  .   .   .

Back from the Kaweahs

Sundown, Timber Gap
            —sat down—
                  dark firs.
   dirty;   cold;
too tired to talk
                  .   .   .

Cherry blossoms at Hood river
            rusty sand near Tucson
mudflats of Willapa Bay
                  .   .   .

Pronghorn country

Steering into the sun
            glittering jewel-road
shattered obsidian
                  .   .   .

The mountain walks over the water!
Rain down from the mountain!
            high bleat of a
cow elk
      over blackberries
                  .   .   .

A great freight truck
            lit like a town
through the dark stony desert
                    •   •   •

Drinking hot saké
                toasting fish on coals
    the motorcycle
out   parked in the rain.
                    •   •   •

Switchback

turn, turn,
and again,   hard-
scrabble
steep travel a-
head.

[1968]

LINDA PASTAN   [b. 1932]

love poem

I want to write you
a love poem as headlong
as our creek
after thaw
when we stand   5
on its dangerous
banks and watch it carry
with it every twig
every dry leaf and branch
in its path   10
every scruple
when we see it
so swollen
with runoff
that even as we watch   15
we must grab
each other
and step back
we must grab each
other or   20
get our shoes

soaked we must
grab each other

[1988]

GEOFFREY HILL   [b. 1932]

In Memory of Jane Fraser

When snow like sheep lay in the fold
And winds went begging at each door,
And the far hills were blue with cold,
And a cold shroud lay on the moor,

She kept the siege. And every day   5
We watched her brooding over death
Like a strong bird above its prey.
The room filled with the kettle's breath.

Damp curtains glued against the pane
Sealed time away. Her body froze   10
As if to freeze us all, and chain
Creation to a stunned repose.

She died before the world could stir.
In March the ice unloosed the brook
And water ruffled the sun's hair.   15
Dead cones upon the alder shook.

[1959]

SYLVIA PLATH   [1932–1963]

Metaphors

I'm a riddle in nine syllables,
An elephant, a ponderous house,
A melon strolling on two tendrils.
O red fruit, ivory, fine timbers!
This loaf's big with its yeasty rising.   5
Money's new-minted in this fat purse.
I'm a means, a stage, a cow in calf.
I've eaten a bag of green apples,
Boarded the train there's no getting off.

[1960]

SYLVIA PLATH   [1932–1963]

Morning Song

Love set you going like a fat gold watch.
The midwife slapped your footsoles, and your bald cry
Took its place among the elements.

Our voices echo, magnify your arrival. New statue.
In a drafty museum, your nakedness   5
Shadows our safety. We stand round blankly as walls.

I'm no more your mother
Than the cloud that distills a mirror to reflect its own slow
Effacement at the wind's hand.

All night your moth-breath   10
Flickers among the flat pink roses. I wake to listen:
A far sea moves in my ear.

One cry, and I stumble from bed, cow-heavy and floral
In my Victorian nightgown.
Your mouth opens clean as a cat's. The window square   15

Whitens and swallows its dull stars. And now you try
Your handful of notes;
The clear vowels rise like balloons.

[1961]

SYLVIA PLATH   [1932–1963]

Daddy

You do not do, you do not do
Any more, black shoe
In which I have lived like a foot
For thirty years, poor and white,
Barely daring to breathe or Achoo.   5

Daddy, I have had to kill you.
You died before I had time—
Marble-heavy, a bag full of God,
Ghastly statue with one grey toe
Big as a Frisco seal   10

And a head in the freakish Atlantic
Where it pours bean green over blue
In the waters off beautiful Nauset.
I used to pray to recover you.
Ach, du.°   *Oh, you (German)* 15

In the German tongue, in the Polish town
Scraped flat by the roller
Of wars, wars, wars.
But the name of the town is common.
My Polack friend   20

Says there are a dozen or two.
So I never could tell where you
Put your foot, your root,
I never could talk to you.
The tongue stuck in my jaw.   25

It stuck in a barb wire snare.
Ich, ich, ich, ich,°   *I (German)*
I could hardly speak.
I thought every German was you.
And the language obscene   30

An engine, an engine
Chuffing me off like a Jew.
A Jew to Dachau, Auschwitz, Belsen.°
I began to talk like a Jew.
I think I may well be a Jew.   35

The snows of the Tyrol,° the clear beer of Vienna
Are not very pure or true.
With my gypsy ancestress and my weird luck
And my Taroc pack and my Taroc pack
I may be a bit of a Jew.   40

I have always been scared of *you*,
With your Luftwaffe,° your gobbledygoo.
And your neat moustache
And your Aryan eye, bright blue.
Panzer°-man, panzer-man, O You—   45

33. **Dachau, Auschwitz, Belsen:** Nazi concentration camps.
36. **the Tyrol:** An alpine region in western Austria and northern Italy.
42. **Luftwaffe:** The Nazi air force in World War II.
45. **Panzer:** An armored unit in the German army in World War II.

Not God but a swastika
So black no sky could squeak through.
Every woman adores a Fascist,
The boot in the face, the brute
Brute heart of a brute like you.   50

You stand at the blackboard, daddy,
In the picture I have of you,
A cleft in your chin instead of your foot
But no less a devil for that, no not
Any less the black man who   55

Bit my pretty red heart in two.
I was ten when they buried you.
At twenty I tried to die
And get back, back, back to you.
I thought even the bones would do.   60

But they pulled me out of the sack,
And they stuck me together with glue.
And then I knew what to do.
I made a model of you,
A man in black with a Meinkampf° look   65

And a love of the rack and the screw.
And I said I do, I do.
So daddy, I'm finally through.
The black telephone's off at the root,
The voices just can't worm through.   70

If I've killed one man, I've killed two—
The vampire who said he was you
And drank my blood for a year,
Seven years, if you want to know.
Daddy, you can lie back now.   75

There's a stake in your fat black heart
And the villagers never liked you.
They are dancing and stamping on you.
They always *knew* it was you.
Daddy, daddy, you bastard, I'm through.   80

[1962]

65. *Mein Kampf:* *My Struggle*, the title of Adolf Hitler's autobiography.

ETHERIDGE KNIGHT   [1933–1991]

Hard Rock Returns to Prison from the Hospital for the Criminal Insane

Hard Rock / was / "known not to take no shit
From nobody," and he had the scars to prove it:
Split purple lips, lumbed ears, welts above
His yellow eyes, and one long scar that cut
Across his temple and plowed through a thick   5
Canopy of kinky hair.

The WORD / was / that Hard Rock wasn't a mean nigger
Anymore, that the doctors had bored a hole in his head,
Cut out part of his brain, and shot electricity
Through the rest. When they brought Hard Rock back,   10
Handcuffed and chained, he was turned loose,
Like a freshly gelded stallion, to try his new status.
And we all waited and watched, like a herd of sheep,
To see if the WORD was true.

As we waited we wrapped ourselves in the cloak   15
Of his exploits: "Man, the last time, it took eight
Screws° to put him in the Hole."° "Yeah, remember when he
Smacked the captain with his dinner tray?" "He set
The record for time in the Hole—67 straight days!"
"Ol Hard Rock! man, that's one crazy nigger."   20
And then the jewel of a myth that Hard Rock had once bit
A screw on the thumb and poisoned him with syphilitic spit.

The testing came, to see if Hard Rock was really tame.
A hillbilly called him a black son of a bitch
And didn't lose his teeth, a screw who knew Hard Rock   25
From before shook him down and barked in his face.
And Hard Rock did *nothing*. Just grinned and looked silly,
His eyes empty like knot holes in a fence.

And even after we discovered that it took Hard Rock
Exactly 3 minutes to tell you his first name,   30
We told ourselves that he had just wised up,
Was being cool; but we could not fool ourselves for long,

17. **Screws:** Guards; **Hole:** Solitary confinement.

And we turned away, our eyes on the ground. Crushed.
He had been our Destroyer, the doer of things
We dreamed of doing but could not bring ourselves to do,   35
The fears of years, like a biting whip,
Had cut deep bloody grooves
Across our backs.

[1968]

JIM BARNES   [b. 1933]

Return to La Plata, Missouri

The warping bandstand reminds you of the hard rage
you felt in the heart of the town the day you said goodbye
to the park, silver jet, and cicadas dead in the sage.

The town is basic red, although it browns. A cry
of murder, rape, or wrong will always bend the night   5
hard into the broken grass. You listen close for sighs

of lovers on the ground. The darkness gathers light
and throws it down: something glows that you cannot name,
something fierce, abstract, given time and space you might

on a journey leave behind, a stone to carve your fame   10
on, or a simple word like *love*. The sun is down
or always going down in La Plata, the same

sun. Same too the child's cry that turns the mother's frown
brittle as chalk or the town's face against the moon.
Same too the moan of dog and diesel circling the town   15

in an air so heavy with cloud that there is little room
for breath or moon. Strange: in a town so country, so
foreign, you never hear a song nor see a loom

pattern dark threads into a history you would know
and would not know. You think you see one silver star.   20
But the town offers only itself, and you must go.

[1982]

AUDRE LORDE   [1934–1992]

Coal

I   is the total black
being spoken
from the earth's inside.

There are many kinds of open
how a diamond comes   5
into a knot of flame
how sound comes into a word
colored
by who pays what for speaking.

Some words are open   10
diamonds on a glass window
singing out within the crash
of passing sun
other words are stapled wagers
in a perforated book   15
buy and sign and tear apart
and come whatever wills all chances
the stub remains
an ill-pulled tooth
with a ragged edge.   20

Some words live in my throat
breeding like adders
others
know sun
seeking like gypsies   25
over my tongue
to explode through my lips
like young sparrows
bursting from shell.

Some words   30
bedevil me.

Love is a word, another kind of open.
As the diamond comes

into a knot of flame
I am Black   35
because I come from the earth's inside
take my word for jewel
in the open light.

[1962; rev. 1992]

MARK STRAND   [b. 1934]

Eating Poetry

Ink runs from the corners of my mouth.
There is no happiness like mine.
I have been eating poetry.

The librarian does not believe what she sees.
Her eyes are sad   5
and she walks with her hands in her dress.

The poems are gone.
The light is dim.
The dogs are on the basement stairs and coming up.

Their eyeballs roll,   10
their blond legs burn like brush.
The poor librarian begins to stamp her feet and weep.

She does not understand.
When I get on my knees and lick her hand,
she screams.   15

I am a new man.
I snarl at her and bark.
I romp with joy in the bookish dark.

[1968]

JEAN VALENTINE   [b. 1934]

December 21st

How will I think of you
"God-with-us"
a name: a word

and trees paths stars this earth
how will I think of them   5

and the dead I love   and all absent friends
here-with-me

and table: hand: white coffee mug:
a northern still life:

and you   10
without a body

quietness

and the infant's red-brown mouth   a star
at the star of a girl's nipple . . .

[1979]

WENDELL BERRY   [b. 1934]

The Peace of Wild Things

When despair for the world grows in me
and I wake in the night at the least sound
in fear of what my life and my children's lives may be,
I go and lie down where the wood drake
rests in his beauty on the water, and the great heron feeds.   5
I come into the peace of wild things
who do not tax their lives with forethought
of grief. I come into the presence of still water.
And I feel above me the day-blind stars
waiting with their light. For a time   10
I rest in the grace of the world, and am free.

[1968]

PAUL ZIMMER   [b. 1934]

Zimmer Imagines Heaven

for Merrill Leffler

I sit with Joseph Conrad in Monet's garden.
We are listening to Yeats chant his poems,
A breeze stirs through Thomas Hardy's moustache,
John Skelton has gone to the house for beer,
Wanda Landowska lightly fingers a harpsichord,   5
Along the spruce tree walk Roberto Clemente and
Thurman Munson whistle a baseball back and forth.
Mozart chats with Ellington in the roses.

Monet smokes and dabs his canvas in the sun,
Brueghel and Turner set easels behind the wisteria.   10
The band is warming up in the Big Studio:
Bean, Brute, Bird, and Serge on saxes,
Kai, Bill Harris, Lawrence Brown trombones,
Little Jazz, Clifford, Fats, Diz on trumpets,
Klook plays drums, Mingus bass, Bud the piano.   15
Later Madam Schuman-Heink will sing Schubert,
The monks of Benedictine Abbey will chant.
There will be more poems from Emily Dickinson,
James Wright, John Clare, Walt Whitman.
Shakespeare rehearses players for *King Lear*.   20

At dusk Alice Toklas brings out platters
Of sweetbreads, Salad Livonière,
And a tureen of Gazpacho of Málaga.
After the meal Brahms passes fine cigars.
God comes then, radiant with a bottle of cognac,   25
She pours generously into the snifters,
I tell Her I have begun to learn what
Heaven is about. She wants to hear.
It is, I say, being thankful for eternity.
Her smile is the best part of the day.   30

[1996]

CHARLES WRIGHT   [b. 1935]

Reunion

Already one day has detached itself from all the rest up ahead.
It has my photograph in its soft pocket.
It wants to carry my breath into the past in its bag of wind.

I write poems to untie myself, to do penance and disappear
Through the upper right-hand corner of things, to say grace.

[1977]

MARY OLIVER   [b. 1935]

First Snow

The snow
began here
this morning and all day
continued, its white
rhetoric everywhere   5
calling us back to *why, how,*
whence such beauty and *what*
the meaning; such
an oracular fever! flowing
past windows, an energy it seemed   10
would never ebb, never settle
less than lovely! and only now,
deep into night,
it has finally ended.
The silence   15
is immense,
and the heavens still hold
a million candles; nowhere
the familiar things:
stars, the moon,   20
the darkness we expect
and nightly turn from. Trees
glitter like castles
of ribbons, the broad fields

smolder with light, a passing   25
creekbed lies
heaped with shining hills;
and though the questions
that have assailed us all day
remain—not a single   30
answer has been found—
walking out now
into the silence and the light
under the trees,
and through the fields,   35
feels like one.

[1983]

MARGE PIERCY   [b. 1936]

Barbie Doll

This girlchild was born as usual
and presented dolls that did pee-pee
and miniature GE stoves and irons
and wee lipsticks the color of cherry candy.
Then in the magic of puberty, a classmate said: 5
You have a great big nose and fat legs.

She was healthy, tested intelligent,
possessed strong arms and back,
abundant sexual drive and manual dexterity.
She went to and fro apologizing.   10
Everyone saw a fat nose on thick legs.

She was advised to play coy,
exhorted to come on hearty,
exercise, diet, smile and wheedle.
Her good nature wore out   15
like a fan belt.
So she cut off her nose and her legs
and offered them up.

In the casket displayed on satin she lay
with the undertaker's cosmetics painted on,   20

a turned-up putty nose,
dressed in a pink and white nightie.
Doesn't she look pretty? everyone said.
Consummation at last.
To every woman a happy ending.   25

[1973]

NANCY WILLARD   [b. 1936]

Questions My Son Asked Me,
Answers I Never Gave Him

1. Do gorillas have birthdays?
   Yes. Like the rainbow, they happen.
   Like the air, they are not observed.

2. Do butterflies make a noise?
   The wire in the butterfly's tongue   5
   hums gold. Some men hear butterflies
   even in winter.

3. Are they part of our family?
   They forgot us, who forgot how to fly.

4. Who tied my navel? Did God tie it?   10
   God made the thread: O man, live forever!
   Man made the knot: enough is enough.

5. If I drop my tooth in the telephone
   will it go through the wires and bite someone's ear?
   I have seen earlobes pierced by a tooth of steel.   15
   It loves what lasts.
   It does not love flesh.
   It leaves a ring of gold in the wound.

6. If I stand on my head
   will the sleep in my eye roll up into my head?   20
   Does the dream know its own father?
   Can bread go back to the field of its birth?

7. Can I eat a star?
   Yes, with the mouth of time
   that enjoys everything.   25

8. Could we Xerox the moon?
   This is the first commandment:
   I am the moon, thy moon.
   Thou shalt have no other moons before thee.

9. Who invented water?   30
   The hands of the air, that wanted to wash each other.

10. What happens at the end of numbers?
    I see three men running toward a field.
    At the edge of the tall grass, they turn into light.

11. Do the years ever run out?   35
    God said, I will break time's heart.
    Time ran down like an old phonograph.
    It lay flat as a carpet.
    At rest on its threads, I am learning to fly.

[1982]

LUCILLE CLIFTON   [1936–2010]

homage to my hips

these hips are big hips
they need space to
move around in.
they don't fit into little
petty places. these hips   5
are free hips.
they don't like to be held back.
these hips have never been enslaved,
they go where they want to go
they do what they want to do.   10
these hips are mighty hips.
these hips are magic hips.
i have known them
to put a spell on a man and
spin him like a top!   15

[1980]

LUCILLE CLIFTON   [1936–2010]

at the cemetery, walnut grove plantation, south carolina, 1989

among the rocks
at walnut grove
your silence drumming
in my bones,
tell me your names.   5

nobody mentioned slaves
and yet the curious tools
shine with your fingerprints.
nobody mentioned slaves
but somebody did this work   10
who had no guide, no stone,
who moulders under rock.

tell me your names,
tell me your bashful names
and i will testify.   15

the inventory lists ten slaves
but only men were recognized.

among the rocks
at walnut grove
some of these honored dead   20
were dark
some of these dark
were slaves

some of these slaves
were women   25
some of them did this
honored work.
tell me your names
foremothers, brothers,
tell me your dishonored names.   30
here lies
here lies

here lies
here lies
hear   35

[1991]

CHARLES SIMIC   [b. 1938]
Begotten of the Spleen°

The Virgin Mother° walked barefoot
Among the land mines.
She carried an old man in her arms
Like a howling babe.

The earth was an old people's home.   5
Judas was the night nurse,
Emptying bedpans into the river Jordan,
Tying people on a dog chain.

The old man had two stumps for legs.
St. Peter came pushing a cart   10
Loaded with flying carpets.
They were not flying carpets.

They were piles of bloody diapers.
The Magi° stood around
Cleaning their nails with bayonets.   15
The old man gave little Mary Magdalene°

A broken piece of a mirror.
She hid in the church outhouse.
When she got thirsty she licked
the steam off the glass.   20

Spleen: Once believed to be the source in a person either of high spirit, courage, and resolute mind or of ill-nature, ill-humor, and irritable or peevish temper.
1. The Virgin Mother: Mary, the mother of Jesus.
14. Magi: The wise men from the East who visited the baby Jesus.
16. Mary Magdalene: A follower of Jesus who was present at his crucifixion and burial and who went to the tomb on Easter Sunday to anoint his body.

That leaves Joseph.° Poor Joseph,
Standing naked in the snow.
He only had a rat
To load his suitcases on.

The rat wouldn't run into its hole.   25
Even when the lights came on—
And the lights came on:
The floodlights in the guard towers.

[1980; rev. 1999]

21. **Joseph:** The husband of Mary, the mother of Jesus.

MICHAEL S. HARPER   [b. 1938]

Nightmare Begins Responsibility

I place these numbed wrists to the pane
watching white uniforms whisk over
him in the tube-kept
prison
fear what they will do in experiment   5
watch my gloved stickshifting gasolined hands
breathe *boxcar-information-please* infirmary tubes
distrusting white-pink mending paperthin
silkened end hairs, distrusting tubes
shrunk in his *trunk-skincapped*   10
shaven head, in thighs
distrusting-white-hands-picking-baboon-light
on this son who will not make his second night
of this wardstrewn intensive airpocket
where his father's asthmatic   15
hymns of *night-train*, train done gone
his mother can only know that he has flown
up into essential calm unseen corridor
going boxscarred home, *mamaborn, sweetsonchild*
gonedowntown into *researchtestingwarehousebatteryacid*   20
mama-son-done-gone/me telling her 'nother
train tonight, no music, no breathstroked
heartbeat in my infinite distrust of them:

and of my distrusting self
white-doctor-who-breathed-for-him-all-night   25
say it for two sons gone,
say nightmare, say it loud
panebreaking heartmadness:
nightmare begins responsibility.

[1975]

SEAMUS HEANEY   [b. 1939]

Digging

Between my finger and my thumb
The squat pen rests; snug as a gun.

Under my window, a clean rasping sound
When the spade sinks into gravelly ground:
My father, digging. I look down   5

Till his straining rump among the flowerbeds
Bends low, comes up twenty years away
Stooping in rhythm through potato drills
Where he was digging.

The coarse boot nestled on the lug, the shaft   10
Against the inside knee was levered firmly.
He rooted out tall tops, buried the bright edge deep
To scatter new potatoes that we picked
Loving their cool hardness in our hands.

By God, the old man could handle a spade.   15
Just like his old man.

My grandfather cut more turf in a day
Than any other man on Toner's bog.
Once I carried him milk in a bottle
Corked sloppily with paper. He straightened up   20
To drink it, then fell to right away
Nicking and slicing neatly, heaving sods
Over his shoulder, going down and down
For the good turf. Digging.

The cold smell of potato mould, the squelch and slap   25
Of soggy peat, the curt cuts of an edge
Through living roots awaken in my head.
But I've no spade to follow men like them.

Between my finger and my thumb
The squat pen rests.   30
I'll dig with it.

[1966]

SEAMUS HEANEY   [b. 1939]

Mid-Term Break

I sat all morning in the college sick bay
Counting bells knelling classes to a close.
At two o'clock our neighbours drove me home.

In the porch I met my father crying—
He had always taken funerals in his stride—   5
And Big Jim Evans saying it was a hard blow.

The baby cooed and laughed and rocked the pram
When I came in, and I was embarrassed
By old men standing up to shake my hand

And tell me they were "sorry for my trouble."   10
Whispers informed strangers I was the eldest,
Away at school as my mother held my hand

In hers and coughed out angry tearless sighs.
At ten o'clock the ambulance arrived
With the corpse, stanched and bandaged by the nurses.   15

Next morning I went into the room. Snowdrops
and candles soothed the bedside; I saw him
For the first time in six weeks. Paler now,

Wearing a poppy bruise on his left temple,
He lay in the four-foot box as in his cot.   20
No gaudy scars, the bumper knocked him clear.

A four-foot box, a foot for every year.

[1966]

SEAMUS HEANEY   [b. 1939]

Glanmore° Sonnets 4

I used to lie with an ear to the line
For that way, they said, there should come a sound
Escaping ahead, an iron tune
Of flange and piston pitched along the ground,
But I never heard that. Always instead,   5
Struck couplings and shuntings two miles away
Lifted over the woods. The head
Of a horse swirled back from a gate, a grey
Turnover of haunch and mane, and I'd look
Up to the cutting where she'd soon appear.   10
Two fields back, in the house, small ripples shook
Silently across our drinking water
(As they are shaking now across my heart)
And vanished into where they seemed to start.

[1979]

Glanmore: A village in County Wicklow, Ireland. Heaney and his family lived there
from 1972 to 1976.

TED KOOSER   [b. 1939]

Abandoned Farmhouse

He was a big man, says the size of his shoes
on a pile of broken dishes by the house;
a tall man too, says the length of the bed
in an upstairs room; and a good, God-fearing man,
says the Bible with a broken back   5
on the floor below the window, dusty with sun;
but not a man for farming, say the fields
cluttered with boulders and the leaky barn.

A woman lived with him, says the bedroom wall
papered with lilacs and the kitchen shelves   10
covered with oilcloth, and they had a child,
says the sandbox made from a tractor tire.
Money was scarce say the jars of plum preserves
and canned tomatoes sealed in the cellar hole.

And the winters cold, say the rags in the window frames.   15
It was lonely here, says the narrow country road.

Something went wrong, says the empty house
in the weed-choked yard. Stones in the fields
say he was not a farmer; the still-sealed jars
in the cellar say she left in a nervous haste.   20
And the child? Its toys are strewn in the yard
like branches after a storm—a rubber cow,
a rusty tractor with a broken plow,
a doll in overalls. Something went wrong, they say.

[1980]

AL YOUNG   [b. 1939]

A Dance for Ma Rainey

I'm going to be just like you, Ma
Rainey this monday morning
clouds puffing up out of my head
like those balloons
that float above the faces of white people   5
in the funnypapers
I'm going to hover in the corners
of the world, Ma
& sing from the bottom of hell
up to the tops of high heaven   10
& send out scratchless waves of yellow
& brown & that basic black honey
misery

I'm going to cry so sweet
& so low   15
& so dangerous,
Ma,
that the message is going to reach you
back in 1922
where you shimmer   20
snaggle-toothed
perfumed &
powdered
in your bauble beads

hair pressed & tied back   25
throbbing with that sick pain
I know
& hide so well
that pain that blues
jives the world with   30
aching to be heard
that downness
that bottomlessness
first felt by some stolen delta nigger
swamped under with redblooded american agony;   35
reduced to the sheer shit
of existence
that bred
& battered us all,
Ma,   40
the beautiful people
our beautiful brave black people
who no longer need to jazz
or sing to themselves in murderous vibrations
or play the veins of their strong tender arms   45
with needles
to prove we're still here

                                                          [1969]

QUINCY TROUPE   [b. 1939]

A Poem for "Magic"°

*for Earvin "Magic" Johnson, Donnell Reid
& Richard Franklin*

take it to the hoop, "magic" johnson,
take the ball dazzling down the open lane
herk & jerk & raise your six-feet, nine-inch frame
into air sweating screams of your neon name

"Magic": Earvin "Magic" Johnson Jr. (b. 1959), star basketball player at Everett
High School in Lansing, Michigan (1973–77), at Michigan State University (1977–
79), and for the Los Angeles Lakers (1979–91 and 1996). He was honored in 1996
as one of the "50 Greatest Players" in National Basketball Association history.

"magic" johnson, nicknamed "windex" way back   5
in high school
                    cause you wiped glass blackboards
so clean, where you first juked & shook
wiled your way to glory
                    a new-style fusion of shake-&-bake   10
energy, using everything possible, you created your own
space to fly through—any moment now
we expect your wings to spread feathers for that spooky takeoff
of yours—then, shake & glide & ride up in space
till you hammer home a clothes-lining duece off glass   15
now, come back down with a reverse hoodoo gem
off the spin & stick in sweet, popping nets clean
from twenty feet, right side
put the ball on the floor again, "magic"
slide the dribble behind your back, ease it deftly   20
between your bony stork legs, head bobbing everwhichaway
up & down, you see everything on the court
off the high yoyo patter
                    stop & go dribble
you thread a needle-rope pass sweet home   25
to kareem° cutting through the lane
                                   his skyhook pops the cords
now, lead the fastbreak, hit worthy° on the fly
now, blindside a pinpoint behind-the-back pass for two more
off the fake, looking the other way, you raise off-balance   30
into electric space
sweating chants of your name
turn, 180 degrees off the move, your legs scissoring space
like a swimmer's yoyoing motion in deep water
stretching out now toward free flight   35
you double pump through human trees
                    hang in place
slip the ball into your left hand
then deal it like a las vegas card dealer off squared glass
into nets, living up to your singular nickname   40
so "bad" you cartwheel the crowd toward frenzy
wearing now your electric smile, neon as your name

in victory, we suddenly sense your glorious uplift
your urgent need to be champion

26, 28. kareem, worthy: Kareem Abdul-Jabbar and James Worthy, teammates of
Johnson on the Los Angeles Lakers.

& so we cheer with you, rejoice with you   45
                  for this quicksilver, quicksilver,
quicksilver moment of fame
so put the ball on the floor again, "magic"
juke & dazzle, shake & bake down the lane
take the sucker to the hoop, "magic" johnson,   50
recreate reverse hoodoo gems off the spin
deal alley-oop dunkathon magician passes
now, double-pump, scissor, vamp through space
hang in place
            & put it all up in the sucker's face, "magic" johnson, 55
& deal the roundball like the juju man that you am
like the sho-nuff shaman that you am, "magic,"
like the sho-nuff spaceman you am

                             [1991; rev. 1996]

MARGARET ATWOOD   [b. 1939]

True Stories

I

Don't ask for the true story;
why do you need it?

It's not what I set out with
or what I carry.

What I'm sailing with,   5
a knife, blue fire,

luck, a few good words
that still work, and the tide.

II

The true story was lost
on the way down to the beach, it's something   10

I never had, that black tangle
of branches in a shifting light,

my blurred footprints
filling with salt

water, this handful   15
of tiny bones, this owl's kill;

a moon, crumpled papers, a coin,
the glint of an old picnic,

the hollows made by lovers
in sand a hundred   20

years ago: no clue.

III

The true story lies
among the other stories,

a mess of colours, like jumbled clothing
thrown off or away,   25

like hearts on marble, like syllables, like
butchers' discards.

The true story is vicious
and multiple and untrue

after all. Why do you   30
need it? Don't ever

ask for the true story.

[1981]

JAMES WELCH   [1940–2003]

Christmas Comes to Moccasin Flat

Christmas comes like this: Wise men
unhurried, candles bought on credit (poor price
for calves), warriors face down in wine sleep.
Winds cheat to pull heat from smoke.

Friends sit in chinked cabins, stare out   5
plastic windows and wait for commodities.
Charlie Blackbird, twenty miles from church
and bar, stabs his fire with flint.

When drunks drain radiators for love
or need, chiefs eat snow and talk of change,   10
an urge to laugh pounding their ribs.
Elk play games in high country.

Medicine Woman, clay pipe and twist tobacco,
calls each blizzard by name and predicts
five o'clock by spitting at her television.   15
Children lean into her breath to beg a story:

Something about honor and passion,
warriors back with meat and song,
a peculiar evening star, quick vision of birth.
Blackbird feeds his fire. Outside, a quick 30 below.   20

[1976]

ROBERT PINSKY   [b. 1940]

Shirt

The back, the yoke, the yardage. Lapped seams,
The nearly invisible stitches along the collar
Turned in a sweatshop by Koreans or Malaysians

Gossiping over tea and noodles on their break
Or talking money or politics while one fitted   5
This armpiece with its overseam to the band

Of cuff I button at my wrist. The presser, the cutter,
The wringer, the mangle. The needle, the union,
The treadle, the bobbin. The code. The infamous blaze

At the Triangle Factory° in nineteen-eleven.   *(in New York City)* 10
One hundred and forty-six died in the flames
On the ninth floor, no hydrants, no fire escapes—

The witness in a building across the street
Who watched how a young man helped a girl to step
Up to the windowsill, then held her out   15

Away from the masonry wall and let her drop.
And then another. As if he were helping them up
To enter a streetcar, and not eternity.

A third before he dropped her put her arms
Around his neck and kissed him. Then he held   20
Her into space, and dropped her. Almost at once

He stepped to the sill himself, his jacket flared
And fluttered up from his shirt as he came down,
Air filling up the legs of his gray trousers—

Like Hart Crane's Bedlamite, "shrill shirt ballooning."   25
Wonderful how the pattern matches perfectly
Across the placket and over the twin bar-tacked

Corners of both pockets, like a strict rhyme
Or a major chord. Prints, plaids, checks,
Houndstooth, Tattersall, Madras. The clan tartans   30

Invented by mill-owners inspired by the hoax of Ossian,°
To control their savage Scottish workers, tamed
By a fabricated heraldry: MacGregor,

Bailey, MacMartin. The kilt, devised for workers
To wear among the dusty clattering looms.   35
Weavers, carders, spinners. The loader,

The docker, the navvy. The planter, the picker, the sorter
Sweating at her machine in a litter of cotton
As slaves in calico headrags sweated in fields:

George Herbert,° your descendant is a Black   40
Lady in South Carolina, her name is Irma
And she inspected my shirt. Its color and fit

And feel and its clean smell have satisfied
Both her and me. We have culled its cost and quality
Down to the buttons of simulated bone,   45

The buttonholes, the sizing, the facing, the characters
Printed in black on neckband and tail. The shape,
The label, the labor, the color, the shade. The shirt.

[1990]

31. **Ossian:** Legendary Gaelic poet, hero of a cycle of traditional tales and poems that place him in the third century C.E. The hoax involved Scottish author James Macpherson (1736–1796), who published two epic poems that he said were translations of works written by Ossian but were in fact mostly composed by Macpherson himself.
40. **George Herbert:** English metaphysical poet (1593–1633). See pages 20 and 21.

BILLY COLLINS   [b. 1941]

Litany

You are the bread and the knife,
The crystal goblet and the wine.
—Jacques Crickillon

You are the bread and the knife,
the crystal goblet and the wine.
You are the dew on the morning grass,
and the burning wheel of the sun.
You are the white apron of the baker   5
and the marsh birds suddenly in flight.

However, you are not the wind in the orchard,
the plums on the counter,
or the house of cards.
And you are certainly not the pine-scented air.   10
There is no way you are the pine-scented air.

It is possible that you are the fish under the bridge,
maybe even the pigeon on the general's head,
but you are not even close
to being the field of cornflowers at dusk.   15

And a quick look in the mirror will show
that you are neither the boots in the corner
nor the boat asleep in its boathouse.

It might interest you to know,
speaking of the plentiful imagery of the world,   20
that I am the sound of rain on the roof.

I also happen to be the shooting star,
the evening paper blowing down an alley,
and the basket of chestnuts on the kitchen table.

I am also the moon in the trees   25
and the blind woman's teacup.
But don't worry, I am not the bread and the knife.
You are still the bread and the knife.
You will always be the bread and the knife,
not to mention the crystal goblet and—somehow—   30
   the wine.

[2002]

TOI DERRICOTTE   [b. 1941]

A Note on My Son's Face

I

Tonight, I look, thunderstruck
at the gold head of my grandchild.
Almost asleep, he buries his feet
between my thighs;
his little straw eyes   5
close in the near dark.
I smell the warmth of his raw
slightly foul breath, the new death
waiting to rot inside him.
Our breaths equalize our heartbeats;   10
every muscle of the chest uncoils,
the arm bones loosen in the nest
of nerves. I think of the peace
of walking through the house,
pointing to the name of this, the name of that,   15
an educator of a new man.

Mother. Grandmother. Wise
Snake-woman who will show the way;
Spider-woman whose black tentacles
hold him precious. Or will tear off his head,   20
her teeth over the little husband,
the small fist clotted in trust at her breast.

This morning, looking at the face of his father,
I remembered how, an infant, his face was too dark,
nose too broad, mouth too wide.   25
I did not look in that mirror
and see the face that could save me
from my own darkness.
Did he, looking in my eye, see
what I turned from: 30
my own dark grandmother
bending over gladioli in the field,
her shaking black hand defenseless
at the shining cock of flower?

I wanted that face to die,   35
to be reborn in the face of a white child.

I wanted the soul to stay the same,
for I loved to death,
to damnation and God-death,
the soul that broke out of me.   40
I crowed: My Son! My Beautiful!
But when I peeked in the basket,
I saw the face of a black man.

Did I bend over his nose
and straighten it with my fingers   45
like a vine growing the wrong way?
Did he feel my hand in malice?

Generations we prayed and fucked
for this light child,
the shining god of the second coming;   50
we bow down in shame
and carry the children of the past
in our wallets, begging forgiveness.

II

A picture in a book,
a lynching.   55
The bland faces of men who watch
a Christ go up in flames, smiling,
as if he were a hooked
fish, a felled antelope, some
wild thing tied to boards and burned.   60
His charring body
gives off light—a halo
burns out of him.
His face scorched featureless;
the hair matted to the scalp   65
like feathers.
One man stands with his hand on his hip,
another with his arm
slung over the shoulder of a friend,
as if this moment were large enough   70
to hold affection.

III

How can we wake
from a dream

we are born into,
that shines around us,   75
the terrible bright air?

Having awakened,
having seen our own bloody hands,
how can we ask forgiveness,
bring before our children the real   80
monster of their nightmares?

The worst is true.
Everything you did not want to know.

[1989]

SIMON J. ORTIZ   [b. 1941]

Speaking

I take him outside
under the trees,
have him stand on the ground.
We listen to the crickets,
cicadas, million years old sound.   5
Ants come by us.
I tell them,
"This is he, my son.
This boy is looking at you.
I am speaking for him."   10

The crickets, cicadas,
the ants, the millions of years
are watching us,
hearing us.
My son murmurs infant words,   15
speaking, small laughter
bubbles from him.
Tree leaves tremble.
They listen to this boy
speaking for me.   20

[1977]

RICHARD GARCIA   [b. 1941]

Why I Left the Church

Maybe it was
because the only time
I hit a baseball
it smashed the neon cross
on the church across   5
the street. Even
twenty-five years later
when I saw Father Harris
I would wonder
if he knew it was me.   10
Maybe it was the demon-stoked
rotisseries of purgatory
where we would roast
hundreds of years
for the smallest of sins.   15
Or was it the day
I wore my space helmet
to catechism? Clear plastic
with a red-and-white
inflatable rim.   20
Sister Mary Bernadette
pointed toward the door
and said, "Out! Come back
when you're ready."
I rose from my chair   25
and kept rising
toward the ceiling
while the children
screamed and Sister
kept crossing herself.   30
The last she saw of me
was my shoes disappearing
through cracked plaster.
I rose into the sky and beyond.
It is a good thing   35
I am wearing my helmet,
I thought as I floated
and turned in the blackness

and brightness of outer space,
my body cold on one side and hot   40
on the other. It would
have been very quiet
if my blood had not been
rumbling in my ears so loud.
I remember thinking,   45
Maybe I will come back
when I'm ready.
But I won't tell
the other children
what it was like.   50
I'll have to make something up.

[1993]

SHARON OLDS   [b. 1942]

The One Girl at the Boys' Party

When I take our girl to the swimming party
I set her down among the boys. They tower
and bristle, she stands there smooth and sleek,
her math scores unfolding in the air around her.
They will strip to their suits, her body hard and   5
indivisible as a prime number,
they'll plunge in the deep end, she'll subtract
her height from ten feet, divide it into
hundreds of gallons of water, the numbers
bouncing in her mind like molecules of chlorine   10
in the bright-blue pool. When they climb out,
her ponytail will hang its pencil lead
down her back, her narrow silk suit
with hamburgers and french fries printed on it
will glisten in the brilliant air, and they will   15
see her sweet face, solemn and
sealed, a factor of one, and she will
see their eyes, two each,
their legs, two each, and the curves of their sexes,
one each, and in her head she'll be doing her   20

wild multiplying, as the drops
sparkle and fall to the power of a thousand from her body.

[1984]

SHARON OLDS   [b. 1942]

I Go Back to May 1937

I see them standing at the formal gates of their colleges,
I see my father strolling out
under the ochre sandstone arch, the
red tiles glinting like bent
plates of blood behind his head, I   5
see my mother with a few light books at her hip
standing at the pillar made of tiny bricks with the
wrought-iron gate still open behind her, its
sword-tips black in the May air,
they are about to graduate, they are about to get married,   10
they are kids, they are dumb, all they know is they are
innocent, they would never hurt anybody.
I want to go up to them and say Stop,
don't do it—she's the wrong woman,
he's the wrong man, you are going to do things   15
you cannot imagine you would ever do,
you are going to do bad things to children,
you are going to suffer in ways you never heard of,
you are going to want to die. I want to go
up to them there in the late May sunlight and say it,   20
her hungry pretty blank face turning to me,
her pitiful beautiful untouched body,
his arrogant handsome blind face turning to me,
his pitiful beautiful untouched body,
but I don't do it. I want to live. I   25
take them up like the male and female
paper dolls and bang them together
at the hips like chips of flint as if to
strike sparks from them, I say
Do what you are going to do, and I will tell about it.   30

[1987]

MARILYN HACKER   [b. 1942]

Villanelle°

Every day our bodies separate,
explode torn and dazed.
Not understanding what we celebrate

we grope through languages and hesitate
and touch each other, speechless and amazed;   5
and every day our bodies separate

us further from our planned, deliberate
ironic lives. I am afraid, disphased,
not understanding what we celebrate

when our fused limbs and lips communicate   10
the unlettered power we have raised.
Every day our bodies' separate

routines are harder to perpetuate.
In wordless darkness we learn wordless praise,
not understanding what we celebrate;   15

wake to ourselves, exhausted, in the late
morning as the wind tears off the haze,
not understanding how we celebrate
our bodies. Every day we separate.

[1974]

Villanelle: See Glossary, page 409.

ELLEN BRYANT VOIGT   [b. 1943]

The Lotus Flowers

The surface of the pond was mostly green—
bright green algae reaching out from the banks,
then the mass of waterlilies, their broad round leaves
rim to rim, each white flower spreading
from the center of a green saucer.   5
We teased and argued, choosing the largest,
the sweetest bloom, but when the rowboat

lumbered through and rearranged them,
we found the plants were anchored, the separate
muscular stems descending in the dense water—   10
only the most determined put her hand
into that frog-slimed pond
to wrestle with a flower. Back and forth
we pumped across the water, in twos and threes,
full of brave adventure. On the marshy shore,   15
the others hollered for their turns,
or at the hem of where we pitched the tents
gathered firewood—
                    this was wilderness,
although the pond was less than half an acre   20
and we could still see the grand magnolias
in the village cemetary, their waxy
white conical blossoms gleaming in the foliage.
A dozen girls, the oldest only twelve, two sisters
with their long braids, my shy neighbor,   25
someone squealing without interruption:
all we didn't know about the world buoyed us,
as the frightful water sustained and moved the flowers
tethered at a depth we couldn't see.

In the late afternoon, before they'd folded   30
into candles on the dark water,
I went to fill the bucket at the spring.
Deep in the pines, exposed tree roots
formed a natural arch, a cave of black loam.
I raked off the skin of leaves and needles,   35
leaving a pool so clear and shallow
I could count the pebbles
on the studded floor. The sudden cold
splashing up from the bucket to my hands
made me want to plunge my hand in—   40
and I held it under, feeling the shock that wakes
and deadens, watching first my fingers,
then the ledge beyond me,
the snake submerged and motionless,
the head propped on its coils the way a girl   45
crosses her arms before her on the sill
and rests her chin there.
                    Lugging the bucket
back to the noisy clearing, I found nothing changed,

the boat still rocked across the pond,   50
the fire straggled and cracked as we fed it
branches and debris into the night,
leaning back on our pallets—
spokes in a wheel—learning the names of the many
constellations, learning how each fixed   55
cluster took its name:
not from the strongest light, but from the pattern
made by stars of lesser magnitude,
so like the smaller stars we rowed among.

                                                            [1987]

LOUISE GLÜCK   [b. 1943]

The Wild Iris

At the end of my suffering
there was a door.

Hear me out: that which you call death
I remember.

Overhead, noises, branches of the pine shifting.   5
Then nothing. The weak sun
flickered over the dry surface.

It is terrible to survive
as consciousness
buried in the dark earth.   10

Then it was over: that which you fear, being
a soul and unable
to speak, ending abruptly, the stiff earth
bending a little. And what I took to be
birds darting in low shrubs.   15

You who do not remember
passage from the other world
I tell you I could speak again: whatever
returns from oblivion returns
to find a voice: 20

from the center of my life came
a great fountain, deep blue
shadows on azure seawater.

[1992]

JAMES TATE   [b. 1943]

The Wheelchair Butterfly

O sleepy city of reeling wheelchairs
where a mouse can commit suicide if he can

concentrate long enough
on the history book of rodents
in this underground town   5

of electrical wheelchairs!
The girl who is always pregnant and bruised
like a pear

rides her many-stickered bicycle
backward up the staircase   10
of the abandoned trolleybarn.

Yesterday was warm. Today a butterfly froze
in midair; and was plucked like a grape
by a child who swore he could take care

of it. O confident city where   15
the seeds of poppies pass for carfare,

where the ordinary hornets in a human's heart
may slumber and snore, where bifocals bulge

in an orange garage of daydreams,
we wait in our loose attics for a new season   20

as if for an ice-cream truck.
An Indian pony crosses the plains

whispering Sanskrit prayers to a crater of fleas.
Honeysuckle says: I thought I could swim.

The Mayor is urinating on the wrong side   25
of the street! A dandelion sends off sparks:
beware your hair is locked!

Beware the trumpet wants a glass of water!
Beware a velvet tabernacle!

Beware the Warden of Light has married   30
an old piece of string!

[1969]

EAVAN BOLAND   [b. 1944]

The Pomegranate

The only legend I have ever loved is
the story of a daughter lost in hell.
And found and rescued there.
Love and blackmail are the gist of it.
Ceres° and Persephone the names.   5
And the best thing about the legend is
I can enter it anywhere. And have.
As a child in exile in
a city of fogs and strange consonants,
I read it first and at first I was   10
an exiled child in the crackling dusk of
the underworld, the stars blighted. Later
I walked out in a summer twilight
searching for my daughter at bed-time.

---

5. Ceres: Roman name of Demeter, the goddess of crops and harvest. Her daughter Persephone was kidnapped by Pluto (or Hades) and taken to the underworld.
Demeter, grieving and angry, refused to let seeds germinate or crops grow. To save
the human race from extinction, Zeus finally ordered Pluto to release Persephone.
Pluto told her she was free to leave but tricked her by offering a pomegranate
seed; anyone who eats food in the underworld must return there. Zeus therefore
arranged a compromise: Persephone would spend a third of each year in the land
of the dead with Pluto (winter, when Demeter went into mourning); but she would
be with her mother for the other two-thirds of each year (spring and summer).

When she came running I was ready   15
to make any bargain to keep her.
I carried her back past whitebeams
and wasps and honey-scented buddleias.
But I was Ceres then and I knew
winter was in store for every leaf   20
on every tree on that road.
Was inescapable for each one we passed.
And for me.
              It is winter
and the stars are hidden.   25
I climb the stairs and stand where I can see
my child asleep beside her teen magazines,
her can of Coke, her plate of uncut fruit.
The pomegranate! How did I forget it?
She could have come home and been safe   30
and ended the story and all
our heart-broken searching but she reached
out a hand and plucked a pomegranate.
She put out her hand and pulled down
the French sound for apple° and   *pomme* 35
the noise of stone° and the proof   *granite*
that even in the place of death,
at the heart of legend, in the midst
of rocks full of unshed tears
ready to be diamonds by the time   40
the story was told, a child can be
hungry. I could warn her. There is still a chance.
The rain is cold. The road is flint-coloured.
The suburb has cars and cable television.
The veiled stars are above ground.   45
It is another world. But what else
can a mother give her daughter but such
beautiful rifts in time?
If I defer the grief I will diminish the gift.
The legend will be hers as well as mine.   50
She will enter it. As I have.
She will wake up. She will hold
the papery flushed skin in her hand.
And to her lips. I will say nothing.

                                                        [1994; 1995]

ANNE WALDMAN   [b. 1945]

Icy Rose

(To The Delicately Winter Coming On)

        all day feeling space
        my face is empty space
        & nighttime too

the space   the space   the space   the space

        & nighttime too   5
        I'm going blank

          Blank.

Where has that last sentence (speaking—you were speaking—gone?
& where have the birds really gone?
& where is the Ice Age now?   10
& who does this poet think he is?   or she is?

She is a far cry from Womanhood

                  O
           T-T-T-TAKE ME BACK!

                                  I stammer   15
      I go down under the moon
      I dance with the big brown bear
                    I kiss the foot

      Down to 6 below last night
      I ran thru the snow like a young puppy   20

      I got the Dashboard Blues
      I threw in the towel

      I reacted like a Crazy Lady
               —well—
                        —well—   25
                 not exactly

YOU SEE ALL THIS FREEDOM?????????????

You see where it gets you?

You see what I mean????

mean?   30

o calm down   cough up   curl under   crawl in
creep along   crouch down   come on

COME ON

there's nothing to fear except fear itself

Get off my fear itself!   35

(it fears itself)

Rather

think of Copernicus

De Revolutionibus Orbium Coelestium°

& Liu Shui°   40

(flowing water)

& you: My Boldest Dream

it's so easy
makes me sleepy

but WHO ARE YOU?   45

& why do you dress so strange?

& who are your parents?

& whence have you come?

[1971]

---

39. *De Revolutionibus Orbium Coelestium*: A major work by astronomer Nicolaus Copernicus that argued for a heliocentric, or sun-centered, solar system, as opposed to an earth-centered one. It was published in 1543 and was subsequently banned by the Roman Catholic Church.

40. Liu Shui: "Flowing water" in Chinese. It is also the title of an ancient Chinese musical piece, still played and recorded today.

MARILYN NELSON   [b. 1946]

Minor Miracle

Which reminds me of another knock-on-wood
memory. I was cycling with a male friend,
through a small midwestern town. We came to a 4-way
stop and stopped, chatting. As we started again,
a rusty old pick-up truck, ignoring the stop sign,   5
hurricaned past scant inches from our front wheels.
My partner called, "Hey, that was a 4-way stop!"
The truck driver, stringy blond hair a long fringe
under his brand-name beer cap, looked back and yelled,
    "You fucking niggers!"   10
And sped off.
My friend and I looked at each other and shook our heads.
We remounted our bikes and headed out of town.
We were pedaling through a clear blue afternoon
between two fields of almost-ripened wheat   15
bordered by cornflowers and Queen Anne's lace
when we heard an unmuffled motor, a honk-honking.
We stopped, closed ranks, made fists.
It was the same truck. It pulled over.
A tall, very much in shape young white guy slid out: 20
greasy jeans, homemade finger tattoos, probably
a Marine Corps boot-camp footlockerful
of martial arts techniques.

"What did you say back there!" he shouted.
My friend said, "I said it was a 4-way stop.   25
You went through it."
"And what did I say?" the white guy asked.
"You said: "'You fucking niggers.'"
The afternoon froze.

"Well," said the white guy,   30
shoving his hands into his pockets
and pushing dirt around with the pointed toe of his boot,
"I just want to say I'm sorry."
He climbed back into his truck
and drove away.   35

                                                        [1997]

LARRY LEVIS   [1946–1996]

The Poem You Asked For

My poem would eat nothing.
I tried giving it water
but it said no,

worrying me.
Day after day,   5
I held it up to the light,

turning it over,
but it only pressed its lips
more tightly together.

It grew sullen, like a toad   10
through with being teased.
I offered it all my money,

my clothes, my car with a full tank.
But the poem stared at the floor.
Finally I cupped it in   15

my hands, and carried it gently
out into the soft air, into the
evening traffic, wondering how

to end things between us.
For now it had begun breathing,   20
putting on more and

more hard rings of flesh.
And the poem demanded the food,
it drank up all the water,

beat me and took my money,   25
tore the faded clothes
off my back,

said Shit,
and walked slowly away,
slicking its hair down.   30

Said it was going
over to your place.

[1972]

YUSEF KOMUNYAKAA   [b. 1947]

Facing It

My black face fades,
hiding inside the black granite.
I said I wouldn't,
dammit: No tears.
I'm stone. I'm flesh.   5
My clouded reflection eyes me
like a bird of prey, the profile of night
slanted against morning. I turn
this way—the stone lets me go.
I turn that way—I'm inside   10
the Vietnam Veterans Memorial
again, depending on the light
to make a difference.
I go down the 58,022 names,
half-expecting to find   15
my own in letters like smoke.
I touch the name Andrew Johnson;
I see the booby trap's white flash.
Names shimmer on a woman's blouse
but when she walks away   20
the names stay on the wall.
Brushstrokes flash, a red bird's
wings cutting across my stare.
The sky. A plane in the sky.
A white vet's image floats   25
closer to me, then his pale eyes
look through mine. I'm a window.
He's lost his right arm
inside the stone. In the black mirror
a woman's trying to erase names: 30
No, she's brushing a boy's hair.

[1988]

JANE KENYON   [1947–1995]

Let Evening Come

Let the light of late afternoon
shine through chinks in the barn, moving
up the bales as the sun moves down.

Let the cricket take up chafing
as a woman takes up her needles   5
and her yarn. Let evening come.

Let dew collect on the hoe abandoned
in long grass. Let the stars appear
and the moon disclose her silver horn.

Let the fox go back to its sandy den.   10
Let the wind die down. Let the shed
go black inside. Let evening come.

To the bottle in the ditch, to the scoop
in the oats, to air in the lung
let evening come.   15

Let it come, as it will, and don't
be afraid. God does not leave us
comfortless, so let evening come.

[1996]

LINDA HOGAN   [b. 1947]

Crow Law

The temple where crow worships
walks forward in tall, black grass.
Betrayal is crow's way of saying grace
to the wolf
so it can eat   5
what is left
when blood is on the ground,
until what remains of moose
is crow
walking out   10

the sacred temple of ribs
in a dance of leaving
the red tracks of scarce and private gods.
It is the oldest war
where moose becomes wolf and crow,   15
where the road ceases
to become the old forest
where crow is calling,
where we are still afraid.

[1993]

AI   [1947–2010]

Why Can't I Leave You?

You stand behind the old black mare,
dressed as always in that red shirt,
stained from sweat, the crying of the armpits,
that will not stop for anything,
stroking her rump, while the barley goes unplanted.   5
I pick up my suitcase and set it down,
as I try to leave you again.
I smooth the hair back from your forehead.
I think with your laziness and the drought too,
you'll be needing my help more than ever.   10
You take my hands, I nod
and go to the house to unpack,
having found another reason to stay.

I undress, then put on my white lace slip
for you to take off, because you like that   15
and when you come in, you pull down the straps
and I unbutton your shirt.
I know we can't give each other any more
or any less than what we have.
There is safety in that, so much   20
that I can never get past the packing,
the begging you to please, if I can't make you happy,
come close between my thighs
and let me laugh for you from my second mouth.

[1972]

LESLIE MARMON SILKO   [b. 1948]

Prayer to the Pacific

I traveled to the ocean
        distant
                from my southwest land of sandrock
                to the moving blue water
            Big as the myth of origin.   5

Pale
pale water in the yellow-white light of
                sun   floating west
                    to China
                where ocean herself was born.   10
Clouds that blow across the sand are wet.

Squat in the wet sand and speak to the Ocean:
         I return to you   turquoise   the red coral you sent us,
                sister spirit of Earth.
Four round stones in my pocket   I carry back the ocean   15
                to suck and to taste.

Thirty thousand years ago
                Indians came riding across the ocean
              carried by giant sea turtles.

Waves were high that day   20
          great sea turtles waded   slowly out
                  from the gray sundown sea.

Grandfather Turtle rolled in the sand   four times
               and disappeared
                swimming into the sun.   25
And so from that time
      immmemorial,
              as the old people say,
rain clouds drift from the west
              gift from the ocean.   30

Green leaves in the wind
Wet earth on my feet
        swallowing raindrops
             clear from China.

                               [1981]

HEATHER McHUGH   [b. 1948]

What He Thought

for Fabbio Doplicher

We were supposed to do a job in Italy
and, full of our feeling for
ourselves (our sense of being
Poets from America) we went
from Rome to Fano, met   5
the mayor, mulled
a couple matters over (what's
cheap date, they asked us; what's
flat drink). Among Italian literati

we could recognize our counterparts: 10
the academic, the apologist,
the arrogant, the amorous,
the brazen and the glib—and there was one

administrator (the conservative), in suit
of regulation gray, who like a good tour guide   15
with measured pace and uninflected tone narrated
sights and histories the hired van hauled us past.
Of all, he was most politic and least poetic,
so it seemed. Our last few days in Rome
(when all but three of the New World Bards had flown)   20
I found a book of poems this
unprepossessing one had written: it was there
in the *pensione* room (a room he'd recommended)
where it must have been abandoned by
the German visitor (was there a bus of *them?*)   25
to whom he had inscribed and dated it a month before.
I couldn't read Italian, either, so I put the book
back into the wardrobe's dark. We last Americans

were due to leave tomorrow. For our parting evening then
our host chose something in a family restaurant, and there   30
we sat and chatted, sat and chewed,
till, sensible it was our last
big chance to be poetic, make
our mark, one of us asked
                        "What's poetry?   35

Is it the fruits and vegetables and
marketplace of Campo dei Fiori, or
the statue there?" Because I was

the glib one, I identified the answer
instantly, I didn't have to think—"The truth   40
is both, it's both," I blurted out. But that
was easy. That was easiest to say. What followed
taught me something about difficulty,
for our underestimated host spoke out,
all of a sudden, with a rising passion, and he said: 45

The statue represents Giordano Bruno,
brought to be burned in the public square
because of his offense against
authority, which is to say
the Church. His crime was his belief   50
the universe does not revolve around
the human being: God is no
fixed point or central government, but rather is
poured in waves through all things. All things
move. "If God is not the soul itself, He is   55
the soul of the soul of the world." Such was
his heresy. The day they brought him
forth to die, they feared he might
incite the crowd (the man was famous
for his eloquence). And so his captors   60
placed upon his face
an iron mask, in which
he could not speak. That's
how they burned him. That is how
he died: without a word, in front   65
of everyone.

       And poetry—

          (we'd all
put down our forks by now, to listen to
the man in gray; he went on   70
softly)—

       poetry is what

he thought, but did not say.

                      [1994]

SEKOU SUNDIATA   [1948–2007]

Blink Your Eyes

Remembering Sterling A. Brown

I was on my way to see my woman
but the Law said I was on my way
thru a red light red light red light
and if you saw my woman
you could understand,   5
I was just being a man
It wasn't about no light
it was about my ride
and if you saw my ride
you could dig that too, you dig?   10
Sunroof stereo radio black leather
bucket seats sit low you know,
the body's cool, but the tires are worn.
Ride when the hard time come, ride
when they're gone, in other words   15
the light was green.

I could wake up in the morning
without a warning
and my world could change:
blink your eyes.   20
All depends, all depends on the skin,
all depends on the skin you're living in.

Up to the window comes the Law
with his hand on his gun
what's up? what's happening?   25
I said I guess
that's when I really broke the law.
He said *a routine, step out the car*
a routine, assume the position.
Put your hands up in the air   30
you know the routine, like you just don't care.
License and registration.
Deep was the night and the light
from the North Star on the car door, deja vu
we've been through this before,   35
why did you stop me?

Somebody had to stop you.
I watch the news, you always lose.
You're unreliable, that's undeniable.
This is serious, you could be dangerous.   40

I could wake up in the morning
without a warning
and my world could change:
blink your eyes.
All depends, all depends on the skin,   45
all depends on the skin you're living in.

New York City, they got laws
can't no bruthas drive outdoors,
in certain neighborhoods, on particular streets
near and around certain types of people.   50
They got laws.
All depends, all depends on the skin,
all depends on the skin you're living in.

[1995]

AGHA SHAHID ALI   [1949–2001]

I Dream It Is Afternoon
When I Return to Delhi

At Purana Qila I am alone, waiting
for the bus to Daryaganj. I see it coming,
but my hands are empty.
"Jump on, jump on," someone shouts,
"I've saved this change for you   5
for years. Look!"
A hand opens, full of silver rupees.
"Jump on, jump on." The voice doesn't stop.
There's no one I know. A policeman,
handcuffs silver in his hands,   10
asks for my ticket.

I jump off the running bus,
sweat pouring from my hair.
I run past the Doll Museum, past

headlines on the Times of India   15
building, PRISONERS BLINDED IN A BIHAR
JAIL, HARIJAN VILLAGES BURNED BY LANDLORDS.
Panting, I stop in Daryaganj,
outside Golcha Cinema.

Sunil is there, lighting   20
a cigarette, smiling. I say,
"It must be ten years, you haven't changed,
it was your voice on the bus!"
He says, "The film is about to begin,
I've bought an extra ticket for you,"   25
and we rush inside:

Anarkali is being led away,
her earrings lying on the marble floor.
Any moment she'll be buried alive.
"But this is the end," I turn   30
toward Sunil. He is nowhere.
The usher taps my shoulder, says
my ticket is ten years old.

Once again my hands are empty.
I am waiting, alone, at Purana Qila.   35
Bus after empty bus is not stopping.
Suddenly, beggar women with children
are everywhere, offering
me money, weeping for me.

                                                        [1987]

VICTOR HERNÁNDEZ CRUZ   [b. 1949]

Problems with Hurricanes

A campesino looked at the air
And told me:
With hurricanes it's not the wind
or the noise or the water.
I'll tell you he said: 5
it's the mangoes, avocados
Green plantains and bananas
flying into town like projectiles.

How would your family
feel if they had to tell   10
The generations that you
got killed by a flying
Banana.

Death by drowning has honor
If the wind picked you up   15
and slammed you
Against a mountain boulder
This would not carry shame
But
to suffer a mango smashing   20
Your skull
or a plantain hitting your
Temple at 70 miles per hour
is the ultimate disgrace.

The campesino takes off his hat—   25
As a sign of respect
towards the fury of the wind
And says:
Don't worry about the noise
Don't worry about the water   30
Don't worry about the wind—
If you are going out
beware of mangoes
And all such beautiful
sweet things.   35

[1991]

JULIA ALVAREZ   [b. 1950]

Bilingual Sestina°

Some things I have to say aren't getting said
in this snowy, blond, blue-eyed, gum-chewing English:
dawn's early light sifting through *persianas*° closed   *blinds*
the night before by dark-skinned girls whose words

Sestina: See Glossary, page 406.

evoke *cama, aposento, sueños°* in *nombres°*   *bed, room, dreams/names*   5
from that first world I can't translate from Spanish.

Gladys, Rosario, Altagracia—the sounds of Spanish
wash over me like warm island waters as I say
your soothing names: a child again learning the *nombres*
of things you point to in the world before English   10
turned *sol, tierra, cielo, luna* to vocabulary words—
sun, earth, sky, moon. Language closed

like the touch-sensitive *morivivî°* whose leaves closed   *touch-me-not plant*
when we kids poked them, astonished. Even Spanish
failed us back then when we saw how frail a word is   15
when faced with the thing it names. How saying
its name won't always summon up in Spanish or English
the full blown genie from the bottled *nombre.*

Gladys, I summon you back by saying your *nombre.*
Open up again the house of slatted windows closed   20
since childhood, where *palabras°* left behind for English   *words*
stand dusty and awkward in neglected Spanish.
Rosario, muse of *el patio,°* sing in me and through me say   *the patio*
that world again, begin first with those first words

you put in my mouth as you pointed to the world—   25
not Adam, not God, but a country girl numbering
the stars, the blades of grass, warming the sun by saying,
¡Qué calor!° as you opened up the morning closed   *How hot!*
inside the night until you sang in Spanish,
Estas son las mañanitas,° and listening in bed, no English   30

yet in my head to confuse me with translations, no English
doubling the world with synonyms, no dizzying array of words
—the world was simple and intact in Spanish—
luna, sol, casa, luz, flor,° as if the *nombres*   *moon, sun, house, light, flower*
were the outer skin of things, as if words were so close   35
one left a mist of breath on things by saying

their names, an intimacy I now yearn for in English—
words so close to what I mean that I almost hear my Spanish
heart beating, beating inside what I say *en inglés.*

[1995]

---

30. *Estas . . . mañanitas:* The opening words of a traditional Mexican birthday
song; literally, "These are the songs (that King David sang. Today . . . we sing them
to you)."

CAROLYN FORCHÉ   [b. 1950]

The Colonel

What you have heard is true. I was in his house. His ᵥ
coffee and sugar. His daughter filed her nails, his son weₙₜ
night. There were daily papers, pet dogs, a pistol on the cushion ᵦᵤ
him. The moon swung bare on its black cord over the house. On the television was a cop show. It was in English. Broken bottles were embedded
in the walls around the house to scoop the kneecaps from a man's legs or
cut his hands to lace. On the windows there were gratings like those in
liquor stores. We had dinner, rack of lamb, good wine, a gold bell was on
the table for calling the maid. The maid brought green mangoes, salt, a
type of bread. I was asked how I enjoyed the country. There was a brief
commercial in Spanish. His wife took everything away. There was some
talk then of how difficult it had become to govern. The parrot said hello
on the terrace. The colonel told it to shut up, and pushed himself from
the table. My friend said to me with his eyes: say nothing. The colonel
returned with a sack used to bring groceries home. He spilled many human ears on the table. They were like dried peach halves. There is no
other way to say this. He took one of them in his hands, shook it in our
faces, dropped it into a water glass. It came alive there. I am tired of fool-
ing around he said. As for the rights of anyone, tell your people they can
go fuck themselves. He swept the ears to the floor with his arm and held
the last of his wine in the air. Something for your poetry, no? he said.
Some of the ears on the floor caught this scrap of his voice. Some of the
ears on the floor were pressed to the ground.

[1978]

RAY A. YOUNG BEAR   [b. 1950]

From the Spotted Night

In the blizzard
while chopping wood
the mystical whistler
beckons my attention.
Once there were longhouses   5
here. A village.
In the abrupt spring floods

mers retrieved our belief.
their spirit remains.
rom the spotted night   10
distant jets transform
into fireflies who float
towards me like incandescent
snowflakes.
The leather shirt   15
which is suspended
on a wire hanger
above the bed's headboard
is humanless; yet when one
stands outside the house,   20
the strenuous sounds
of dressers and boxes
being moved can be heard.
We believe someone wears
the shirt and rearranges   25
the heavy furniture,
although nothing
is actually changed.
Unlike the Plains Indian shirts
which repelled lead bullets,   30
ricocheting from them
in fiery sparks,
this shirt is the means;
this shirt *is* the bullet.

[1990]

JOY HARJO   [b. 1951]

She Had Some Horses

She had some horses.

She had horses who were bodies of sand.
She had horses who were maps drawn of blood.
She had horses who were skins of ocean water.
She had horses who were the blue air of sky.   5
She had horses who were fur and teeth.

She had horses who were clay and would break.
She had horses who were splintered red cliff.

She had some horses.

She had horses with long, pointed breasts.   10
She had horses with full, brown thighs.
She had horses who laughed too much.
She had horses who threw rocks at glass houses.
She had horses who licked razor blades.

She had some horses.   15

She had horses who danced in their mothers' arms.
She had horses who thought they were the sun and their
bodies shone and burned like stars.
She had horses who waltzed nightly on the moon.
She had horses who were much too shy, and kept quiet   20
in stalls of their own making.

She had some horses.

She had horses who liked Creek Stomp Dance songs.
She had horses who cried in their beer.
She had horses who spit at male queens who made   25
them afraid of themselves.
She had horses who said they weren't afraid.
She had horses who lied.
She had horses who told the truth, who were stripped
bare of their tongues.   30

She had some horses.

She had horses who called themselves, "horse."
She had horses who called themselves, "spirit," and kept
their voices secret and to themselves.
She had horses who had no names.   35
She had horses who had books of names.

She had some horses.

She had horses who whispered in the dark, who were afraid to speak.
She had horses who screamed out of fear of the silence, who
carried knives to protect themselves from ghosts.   40
She had horses who waited for destruction.
She had horses who waited for resurrection.

She had some horses.

She had horses who got down on their knees for any saviour.
She had horses who thought their high price had saved them.   45
She had horses who tried to save her, who climbed in her
bed at night and prayed as they raped her.

She had some horses.

She had some horses she loved.
She had some horses she hated.   50

These were the same horses.

[1983]

GARRETT KAORU HONGO   [b. 1951]

Yellow Light

One arm hooked around the frayed strap
of a tar-black, patent-leather purse,
the other cradling something for dinner:
fresh bunches of spinach from a J-Town *yaoya*,°   *vegetable stand or seller*
sides of split Spanish mackerel from Alviso's,   5
maybe a loaf of Langendorf;° she steps
off the hissing bus at Olympic and Fig,
begins the three-block climb up the hill,
passing gangs of schoolboys playing war,
Japs against Japs, Chicanas chalking sidewalks   10
with the holy double-yoked crosses of hopscotch,
and the Korean grocer's wife out for a stroll
around this neighborhood of Hawaiian apartments
just starting to steam with cooking
and the anger of young couples coming home   15
from work, yelling at kids, flicking on
TV sets for the Wednesday Night Fights.

If it were May, hydrangeas and jacaranda
flowers in the streetside trees would be
blooming through the smog of late spring.   20
Wisteria in Masuda's front yard would be
shaking out the long tresses of its purple hair.

6. Langendorf: A well-known bakery in California.

Maybe mosquitoes, moths, a few orange butterflies
settling on the lattice of monkey flowers
tangled in chain-link fences by the trash.   25

But this is October, and Los Angeles
seethes like a billboard under twilight.
From used-car lots and the movie houses uptown,
long silver sticks of light probe the sky.
From the Miracle Mile, whole freeways away,   30
a brilliant fluorescence breaks out
and makes war with the dim squares
of yellow kitchen light winking on
in all the side streets of the Barrio.

She climbs up the two flights of flagstone   35
stairs to 201-B, the spikes of her high heels
clicking like kitchen knives on a cutting board,
props the groceries against the door,
fishes through memo pads, a compact,
empty packs of chewing gum, and finds her keys.   40

The moon then, cruising from behind
a screen of eucalyptus across the street,
covers everything, everything in sight,
in a heavy light like yellow onions.

[1982]

JIMMY SANTIAGO BACA   [b. 1952]

Family Ties

Mountain barbecue.
They arrive, young cousins singly,
older aunts and uncles in twos and threes,
like trees. I play with a new generation
of children, my hands in streambed silt   5
of their lives, a scuba diver's hands, dusting
surface sand for buried treasure.
Freshly shaved and powdered faces
of uncles and aunts surround taco
and tamale tables. Mounted elk head on wall,   10

brass rearing horse cowboy clock
on fireplace mantle. Sons and daughters
converse round beer and whiskey table.
Tempers ignite on land grant issues.
Children scurry round my legs.   15
Old bow-legged men toss horseshoes on lawn,
other farmhands from Mexico sit on a bench,
broken lives repaired for this occasion.
I feel no love or family tie here. I rise
to go hiking, to find abandoned rock cabins   20
in the mountains. We come to a grass clearing,
my wife rolls her jeans up past ankles,
wades ice cold stream, and I barefooted,
carry a son in each arm and follow.
We cannot afford a place like this.   25
At the party again, I eat bean and chile
burrito, and after my third glass of rum,
we climb in the car and my wife drives
us home. My sons sleep in the back,
dream of the open clearing,   30
they are chasing each other with cattails
in the sunlit pasture, giggling,
as I stare out the window
at no trespassing signs white flashing past.

                                                    [1989]

JUDITH ORTIZ COFER   [b. 1952]

Cold as Heaven

Before there is a breeze again
before the cooling days of Lent, she may be gone.
My grandmother asks me to tell her
again about the snow.
We sit on her white bed   5
in this white room, while outside
the Caribbean sun winds up the world
like an old alarm clock. I tell her
about the enveloping blizzard I lived through

that made everything and everyone the same; 10
how we lost ourselves in drifts so tall
we fell through our own footprints;
how wrapped like mummies in layers of wool
that almost immobilized us, we could only
take hesitant steps like toddlers 15
toward food, warmth, shelter.
I talk winter real for her,
as she would once conjure for me to dream
at sweltering siesta time,
cool stone castles in lands far north. 20
Her eyes wander to the window,
to the teeming scene of children
pouring out of a yellow bus, then to the bottle
dripping minutes through a tube
into her veins. When her eyes return to me, 25
I can see she's waiting to hear more
about the purifying nature of ice,
how snow makes way for a body,
how you can make yourself an angel
by just lying down and waving your arms 30
as you do when you say
good-bye.

[1995]

NAOMI SHIHAB NYE   [b. 1952]

Kindness

Before you know what kindness really is
you must lose things,
feel the future dissolve in a moment
like salt in a weakened broth.
What you held in your hand, 5
what you counted and carefully saved,
all this must go so you know
how desolate the landscape can be
between the regions of kindness.
How you ride and ride 10

thinking the bus will never stop,
the passengers eating maize and chicken
will stare out the window forever.

Before you learn the tender gravity of kindness,
you must travel where the Indian in a white poncho   15
lies dead by the side of the road.
You must see how this could be you,
how he too was someone
who journeyed through the night with plans
and the simple breath that kept him alive.   20

Before you know kindness as the deepest thing inside,
you must know sorrow as the other deepest thing.
You must wake up with sorrow.
You must speak to it till your voice
catches the thread of all sorrows   25
and you see the size of the cloth.

Then it is only kindness that makes sense anymore,
only kindness that ties your shoes
and sends you out into the day to mail letters and purchase bread,
only kindness that raises its head   30
from the crowd of the world to say
It is I you have been looking for,
and then goes with you everywhere
like a shadow or a friend.

[1980]

NAOMI SHIHAB NYE   [b. 1952]

The Small Vases from Hebron°

Tip their mouths open to the sky.
Turquoise, amber,
the deep green with fluted handle,
pitcher the size of two thumbs,
tiny lip and graceful waist.   5

Hebron: An ancient city in the West Bank area of Israel, a sacred place for both
Muslims and Jews. It has been a focus of tension between Israelis and Palestinians
since the 1967 Arab-Israeli war.

Here we place the smallest flower
which could have lived invisibly
in loose soil beside the road,
sprig of succulent rosemary,
bowing mint.   10

They grow deeper in the center of the table.

Here we entrust the small life,
thread, fragment, breath.
And it bends. It waits all day.
As the bread cools and the children   15
open their gray copybooks
to shape the letter that looks like
a chimney rising out of a house.

And what do the headlines say?

Nothing of the smaller petal   20
perfectly arranged inside the larger petal
or the way tinted glass filters light.
Men and boys, praying when they died,
fall out of their skins.
The whole alphabet of living,   25
heads and tails of words,
sentences, the way they said,
"Ya'Allah!" when astonished,
or "ya'ani" for "I mean"—
a crushed glass under the feet   30
still shines.
But the child of Hebron sleeps
with the thud of her brothers falling
and the long sorrow of the color red.

[1998]

GARY SOTO   [b. 1952]

Moving Away

Remember that we are moving away   brother
From those years
In the same house with a white stepfather
What troubled him has been forgotten

But what troubled us has settled   5
Like dirt
In the nests of our knuckles
And cannot be washed away

All those times you woke shivering
In the night   10
From a coldness I
Could not understand
And cupped a crucifix beneath the covers

All those summers we hoed our yard
In the afternoon sun   15
The heat waving across our faces
And we waved back wasps
While the one we hated
Watched us from under a tree and said nothing

We will remember those moments   brother   20

And now that we are far
From one another
What I want to speak of
Is the quiet of a room just before a daybreak
And you next to me   sleeping   25

[1977]

RITA DOVE   [b. 1952]

Fifth Grade Autobiography

I was four in this photograph fishing
with my grandparents at a lake in Michigan.
My brother squats in poison ivy.
His Davy Crockett cap
sits squared on his head so the raccoon tail   5
flounces down the back of his sailor suit.

My grandfather sits to the far right
in a folding chair,
and I know his left hand is on

the tobacco in his pants pocket   10
because I used to wrap it for him
every Christmas. Grandmother's hips
bulge from the brush, she's leaning
into the ice chest, sun through the trees
printing her dress with soft   15
luminous paws.

I am staring jealously at my brother;
the day before he rode his first horse, alone.
I was strapped in a basket
behind my grandfather.   20
He smelled of lemons. He's died—

but I remember his hands.

[1989]

ALBERTO RÍOS   [b. 1952]

Nani°

Sitting at her table, she serves
the sopa de arroz° to me   *Mexican rice soup*
instinctively, and I watch her,
the absolute *mamá*, and eat words
I might have had to say more   5
out of embarrassment. To speak,
now-foreign words I used to speak,
too, dribble down her mouth as she serves
me albondigas.° No more   *meatballs*
than a third are easy to me.   10
By the stove she does something with words
and looks at me only with her
back. I am full. I tell her
I taste the mint, and watch her speak
smiles at the stove. All my words   15
make her smile. Nani never serves

Nani: Diminutive for *grandmother*.

herself, she only watches me
with her skin, her hair. I ask for more.

I watch the *mamá* warming more
tortillas for me. I watch her   20
fingers in the flame for me.
Near her mouth, I see a wrinkle speak
of a man whose body serves
the ants like she serves me, then more words
from more wrinkles about children, words   25
about this and that, flowing more
easily from these other mouths. Each serves
as a tremendous string around her,
holding her together. They speak
nani was this and that to me   30
and I wonder just how much of me
will die with her, what were the words
I could have been, was. Her insides speak
through a hundred wrinkles, now, more
than she can bear, steel around her,   35
shouting, then, What is this thing she serves?

She asks me if I want more.
I own no words to stop her.
Even before I speak, she serves.

[1982]

MARY RUEFLE   [b. 1952]

Barbarians

Here and there, between trees,
cows lie down in the forest
in the mid-afternoon
as though sleep were an idea
for which they were willing   5
to die.

[1987]

ANITA ENDREZZE   [b. 1952]

The Girl Who Loved the Sky

Outside the second grade room,
the jacaranda tree blossomed
into purple lanterns, the papery petals
drifted, darkening the windows.
Inside, the room smelled like glue.   5
The desks were made of yellowed wood,
the tops littered with eraser rubbings,
rulers, and big fat pencils.
Colored chalk meant special days.
The walls were covered with precise   10
bright tulips and charts with shiny stars
by certain names. There, I learned
how to make butter by shaking a jar
until the pale cream clotted
into one sweet mass. There, I learned   15
that numbers were fractious beasts
with dens like dim zeros. And there,
I met a blind girl who thought the sky
tasted like cold metal when it rained
and whose eyes were always covered   20
with the bruised petals of her lids.

She loved the formless sky, defined
only by sounds, or the cool umbrellas
of clouds. On hot, still days
we listened to the sky falling   25
like chalk dust. We heard the noon
whistle of the pig-mash factory,
smelled the sourness of home-bound men.
I had no father; she had no eyes;
we were best friends. The other girls   30
drew shaky hop-scotch squares
on the dusty asphalt, talked about
pajama parties, weekend cook-outs,
and parents who bought sleek-finned cars.
Alone, we sat in the canvas swings,   35
our shoes digging into the sand, then pushing,
until we flew high over their heads,

our hands streaked with red rust
from the chains that kept us safe.

I was born blind, she said, an act of nature.   40
Sure, I thought, like birds born
without wings, trees without roots.
I didn't understand. The day she moved
I saw the world clearly; the sky
backed away from me like a departing father.   45
I sat under the jacaranda, catching
the petals in my palm, enclosing them
until my fist was another lantern
hiding a small and bitter flame.

                                                    [1988]

DAVID MURA   [b. 1952]

Grandfather-in-Law

It's nothing really, and really, it could have been worse, and of course,
        he's now several years dead,
and his widow, well, if oftentimes she's somewhat distracted, overly
        cautious when we visit—
after all, Boston isn't New York—she seems, for some reason, enormously
        proud that there's now a writer in the family,
and periodically, sends me clippings about the poet laureate, Thoreau,
        Anne Sexton's daughter, Lowell, New England literary lore—
in which I fit, if I fit at all, simply because I write in English—as if color
        of skin didn't matter anymore.   5
Still, years ago, during my first visit to Boston, when we were all asleep,
he, who used to require that my wife memorize lines of Longfellow or
        Poe and recite them on the phone,
so that, every time he called, she ran outdoors and had to be coaxed back,
        sometimes with threats, to talk to Pops
(though she remembers too his sly imitations of Lincoln, ice cream at
        Brighams, burgers and fries, all the usual grandfatherly treats),
he, who for some reason was prejudiced against Albanians—where on
        earth did he find them I wondered—   10
who, in the thirties, would vanish to New York, catch a show, buy a suit,
        while up north,
the gas and water bills pounded the front door (his spendthrift ways
        startled me with my grandfather's resemblance),

who for over forty years came down each morning, "How's the old goat?"
    with a tie only his wife could knot circling his neck,
he slipped into my wife's room—we were unmarried at the time—and
    whispered so softly she thought
he almost believed she was really asleep, and was saying this like a wish
    or spell, some bohunk miscalculated Boston sense of duty: 15
"Don't make a mistake with your life, Susie. Don't make a mistake . . ."
Well. The thing that gets me now, despite the dangling rantings I've let
    go, is that, at least at that time,
he was right: There was, inside me, some pressing, raw unpeeled
    persistence, some libidinous desire for dominance
that, in the scribbled first drafts of my life, seemed to mark me as wastrel
    and rageful, bound to be unfaithful,
to destroy, in some powerful, nuclear need, fissioned both by childhood
    and racism, whatever came near—   20
And I can't help but feel, forgiving him now, that if she had listened, if
    she had been awake,
if this flourishing solace, this muscled-for-happiness, shared by us now,
    had never awakened,
he would have become for me a symbol of my rage and self-destruction,
    another raw, never healing wound,
and not this silenced grandfatherly presence, a crank and scoundrel, red-
    necked Yankee who created the delicate seed of my wife, my child.

[1989]

RAY GONZÁLEZ   [b. 1952]

Praise the Tortilla,
Praise Menudo,
Praise Chorizo

I praise the tortilla in honor of El Panzón,
who hit me in school every day and made me see
how the bruises on my arms looked like
the brown clouds on my mother's tortillas.
I praise the tortilla because I know   5
they can fly into our hands like
eager flesh of the one we love,
those soft yearnings we delight in biting
as we tear the tortilla and wipe the plate clean.

I praise the menudo° as visionary food that it is,   10
the tripas y posole° tight flashes of color   *tripe and hominy*
we see as the red caldo° smears across our notebooks   *soup*
like a vision we have not had in years,
our lives going down like the empty bowl
of menudo exploding in our stomachs   15
with the chili piquin° of our poetic dreams.

I praise the chorizo° and smear it   *Mexican sausage*
across my face and hands,
the dayglow brown of it painting me
with the desire to find out   20
what happened to la familia,
why the chorizo sizzled in the pan
and covered the house with a smell
of childhood we will never have again,
the chorizo burrito hot in our hands,   25
as we ran out to play and show the vatos°   *guys*
it's time to cut the chorizo,
tell it like it is before la manteca° runs down   *lard or grease*
our chins and drips away.

[1992]

10. menudo: Mexican soup made with hominy and tripe; said to have special
powers.
16. chili piquin: Type of pepper, added to menudo or other soups.

JANE HIRSHFIELD   [b. 1953]

To Drink

I want to gather your darkness
in my hands, to cup it like water
and drink.
I want this in the same way
as I want to touch your cheek—   5
it is the same—
the way a moth will come
to the bedroom window in late September,
beating and beating its wings against cold glass;

the way a horse will lower   10
his long head to water, and drink,
and pause to lift his head and look,
and drink again,
taking everything in with the water,
everything.   15

[1988]

MARK DOTY   [b. 1953]

Tiara

Peter died in a paper tiara
cut from a book of princess paper dolls;
he loved royalty, sashes

and jewels. *I don't know,*
he said, when he woke in the hospice,   5
I was watching the Bette Davis film festival

on Channel 57 and then—
At the wake, the tension broke
when someone guessed

the casket closed because   10
he was *in there in a big wig
and heels*, and someone said,

*You know he's always late,
he probably isn't here yet—
he's still fixing his makeup.*   15

And someone said he asked for it.
Asked for it—
when all he did was go down

into the salt tide
of wanting as much as he wanted,   20
giving himself over so drunk

or stoned it almost didn't matter who,
though they were beautiful,
stampeding into him in the simple,

ravishing music of their hurry.   25
I think heaven is perfect stasis
poised over the realms of desire,

where dreaming and waking men lie
on the grass while wet horses
roam among them, huge fragments   30

of the music we die into
in the body's paradise.
Sometimes we wake not knowing

how we came to lie here,
or who has crowned us with these temporary,   35
precious stones. And given

the world's perfectly turned shoulders,
the deep hollows blued by longing,
given the irreplaceable silk

of horses rippling in orchards,   40
fruit thundering and chiming down,
given the ordinary marvels of form

and gravity, what could he do,
what could any of us ever do
but ask for it?   45

[1991]

RICHARD JONES   [b. 1953]

Cathedral

Songbirds live
in the old cathedral,
caged birds bought at the street market
and freed as a kind of offering.
Now doves and finches and parakeets   5
nest in the crooks of the nave's highest arches,
roosting on the impossibly high
sills of stained glass windows,
looking down into the valley of the altar
as if from cliffs.   10

Twice a day, you'll hear them singing:
at dawn
when the blue light
of angels' wings
and the yellow light of halos   15
flood into their nests to wake them;
and during mass
when the organ fills
the valley below with thunder.
These birds love thunder,   20
never having seen a drop of rain.
They love it when the people below stand up
and sing. They fly
in mad little loops
from window to window,   25
from the tops of arches
down toward the candles and tombs,
making the sign of the cross.

If you look up during mass
to the world's light falling   30
through the arms of saints,
you can see birds flying
through blue columns of incense
as if it were simple wood smoke
rising from a cabin's chimney   35
in a remote and hushed forest.

[1994]

THYLIAS MOSS   [b. 1954]

The Lynching

They should have slept, would have
but had to fight the darkness, had
to build a fire and bathe a man in
flames. No

other soap's as good when   5
the dirt is the skin. Black since
birth, burnt by birth. His father
is not in heaven. No parent

of atrocity is in heaven. My father chokes
in the next room. It is night, darkness   10
has replaced air. We are white like
incandescence

yet lack light. The God in my father
does not glow. The only lamp
is the burning black man. Holy   15
burning, holy longing, remnants of

a genie after greed. My father
baptizes by fire same as Jesus will.
Becomes a holy ghost when
he dons his sheet, a clerical collar   20

out of control, Dundee Mills percale,
fifty percent cotton, dixie, confederate
and fifty percent polyester, man-made, man-
ipulated, unnatural, mulatto fiber, warp

of miscegenation.   25
After the bath, the man is hung as if
just his washed shirt, the parts
of him most capable of sin removed.

Charred, his flesh is bark, his body
a trunk. No sign of roots. I can't leave   30
him. This is limbo. This is the life after
death coming if God is an invention as were

slaves. So I spend the night, his thin moon-begot
shadow as mattress; something smoldering
keeps me warm. Patches of skin fall onto me   35
in places I didn't know needed mending.

                                              [1991]

LORNA DEE CERVANTES   [b. 1954]

Freeway 280

Las casitas° near the gray cannery,   *little houses*
nestled amid wild abrazos° of climbing roses   *bear hugs*
and man-high red geraniums

are gone now. The freeway conceals it
all beneath a raised scar.   5

But under the fake windsounds of the open lanes,
in the abandoned lots below, new grasses sprout,
wild mustard remembers, old gardens
come back stronger than they were,
trees have been left standing in their yards.   10
Albaricoqueros, cerezos, nogales° . . .   *apple, cherry, walnut trees*
Viejitas° come here with paper bags to gather greens.   *old women*
Espinaca, verdolagas, yerbabuena° . . .   *spinach, purslane, mint*

I scramble over the wire fence
that would have kept me out.   15
Once, I wanted out, wanted the rigid lanes
to take me to a place without sun,
without the smell of tomatoes burning
on swing shift in the greasy summer air.

Maybe it's here   20
en los campos extraños de esta ciudad°
where I'll find it, that part of me
mown under
like a corpse
or a loose seed.   25

[1981]

21. en . . . ciudad: In the strange fields of this city.

MARY JO SALTER   [b. 1954]

Half a Double Sonnet
for Ben

Their ordeal over, now the only trouble
was conveying somehow to a boy of three
that for a week or two he'd be seeing double.
Surely he wouldn't recall the surgery
years later, but what about the psychic scars?   5
And so, when the patch came off, they bought the toy

he'd wanted most. He held it high. "Two cars!"
he cried; and drove himself from joy to joy.
Two baby sisters . . . One was enough of Clare,
but who could complain?—considering that another   10
woman had stepped forward to take care
of the girls, which left him all alone with Mother.
Victory! Even when he went to pee,
he was seconded in his virility.

[1994]

DONALD REVELL   [b. 1954]

Mignonette

The metaphors are what has really happened. When
the stars go, it's a person going, or an old
religion folding like a lawn chair, only less
dramatic, less whatever you would call a girl
with cancer or a star that fell. The metaphors   5

are at the convent where she had so many friends,
so many things to talk about, and they are the blue
green of an ocean, only more like stars. The white
embroidery, her body white and smooth beneath
it, folded in a chair is wonderful to think   10

of when the moon's in Cancer. She would dream about
the lawn or of the convent moon where men betray
themselves. A lawn could only think of dreaming. Think
about a girl you saw by moonlight, dancing on
the lawn. You see a window seat from where you see   15

a chair in which a girl is dying. Cancer kills,
and only stars can help her. Mignonette, the love
of whom is dancing on the lawn like convent stars,
could never have religion, white as she could be
for anyone who talked to her or sat beside   20

her in the little chair, not even now with stars
about to fall and cancer. Metaphors are what
a girl depends on at a time like this, because

the way they work is musical, and music makes
you feel good, even if you're not religious. Life   25

is any convent, any constellation or
a chair to die in, dreaming of the way a lawn
can look. You looked at her again to see
a proof of something, but you didn't find it, didn't
betray yourself. The metaphors are what you said   30

would happen: stars around a chair, the cancer of
a girl who dances on the lawn and likes to talk
about religion when the moon's up. What you said
is that you dreamed of watching. Music dreamed. The silk,
what is so white around her folded body, watched.   35

                                                        [1983]

CORNELIUS EADY   [b. 1954]

My Mother,
If She Had Won Free Dance Lessons

Would she have been a person
With a completely different outlook on life?
There are times when I visit
And find her settled on a chair
In our dilapidated house,   5
The neighborhood crazy lady
Doing what the neighborhood crazy lady is supposed to do,
Which is absolutely nothing

And I wonder as we talk our sympathetic talk,
Abandoned in easy dialogue,   10
I, the son of the crazy lady,
Who crosses easily into her point of view
As if yawning
Or taking off an overcoat.
Each time I visit   15
I walk back into our lives

And I wonder, like any child who wakes up one day to find themself
Abandoned in a world larger than their

   Bad dreams,
I wonder as I see my mother sitting there,   20
Landed to the right-hand window in the living room,
Pausing from time to time in the endless loop of our dialogue
To peek for rascals through the
Venetian blinds,

I wonder a small thought.   25
I walk back into our lives.
Given the opportunity,
How would she have danced?
Would it have been as easily

As we talk to each other now,   30
The crazy lady
And the crazy lady's son,
As if we were old friends from opposite coasts
Picking up the thread of a long conversation,

Or two ballroom dancers   35
Who only know
One step?

What would have changed
If the phone had rung like a suitor,
If the invitation had arrived in the mail   40
Like Jesus, extending a hand?

                             [1986]

CATHY SONG   [b. 1955]

Girl Powdering Her Neck

From a Ukiyo-e Print by Utamaro

The light is the inside
sheen of an oyster shell,
sponged with talc and vapor,
moisture from a bath.

A pair of slippers   5
are placed outside

Utamaro Kitagawa (1753–1806), *Girl Powdering Her Neck*
(Musée Guimet, Paris).

the rice-paper doors.
She kneels at a low table
in the room,
her legs folded beneath her   10
as she sits on a buckwheat pillow.

Her hair is black
with hints of red,
the color of seaweed
spread over rocks.   15

Morning begins the ritual
wheel of the body,
the application of translucent skins.
She practices pleasure:
the pressure of three fingertips   20
. applying powder.
Fingerprints of pollen
some other hand will trace.

The peach-dyed kimono
patterned with maple leaves   25
drifting across the silk,
falls from right to left
in a diagonal, revealing
the nape of her neck
and the curve of a shoulder   30
like the slope of a hill
set deep in snow in a country
of huge white solemn birds.
Her face appears in the mirror,
a reflection in a winter pond,   35
rising to meet itself.

She dips a corner of her sleeve
like a brush into water
to wipe the mirror;
she is about to paint herself.   40
The eyes narrow
in a moment of self-scrutiny.
The mouth parts
as if desiring to disturb
the placid plum face;   45
break the symmetry of silence.
But the berry-stained lips,

stenciled into the mask of beauty,
do not speak.

Two chrysanthemums   50
touch in the middle of the lake
and drift apart.

[1983]

MARILYN CHIN   [b. 1955]

How I Got That Name
an essay on assimilation

I am Marilyn Mei Ling Chin.
Oh, how I love the resoluteness
of that first person singular
followed by that stalwart indicative
of "be," without the uncertain i-n-g   5
of "becoming." Of course,
the name had been changed
somewhere between Angel Island° and the sea,
when my father the paperson°
in the late 1950s   10
obsessed with a bombshell blonde
transliterated "Mei Ling" to "Marilyn."
And nobody dared question
his initial impulse—for we all know
lust drove men to greatness,   15
not goodness, not decency.
And there I was, a wayward pink baby,
named after some tragic white woman
swollen with gin and Nembutal.°
My mother couldn't pronounce the "r."   20

8. **Angel Island:** Island in San Francisco Bay and site of the immigration station that processed approximately one million Asian immigrants between 1910 and 1940.
9. **paperson:** A "paper son" is a term used for young Chinese males entering the United States who claimed to be sons of U.S. citizens but were, in fact, sons on paper only.
19. **Nembutal:** A short-acting barbiturate (Pentobarbital) prescribed as a sedative but also used as an intoxicant.

She dubbed me "Numba one female offshoot"
for brevity: henceforth, she will live and die
in sublime ignorance, flanked
by loving children and the "kitchen deity."
While my father dithers,   25
a tomcat in Hong Kong trash—
a gambler, a petty thug,
who bought a chain of chopsuey joints
in Piss River, Oregon,
with bootlegged Gucci cash.   30
Nobody dared question his integrity given
his nice, devout daughters
and his bright, industrious sons
as if filial piety were the standard
by which all earthly men were measured.   35

Oh, how trustworthy our daughters,
how thrifty our sons!
How we've managed to fool the experts
in education, statistics and demography—
We're not very creative but not adverse to rote-learning.   40
Indeed, they can *use* us.
But the "Model Minority" is a tease.
We know you are watching now,
so we refuse to give you any!
Oh, bamboo shoots, bamboo shoots!   45
The further west we go, we'll hit east;
the deeper down we dig, we'll find China.
History has turned its stomach
on a black polluted beach—
where life doesn't hinge   50
on that red, red wheelbarrow,°
but whether or not our new lover
in the final episode of "Santa Barbara"°
will lean over a scented candle
and call us a "bitch."   55
Oh God, where have we gone wrong?
We have no inner resources!

Then, one redolent spring morning
the Great Patriarch Chin

51. red wheelbarrow: See the poem by William Carlos Williams on page 116.
53. "Santa Barbara": American television soap opera (1984–1993) that focused
on the lives of the wealthy Capwell family of Santa Barbara, California.

peered down from his kiosk in heaven   60
and saw that his descendants were ugly.
One had a squarish head and a nose without a bridge.
Another's profile—long and knobbed as a gourd.
A third, the sad, brutish one
may never, never marry.   65
And I, his least favorite—
"not quite boiled, not quite cooked,"
a plump pomfret° simmering in my juices—
too listless to fight for my people's destiny.
"To kill without resistance is not slaughter"   70
says the proverb. So, I wait for imminent death.
The fact that this death is also metaphorical
is testament to my lethargy.

So here lies Marilyn Mei Ling Chin,
married once, twice to so-and-so, a Lee and a Wong,   75
granddaughter of Jack "the patriarch"
and the brooding Suilin Fong,
daughter of the virtuous Yuet Kuen Wong
and G. G. Chin the infamous,
sister of a dozen, cousin of a million,   80
survived by everybody and forgotten by all.
She was neither black nor white,
neither cherished nor vanquished,
just another squatter in her own bamboo grove
minding her poetry—   85
when one day heaven was unmerciful,
and a chasm opened where she stood.
Like the jowls of a mighty white whale,°
or the jaws of a metaphysical Godzilla,°
it swallowed her whole.   90
She did not flinch nor writhe,
nor fret about the afterlife,
but stayed! Solid as wood, happily
a little gnawed, tattered, mesmerized
by all that was lavished upon her   95
and all that was taken away!

[1994]

68. **pomfret:** Type of fish served as a popular dish in South Asia.
88. **mighty white whale:** The whale in Herman Melville's 1851 novel, *Moby-Dick*.
89. **Godzilla:** A monster that appeared first in Ishirō Honda's 1954 film *Godzilla* and became a pop-culture icon in twenty-eight additional films.

KIMIKO HAHN   [b. 1955]

Mother's Mother

. . . There is no mother tongue.
—Elaine Showalter

The mother draws the shade down halfway
so the sunlight does not blind the pages
and she reads the story, *mukashi mukashi aruhi,*°
which is the way every story begins
whether about a boy riding a tortoise beneath the sea   5
or a girl born from a bamboo stalk.
Her daughter does not speak Japanese
though she can write her name in the *kana*°
that resembles tv antennae

キ ミ コ °

and she knows not everyone speaks the same language: 10
see you, ciao, adios, sayonara. She knows
her mother knows more than one way to say things
and Japanese, which is also how she *looks,*
is the language her mother was taught,
like the island of Japan,   15
almost as far from this little house on the island of Maui.

The chickens are so loud grandma.
Ursuai ne.°
So dusty.
Kitanai°   20
So—

She wants to learn every word her grandma knows.
She wants to be like her grandma
who she sees her mother loves and does not want to leave.

---

3. *mukashi mukashi aruhi:* Once upon a time.
8. *kana:* A general term for the syllabic Japanese scripts *hiragana* and *katakana,*
which were adapted from the logographic characters of Chinese origin known in
Japan as *Kanji* and are easier to master.
9. キ ミ コ: Ki - mi - ko.
18. *Ursuai ne:* Annoying, isn't it?
20. *Kitanai:* Dirty, filthy.

She wants to stay with her grandma also   25
and knows from her mother's shoulders they will not see her again.

If there is no mother tongue for women
there is for immigrant children
who play on the black volcanic beaches,
on the sharp coral reefs, in the salty rain, the plantation houses,   30
the fields of burning cane, the birds-of-paradise.
Who see the shark fins in the sunlight and linger on the blanket.

There is a mother's tongue and it is conveyed
by this mother to her daughters
who will carry the words at least in song   35
because when mother dies there will be no one else
unless there is an aunt or cousin
to correct the tense or word choice
with such affection and cause.

                    そう ト ね 。°

The same cause found in domestic arts and survival.   40
When the mother dies the daughter
or the daughter-in-law, or even the son,
becomes that figure in part
and the words the older woman knew
are the words this person will parent   45
despite lineage and its repressive roots.
Its often awful branches.
The root words and radicals the daughter memorizes.

                    永   シ °

So when I toss my hair from my eyes I feel
it's mother tossing her head and when I cough   50
it is her cough I hear.
And when I tell my child to say *mama*
it may be that I am speaking to myself
as much as I am speaking to the small mouth
a few inches from my face.   55

                                                        [1999]

39. そう ト ね .: That's just the way it is, isn't it?
48. 永   シ : It is endless (the process of learning Japanese characters).

LI-YOUNG LEE   [b. 1957]

Eating Alone

I've pulled the last of the year's young onions.
The garden is bare now. The ground is cold,
brown and old. What is left of the day flames
in the maples at the corner of my
eye. I turn, a cardinal vanishes.   5
By the cellar door, I wash the onions,
then drink from the icy metal spigot.

Once, years back, I walked beside my father
among the windfall pears. I can't recall
our words. We may have strolled in silence. But   10
I still see him bend that way—left hand braced
on knee, creaky—to lift and hold to my
eye a rotten pear. In it, a hornet
spun crazily, glazed in slow, glistening juice.

It was my father I saw this morning   15
waving to me from the trees. I almost
called to him, until I came close enough
to see the shovel, leaning where I had
left it, in the flickering, deep green shade.

White rice steaming, almost done. Sweet green peas   20
fried in onions. Shrimp braised in sesame
oil and garlic. And my own loneliness.
What more could I, a young man, want.

[1986]

LI-YOUNG LEE   [b. 1957]

The Gift

To pull the metal splinter from my palm
my father recited a story in a low voice.
I watched his lovely face and not the blade.
Before the story ended, he'd removed
the iron sliver I thought I'd die from.   5

I can't remember the tale,
but hear his voice still, a well

of dark water, a prayer.
And I recall his hands,
two measures of tenderness   10
he laid against my face,
the flames of discipline
he raised above my head.

Had you entered that afternoon
you would have thought you saw a man   15
planting something in a boy's palm,
a silver tear, a tiny flame.
Had you followed that boy
you would have arrived here,
where I bend over my wife's right hand.   20

Look how I shave her thumbnail down
so carefully she feels no pain.
Watch as I lift the splinter out.
I was seven when my father
took my hand like this,   25
and I did not hold that shard
between my fingers and think,
Metal that will bury me,
christen it Little Assassin,
Ore Going Deep for My Heart.   30
And I did not lift up my wound and cry,
Death visited here!
I did what a child does
when he's given something to keep.
I kissed my father.   35

[1986]

MARTÍN ESPADA   [b. 1957]

The Saint Vincent de Paul
Food Pantry Stomp

Madison, Wisconsin, 1980

Waiting for the carton of food
given with Christian suspicion
even to agency-certified charity cases

like me,
thin and brittle   5
as uncooked linguini,
anticipating the factory-damaged cans
of tomato soup, beets, three-bean salad
in a welfare cornucopia,
I spotted a squashed dollar bill   10
on the floor, and with
a Saint Vincent de Paul food pantry stomp
pinned it under my sneaker,
tied my laces meticulously,
and stuffed the bill in my sock   15
like a smuggler of diamonds,
all beneath the plaster statue wingspan
of Saint Vinnie,
who was unaware
of the dance   20
named in his honor
by a maraca shaker
in the salsa band
of the unemployed.

[1990]

WANG PING   [b. 1957]

Syntax

She walks to a table
She walk to table

She is walking to a table
She walk to table now

What difference does it make   5
What difference it make

In Nature, no completeness
No sentence really complete thought

Language, like woman,
Look best when free, undressed.   10

[1999]

BOB HICOK   [b. 1960]

In the loop

I heard from people after the shootings.° People
I knew well or barely or not at all. Largely
the same message: how horrible it was, how little
there was to say about how horrible it was.
People wrote, called, mostly e-mailed   5
to say, there's nothing to say. Eventually
I answered these messages: there's nothing
to say back except of course there's nothing
to say, thank you for your willingness to say it.
Because this was about nothing. A boy who felt   10
that he was nothing, who erased and entered
that erasure, and guns that are good for nothing,
and talk of guns that is good for nothing,
and spring that is good for flowers, and Jesus
for some, and scotch for others, and "and"   15
for me in this poem, "and" that is good
for sewing the minutes together, which otherwise
go about going away, bereft of us and us
of them, like a scarf left on a train
and nothing like a scarf left on a train,   20
like the train, empty of everything but a scarf,
and still it opens its doors at every stop,
because this is what a train does,
this is what a man does with his hand on a lever,
because otherwise why the lever, why the hand,   25
and then it was over, and then it had just begun.

[2010]

1. **the shootings:** On 16 April 2007, a senior English major at Virginia Tech University (where Bob Hicok teaches) shot and killed thirty-two people and wounded seventeen others.

ATSURO RILEY   [b. 1960]

Drill

Mama talks in this one.
Here's us, backing down our driveway's maze of red-dirt dog-legs, her
at the wheel (with a fresh-forged license), me turned around navigating,

the yard black-dark but flushed now (and now) and now with brake-lights, her Kool-tip flaring on every hard in-breath, river-reek and oil-scorch and marsh-gas mingling, our under-chassis (and rear axle, eyeteeth) chuttering due to roots and rain-ruts, our rust-crusting Rambler swerving and fishtailing and near-missing trees.

At the mailbox, gears knock, gnaw, grind, find Forward eventually: we're missile-heading straight (more or less) for the Low Country fairgrounds; here's us, late, loud, breaknecking her blue-ribbon hoard to the Fair.

Everything is home-made.

Not just our back-seat freight of gem-flame jelly-jars (slip-skin grape, beet, black- and blueberry, brunt-apple, seed-splacked fig) and payload of pressure-torqued pickle-jars (wrick-kinked banana-peppers, lethal hot-hat peppers, (green) tear-tomatoes, hairy okra, baby-dills in brine), but also the crazy-quilt safe-swaddling them, the gummed saliva-labels neat-naming them, my mama's name—hieroglyphical, grease-penciled, "KAY" (KAZUE) HUTTO—branding lids.

Do you reckon tomorrow they'll put my picture in the paper?
Will somebody do a write-up when I win?

[2010]

DENISE DUHAMEL   [b. 1961]

One Afternoon when Barbie Wanted to Join the Military

It was a crazy idea, she admits now,
but camouflage was one costume she still hadn't tried.
Barbie'd gone mod with go-go boots° during Vietnam.
Throughout Panama° she was busy playing with a Frisbee
the size of a Coke bottle cap. And while troops   5
were fighting in the Gulf,
she wore a gown inspired by Ivana Trump.°

---

3. go-go boots: Low-heeled, knee-length women's fashion boot, worn initially in the mid-sixties with miniskirts.
4. Panama: U.S. invasion of Panama on 20 December 1989 in order to remove military dictator Manuel Noriega.
7. Ivana Trump: A former Czechoslovakian Olympic skier and fashion model (b. 1949) who was married to magnate Donald Trump from 1977 to 1991.

When Mattel told her, hell no—she couldn't go,
Barbie borrowed GI Joe's° fatigues,
safety pinning his pants's big waist   10
to better fit her own.
She settled on his olive tank.
But Barbie thought it was boring.
"Why don't you try running over something small?"
coaxed GI Joe, who sat naked behind the leg   15
of a human's living room chair.
Barbie saw imaginary bunnies
hopping through the shag carpet.
"I can't," she said.
GI Joe suggested she gun down the enemy,   20
who was sneaking up behind her.
Barbie couldn't muster up the rage
for killing, even if it was only play.
Maybe if someone tried to take her parking space
or scratched her red Trans Am.   25
Maybe if someone had called her a derogatory name.
But what had this soldier from the other side done?
GI Joe, seeing their plan was a mistake,
asked her to return his clothes,
making Barbie promise not to tell anyone.   30
As she slipped back into her classic baby blue
one-piece swimsuit, she realized
this would be her second secret.
She couldn't tell about the time
she posed nude for *Hustler*.   35
A young photographer who lived in the house
dipped her legs in a full bottle of Johnson's Baby Oil,
then swabbed some more on her torso.
Barbie lounged on the red satin lining
of the kid's Sunday jacket. He dimmed   40
the lights and lit a candle
to create a glossy centerfold mood.
"Lick your lips," he kept saying,
forgetting Barbie didn't have a tongue.
She couldn't pout. She couldn't even bite   45
the maraschino cherry he dangled in front of her mouth.

9. GI Joe: An American soldier. *G. I.* is an abbreviation for *government issue*, used for equipment designed or provided for members of the U.S. armed forces. The poem refers to the G.I. Joe toy action figure.

Luckily there was no film in his sister's camera,
so the boy's pictures never came out.
Luckily GI Joe wasn't in the real Army
or he said he would risk being court-martialed—   50
he wasn't supposed to lend his uniform
to anyone, especially a girl.
Just then a human hand deposited Ken from the sky.
Somewhere along the way he'd lost his sandals.
"What have you two been up to?" he asked.   55
Barbie didn't have the kind of eyes that could shift away
so she lost herself in the memory of a joke
made by her favorite comedian Sandra Bernhard,°
who said she liked her dates to be androgynous
because if she was going to be with a man   60
she didn't want to have to face that fact.
Barbie was grateful for Ken's plastic flat feet
and plastic flat crotch. No military
would ever take him, even if there was a draft.
As GI Joe bullied Ken into a headlock,   65
Barbie told the boys to cut it out. She threatened
that if he kept it up, GI Joe would
never get that honorable discharge.

[1997]

58. Sandra Bernhard: American comedian and actress (b. 1955).

VIRGIL SUÁREZ   [b. 1962]

Tea Leaves, *Caracoles*, Coffee Beans

My mother, who in those Havana days believed in divination,
found her tea leaves at *El Volcán*, the Chinese market/apothecary,

brought the leaves in a precious silk paper bundle, unwrapped
them as if unwrapping her own skin, and then boiled water

to make my dying grandmother's tea; while my mother read   5
its leaves, I simply saw *leaves floating* in steaming water,

vapor kissed my skin, my nose became moist as a puppy's.
My mother did this because my grandmother, her mother-in-law,

believed in all things. Her appetite for knowledge was vast,
the one thing we all agreed she passed down to me, the skinny   10

kid sent to search for *caracoles*, these snail shells
that littered the underbrush of the empty lot next door.

My mother threw them on top of the table, cleaned them of dirt,
kept them in a mason jar and every morning before breakfast,

read them on top of the table, their way of falling, some up,   15
some down, their ridges, swirls of creamy lines, their broken

edges. . . . Everything she read looked bad, for my grandmother,
for us, for staying in our country, this island of suspended

disbelief. My mother read coffee beans too, with their wrinkled,
fleshy green and red skin. Orange-skinned beans she kept aside.   20

Orange meant death, and my mother didn't want to accept it.
I learned mostly of death from the way a sparrow fell

when I hit it in the chest with my slingshot and a lead pellet
I made by melting my toy soldiers. The sparrow's eyes

always hid behind droopy eyelids, which is how my grandmother   25
died, by closing her eyes to the world; truth became this fading

light, a tunnel, as everybody says, but instead of heaven
she went into the ground, to that one place that still nourishes

the tea leaves, *caracoles*, and the coffee beans, which, if I didn't
know better, I'd claim shone; those red-glowing beans   30

in starlight were the eyes of the dead looking out through
the darkness as those of us who believed in such things walked

through life with a lightness of feet, spirit, a vapor-aura
that could be read or sung.

[2005]

VIEVEE FRANCIS   [b. 1963]

1864, A Pocket Full of Rye

Confederate anticipating Colored Union troops

The trees are so full in this light—
green petticoats the balls will mow flat.

If I hide tonight, beneath a mound
of dirt I will still die, trampled

by boot, or impaled on the dark beak   5
of a rifle. I long for my field,

my plow, my good wife,
the farm and its smell.

It took two years to clear a small plot.
I took down the black gums   10

with swings I then thought mighty,
muled the stumps, fought the weed,

spread the mulch, succulent
as flowers. I miss my daughters—

hear that? a rumble—rage from the portholes—   15
and I would have it over soon and

done. I won't survive these musings.
Into the pitch   the caws,

the crows rising quick, as if suddenly freed
from some great pie, a mad and mocking flock.   20

                                                    [2006]

CATHERINE TUFARIELLO   [b. 1963]

This Child

This child, in whose improbable red hair
My mother soon will see a fair colleen°—   *girl (Anglo Irish)*
The dormant Shea genes slipped from quarantine—
While yours will find a beauty to compare
With her own mother Rose, a *gingy*° too,   *redhead*   5
Belongs, for this first night, to me and you.

Straight-jacketed, the sometime acrobat
Lies still now, punch-drunk from the din and glare
That hauled her howling, flailing, from her lair
Like a furious pink rabbit from a hat.   10
She has fine lungs (Italian, we suppose),
Whether an Irish or a Jewish Rose.

So furtively you'd think a watchful warden
Might interrupt, we pull the cap away—

Conspirators again, as on the day   15
We took our vows in the judge's tiny garden,
Hopeful and ignorant of what they'd mean,
Framed with magnolia's cream and tangled green.

She's really here, resistant as the world,
Marvelous as an unexpected joke,   20
A gift to be unwrapped. Shyly we stroke
Damp head, clown feet, tease starfish hands uncurled,
That copper down, startlingly bright and fine,
Closing the circuit between your hand and mine.

Meanwhile, neither of her world nor of this,   25
She gazes past us, toward the sunless void
She'd crossed to meet us like an asteroid—
The proof of an absurd hypothesis
We'd stubbornly defended all the same,
While all the time we hoarded this pure flame.   30

[2004]

A. VAN JORDAN   [b. 1965]

From

from (⇨) *prep.* 1. Starting at (a particular place or time): As in, John was *from* Chicago, but he played guitar straight *from* the Delta; he wore a blue suit *from* Robert Hall's; his hair smelled like coconut; his breath, like mint and bourbon; his hands felt like they were *from* slave times when he touched me—hungry, stealthy, trembling. 2. Out of: He pulled a knot of bills *from* his pocket, paid the man and we went upstairs. 3. Not near to or in contact with: He smoked the weed, but, surprisingly, he kept it *from* me. He said it would make me too self-conscious, and he wanted those feelings as far away *from* us as possible; he said a good part of my beauty was that I wasn't conscious of my beauty. Isn't that funny? So we drank Bloody Mothers (Hennessey and tomato juice), which was hard to keep *from* him—he always did like to drink. 4. Out of the control or authority of: I was released *from* my mama's house, *from* dreams of hands holding me down, *from* the threat of hands not pulling me up, *from* the man that knew me, but of whom I did not know; released *from* the dimming of twilight, *from* the brightness of morning; *from* the love I thought had to look like love; *from* the love I thought had to taste like love, *from* the love I thought I had to love like love. 5. Out of the totality of: I came *from* a family full of women; I came *from* a family full of believers; I came *from* a pack of witches—I'm just waiting to conjure my powers; I came *from* a legacy of lovers—I'm just waiting to seduce my seducer; I came *from* a pride of proud women, and we take good care of our young. 6. As being other or another than: He couldn't tell me *from* his mother; he couldn't tell me *from* his sister; he couldn't tell me *from* the last woman he had before me, and why should he—we're all the same woman. 7. With (some person, place, or thing) as the instrument, maker, or source: Here's a note *from* my mother, and you can take it as advice *from* me: A weak lover is more dangerous than a strong enemy; if you're going to love someone, make sure you know where they're coming *from*. 8. Because of: Becoming an alcoholic, learning to walk away, being a good speller, being good in bed, falling in love—they all come *from* practice. 9. Outside or beyond the possibility of: In the room, he kept me *from* leaving by keeping me curious; he kept me *from* drowning by holding my breath in his mouth; yes, he kept me *from* leaving till the next day when he said *Leave*. Then, he couldn't keep me *from* coming back.

[2004]

NATASHA TRETHEWEY   [b. 1966]

History Lesson

I am four in this photograph, standing
on a wide strip of Mississippi beach,
my hands on the flowered hips

of a bright bikini. My toes dig in,
curl around wet sand. The sun cuts   5
the rippling Gulf in flashes with each

tidal rush. Minnows dart at my feet
glinting like switchblades. I am alone
except for my grandmother, other side

of the camera, telling me how to pose.   10
It is 1970, two years after they opened
the rest of this beach to us,

forty years since the photograph
where she stood on a narrow plot
of sand marked *colored*, smiling,   15

her hands on the flowered hips
of a cotton meal-sack dress.

[2000]

SHERMAN ALEXIE   [b. 1966]

Postcards to Columbus

Beginning at the front door of the White House, travel west
for 500 years, pass through small towns and house fires, ignore
hitchhikers and stranded motorists, until you find yourself
back at the beginning of this journey, this history and country

folded over itself like a Mobius strip. Christopher Columbus   5
where have you been? Lost between Laramie and San Francisco
or in the reservation HUD house, building a better mousetrap?
Seymour saw you shooting free throws behind the Tribal School

in a thunderstorm. Didn't you know lightning strikes the earth
800 times a second? But, Columbus, how could you ever imagine   10
how often our lives change? *Electricity is lightning pretending
to be permanent* and when the Indian child pushes the paper clip

into the electrical outlet, it's applied science, insane economics
of supply and demand, the completion of a 20th century circuit.
Christopher Columbus, you are the most successful real estate agent   15
who ever lived, sold acres and acres of myth, a house built on stilts

above the river salmon travel by genetic memory. Beneath the burden
of 15,000 years my tribe celebrated this country's 200th birthday
by refusing to speak English and we'll honor the 500th anniversary
of your invasion, Columbus, by driving blindfolded cross-country   20

naming the first tree we destroy *America*. We'll make the first guardrail
we crash through our national symbol. Our flag will be a white sheet
stained with blood and piss. Columbus, can you hear me over white noise
of your television set? Can you hear ghosts of drums approaching?

[1993]

ANNA MARIA HONG

The Frog-Prince

"You're just like every toad I've ever met,"
said the Princess to her smooth companion.
"Except maybe more persistent," she thought
quietly. "I'm still not sure why a person

like me should bother with a totally slimy,   5
webfooted *thing*, when I'm so perfectly
content with my ball and myself." "I see,"
said the frog laconically. "Perfectly

content." Something about his tone—half-burp,
so sure—instantly enraged the Princess, who   10
then grabbed the frog's slick carapace and threw

it at the wall, which broke the beast into
his handsome, manly origins. "How warped,"
said the plussed Princess. "Now what do I do?"

[2013]

THOM SATTERLEE   [b. 1967]

Question 4:
Whether, Once Wounded by Love,
One Ever Heals Completely?

It's like picking at a scab, this love.
I'm a boy again with crusted skin
on my knee. It's best to let it be, but I shove
my nails underneath, and the pleasure-pain
first shocks, then throbs, then only feels uncovered.   5
So it is when I hear her singing in the yard.
I know I shouldn't look, but overpowered
I do—I turn—I gaze—quickly but hard.
Then I feel as if I've ripped off all my skin:
behind this desk I'm bones and a beating heart—   10

pitiful, raw, and promising once again
this time's the last. I beg the healing to start,
layer upon layer, until I'm so scabbed over
no one, not even I, can penetrate the cover.

[2006]

HONORÉE FANONNE JEFFERS   [b. 1967]

Unidentified Female Student, Former Slave (Talladega College, circa 1885)

You might have heard a story like this one well
but I'm telling this one to you now.
I was five when the soldiers came.

Master worked me twenty years longer.
How could I know? One day he left me alone   5
and an unwatched pot started to boil. By the time

he came back home I was cleaned of him and singing,
There's a man going round taking names.
Ready, set, and I was gone, walking. Could I see

beyond his yard? Did I have a thought to read or write   10
or count past God's creation? A barefooted
girl—and you remember, you woman who will take

your pen to write my life. This is what the truth was like:
Master's clouds followed me to the steps of this school.
Dear reader, when you think on this years after I have died   15

and I am dust, think on a great and awful morning
when I learned my freedom. Think that the skin on my
back was scared when I dared step out into the world,

when my Master stood trembling and weeping
on his front porch and he cursed me beyond knowing.   20

[2003]

ALLISON JOSEPH   [b. 1967]

On Being Told I Don't Speak
Like a Black Person

Emphasize the "h," you hignorant ass,
was what my mother was told
when colonial-minded teachers
slapped her open palm with a ruler
in that Jamaican schoolroom.   5
Trained in England, they tried
to force their pupils to speak
like Eliza Doolittle° after
her transformation, fancying themselves
British as Henry Higgins,°   10
despite dark, sun-ripened skin.
Mother never lost her accent,
though, the music of her voice
charming everyone, an infectious lilt
I can imitate, not duplicate.   15
No one in the States told her
to eliminate the accent,
my high school friends adoring
the way her voice would lift
when she called me to the phone,   20
A-ll-i-son, it's friend Cathy.
Why don't you sound like her?,
they'd ask. I didn't sound
like anyone or anything,
no grating New Yorker nasality,   25
no fastidious British mannerisms
like the ones my father affected
when he wanted to sell someone
something. And I didn't sound
like a Black American,   30
college acquaintances observed,
sure they knew what a black person

8–10. Eliza Doolittle ... Henry Higgins: Flower-girl with a strong Cockney (working-class) accent in George Bernard Shaw's play *Pygmalion* and the musical based on it, *My Fair Lady*. Henry Higgins, a linguistics professor, takes on the challenge of teaching her how to speak (and act and dress) like a proper British lady.

was supposed to sound like.
Was I supposed to sound lazy,
dropping syllables here, there,   35
not finishing words but
slurring the final letter so that
each sentence joined the next,
sliding past the listener?
Were certain words off limits,   40
too erudite, too scholarly
for someone with a natural tan?
I asked what they meant,
and they stuttered, blushed,
said you know, Black English,   45
applying what they'd learned
from that semester's text.
Does everyone in your family
speak alike?, I'd question,
and they'd say don't take this the   50
wrong way, nothing personal.

Now I realize there's nothing
more personal than speech,
that I don't have to defend
how I speak, how any person,   55
black, white, chooses to speak.
Let us speak. Let us talk
with the sounds of our mothers
and fathers still reverberating
in our minds, wherever our mothers   60
or fathers come from:
Arkansas, Belize, Alabama,
Brazil, Aruba, Arizona.
Let us simply speak
to one another,   65
listen and prize the inflections,
differences, never assuming
how any person will sound
until her mouth opens,
until his mouth opens,   70
greetings familiar
in any language.

[1999]

A. E. STALLINGS   [b. 1968]

Olives

Sometimes a craving comes for salt, not sweet,
For fruits that you can eat
Only if pickled in a vat of tears—
A rich and dark and indehiscent° meat
Clinging tightly to the pit—on spears   5

Of toothpicks maybe, drowned beneath a tide
Of vodka and vermouth,
Rocking at the bottom of a wide,
Shallow, long-stemmed glass, and gentrified,
Or rustic, on a plate cracked like a tooth,   10

A miscellany of the humble hues
Eponymously° drab—
Brown greens and purple browns, the blacks and blues
That chart the slow chromatics of a bruise—
Washed down with swigs of barrel wine that stab   15

The palate with pine-sharpness. They recall
The harvest and its toil,
The nets spread under silver trees that foil
The blue glass of the heavens in the fall—
Daylight packed in treasuries of oil,   20

Paradigmatic° summers that decline
Like singular archaic nouns, the troops
Of hours in retreat. These fruits are mine—
Small bitter drupes°
Full of the golden past and cured in brine.   25

[2012]

---

4. indehiscent: Not splitting open at maturity to discharge seeds or spores.
12. Eponymously: Giving its name to something.
21. Paradigmatic: Exemplary, typical, model.
24. drupes: Fruits consisting of an outer skin, a pulpy middle layer, and hard and woody inner shell enclosing a single seed.

KEVIN YOUNG   [b. 1970]

Song of Smoke

To watch you walk
cross the room in your black

corduroys is to see
civilization start—

the *wish-*   5
whish-whisk

of your strut is flint
striking rock—the spark

of a length of cord
rubbed till   10

smoke starts—you stir
me like coal

and for days smoulder.
I am no more

a Boy Scout and, besides,   15
could never

put you out—you
keep me on

all day like an iron, out
of habit—   20

you threaten, brick-
house, to burn

all this down. You leave me
only a chimney.

[2003]

TERRANCE HAYES   [b. 1971]

Talk

like a nigger now, my white friend, M, said
after my M.L.K.° and Ronald Reagan impersonations,
the two of us alone and shirtless in the locker room,

and if you're thinking my knuckles knocked
a few times against his jaw or my fingers knotted   5
at his throat, you're wrong because I pretended

I didn't hear him, and when he didn't ask it again,
we slipped into our middle school uniforms
since it was November, the beginning

of basketball season, and jogged out   10
onto the court to play together
in that vision all Americans wish for

their children, and the point is we slipped
into our uniform harmony, and spit out *Go Team!*,
our hands stacked on and beneath the hands   15

of our teammates and that was as close
as I have come to passing for one
of the members of The Dream, my white friend

thinking I was so far from that word
that he could say it to me, which I guess   20
he could since I didn't let him taste the salt

and iron in the blood, I didn't teach him
what it's like to squint through a black eye,
and if I had I wonder if he would have grown

up to be the kind of white man who believes   25
all blacks are thugs or if he would have learned
to bite his tongue or let his belly be filled

by shame, but more importantly, would I be
the kind of black man who believes silence
is worth more than talk or that it can be   30

---

2. M.L.K.: Martin Luther King.

a kind of grace, though I'm not sure
that's the kind of black man I've become,
and in any case, M, wherever you are,

I'd just like to say I heard it, but let it go
because I was afraid to lose our friendship   35
or afraid we'd lose the game—which we did anyway.

[2006]

RANDALL MANN   [b. 1972]

The Heron

A pond the color of Oriental teas.
A heron refusing to look anywhere but east.

Mangroves° flecked with a fire,
deep-set birches rife

with the wait for night. In stone,   5
the heron stares: the stoic tones

of the sky a storied procession of palms;
their red-tipped fronds,° overhanging lamps.

Water-bird, it has been centuries since I felt
anything for you. You have been left: 10

look around. Why does the owl
rest on a goddess's shoulder° while you wade so low?

[2004]

3. mangroves: Tropical medium-height trees or shrubs that grow in marshes or
tidal shores.
8. fronds: Large compound leaves, as found on some palm trees.
12. goddess's shoulder: Athena, the Greek goddess of wisdom, is frequently
depicted with an owl perched on her head or shoulder.

ERIKA MEITNER   [b. 1975]

North Country Canzone°

Here in the Adirondacks the last saffron and orange leaves
shade everything in a strange golden light. My mother
writes *be careful of ticks* — to her, any form of nature leaves
open the possibility for disease and alarm — but these leaves
are an innocuous visitation, relics lashed to boughs gone   5
nearly bare. Two weeks ago I packed the car and left
D.C. the way an explorer in a booby-trapped cave flees
when he hears a specific crack or rolling pebble. The deer
are docile and unflappable here, flicking up their snowy deer
tails when they bend their necks to eat around fallen leaves.   10
Snowy is a cliché adjective, I know, but I'm pregnant,
the fuzziness and memory-lapse a side effect of this baby,

along with the loose joints and breathlessness of pregnancy.
Even the slowest stroll to the old airplane hangar leaves
me winded. My lungs have less room, claims *The Pregnancy*   15
Book, to expand, so my body is protesting the baby
by gasping. Aren't all our bodies protesting? My grandmother
turned ninety-four this week, and her left leg is pregnant
with a clot, blocking the circulation. She said that if the baby
kicks in the fourth month, it will be a boy. Her leg will be gone   20
by next week, amputated. When all the color is gone,
how will it look here? I sit quietly, but I can't feel the baby
moving yet. Without the sun, the leaves are as brown as the deer;
soon the trees will be completely bare. I write a letter that starts, *Dear*
husband, and never send it: *last night I dreamed of white-tailed deer,*   25
and a trail of blood. I was a failed truck-stop waitress; you left me pregnant
with untranslatable emotion. My grandmother's terms of endearment
for me when she calls are *mein shayna maidel*° or *bubbeleh.*° The deer
here have *coyach*, the Yiddish word for strength; when they leave
the woods hurriedly, the ground quakes with their heavy deer   30
bounding, which seems incongruous with their gracefulness. Dear
missing left leg. Dear future child. Your great-grandmother
insisted on the phone that if I looked big at four months, I'd be mother
to a boy. She was high and slurred on hospital Oxycontin.° The dear

---

Canzone: See Glossary, page 395.
28. *mein shayna maidel:* My pretty, or dear, or good, girl (Yiddish); *bubbeleh:* A
term of endearment (dear, darling, honey).
34. Oxycontin: Oxycodone, a narcotic pain reliever used to treat moderate to
severe pain.

price of outliving everyone, her silent litany of what's gone   35
too long to mention, only recited when she weeps over candles on

Shabbos° with her eyes covered. I have two hearts, and the second one
beats faster. My anxious dreams. Dr. Sears° explains REM,° hormones,
   says *hear*
your dreams—really *listen* and rewrite them with a happy ending. On
my daily walk here I'm often struck with irrational panic—a fear that
   I've gone   40
too far, won't have the *coyach* to come back. My mother says this
   pregnancy
gives Baba° strength. I traveled here via Aunt Mary's in Livingston
to see my grandmother before her operation. Aunt Mary drives us in her
   Lincoln
to Daughters of Israel while Mandy Patinkin° croons *Hey, Tsigelekh.*° Wet
   leaves
carpet the Jersey roads in rust; tentlike sukkahs° adorned with fruit and
   leaves   45
and lights grace each Jewish yard of West Orange. They'll be gone
in a week. They have a sukkah at the rehab center, but my grandmother
refuses to take meals there, says the harvest festival is only for men. My
   grandmother
is stubborn. She insists on eating in the dining room with her other
table-ladies even though we offer to take her out. Her *coyach* is gone,   50
she says. The pink and beige room seem filled with every Jewish
   grandmother
in the tri-state area. Baba immediately sends her diabetic macaroni back;
   another
grandmother taps me on the shoulder and hands me an album of her dear
grandchildren (*three in Canada—I never get to see them*). My grandmother
has successfully negotiated for waffles instead of herring. Each
   grandmother   55

37. Shabbos: Shabbat, the Sabbath, the seventh day of the Jewish week and the
Jewish day of rest.
38. Dr. Sears: William Penton Sears ("Dr. Bill," b. 1939), American pediatrician
and author or coauthor of more than thirty parenting books; **REM:** Normal stage
of sleep characterized by rapid (and random) movement of the eyes and associated with vivid dreams.
42. Baba: Grandmother.
44. Mandy Patinkin: Mandel Bruce Patinkin (b. 1952), American actor and vocal-
ist; *Hey, Tsigelekh:* "Hey, little goats," Yiddish song about a shepherd's longing for
his lost love, recorded by Mandy Patinkin.
45. sukkahs: Temporary huts, or booths, constructed for use during the week-
long Jewish festival of Sukkot.

dutifully wears a long white napkin that slips over the head, like a baby's
bib. The ladies at the table that can still hear ask me about my pregnancy.
We try to get Baba to eat more, so Aunt Mary tells a long story about my
    mother
and the hot summer waffles on the boardwalk in Far Rockaway before
    we leave
Baba to go for dinner. Here, the oaks and beech cling willfully to their
    last leaves.   60

O mother of leaves
and sweetness, my grandmother
is not nearly gone.
She is rising like a deer
from the meadow. She is dancing with a baby   65
                      in her arms.

                                [2010]

ARACELIS GIRMAY   [b. 1977]

Snail, or, To a House

I can not say what was on the bed the day we left
& if the blinds were drawn over the windows.
How does one hold
a whole live house
in a brain?   5

But there were bowls, & glass,
cereals in the pantry, cloves, folded
clothes.

Back then
the snails gathered at the water hose, their feelers   10
prodding alien in the dusky afternoon, summer of wasps
with their mud cities
hanging down.

The pots caught drops & drops of rain
while gardens grew for morning, out in back.   15

Our house, that house & nation of beams
all crossed with wooden light above the people,
I loved you.

& it is only love to see you
obese in this new city   20
following me on the train & at the job.

Forgive me then, I did not even look twice,
or good & hard like in a mirror.
I could not even know
that we were leaving.   25

The story goes: it was the best thing
to leave you & the king,
to have start-
        ed
    all over with   30
only those things

we carried on
    our backs.

[2007]

How to Write about a Poem — and Why

WHY WRITE ABOUT A POEM?

When we are interested in and excited about a particular movie or sports event or piece of music, we usually want to share our enthusiasm with someone else. We often start by talking to someone, texting or tweeting friends, or posting on Facebook about the parts we liked, how we reacted, what we experienced or realized that was important to us. That should be true of poetry as well: If we like a poem, if we are enthusiastic about a poem, if we were touched or moved by a poem, we will want to share that with someone else who likes poetry, comparing our reactions and discussing lines or phrases or images that meaningfully struck us.

Writing about a poem is simply an extension of thinking and talking about it. Writing can be regarded as transforming and transferring such thinking and talking to a piece of paper or an electronic screen. That transfer, however, offers the following advantages over talking:

• The kind of writing we mean — developing thoughts more fully than when text messaging, and thoughtfully revising them — helps us pin down our ideas and responses. Almost all serious writers have said something like author Joan Didion who is quoted as saying, "I don't know what I think until I write it down." When we write, we usually try harder to find exactly the right words and phrases to express our precise meaning than when we talk. Often we don't figure out exactly what we really think and how to articulate it until we make the effort to write it out.

• This kind of writing enables us to keep a record of our thoughts and responses. We can go back to them, remind ourselves what we thought and felt earlier, and add to or refine what we wrote.

• This kind of writing allows us to participate in an ongoing conversation about poetry and literature. Some of this conversation is personal, some public; it covers a seemingly endless range of subjects. Authors read other authors and respond to them. Scholars and critics publish their ideas and others respond to what they've said. When we write about literature, we are taking part in this continuing conversation, adding our own two cents' worth to the table talk.

• This kind of writing actually leads to a more personally meaningful experience of the work. We often assume we know what we think and feel, but when we put our responses into words, we come to new realizations, realizations that can enlarge our own humanity and lead us to a more complex understanding of others and the worlds they live in.

WHAT TO WRITE ABOUT A POEM

When you are deciding what to write about, you might start in the "How to Read a Poem—and Why" section at the beginning of this book (pp. 1–5). It suggests that a good way to approach poetry is by asking the question, "What does poetry do?" Writing about poetry can start at the same place. We can write about what a particular poem does: about the subject the poem gives voice to; the way it tells a story; the way it describes; the way it captures memories; the way it expresses, embodies, or kindles emotions; and the way it uses language. We can write about the images a poem uses, the sounds it captures or creates, its rhythms, its form, and its use of similes or metaphors or other figures of speech. The glossary at the back of the book clarifies these aspects of poetry and points toward many other features to watch for and write about. We can write about the connections we find in and through poetry, about what a poem says to us, or about what in a poem moves, excites, appeals to, puzzles, or enrages us.

When deciding on a topic, look first for a poem you connect with and find yourself thinking about, one that grabs you in some way. You may have to read a dozen or more before you come upon one that hits you. That's normal. Usually you will write best when you deal with a work you enjoy. Once you've found a poem you think you could like writing about, reread it several times, with your intellect, imagination, and feelings fully engaged. Notice the way the poet uses the various elements of poetry; pay attention to every image, figure of speech, sentence, and line, even to every word.

It helps if you spread your rereadings over at least a week. So get started way before your deadline! Coming back to a poem every day can lead you to see things that reading it several times in one sitting can not. Sometimes read the poem aloud, sometimes—if you can arrange it— listen to someone else read it. Each time you read the poem, focus on a different aspect: one time on the speaker, another on images, another on line breaks, another on rhythm, and so on.

Then begin to think about things you feel confident you could write about. Poetry often involves transforming an experience into words: A paper could focus on the experience explored in a poem and why the poet might have wanted to preserve it. Or a paper could examine the kind of techniques the poet uses. For this kind of paper, you could pay attention to what stands out, what seems big and important to the way the poem is handled, or you could focus on little things that might escape initial notice but turn out to be very significant in shaping the poem's effect. The way a poem handles the beginning or the ending or descriptive details or imaginative comparisons or lines or dashes can become the entire focus of a literary analysis paper.

For another kind of paper, a thematic analysis, you could focus on ideas that are explored in the poem. Be sure to pick ones that appeal to or challenge you enough that you can discuss them in detail, and be sure to support the points you make with specific examples and quotations from the poem. A paper could also combine literary analysis with the ideas in a poem, looking at how what is stated or depicted is affected by the way the poem is written. ("Theme and technique in . . ." can be an especially safe, solid topic for a short paper.) If you are particularly interested in society and culture, you could write a paper on how a poem speaks to or is influenced by its social or cultural context.

Ask and keep asking questions: What is the poem revealing? Why is this or that handled the way it is? What is the effect or impact of the poet's use of particular poetic elements? What if it were written differently? Why does the poem suddenly shift in tone? What role does the title play? Why did the poet work with unsettling material? Why is the poem organized the way it is? How else might the poem have ended and what would be different if it had?

HOW TO WRITE ABOUT A POEM

Writing doesn't start when we begin typing words into our computers. Writing is a process. It begins with reading and reacting with our minds, emotions, and imaginations—what we've already been discussing as we considered what to write about. The process then moves on to marking up the text, taking notes, and perhaps outlining possible points. It continues with drafting, revising, and checking. The pages ahead move through this process by looking at three kinds of writing about poetry: writing in the margins, writing in response to a poem, and writing a short paper about a poem.

1. Writing in the Margins

The first and most fundamental way to write about a poem is something many people do as part of their reading process: They mark up the text.

They underline or highlight favorite lines, and they jot ideas, questions, exclamation points, stars, and other symbols in the margins. This helps them remember and relocate the parts they may end up working with and so can become a valuable early step when they start drafting a paper. (Of course you should only mark up a book if you own it; if you don't own the book, make a photocopy of the poem for this step.)

Writing in a book is one way of engaging with a work as an active reader: talking back to the work, agreeing with it, interrogating it, connecting with it, challenging it. Here are some suggestions for getting started with this kind of writing:

- *Underline or highlight key parts.* Underline sentences or phrases that you really like or that strike you as important. But don't underline or highlight *everything*—then nothing stands out. Circle particular words you find especially noteworthy.

- *Flag key lines in the poem.* Put a star, a question mark, or an exclamation point, especially during a first reading, next to lines or sections you might want to read again to understand them better or to think about them in light of what comes later.

- *Talk back to the poem.* Write comments in the margins as you move through a work (i.e., What does this mean? Important line! Tone shifts).

- *Talk to yourself about the poem.* Jot down thoughts that occur to you as you read—personal realizations or things that remind you of other works you've read, for example, or that connect with a movie or song you like or with something you learned in a biology, history, psychology, or religion course.

- *Jot notes about the poem.* Write out definitions and explanations of words and details you had to look up.

This form of "engaged reading," writing in a book, is an ancient and honored tradition. Reading the marginal notes (or *marginalia*) that people centuries ago, or very recently, wrote in their books can be interesting and valuable, letting us know a great deal about their tastes, values, and judgments.

To illustrate what we mean (not to prescribe how it should be done), here is some writing in the margins of Mary Oliver's poem "First Snow." It was written by Sunkyo Hong, a student responding to the assignment to "write a two- to three-page paper discussing how one of the following poems explores an author's experience with nature—James Wright's 'A Blessing' (p. 181), William Stafford's 'Traveling through the Dark' (p. 158), or Mary Oliver's 'First Snow' (p. 204)."

MARY OLIVER   [b. 1935]

First Snow

why is the first snow special?

The snow
began here
this morning and all day
continued, its white   *lots of alliteration*
rhetoric everywhere   *and assonance*   5
calling us back to *why, how,*
whence such beauty and *what*
the meaning; such
an oracular fever! flowing   *active verbs*
past windows, an energy it seemed   10
would never ebb, never settle   *ebb: flow back*
less than lovely! and only now,
deep into night,
it has finally ended.
The silence   15
is immense,   *how can silence be large?*
and the heavens still hold
a million candles; nowhere ◄—— *(they are there, but she*
the familiar things: *can't see them)*
stars, the moon,   20
the darkness we expect
and nightly turn from. Trees
glitter like castles   ❋ *lovely!*
of ribbons, the broad fields
smolder with light, a passing   25
creekbed lies
heaped with shining hills;
and though the questions   *Three long*
that have assailed us all day   *sentences*
remain—not a single   30
answer has been found—
walking out now
into the silence and the light
under the trees,
and through the fields,   35
feels like one.
     why/how does it feel
     like an answer?

[1983]

Annotations (left and right margins):

persuasive use of language → (white)

why? how? → (why) (whence) (what) (back)

what is the meaning? →

an inspired & authoritative statement, as from an oracle

metaphor — a million candles

simile — (glitter)

metaphor — (smolder)

metaphor — (heaped)

2. Writing in Response to a Poem

After reading a poem and writing in the margins, many readers find it helpful to write a brief response or reaction to the poem, and doing so can be a valuable step in the writing process. Often they keep such responses in a journal. Sometimes teachers assign journals as a way to encourage students to write out their responses to literary works.

Think of a journal, whether assigned or something you do on your own, as halfway between a diary and a course notebook. It's not intimate or confessional as diaries often are, nor is it as objective, remote, and impersonal as a notebook. In addition to being a good place to write responses and reactions, a journal is useful for storing information, like the titles of poems you like, lines you want to remember, and things you were drawn to or put off by. Keeping a journal can help you trace your own development and growth as a reader, in taste, judgment, and attitudes.

This kind of writing asks you to pause after reading to reflect on the reading experience and then put into words how it affected you intellectually, emotionally, imaginatively, or in some other way. Spend time thinking about how to express your reaction; then plunge in, being honest and genuine about what you say.

The following are some tips for effective response writing.

- *Don't put it off.* Jot down your notes and reactions soon after you've read the poem, while your thoughts and emotions are fresh. Later you can add your further reflections.
- *Be honest.* Express your genuine responses and opinions, not what you think you "ought" to write or what might impress others. Jot down details and examples that support your responses and opinions.
- *Make quotations apparent.* Include some quotations of favorite lines and passages to help you remember them and recall or find them. Be careful to quote accurately and to mark clearly what is quotation and what is summary or paraphrase.
- *Include line numbers and page numbers.* Check to be sure you include titles and line numbers and page numbers so you can find poems and passages easily. This too can save you valuable time later.

On the next page is the response Sunkyo wrote on "First Snow." Notice the places where he carries over ideas from his marginal notations and elaborates on or changes them.

Mary Oliver, "First Snow" (pp. 204–05)

The poem obviously is about snow, as indicated by the title and the first line "The snow." The speaker (who seems to be pretty much the same as the author) really likes the snow and portrays it beautifully and appealingly through her descriptions. The things that happen in the poem are simple and straightforward: It snows all day; it stops snowing at night; and the speaker and her friends walk out in the snow after it has stopped snowing and they somehow feel good or at peace about it. Aside from the action, the poem consists of the author's descriptions of the snow, of the snow-covered scene, and her being full of wonder at the beauty of what she has experienced, and at the way the beauty seems meaningful. Words to look up: rhetoric (line 5); oracular (9); ebb (11). Figures of speech to reflect on: "the heavens still hold / a million candles" (17–18); "Trees / glitter like castles / of ribbons" (22–24). Favorite lines: "walking out now / into the silence and the light / . . . / feels like one" (32–36).

3. Writing a Short Paper about a Poem

Response writing can be valuable in and of itself, and it can also be a valuable part of the writing process, as a step toward composing a short paper about a poem. Formal papers are generally longer than responses: While a response is often a single paragraph, a short paper will have several or many paragraphs and be two to five pages long. Response writing can summarize one's reaction to a poem and make scattered comments about the poem and the experience of reading it; a paper, on the other hand, needs to have a "thesis," or central claim, that it develops in an organized, carefully supported way. The following steps in the writing process cover additional issues you need to consider when you write a paper.

Limit Your Topic

After you've done the kind of attentive reading and thinking discussed above and decided on a subject, you need to consider whether the size of the topic is appropriate for the length of the assigned paper and the amount of time available for working on it. Too large a topic for the length (such as "Nature as a unifying theme in the poetry of Mary Oliver" for a five-page assignment) will prove frustrating and ineffective. Too small a topic ("Silence in Mary Oliver's 'First Snow'") can leave you without enough to say to fill the required pages. Taking on too large a topic happens more often than choosing one that is too small. To avoid trying to do too much, you may need to concentrate on one aspect of the initial subject or make just one point instead of covering several or concentrate on part of a poem instead of discussing all parts in equal detail. It's usually better to cover a limited topic in more depth than it is to cover a lot in a superficial way.

Make a Central Point or Claim

Once you've limited the topic, you should concentrate on the point or points you want to make about that topic. You need to do more than merely summarize or describe the poem—which is seldom interesting or valuable for you or your reader. Readers can read the poem for themselves: They can follow what it says and pick out its images. But what they can't know in any other way are *your* explanations, interpretations, observations, perceptions, and connections. That's what you need to get across, in as clear, inviting, and accessible a way as possible. Your challenge is to develop a central idea or make a claim that has insight, interest, and significance. Your job is not just to lay out your views but to show readers that your views are sound and convincing.

Include a Thesis

The central point you want to make should be stated as a thesis, a proposition put forward for consideration and placed, usually, at or near the end of the first paragraph. It's important to notice the difference between a topic and a thesis. A *topic* just names a subject area: for example, "Images of snow in Mary Oliver's 'First Snow.'" It states a fact. A *thesis* on the other hand adds a *comment* about the subject and turns it into something requiring persuasive support: for example, "The most significant aspect of 'First Snow' is the way the poem asserts that the season's first snow is not just beautiful but conveys meaning in a wonder-filled way." A thesis states an idea that readers could disagree with or reject and that needs to be developed and supported with explanations and evidence.

Start Paragraphs with Idea Sentences

The way you start the paragraphs in the body of a paper is very important. Just as the thesis of your paper must state an idea, not just a fact, so should the first sentence—or topic sentence—of each paragraph. The opening sentence of a paragraph is a mini-thesis: It should state briefly the point or idea to be developed in that paragraph. If a paragraph starts with a statement of fact, rather than with a statement of idea, the rest of the paragraph is likely to consist of summary and more factual statements and not explore an idea or develop an argument. Often the second sentence of the paragraph is used to expand on the point or idea stated briefly in the topic sentence, bringing out its significance and implications, and the rest of the paragraph must develop and support the point or idea. The final paragraph of Sunkyo's paper on "First Snow" (pp. 316–18) provides a good example of this strategy.

Illustrate and Explain

As you write paragraphs developing the points in your outline, you need to include two things: (1) details from the poem and (2) your explanations of the details. The two need to go together. Details by themselves do not prove anything. Your explanations are needed to indicate what is important about the details and to tie them in to the whole fabric you are weaving in the paper. Likewise, explanations without supporting details are not specific enough and do not anchor themselves to the work. The key to a successful paper lies in its development and illustration of its ideas: explaining ideas so readers understand them readily and supporting ideas with details so readers have confidence that the points are well grounded and worth considering.

Include Quotations

In any literary paper, some of the supporting evidence must be in the form of quotations from the literary work. Quotations connect your explanations and interpretations directly to the work(s) and show that they are firmly based. Be careful that the phrases or sentences as you quote them continue to convey what they mean *in their context*. The way words are selected for quotation must never distort the way they are used in the original text. Here are some tips on quoting poetry effectively:

- Avoid long quotations whenever possible. Often the best approach is to combine quotations with summary and to gracefully blend quoted extracts into your prose style. Notice how Sunkyo does this in his paper.

- Quotations can be shortened by the omission of words, phrases, or even sentences. Such omissions must be signaled by the use of ellipses (. . .). If you omit a complete line or more than one line, indicate this by a row of spaced periods as long as a line of the poem.

- When you quote fewer than four lines of poetry, blend the lines into your sentence, using a slash with a space before and after it to indicate line divisions, as in this example that Sunkyo used in his paper: "The snow/began here/this morning" (lines 1–3).

- If you quote four or more lines, type them as a block quotation with each line on a separate line, each indented an inch and a half or two inches from the left margin. The passage should look the same way it looks in the book, with identical indentation and spacing. See the example in Sunkyo's paper on page 317.

- Identify lines quoted or cited by supplying line numbers in parentheses. For the first reference, include the word "line" (not abbreviated); for later references, give the numbers alone. Page numbers for the poem will be included on the Works Cited page, if requested.

- A paragraph should not begin with a quotation. The paragraph needs an opening topic sentence, setting up the point you want to develop, stated in your own words.

- Don't automatically start a new paragraph after a quotation. Usually each quotation should be followed with an explanation or comment in your words on the point being illustrated, tying it in to the point the paragraph is developing.

Focus on Key Passages

When you write about a poem, you may be tempted to start at the poem's beginning and follow it through to the end. That sometimes works well, but it can lead to summarizing instead of examining and discussing the poem in detail. Therefore it's often preferable to organize the paper by topics or ideas—a series of techniques or a series of points about your central idea—especially if you're writing about a long poem. One way to be specific and detailed without lapsing into summary is to focus on *key passages*. As we listen to and read a poem, we try to take the whole work into consideration, to grasp its essence. In doing so, we usually find that a particular section—an image, a line, a sentence, a stanza, a metaphor—seems to shed light on all the other parts of the poem.

It was teacher-critic Benjamin De Mott who first called such sections "key passages." They are not something writers insert deliberately into a work, as clues to readers; they are simply parts of the work that appear particularly meaningful to an individual reader in relation to that reader's interpretation. So, instead of trying to discuss every line in a part, you can focus on a key passage in depth, or perhaps two or three key passages, and use it or them to represent, connect with, and illuminate what is occurring in the work as a whole.

Write with Readers in Mind

As you think about writing and as you write, you need to be aware of the audience you are addressing. When you write a paper for a literature course, address the same group you talk to in class. Visualize your fellow students as well as your teacher as readers. Assume that your audience has read the poem you are writing about. Therefore, you don't need to retell or summarize the work. Take for granted that your audience knows what the poem is about generally, but assume that your readers could benefit from your help in understanding the work more fully or in seeing the implications you saw. Think of your paper as part of the continuing conversation, helping interested readers by talking clearly about things they would like to think more about.

Revise Thoroughly

Once you finish a draft of the paper, the next steps are to revise and then proofread it. Notice that these are separate steps. Revising doesn't mean correcting spelling and grammar errors: That's proofreading, the final step. Revising comes first. The word *revision* derives from the Latin words for *look* and *again*: Revising means examining closely what you've written, thinking it through again, and trying to find ways to improve its content, organization, and expression. Revision is crucial to effective writing: Making your paper the strongest possible usually requires several drafts. You may be able to write one draft and get a passing grade, but the writing simply won't be as thoughtful and engaging as it would be if you revised. And revision is one of the best ways to learn even more about writing.

It's hard to get a fresh look right after you finish writing. You are usually still too close to it to come up with different ways to explain, arrange, and express. Revision often works best if you can lay your paper aside for a day or two or even longer before thinking about changes. It also may help to have someone else read the paper. But make sure it is someone who knows enough about poetry and writing to check that your ideas and organization are clear and adequately supported and who will be straightforward with you.

Proofread Carefully

After revising your paper, proofread and edit it carefully to check for errors in spelling and grammar, for inconsistencies, and for any awkward expressions. If you write your paper on a computer, use its programs to check spelling and grammar. There's no excuse for simple typos when spending a few minutes on spell-checking would catch them.

A computer check, of course, doesn't free you from the need to read closely as well. The computer can tell you that it doesn't recognize *thier* and ask if you intended to write *their;* but it won't notice if you wrote *their* when you should have used *there*. Again, distance (coming back after a couple of days) can be helpful because you may have become so familiar with your essay that it is hard to see what should be different. Some writers proofread by starting at the end and reading backward as a way of looking at the words instead of getting caught up in the meaning. Again, having someone else read your essay is often useful—but only if she or he is an attentive reader and good with spelling and grammar.

Even if you revise and proofread initially on a computer screen, we recommend at least one revision (and the final proofreading and editing) be done from a hard copy. It is helpful to see the sentences and paragraphs the way they will look on paper in the finished product. To save paper, use the back of scrap paper.

Format Correctly

Papers on literature usually follow the guidelines of the Modern Language Association (MLA). In MLA style, papers should be typed (word processed), double-spaced throughout, with one-inch margins all around, and printed in an easily readable 12-point font (such as Times New Roman) on 8½″ × 11″ white paper. Use a paper clip to hold pages together, unless your instructor asks that they be stapled. Use Tab to indent the first line of each paragraph one-half inch.

MLA style does not require a title page. Instead, at the top of the first page, against the left margin, on separate double-spaced lines, place your name, your instructor's name, the course number, and the date. Then, double-space and center your title. See the first page of Sunkyo's paper as an example. (If your instructor requires a title page, ask for formatting guidelines.) Place page numbers (in arabic numerals) preceded by your last name in the upper right-hand corner of each page, one-half inch below the top edge (see Sunkyo's paper).

SAMPLE SHORT PAPER

Sunkyo Hong
Professor Ridl
English 248
15 May 2012

Experiencing "First Snow"

I had seen snow before coming to college in Michigan, but never like this. I woke up one December morning to find yesterday's green lawns a continuous smooth, white expanse. The indifferent ground of the day before now noticed my shoe soles and kept their shape as I took a few experimental steps outside the doorway. Another time, as I walked through the pine grove in the center of campus during a large-flaked snowfall, I could not see a single campus building or a single person. I felt that I had somehow stepped into a gentle winter world without time. It was calming how the falling of a million flaky water-drops could transform a landscape and absorb my attention.

Mary Oliver's poem "First Snow" recalls a similar experience. In the poem, Oliver describes the snowfall, from the morning, when it began, to the night, when it ended. Her chronological tracing of the event allows us to experience the same wonder and admiration she feels in watching the snow and its effects.

The poem begins with the author describing how the snow began: "The snow/began here/this morning" (lines 1-3). With this opening, the author gives the reader a natural starting place. The opening is similar to the common story opening, that is, "Once upon a time in such and such a place."

The poem continues with Oliver describing how the snow fell throughout the day and what it was like. The snow falling had "white/ rhetoric everywhere" (4-5). Rhetoric is persuasive speaking or writing. The next lines say what the snow's "white rhetoric" was doing: "calling us back to *why, how,/whence* such beauty and *what/*the meaning" (6-8). The rhetoric was persuading the author to wonder, in the literal sense, about the beauty and meaning of the snow and wonder at it in the sense of amazement also. The questions of *"why, how, / whence* such beauty" and *"what /* the meaning" indicate that the author is dumbfounded. Her sense of amazement continues into the next line, where she exclaims "such / an oracular fever!" (8-9). *Oracular* means pertaining to an oracle, thus a prophetic utterance, often enigmatic or mysterious. Since there is no indication of illness in the poem, *fever* describes how the snow is moving and the excitement the author is feeling. Thus, the "oracular fever" is both the swirling flurry of snow the author sees and the inspired feeling of awe and mystery she gets from watching it. We share her marvel as we witness the snow-white energy "[flow] / past [the] windows" (9-10) and show no sign of waning or becoming "less than lovely" (12).

Until now, the poem has been about how the snow has fallen throughout the day, and it has been told in the past tense. For the rest of the poem, Oliver focuses on the present, describing how the scene is now blanketed by snow. By line 13 it is night, and the snow has stopped falling. The author can feel the silence because it is "immense" (15-16). Although it is night, the sky still brims with light as if lit by "a million candles" (18). At first, it seems like the million candles are stars, but lines 18-22 show that the skyscape has been transformed so much because of the snow that the stars are not visible:

> nowhere
>
> the familiar things:
> stars, the moon,
> the darkness we expect
> and nightly turn from.

The heavens are bright, with "broad fields / smolder[ing] with light" (24-25) and "a passing / creekbed . . . / heaped with shining hills" (25-27). There is "light / under the trees" (33-34). The "broad fields" and "shining hills" indicate that the landscape has also changed. In this burning landscape, trees glitter with frost "like castles / of ribbons" (22-24), reminding us of some romantic fantasyland.

The final section of the poem shifts from a description of the snow-covered scene to participation in it. Oliver and her companions — let us imagine we are they — walk out into the snow and feel that an answer has been found. "[T]he questions / that have assailed us all day / remain" (28-30) — "*why, how, / whence* such beauty and *what* / the mean-ing" (6-8) — and "not a single / answer has been found" (30-31). We had been wondering at the sight all day. Now, trooping "into the silence and the light / under the trees, / and through the fields" (33-35) — in short, immersing ourselves in the snow that made us wonder — "feels like [an answer]" (36). This is because walking out into the snow places us in the wonder itself, and that experience somehow satisfies our wonder without diminishing it. Thus, the answer is the experience.

"First Snow" presents an impressionistic account of a snowfall. The poem unfolds chronologically, and this ordering enables us to fol-low Oliver's experience vicariously with ease. The author witnesses the seemingly infinite falling of the snow throughout the day, observes the transformed landscape after the snow has stopped falling, and feels the immense silence when walking out into the snow. We share her wonder at each step, and at the end of the poem we share the answer of stepping out into the snow with our imaginations. This experiential answer is what makes every snowfall a "first snow."

Biographical Notes on the Authors
[Arranged Alphabetically]

This section offers brief biographical sketches of the 191 known authors of the poems included in this book. For fuller biographical information, the most convenient print sources are the *Dictionary of Literary Biography* (Detroit: Gale, 1978–), currently at 360 volumes; and *Contemporary Authors*, also published by Gale (original series, 248 volumes; new revised series, currently 312 volumes).

Biographical information for many authors is also found on the Internet. The Academy of American Poets Web site is valuable and convenient; we are indebted to it for many of the entries. The Modern American Poetry Web site also is excellent and very convenient. The Bedford/St. Martin's LitLinks site is another useful resource. Sites for many individual authors are available as well, as are personal home pages for some contemporary poets and sites maintained by scholars or fans of writers old and new.

Poets often work with and are influenced by each other. Whenever poets represented in this anthology appear within a biographical entry, their names are in small capitals as a reminder that their biographical notes will shed further light on the author at hand.

Ai (1947–2010), who described herself as "one-half Japanese, one-eighth Choctaw, one-fourth black, and one-sixteenth Irish," was born Florence Anthony in Albany, Texas, and grew up in Tucson, Arizona. She legally changed her name to "Ai," which means "love" in Japanese. She received a B.A. in Japanese from the University of Arizona and an M.F.A. from the University of California at Irvine. She was the author of nine volumes of poetry, among them *Vice* (1999), which won the National Book Award for Poetry. Her last book was *No Surrender* (2010). She taught at Wayne State University, George Mason University, the University of Kentucky, and Oklahoma State University.

Sherman Alexie (b. 1966), of Spokane/ Coeur d'Alene Indian descent, was born on the Spokane Indian Reservation in Wellpinit, Washington. He earned his B.A. from Washington State University in Pullman. He has published ten books of poetry, ten novels and collections of short fiction, including *The Lone Ranger and Tonto Fistfight in Heaven* (1993), and two screenplays, *Smoke Signals* (1998) and *The Business of Fancydancing* (2002). His most recent books are a collection of poems, *Face* (2009); a novel, *Flight* (2007); a novel for young adults, *The Absolutely True Diary of a Part-Time Indian* (2007), winner of many awards including the 2007 National Book Award for Young People's Literature; and a collection of stories, *Blasphemy: New and Selected Stories* (2012). In 2010 he was honored with the Native Writers' Circle of the Americas Lifetime Achievement Award.

Agha Shahid Ali (1949–2001) was born in New Delhi and grew up Muslim in Kashmir. He was educated at the University of Kashmir, Srinagar, and at the University of Delhi. He earned a Ph.D. from Pennsylvania State University in 1984 and an M.F.A. from the University of Arizona in 1985. He was a poet (author of eight books of poetry), critic (author of *T. S. Eliot as Editor*, 1986), translator (*The Rebel's Silhouette: Selected Poems* by Faiz Ahmed Faiz, 1992), and editor (*Ravishing Disunities: Real Ghazals in English*, 2000). He held teaching positions at the University of Delhi and at several colleges and universities in the United States. "I Dream It Is Afternoon When I Return to Delhi" shows Ali's use of Western formal cultural principles in work that focuses on his own cultural background.

Julia Alvarez (b. 1950) was born in New York City, lived in the Dominican Republic until she was ten, and returned to New York when her father had to flee because he was involved in a plot to overthrow the dictator, Rafael Trujillo. Thus she needed to adjust to a new culture and a new language. Since childhood, she says, she has loved stories—hearing them and telling them, so it was natural for her to decide she wanted to be a writer. She graduated from Middlebury College in Vermont and earned an M.A. in creative writing from Syracuse University. Since 1998, she has been writer in residence at Middlebury. In addition to three volumes of poetry (*Homecoming*, 1984; *The Other Side*, 1995; and *The Woman I Kept to Myself*, 2004), she has published seven novels, many short stories, numerous books for young readers, and a book of essays about herself and her writing life, *Something to Declare* (1998).

Matthew Arnold (1822–1888) was born in the small English village of Laleham and raised at Rugby School, where his father was headmaster. He attended Oxford University and, in 1857, was elected professor of poetry at Oxford, a position he held for ten years, writing mostly literary criticism. He also worked for thirty-five years as an inspector of schools and made two lecture tours of the United States.

John Ashbery (b. 1927) grew up on a farm near Rochester, New York. He graduated from Harvard University and received his M.A. from Columbia University. He studied in France for two years and then stayed on, writing art criticism. Returning to New York, he taught, edited *Art News*, and wrote for *Newsweek*. He is the author of twenty-six books of poetry, including *Some Trees* (1956), which was selected by W. H. AUDEN for the Yale Younger Poets Series, and *Self-Portrait in a Convex Mirror* (1975), which received the Pulitzer Prize for Poetry, the National Book Critics Circle Award, and the National Book Award. His most recent books are *A Worldly Country* (2005), *Where Shall I Wander* (2007), and *Quick Question* (2012). He has also published literary criticism, a book of art criticism, a collection of plays, and a novel.

Margaret Atwood (b. 1939) was born in Ottawa and grew up in northern Ontario, Quebec, and Toronto. She began writing while attending high school in Toronto. She received her undergraduate degree from Victoria College at the University of Toronto and her master's degree from Radcliffe College. She won the E. J. Pratt Medal for her privately printed book of poems, *Double Persephone* (1961), and has published sixteen more collections of poetry. She is perhaps best known for her twelve novels, which include *The Handmaid's Tale* (1983), *The Robber Bride* (1994), and *The Blind Assassin* (2000, winner of the Booker Prize). She has also published seven collections of short stories, seven children's books, and nine books of nonfiction, and edited several anthologies. Her work has been translated into more than thirty languages, including Farsi, Japanese, Turkish, Finnish, Korean, Icelandic, and Estonian.

W.[ystan] H.[ugh] Auden (1907–1973) was born in York, England. He went to private school and then to Oxford University, where he began to write poetry. He supported himself by teaching and publishing and wrote books based on his travels to Iceland, Spain, and China. He also wrote (with Chester Kallman) several librettos, including the one for Igor Stravinsky's *The Rake's Progress* (1951). He lived in the United States from 1939 until his death and became a U.S. citizen in 1946. His work combines lively intelligence, quick wit, careful craftsmanship, and social concern.

Jimmy Santiago Baca (b. 1952) was born in Sante Fe, New Mexico, of Chicano and Apache heritage. Abandoned by his parents at the age of two, he lived with one of his grandparents for several years before being placed in an orphanage. He lived on the streets as a youth and was imprisoned for six years for drug possession. In prison, he taught himself to read and write and began to compose poetry. A fellow inmate convinced him to submit some of his poems for publication. He has since published a dozen books of poetry, a memoir, a collection of stories and essays, a play, a screenplay, and a novel, *A Glass of Water* (2009).

Jim Barnes (b. 1933), born in Oklahoma of Choctaw and Welsh heritage, worked for ten years as a lumberjack. He studied at Southeastern Oklahoma State University and received his M.A. and Ph.D. from the University of Arkansas. He has published many books of poetry, most recently *Visiting Picasso* (2007); several books of translations and criticism; and over 500 poems in more than 100 journals, including *The Chicago Review, The American Scholar, Prairie Schooner*, and *Georgia Review*. He is the founding editor of the Chariton Review Press and editor of *The Chariton Review*. He taught at Truman State University from 1970 to 2003, then at Brigham Young University, and presently lives in Santa Fe.

Wendell Berry (b. 1934) was the first of four children born to Virginia and John Berry, a lawyer and tobacco farmer, in Henry County, Kentucky, where his family has farmed for five generations. He attended Millersburg Military Institute and earned his B.A. and M.A. from the University of Kentucky and was a Wallace Stegner Fellow at Stanford University. A prolific author of poetry, essays, short stories, and novels, he is also recognized for his academic, cultural, environmental, and economic criticism. His work focuses on the life that he deeply values, one that includes sustainable agriculture (since 1965, he has farmed his 125-acre homestead, Lane's Landing), community, a connection to place, local economics, good work, and the interconnectedness of all life. He is a fellow of Britain's Temenos Academy, which is devoted to studying all faiths and spiritual paths.

John Berryman (1914–1972) was born John Smith in McAlester, Oklahoma;

he took the name of his stepfather after his father's suicide. He attended a private school in Connecticut, Columbia College, and Clare College, Cambridge. He taught at Wayne State University, Harvard University, Princeton University, and the University of Minnesota. His early work was traditional, highly crafted, and admired, but only later, when he was in his forties, did his poetry emerge as boldly original and innovative. 77 *Dream Songs*, published in 1964 and awarded a Pulitzer Prize, unveiled the alter egos "Henry" and "Mr. Bones" in a sequence of sonnet-like poems whose unusual diction, difficult syntax, leaps in language and tone, and mixture of lyricism and comedy reached depths of the human spirit and psyche. He added to the sequence in the following years until they totaled nearly four hundred in *The Dream Songs* (1969). Berryman suffered throughout his life from mental and emotional difficulties and commited suicide by jumping off a bridge in Minneapolis.

Elizabeth Bishop (1911–1979), born in Worcester, Massachusetts, was raised in Nova Scotia by her grandparents after her father died and her mother was committed to an asylum. She attended Vassar College, intending to study medicine, but was encouraged by MARIANNE MOORE to be a poet. From 1935 to 1937 she traveled in France, Spain, northern Africa, Ireland, and Italy and then settled in Key West, Florida, for four years, after which she lived in Rio de Janeiro for almost twenty years. She wrote slowly and carefully and produced a small body of poetry (totaling only around one hundred poems), technically sophisticated, formally varied, witty, and thoughtful, revealing in precise, true-to-life images her impressions of the physical world. She served

as Consultant in Poetry to the Library of Congress from 1949 to 1950.[1]

William Blake (1757–1827) was born and lived in London. His only formal schooling was in art—he studied for a year at the Royal Academy and was apprenticed to an engraver. He worked as a professional engraver, doing commissions and illustrations, assisted by his wife, Catherine Boucher. Blake started writing poetry at the age of eleven and later engraved and hand-printed his own poems, in very small batches, with his own hand-colored illustrations. His early work showed a strong social conscience, and his later work turned increasingly mythic and prophetic.

Robert Bly (b. 1926) was born in Madison, Minnesota, and served in the navy during World War II. He studied at St. Olaf College for a year before going to Harvard University. He lived in New York for a few years, then earned an M.A. from the University of Iowa Writers' Workshop. He received a Fulbright grant in 1956 to travel to Norway and began to translate Norwegian poetry into English. In 1966 he founded (with David Ray) American Writers Against the Vietnam War. He has published more than thirty books of poetry—most recently *Talking into the Ear of a Donkey* (2011), many books of translations, and a number of nonfiction books and has edited numerous collections of poetry. A best-selling author, he is also a challenging critic of contemporary

1. The first appointment of a Consultant in Poetry to the Library of Congress was made in 1937. The title was changed to Poet Laureate Consultant in Poetry in 1986. Appointments are made for one year, beginning in September, and sometimes have been renewed for a second year.

consumerist culture (his controversial 1990 best-seller *Iron John* was a key book in the "men's movement"). "Driving to Town Late to Mail a Letter" is an example of his ability to discover a moment of epiphany in the most common of situations.

Eavan Boland (b. 1944) was born in Dublin and educated there and in London and New York. She has taught at Trinity College and University College, Dublin; Bowdoin College; and the University of Iowa. She is currently the Bella Mabury and Eloise Mabury Knapp Professor in Humanities and the Melvin and Bill Lane Professor for the Director of the Creative Writing Program at Stanford University. An influential figure in Irish poetry, Boland has published a dozen volumes of poetry, including *The Journey and Other Poems* (1987), *Night Feed* (1994), *The Lost Land* (1998), *Code* (2001), *New Collected Poems* (2005), and *Domestic Violence* (2007) and has edited several other books including *Three Irish Poets: An Anthology* (2003) and *Irish Writers on Writing* (2007). Her poems and essays have appeared in magazines such as the *New Yorker*, the *Atlantic*, *Kenyon Review*, and *American Poetry Review*. A collection of essays, *A Journey with Two Maps: Becoming a Woman Poet*, was published in 2011. She is a regular reviewer for the *Irish Times*.

Philip Booth (1925–2007) was born in Hanover, New Hampshire, but spent much of his childhood and later life in Castine, Maine, in a house that had been in his mother's family for generations. After serving in the air force in World War II, Booth studied under Robert Frost at Dartmouth, where he returned to teach after earning his M.A. in English at Columbia University. He

left after one year to teach at Wellesley College and later taught at Syracuse University, where he was one of the founders of the creative writing program. His life was very private: He and his family spent much of their lives in the spare, dramatic, and intense landscape of the seacoast of Maine. This locale had a profound impact on the subject, style, and voice of his poems. As R. W. French put it in the *Nation*, "Booth's place is the Maine coast, and he seems not at all sure that a man can find himself there or anywhere else. . . . Booth's landscapes are ominous, forbidding, and his central metaphor is, significantly, that of the tide." Throughout his ten books of poetry, Booth worked with similar subjects, in ever deepening exploration of his material.

Anne Bradstreet (c. 1612–1672), born in Northampton, England, was educated by tutors, reading chiefly religious writings and the Bible. In 1628 she married Simon Bradstreet, a brilliant young Puritan educated at Cambridge. They were among the earliest settlers of the Massachusetts Bay Colony, in 1630, and her father and husband were leading figures in its governance. She wrote regularly in both prose and verse throughout her busy and difficult years in Massachusetts.

Gwendolyn Brooks (1917–2000), born in Topeka, Kansas, was raised in Chicago and wrote her first poems at age seven. She began studying poetry at the Southside Community Art Center. Her second collection of poems, *Annie Allen* (1949), earned the first Pulitzer Prize given to an African American poet. She served as Consultant in Poetry at the Library of Congress from 1985 to 1986 and worked in community programs and poetry workshops in Chicago to encourage young African American writers.

Sterling A. Brown (1901–1989) was born in Washington, D.C., and educated at Dunbar High School, Williams College, and Harvard University. He taught for more than fifty years at Howard University. Like many other black poets of the period, he expresses his concerns about race in America. His first book of poems, *Southern Road* (1932), was well received by critics, and Brown became part of the artistic tradition of the Harlem Renaissance. Brown was deeply interested in African American music and dialect. He became one of the great innovators in developing poetry related to jazz. His work is known for its frank, unsentimental portraits of black people and their experiences and its successful incorporation of African American folklore and contemporary idiom.

Elizabeth Barrett Browning (1806–1861) was born in Durham, England, and studied with her brother's tutor. Her first book of poetry was published when she was thirteen, and she soon became the most famous female poet to that point in English history. A riding accident at the age of sixteen left her a semi-invalid in the house of her possessive father, who had forbidden any of his eleven children to marry. She and ROBERT BROWNING were forced to elope (she was thirty-nine at the time); they lived in Florence, Italy, where she died fifteen years later. Her best-known book of poems was *Sonnets from the Portuguese*, a sequence of forty-four sonnets recording the growth of her love for Robert.

Robert Browning (1812–1889) was the son of a bank clerk in Camberwell, then a suburb of London. As an aspiring poet in 1844, he admired ELIZABETH BARRETT's poetry and began a correspondence with her that led to one of the world's most famous romances. Their courtship lasted until 1846 when they were secretly wed and ran off to Italy, where they lived until Elizabeth's death in 1861. The years in Florence were among the happiest for both of them. To her he dedicated *Men and Women*, which contains his best poetry. Although she was the more popular poet during her lifetime, his reputation grew upon his return to London after her death, assisted somewhat by public sympathy for him. The late 1860s were the peak of his career: He and TENNYSON were mentioned together as the foremost poets of the age.

Charles Bukowski (1920–1994), born in Andernach, Germany, came to the United States at age three and grew up in poverty in Los Angeles. He drifted extensively, but for much of his life made his home in San Pedro, working for many years for the U.S. Postal Service. He was familiar with the people of the streets, skid row residents, hustlers, and a transient lifestyle. He began writing in childhood, and published his first story at age twenty-four and his first poetry when he was thirty-five. In addition to his many books of poetry, he published novels and short stories written in a style reminiscent of that of Ernest Hemingway. He is very popular in Europe. The strong sense of immediacy in his writing and its refusal to embrace standard formal structures reflect the influence of the Beat movement.

Robert Burns (1759–1796) was born in Ayrshire in southwestern Scotland, the son of a poor farming family. His formal education lasted only to about his ninth year, when he was needed to

work on the farm, but he read widely
and voraciously whenever he could
find time. His first book of poems, published in 1785, sold out within a month.
Despite living in poverty, he poured out
a flood of his finest poems in the early
1790s. Burns is regarded as Scotland's
national bard for his ability to depict
with loving accuracy the life of his fellow
rural Scots. His use of dialect brought
a stimulating, much-needed freshness
and raciness into English poetry, but
his greatness extends beyond the limits
of dialect: His poems are written about
Scots, but, in tune with the rising hu-
manitarianism of his day, they apply to
a multitude of universal problems.

George Gordon, Lord Byron (1788–
1824) was one of the great Romantic
poets, although he is best known for
his lighthearted and humorous verse,
such as *Don Juan*. He was born in London and raised in Scotland; he studied
at Harrow and at Trinity College, Cambridge. He inherited the title of sixth
baron Byron (with estate) at age ten.
The last few years of his life were spent
in Italy, and he died in Greece after
joining the Greek forces in their war
for independence.

Lorna Dee Cervantes (b. 1954) was
born in San Francisco and grew up in
San Jose. There she studied at San Jose
City College and San Jose State University. She is the author of four volumes
of poetry: *Emplumada*, winner of an
American Book Award (1981); *From the
Cables of Genocide: Poems on Love and
Hunger* (1991); *Drive: The First Quartet*
(2006); and *Ciento: 100 100-Word Love
Poems* (2011). She is also coeditor of
Red Dirt, a cross-cultural poetry journal, and her work has been included
in many anthologies. Cervantes, who
considers herself "a Chicana writer, a

feminist writer, a political writer,"
taught at the University of Colorado,
Boulder, from 1988 to 2007 and currently lives in San Francisco.

Geoffrey Chaucer (c. 1340–1400) was
born and raised in London, as part of
the growing and prosperous middle
class of his time. His father was an afflu-
ent wine merchant with social connections that enabled Chaucer to become
a page in one of the great aristocratic
households of England, that of the
Countess of Ulster, wife of Lionel, the
second son of King Edward III. There
he acquired the education, manners,
and skills needed for a career in the
service of the ruling class. His life is
unusually well documented for a non-
royal figure of the Middle Ages. In
1359, while in military service with the
English in France, he was captured by
the French and ransomed with royal
funds. Later, he served in King Edward's
household and traveled as a member of
diplomatic missions to Spain in 1366,
France in 1368, and Italy in 1372. From
1374 until 1385, he held the important
position of comptroller of customs in
the port of London, keeping records on
export taxes. After he left that position,
he accepted his most challenging appointment: clerk of the king's works
(1389–91), which included responsibility for the upkeep of the Tower of
London, Westminster Palace, and several royal residences. He also served as
a justice of the peace and member of
Parliament for the county of Kent,
where he lived later in life. All the while,
he was reading and writing poetry. He
was deeply influenced by (and translated) Latin, French, and Italian writers, but he chose to write mostly in the
language of the London of his own day,
what is now referred to as Middle English, a predecessor of modern English.

His most famous work is *The Canterbury Tales*, which he left unfinished when he died. But even if he hadn't written it, he would have been remembered as a major English poet for works like *The House of Fame*, *The Parliament of Fowls*, and especially *Troilus and Criseyde*.

Marilyn Chin (b. 1955) is a first-generation Chinese American, born in Hong Kong and raised in Portland, Oregon. She is the author of three volumes of poetry, *Dwarf Bamboo* (1987), *The Phoenix Gone, The Terrace Empty* (1994), and *Rhapsody in Plain Yellow* (2002), and a novel, *Revenge of the Mooncake Vixen* (2009). She also is a coeditor of *Dissident Song: A Contemporary Asian American Anthology* (1991) and has translated poems by the modern Chinese poet Ai Qing and cotranslated poems by the Japanese poet Gozo Yoshimasu. She has received numerous awards for her poetry, including a Stegner fellowship, the PEN/Josephine Miles Award, and four Pushcart Prizes. She is codirector of the M.F.A. program at San Diego State University.

Lucille Clifton (1936–2010) was born in Depew, New York, and studied at Howard University. She published many books of poetry, including *Blessing the Boats: New and Selected Poems 1988–2000* (2000), which won the National Book Award for Poetry. She also published a memoir and more than twenty books for children. She taught at several colleges and worked in the Office of Education in Washington, D.C. She served as poet laureate for the State of Maryland. Her poems typically reflect her ethnic pride, womanist principles, and race and gender consciousness.

Judith Ortiz Cofer (b. 1952) was born in Hormigueros, Puerto Rico. Her family moved to Paterson, New Jersey, in 1955. For the next decade, she grew up moving between those two very different worlds. She graduated from Augusta College in Georgia, married and had a daughter, completed a graduate degree, and began teaching English. But, she says, something was missing from her life: She realized that she needed to write. Her first book of poetry, *Reaching for the Mainland* (1987), was followed by several others including, most recently, *A Love Story Beginning in Spanish: Poems* (2006). She has also published novels for adults, a memoir—*Silent Dancing: A Partial Remembrance of a Puerto Rican Childhood* (1990)—and a book about writing, *Woman in Front of the Sun: On Becoming a Writer* (2000). She has written several award-winning books for young adults, including *An Island Like You: Stories of the Barrio* (1996), *Call Me Maria* (2004), and *If I Could Fly* (2011). She is Regents' and Franklin Professor of English and Creative Writing at the University of Georgia and lives with her husband on the family farm near Louisville, Georgia.

Samuel Taylor Coleridge (1772–1834) was born in Devonshire and sent to school in London after his father's death. He went to Jesus College, Cambridge, in 1791, and dropped out twice without a degree. In 1798 Coleridge and WILLIAM WORDSWORTH published *Lyrical Ballads*, which initiated the Romantic movement in English poetry and established both of their reputations. After 1802 Coleridge became addicted to opium, used as a treatment for physical discomfort and seizures. He and his wife were separated, his friendship with Wordsworth broke up, and his poetic output stopped. From 1816 to his death he lived under constant medical supervision but still published a journal and wrote several plays, pieces of criticism, and philosophical and religious treatises.

Billy Collins (b. 1941), born and raised in New York City, is the author of numerous collections of poems, most recently *Horoscopes for the Dead* (2011). Perhaps no poet since ROBERT FROST has managed to combine high critical acclaim with such broad popular appeal. The typical Collins poem opens on a clear and hospitable note but soon takes an unexpected turn; poems that begin in irony may end in a moment of lyric surprise. Collins sees his poetry as "a form of travel writing" and considers humor "a door into the serious." Collins is Distinguished Professor of Literature at Lehman College of the City University of New York and a writer-in-residence at Sarah Lawrence College. He was appointed Poet Laureate Consultant in Poetry to the Library of Congress from 2001 to 2003.

Victor Hernández Cruz (b. 1949) was born in Aguas Buenas, Puerto Rico, and moved to New York City with his family at the age of five. His first book of poetry, *Papa Got His Gun, and Other Poems* (1966), was published when he was seventeen. Since then he has published numerous other collections, including *Maraca: New and Selected Poems 1965–2000* (2001) and most recently *The Mountain in the Sea* (2006). In 1971 Cruz visited Puerto Rico and reconnected with his ancestral heritage; eighteen years later, he returned to Puerto Rico to live. He now divides his time between Puerto Rico and New York. Much of his work explores the relation between the English language and his native Spanish, playing with grammatical and syntactical conventions within both languages to create his own bilingual idiom.

Countee Cullen (1903–1946) was born in Louisville, Kentucky, or in Baltimore, Maryland, or (as he himself claimed) in New York City. He was adopted by the Reverend Frederick A. Cullen and his wife and grew up, as he put it, "in the conservative atmosphere of a Methodist parsonage." He studied at New York University and Harvard University. A forerunner of the Harlem Renaissance movement, he was in the 1920s the most popular black literary figure in America. From the 1930s until his death, he wrote less and worked as a junior high school French teacher. For many years after his death, his reputation was eclipsed by that of other Harlem Renaissance writers, particularly LANGSTON HUGHES and Zora Neale Hurston; recently, however, there has been a resurgence of interest in his life and work.

E. E. Cummings (1894–1962) was born in Cambridge, Massachusetts, where his father was a Unitarian minister and a sociology lecturer at Harvard University. He graduated from Harvard and then served as an ambulance driver during World War I. *The Enormous Room* (1922) is an account of his confinement in a French prison camp during the war. After the war, he lived in rural Connecticut and Greenwich Village, with frequent visits to Paris. In his work, Cummings experimented radically with form, punctuation, spelling, and syntax, abandoning traditional techniques and structures to create a new, highly idiosyncratic means of poetic expression. At the time of his death in 1962, he was the second most widely read poet in the United States, after ROBERT FROST.

Toi Derricotte (b. 1941) was born and raised in Detroit. She earned a B.A. in special education from Wayne State

University and an M.A. in English literature from New York University. She is the author of four collections of poetry as well as a memoir, *The Black Notebooks* (1997). With poet CORNELIUS EADY, she cofounded Cave Canem, which offers workshops and retreats for African American poets. Among many honors she has received is the Distinguished Pioneering of the Arts Award from the United Black Artists. Derricotte teaches creative writing at the University of Pittsburgh.

Emily Dickinson (1830–1886) was born in Amherst, Massachusetts, and lived there her entire life, rarely leaving. She briefly attended a women's seminary but became homesick and left before a year was out. Dickinson never married and became reclusive later in life, forgoing even the village routines and revelries she enjoyed. She wrote over 1,700 fresh, often unconventional, carefully crafted poems, marked by striking images, surprising figures of speech, metrical irregularities, frequent slant rhymes, and unique punctuation. Only five were published during her lifetime. Not until 1955 was there a complete edition of her poems attempting to present them as originally written.

John Donne (1572–1631) was born in London to a prosperous Catholic family (through his mother he was related to Sir Thomas More and the playwright John Heywood). Donne studied at Oxford University for several years but did not take a degree. He fought with Sir Walter Raleigh in two naval strikes against Spain. In 1601 Donne's promising political career was permanently derailed by his precipitous marriage to Anne More without her father's consent. He was briefly imprisoned, lost a very promising position with Sir Thomas

Egerton, and spent years seeking further political employment before finally being convinced by King James in 1615 to become a priest of the Church of England. His life was described by Isaac Walton later in the century as being divided into two parts. In Phase I he was "Jack Donne" of Lincoln's Inn: When young, Donne employed a sophisticated urban wit that created in his earlier poetry a sort of jaded tone. "The Flea" presumably appeared during this stage of his life and illustrates its characteristics well (a typical **metaphysical poem**—see the glossary). In Phase II he was John Donne, dean of St. Paul's: After Donne took holy orders in 1615, his poetry became markedly less amorous and more religious in tone. His *Holy Sonnets* (of which "Death, be not proud" is one) are as dense and complex as his earlier work, with his talent now directed toward exploration of his relationship with God.

Hilda Doolittle [H. D.] (1886–1961) was born in Bethlehem, Pennsylvania. She went to private schools in Philadelphia and then dropped out of Bryn Mawr after a year because of ill health. She moved to England, where an old friend (and fiancé for a time), EZRA POUND, encouraged her to write and sent some of her poetry to a journal. H. D. became a leader of Pound's Imagist group but eventually moved away from it. From 1933 to 1934 she visited Sigmund Freud as a patient and later wrote *Tribute to Freud* (1956). Besides poetry, she wrote novels and translated Greek.

Mark Doty (b. 1953) is the author of twelve collections of poetry and three memoirs—*Heaven's Coast* (1996), about the loss of his partner, Wally Roberts; *Firebird* (1999), a gay coming-of-age

story and a chronicle of a gradual process of finding in art a place of personal
belonging; and *Dog Years* (2007), about
the relationships between humans and
the dogs they love. He has taught at
Brandeis University, Sarah Lawrence
College, Vermont College, and the University of Iowa Writers' Workshop. He
now lives in New York City and on Fire
Island, New York, and teaches at Rut-
gers University.

Rita Dove (b. 1952) was born in Akron,
Ohio. Her father was the first research
chemist to break the race barrier in
the tire industry. She graduated from
Miami University in Oxford, Ohio, with
a degree in English; after a year at
Tübingen University in Germany on a
Fulbright Fellowship, she joined the
University of Iowa Writers' Workshop,
where she earned her M.F.A. in 1977.
She has taught at Tuskegee Institute
and Arizona State University and now
is on the faculty of the University of Virginia. She was appointed Poet Laureate Consultant in Poetry to the Library
of Congress in 1993, making her the
youngest person — and the first African
American — to receive this highest official honor in American letters. She is
the author of numerous collections of
poetry, including *Thomas and Beulah*
(1986), a book-length sequence loosely
based on the lives of her grandparents,
which was awarded the Pulitzer Prize
in 1987.

Michael Drayton (1563–1631) was born
a year before Shakespeare and in the
same county, Warwickshire, England.
He wrote sonnets, pastorals, odes, verse
epistles, satires, and historical epics. His
masterpiece is a topographical work
on England titled *Poly-Olbion*, a poem
celebrating all the counties of England
and Wales. He was an influential writer

of religious poetry as well. "Since there's
no help, come let us kiss and part" is
the sixty-first in a sequence of sonnets
addressed to "Idea," the embodiment of
the Platonic idea of virtue and beauty.

Denise Duhamel (b. 1961) was born in
Woonsocket, Rhode Island. She received
her B.F.A. from Emerson College and
her M.F.A. from Sarah Lawrence College. She has published many collections of poetry, most recently *Ka-Ching!*
(2009). She was winner of the Crab Orchard Poetry Prize for her collection
The Star-Spangled Banner (1999). She
has been anthologized widely and has
been included in four volumes of *The
Best American Poetry*. She teaches creative writing at Florida International
University.

Paul Laurence Dunbar (1872–1906)
was the first African American to gain
national eminence as a poet. Born and
raised in Dayton, Ohio, he was the son
of ex-slaves. He was an outstanding
student. The only African American in
his class, he was both class president
and class poet. Although he lived to be
only thirty-three years old, Dunbar was
prolific, writing short stories, novels,
librettos, plays, songs, and essays as
well as the poetry for which he became
well known. He was popular with both
black and white readers of his day. His
style encompasses two distinct voices —
the standard English of the classical
poet and the evocative dialect of the
turn-of-the-century black community
in America.

Cornelius Eady (b. 1954) was born
and raised in Rochester, New York, and
attended Monroe Community College
and Empire State College. He began
writing as a teenager. His poems are
his biography, their subjects ranging

from blues musicians to the witnessing of his father's death. He has published eight volumes of poetry. With poet Toi Derricotte, he cofounded Cave Canem, which offers workshops and retreats for African American poets, and with composer Diedre Murray he has collaborated on two highly acclaimed music-dramas. Formerly the director of the Poetry Center at the State University of New York, Stony Brook, and Distinguished Writer in Residence at the City College of New York, he currently holds the Miller Family Endowed Chair in Literature and Writing at the University of Missouri.

T.[homas] S.[tearns] Eliot (1888–1965) was born and raised in St. Louis. He went to prep school in Massachusetts and to Harvard University, where he earned an M.A. in philosophy in 1910 and started his doctoral dissertation. He studied at the Sorbonne, Paris, and then at Marburg, Germany, in 1914. The war forced him to Oxford, where he married and abandoned philosophy for poetry. After teaching and working in a bank, he became an editor at Faber and Faber and editor of the journal *Criterion* and was the dominant force in English poetry for several decades. He became a British citizen and a member of the Church of England in 1927. He won the Nobel Prize in Literature in 1948. He also wrote plays, essays, and a series of poems on cats that became the basis of a musical by Andrew Lloyd Weber. The poems included in this anthology show Eliot's use of collage techniques to embody the fragmentation he saw in culture and individual psyches in his day.

Elizabeth I (1533–1603) was queen of England from 1558 to 1603. In addition to being well educated and a skillful politician and ruler, she wrote exten-

sively, mostly speeches and translations but also a few original poems in the forms and manner typical of her time. Though the attribution of "When I was fair and young" has been questioned, it is credited to her in the most recent collection of her works.

Anita Endrezze (b. 1952), of Yaqui and European ancestry, was born in Long Beach, California, and earned her M.A. from Eastern Washington University. She is a poet, writer, and painter (in watercolor and acrylics) who also works in fiber and creates handmade books. She is a member of Atlatl, a Native American arts service organization. In addition to four volumes of poetry, she has published a children's novel, short stories, and nonfiction. She lives in Everett, Washington, where she is a storyteller, teacher, and writer.

Martín Espada (b. 1957) was born in Brooklyn and has had an eclectic résumé: radio journalist in Nicaragua, welfare rights paralegal, advocate for mental patients, night desk clerk in a transient hotel, attendant in a primate nursery, groundskeeper at a minor league ballpark, bindery worker in a printing plant, bouncer in a bar, and practicing lawyer in Chelsea, Massachusetts. Author of nine books of poetry, his latest collection is *The Trouble Ball* (2011). His book *Alabanza: New and Selected Poems, 1982–2002* (2003) received the Paterson Award for Sustained Literary Achievement and was named an American Library Association Notable Book of the Year. He is an essayist, editor, and translator as well as a poet. He presently teaches at the University of Massachusetts, Amherst.

Carolyn Forché (b. 1950) was born in Detroit, attended Michigan State University, and earned an M.F.A. from

Bowling Green State University. She achieved immediate success as a writer, winning the Yale Younger Poets Prize in 1976. Her work underwent a remarkable shift following a year spent on a Guggenheim Fellowship in El Salvador, where she worked with human-rights activist Archbishop Oscar Humberto Romero and with Amnesty International. The shock of witnessing countless atrocities in Central America led her to begin writing what she calls "poetry of witness." The volume *The Country Between Us* (1981) stirred immediate controversy because of its overtly political topics and themes. "The Colonel," a prose poem in which the speaker conveys a horrific story with chilling flatness, is probably the most disturbing and memorable poem in the book. She is the author of four books of poetry, most recently *Blue Hour* (2004), and the editor of *Against Forgetting: Twentieth-Century Poetry of Witness* (1993). She has also translated several books of poetry. She is director of the Lannan Center for Poetry and Poetics and holds the Lannan Chair in Poetry at Georgetown University in Washington, D.C.

Vievee Francis (b. 1963) grew up in Detroit and has lived there all her life. In addition to publishing two books of poetry, her work has appeared in many venues, including the *2003 Grolier Prize Annual*, *Callaloo*, *Margie*, and *Crab Orchard Review*. She spent several years doing exhaustive research for her first collection, *Blue-Tail Fly* (2006), a series of persona poems that treat the period of American history between the beginning of the Mexican War and the end of the Civil War. Francis gives voice to outsiders, from soldiers and common folk to influential politicians. Her second book, *Horse in the Dark* (2011), received the 2010 Cave Canem Northwestern University Press Poetry Prize. She

earned her M.F.A. from the University of Michigan, where she was the 2009–2010 poet in residence for the Lloyd Hall Scholars Program. She teaches independent workshops for young adult writers in the Detroit area.

Robert Frost (1874–1963) was born in San Francisco and lived there until he was eleven. When his father died, the family moved to Massachusetts, where Frost did well in school, especially in the classics, but he dropped out of both Dartmouth College and Harvard University. He went unrecognized as a poet until 1913, when he was first published in England, where he had moved with his wife and four children. Upon returning to the United States, he quickly achieved success with more publications and became the most celebrated poet in mid-twentieth-century America. He held a teaching position at Amherst College and received many honorary degrees as well as an invitation to recite a poem at John F. Kennedy's inauguration. Although his work is principally associated with the life and landscape of New England, and although he was a poet of traditional verse forms and meters, he is also a quintessentially modern poet in his adherence to language as it is actually spoken, in the psychological complexity of his portraits, and in the degree to which his work is infused with layers of ambiguity and irony.

Richard Garcia (b. 1941) was born in San Francisco, a first-generation American (his mother was from Mexico, his father from Puerto Rico). While still in high school, he had a poem published by City Lights in a Beat anthology. After publishing his first collection in 1972, however, he did not write poetry again for twelve years, until an unsolicited letter of encouragement from poet

Octavio Paz inspired him to resume. Since then, his work has appeared widely in literary magazines as well as three later books, *The Flying Garcias* (1991), *Rancho Notorious* (2001), and *The Persistence of Objects* (2006). He is also the author of a bilingual children's book, *My Aunt Otilia's Spirits* (1987). For twelve years he was the poet in residence at Children's Hospital Los Angeles, where he conducted poetry and art workshops for hospitalized children. He teaches creative writing in the Antioch University Los Angeles M.F.A. program and at the College of Charleston.

Allen Ginsberg (1926–1997) was born in Newark, New Jersey, and graduated from Columbia University, after several suspensions, in 1948. Several years later, Ginsberg left for San Francisco to join other poets of the Beat movement. His poem "Howl," the most famous poem of the movement, was published in 1956 by Lawrence Ferlinghetti's City Lights Books; the publicity of the ensuing censorship trial brought the Beats to national attention. Ginsberg was co-founder with ANNE WALDMAN of the Jack Kerouac School of Disembodied Poetics at the Naropa Institute in Boulder, Colorado. In his later years he became a distinguished professor at Brooklyn College.

Aracelis Girmay (b. 1977), inheritor of Eritrean, Puerto Rican, and African American traditions, was born in Santa Ana, California, and grew up in southern California. Her future as a writer was indicated when, at age seven, she was given a red typewriter. She earned her B.A. from Connecticut College and her M.F.A. in poetry from New York University. A writer of poetry, essays, and fiction, her works have appeared in numerous journals and magazines. She received the Great Lakes Colleges

Association New Writers Award for her first poetry collection, *Teeth* (2007). Her second collection, *Kingdom Animalia* (2011), was awarded the Isabella Gardner Poetry Award. She teaches writing workshops in New York and California and has served as writer in residence at Hampshire College, where she is now on the faculty. In addition to her poetry collections, she has published a collage-based picture book, *Changing, Changing: Story and Collages* (2005).

Louise Glück (b. 1943) was born in New York City and educated at Sarah Lawrence College and Columbia University. She has published numerous collections of poetry, including *The Triumph of Achilles* (1985), which received the National Book Critics Circle Award and the Poetry Society of America's Melville Kane Award; *Ararat* (1990), which received the Rebekah Johnson Bobbitt National Prize for Poetry; *The Wild Iris* (1992), which received the Pulitzer Prize and the Poetry Society of America's William Carlos Williams Award; and *Averno*, a finalist for the 2006 National Book Award in Poetry. Her most recent collection is *A Village Life* (2009). She has also published a collection of essays, *Proofs and Theories: Essays on Poetry* (1994), which won the PEN/Martha Albrand Award for Nonfiction. She was Poet Laureate Consultant in Poetry to the Library of Congress, 2003–2004. She is the Rosencranz Writer in Residence at Yale University and teaches in the creative writing program of Boston University.

Ray González (b. 1952) received his M.F.A. in creative writing from Southwest Texas State University. He has published ten books of poetry, including *The Heat of Arrivals* (which won the 1997 Josephine Miles Book Award) and *The Hawk Temple at Tierra Grande*, winner of a 2003 Minnesota Book Award in Poetry. He is the author of three books of nonfiction—*Memory Fever*, a memoir about growing up in the Southwest (1999), *The Underground Heart* (2002), which received the 2003 Carr P. Collins/Texas Institute of Letters Award for Best Book of Nonfiction, and *Renaming the Earth* (2008)—and two collections of short stories—*The Ghost of John Wayne* (2001) and *Circling the Tortilla Dragon* (2002)—and is editor of twelve anthologies. He has served as poetry editor for *The Bloomsbury Review* since 1980. He teaches creative writing at the University of Minnesota.

Thomas Gray (1716–1771) was born in London and educated at Eton and at Cambridge University, where he studied literature and history. In November 1741 his father died, and Gray moved with his mother and aunt to the village of Stoke Poges in Buckinghamshire, where he wrote his first important poems, the "Ode on the Spring," "Ode on a Distant Prospect of Eton College," and "Hymn to Adversity," and began his masterpiece, "Elegy Written in a Country Churchyard," called the most famous and diversified of all graveyard poems. These poems solidified his reputation as one of the most important English poets of the eighteenth century. In 1757 he was named poet laureate but refused the position. In 1762 he applied for the Regius Professorship of Modern History at Cambridge but was rejected; however, he was given the position in 1768, when the successful candidate was killed. A painfully shy and private person, he never delivered any lectures as a professor.

Marilyn Hacker (b. 1942) was born in New York City. She is the author of ten books of poetry, including *Presentation Piece* (1974), which was the Lamont

Poetry Selection of the Academy of American Poets and a National Book Award winner, and *Selected Poems, 1965–1990* (1994), which received the Poets' Prize. Her most recent collection is *Essays on Departure: New and Selected Poems* (2006). Her translation of *King of a Hundred Horsemen* (2008) by Marie Étienne won the PEN Award for Poetry in Translation and the Robert Fagles Translation Prize from the National Poetry Series. She has received numerous honors and awards, including the PEN/Voelcker Award for Poetry in 2010. She lives in New York City and Paris. Often labeled a neo-formalist, Hacker often handles traditional forms in fresh ways, as "Villanelle" illustrates.

Kimiko Hahn (b. 1955) was born in Mt. Kisco, New York, to two artists, a Japanese American mother from Hawaii and a German American father from Wisconsin. Hahn majored in English and East Asian studies at the University of Iowa and received an M.A. in Japanese literature at Columbia University. She is the author of eight volumes of poetry, including *The Unbearable Heart* (1996), which received an American Book Award, and, most recently, *Toxic Flora: Poems* (2010). In 1995 she wrote ten portraits of women for a two-hour HBO special titled *Ain't Nuthin' but a She-Thing*. She has taught at Parsons School of Design, the Poetry Project at St. Mark's Church, and Yale University. She lives in New York and is Distinguished Professor in the English Department at Queens College/CUNY.

Thomas Hardy (1840–1928) was born in a cottage in Higher Bockhampton, Dorset, near the regional market town of Dorchester in southwestern England. Apprenticed at age sixteen to an architect, he spent most of the next twenty years restoring old churches. He had always had an interest in literature and started writing novels in his thirties, publishing more than a dozen. In 1896 Hardy gave up prose and turned to poetry, writing until his death at age eighty-eight. He had a consistently bleak, even pessimistic, outlook on life. Many of his works stress the dark effects of "hap" (happenstance, coincidence) in the world.

Joy Harjo (b. 1951) was born in Tulsa, Oklahoma. Her mother was of Cherokee-French descent and her father was Creek. She moved to the Southwest and began writing poetry in her early twenties. She then earned her B.A. at the University of New Mexico and her M.F.A. from the University of Iowa Writers' Workshop. Harjo has published numerous volumes of poetry, including *In Mad Love and War* (1990), which received an American Book Award and the Delmore Schwartz Memorial Award, and *How We Became Human: New and Selected Poems: 1975–2001* (2002). Her most recent book is *Crazy Brave, A Memoir* (2012). She also performs her poetry and plays saxophone with her band, Poetic Justice. She is professor of English at the University of New Mexico, Albuquerque. Of "She Had Some Horses" Harjo has said, "This is the poem I'm asked most about and the one I have the least to say about. I don't know where it came from."

Michael S. Harper (b. 1938) was born in Brooklyn and grew up surrounded by jazz. When his family moved to Los Angeles, he worked at all kinds of jobs, from postal work to professional football. He studied at the City College of Los Angeles; California State University, Los Angeles; and the University of Iowa Writers' Workshop. He has written ten books of poetry, most recently *Selected*

Poems (2002), and edited or coedited several collections of African American poetry. He is University Professor and professor of English at Brown University, where he has taught since 1970. He lives in Barrington, Rhode Island.

Robert Hayden (1913–1980) was raised in a poor neighborhood in Detroit and had an emotionally tumultuous childhood. Because of impaired vision, he was unable to participate in sports and spent his time reading instead. He graduated from high school in 1932 and attended Detroit City College (later Wayne State University). His first book of poems, *Heart-Shape in the Dust*, was published in 1940. After working for newspapers and on other projects, he studied under W. H. AUDEN in the graduate creative writing program at the University of Michigan. He taught at Fisk University and at the University of Michigan. His poetry gained international recognition in the 1960s, and he was awarded the grand prize for poetry at the First World Festival of Negro Arts in Dakar, Senegal, in 1966 for his book *Ballad of Remembrance*. In 1976 he became the first black American to be appointed as Consultant in Poetry to the Library of Congress.

Terrance Hayes (b. 1971) was born in Columbia, South Carolina. In addition to being a writer, he is an accomplished artist and athlete. After receiving a B.A. from Coker College, where he was named Academic All-American for his athletic and academic accomplishments, he earned an M.F.A. from the University of Pittsburgh. His first book of poetry, *Muscular Music* (1999), won both the Whiting Writers Award and the Kate Tufts Discovery Award. His next collection, *Hip Logic* (2002), won the National Poetry Series Award. His most recent book, *Lighthead*, won the National Book Award in Poetry for 2010. After teaching at Xavier University, he returned to Pittsburgh, where he is professor of creative writing at Carnegie Mellon University.

H. D. *See* **Doolittle, Hilda.**

Seamus Heaney (b. 1939) grew up on a small farm near Castledawson, County Derry, Northern Ireland. He was educated at St. Columb's College, a Catholic boarding school in the city of Derry, forty miles from home, and then at Queen's University, Belfast. As a young English teacher in Belfast in the early 1960s, he joined a poetry workshop and began writing verse. Subsequently he became a major force in contemporary Irish literature. The author of many volumes of poetry, translations, and essays as well as two plays, he is well known for his best-selling verse translation of *Beowulf* (2000). He held the chair of professor of poetry at Oxford University from 1989 to 1994. He was awarded the Nobel Prize in Literature in 1995.

George Herbert (1593–1633) was the fifth son in an ancient and wealthy Welsh family. He studied at Cambridge, graduating with honors, and was elected public orator of the university. He served in Parliament for two years but fell out of political favor and become rector of Bemerton near Salisbury. Herbert was a model Anglican priest and an inspiring preacher. All of his poetry, religious in nature, was published posthumously in 1633. "Easter-wings" is among the earliest of **concrete poems**, and, like "Redemption," it illustrates characteristics of **metaphysical poetry.**

Robert Herrick (1591–1674), the son of a well-to-do London goldsmith, was apprenticed to his uncle (also a goldsmith), studied at Cambridge University, then lived for nine years in London, where he hobnobbed with a group of poets that included BEN JONSON. Under familial pressure to do something more worthwhile, Herrick became an Anglican priest. He was given the parish of Dean Prior, Devonshire—a rural place that at first he hated—and there he quietly wrote poems about imagined mistresses and pagan rites (as in his well-known "Corinna's Going A-Maying") and deft but devout religious poems. When he returned to London in 1648, having been ejected from his pulpit by the Puritan revolution, he published his poetry in a volume with two titles, *Hesperides* for the secular poems, *Noble Numbers* for those with sacred subjects. Probably his most famous poem is "To the Virgins, to Make Much of Time," a short lyric on the traditional **carpe diem** theme (see the glossary).

Bob Hicok (b. 1960), in addition to writing poetry, spent years as an automotive die designer and computer system administrator in Ann Arbor, Michigan. His first collection of poetry, *The Legend of Light* (1995), won the Felix Pollack Prize in Poetry and was named a "notable book of the year" by the American Library Association's *Booklist* magazine. He has published five more books: *Plus Shipping* (1998); *Animal Soul* (2001), a finalist for the National Book Critics Circle Award; *Insomnia Diary* (2004); *This Clumsy Living* (2007); and *Words for Empty and Words for Full* (2010). He teaches in the M.F.A. program at Virginia Tech University.

Geoffrey Hill (b. 1932) is a major presence in contemporary British poetry. Born in Bromsgrove, Worcestershire, he attended the local grammar school there before going on to study English language and literature at Keble College, Oxford. He taught at Leeds University from 1954 until 1980, when he moved to Emmanuel College, Cambridge. In 1988 he became University Professor and a professor of literature and religion at Boston University. After returning to England in 2006, he was elected in 2010 to the post of Oxford Professor of Poetry and was knighted in 2012 for his service to literature.

Jane Hirshfield (b. 1953) is the author of numerous award-winning books of poetry, editor and cotranslator of two anthologies of poetry by women, and author of a collection of essays, *Nine Gates: Entering the Mind of Poetry* (1997). A graduate of Princeton University, she studied Soto Zen from 1974 to 1982, including three years of monastic practice, the influence of which is apparent in her work. She has said, "For me, poetry, like Zen practice, is a path toward deeper and more life. There are ways to wake up into the actual texture of one's own existence, to widen it, to deepen and broaden it, and poetry is one of the things that does that." She has taught at the University of California, Berkeley; the University of San Francisco; the University of Cincinnati; and at many writers' conferences.

Linda Hogan (b. 1947), a poet, novelist, essayist, playwright, and activist widely considered to be one of the most influential and provocative Native American figures in the contemporary American literary landscape, was born in Denver. Because her father, who was from the Chickasaw Nation, was in the army and was transferred frequently during Hogan's childhood, she lived in various locations while growing up but considers Oklahoma her true home. In her

late twenties, while working with children with orthopedic disabilities, she began writing during her lunch hours, although she had no previous experience as a writer and little experience reading literature. She pursued her writing by commuting to the University of Colorado, Colorado Springs, for her undergraduate degree and earning an M.A. in English and creative writing at the University of Colorado, Boulder, in 1978. She has published many books — poetry, novels, and nonfiction — and received numerous awards for her work. She is an emeritus professor in the University of Colorado English department and the writer in residence for the Chickasaw Nation.

Anna Maria Hong recently completed a two-collection series of sonnets titled *The Glass Age.* Embracing traditional English and Italian forms as well as more experimental hybrids and departures, her poems sometimes shun the sonnet's formal rhyme schemes and other constraints, bending and torquing to stretch the limits of the form. The 2010–2011 Bunting Fellow in Poetry at Harvard University's Radcliffe Institute for Advanced Study, she earned a B.A. in philosophy at Yale University and an M.F.A. in creative writing from the University of Texas Michener Center for Writers. Her poems have been published in many venues including *Boston Review, Exquisite Corpse, jubilat, Fence, Green Mountains Review, Verse Daily, Fairy Tale Review, Mandorla,* and *POOL.* She is the editor of *Growing Up Asian American,* an anthology of fiction and memoir. A three-time Pushcart Fellowship nominee, she has received residencies from Yaddo, Djerassi, Valparaiso, and AIR West Norway and teaches creative writing at the UCLA Extension Writers' Program.

Garrett Kaoru Hongo (b. 1951) was born in Volcano, Hawaii, grew up on Oahu and in Los Angeles, and did graduate work in Japanese language and literature at the University of Michigan. Hongo has published three books of poetry, including *The River of Heaven* (1988), which was the Lamont Poetry Selection of the Academy of American Poets and a finalist for the Pulitzer Prize. His most recent collection is *Coral Road: Poems* (2011). He has also written *Volcano: A Memoir of Hawai'i* (1995) and edited collections of Asian American verse. He teaches at the University of Oregon, Eugene, where he directed the creative writing program from 1989 to 1993. His work often uses rich textures and sensuous detail to comment on conditions endured by Japanese Americans during World War II and thereafter.

Gerard Manley Hopkins (1844–1889) was born in London, the eldest of eight children. His father was a ship insurer who also wrote a book of poetry. Hopkins studied at Balliol College, Oxford, and, after converting to Catholicism, taught in a school in Birmingham. In 1868 he became a Jesuit and burned all his early poetry, considering it "secular" and worthless. He then worked as a priest and teacher in working-class London, Glasgow, and Merseyside, and later as professor of classics at University College, Dublin. Hopkins went on to write many poems on spiritual themes, but he published little during his lifetime; his poems were not known until they were published by his friend Robert Bridges in 1918. They convey a spiritual sensuality, celebrating the wonder of nature both in their language and in their rhythms (which he called "sprung rhythm"; see the glossary under **accentual meter**).

A. E. Housman (1859–1936) was born in Fockbury, Worcestershire. A promising student at Oxford University, he failed his final exams (because of emotional turmoil possibly caused by his suppressed homosexual love for a fellow student) and spent the next ten years feverishly studying and writing scholarly articles while working as a clerk at the patent office. Housman was rewarded with the chair of Latin at University College, London, and later at Cambridge University. His poetry, like his scholarship, was meticulous, impersonal in tone, and limited in output: two slender volumes—*A Shropshire Lad* (1896) and *Last Poems* (1922)—during his lifetime and a small book titled *More Poems* (1936) after his death. His poems often take up the theme of doomed youths acting out their brief lives in the context of agricultural communities and activities, especially the English countryside and traditions he loved.

Langston Hughes (1902–1967) was born in Joplin, Missouri, and grew up in Lincoln, Illinois, and Cleveland, Ohio. During high school he began writing poetry. He attended Columbia University for a year, then held odd jobs as an assistant cook, a launderer, and a busboy and traveled to Africa and Europe working as a seaman. In 1924 he moved to Harlem. Hughes's first book of poetry, *The Weary Blues*, was published in 1926. He finished his college education at Lincoln University in Pennsylvania three years later. He wrote novels, short stories, plays, songs, children's books, essays, and memoirs as well as poetry and is also known for his engagement with the world of jazz and the influence it had on his writing. His life and work were enormously important in shaping the artistic contributions of the Harlem Renaissance of the 1920s.

Randall Jarrell (1914–1965) was born in Nashville, Tennessee, and earned his B.A. and M.A. at Vanderbilt University. From 1937 to 1939 he taught at Kenyon College, where he met JOHN CROWE RANSOM and ROBERT LOWELL, and afterward he taught at the University of Texas. He served in the air force during World War II. Jarrell's reputation as a poet was established in 1945 with the publication of his second book, *Little Friend, Little Friend*, which documents the intense fears and moral struggles of young soldiers. Other volumes followed, all characterized by great technical skill, empathy with others, and deep sensitivity. Following the war, Jarrell began teaching at the University of North Carolina, Greensboro, and remained there, except for occasional absences to teach elsewhere, until his death. Besides poetry, he wrote a satirical novel, several children's books, numerous poetry reviews— collected in *Poetry and the Age* (1953)— and a translation of Goethe's *Faust*.

Honorée Fanonne Jeffers (b. 1967) has published fiction in addition to three books of poetry, *The Gospel of Barbecue* (2000), which won the 1999 Stan and Tom Wick Prize for Poetry and was a finalist for the 2001 Paterson Poetry Prize; *Outlandish Blues* (2003); and *Red Clay Suite* (2007). She won the 2002 Julia Peterkin Award for Poetry and awards from the Barbara Deming Memorial Fund and the Rona Jaffe Foundation. Her poetry has been published in the anthologies *At Our Core: Women Writing about Power, Dark Eros*, and *Identity Lessons* and in many journals, including *Callaloo, Kenyon Review*, and *Prairie Schooner*. She teaches at the University of Oklahoma.

Robinson Jeffers (1887–1962) was born in Pittsburgh, where his father was a professor of Old Testament literature and biblical history at Western Theology Seminary. He began to learn Greek from his father at the age of five, and his early lessons were followed by travel in Europe, which included schooling in Zurich, Leipzig, and Geneva. He moved with his family to southern California in 1903. After graduating from Occidental College in 1906 and pursuing graduate studies in medicine and forestry, Jeffers decided to concentrate on poetry. In 1914 he settled in Carmel, California, and built a stone cottage and a forty-foot stone tower on land overlooking Carmel Bay and facing Point Lobos, where he lived the rest of his life (Tor House and Hawk Tower are open to the public—see www.torhouse .org). Much of Jeffers's verse celebrates the awesome beauty of the Carmel–Big Sur region, often contrasting the intense, rugged beauty of the landscape with the degraded and introverted condition of modern man.

Richard Jones (b. 1953) was born in London, where his father was serving in the U.S. Air Force, and studied at the University of Virginia. Jones is the author of several books of poems, including *The Blessing: New and Selected Poems*, which received the Midland Authors Award for Poetry for 2000, and most recently *The Correct Spelling & Exact Meaning* (2010). He has also produced a CD on the art of poetry, entitled *Body and Soul*. In addition, he has published two critical anthologies and edited the literary journal *Poetry East* since 1979. He taught at Piedmont College and the University of Virginia and presently is professor of English and director of the creative writing program at DePaul University in Chicago.

Ben Jonson (1572–1637), born in London, was the stepson of a bricklayer (his father died before he was born). He attended Westminster School and then joined the army. Jonson later worked as an actor and wrote comedies such as *Everyman in His Humor* (in which SHAKESPEARE acted the lead), *Volpone*, and *The Alchemist*. He wrote clear, elegant, "classical" poetry that contrasted with the intricate, subtle, "metaphysical" poetry of his contemporaries JOHN DONNE and GEORGE HERBERT. He was named poet laureate and was the idol of a generation of English writers, who dubbed themselves the Sons of Ben.

A. Van Jordan (b. 1965) was born and raised in Akron, Ohio. He earned degrees at Wittenberg University, Howard University, and Warren Wilson College. In 1995 he was awarded a D.C. Commission on the Arts and Humanities Literary Award. He was also a semifinalist for the 1999 "Discovery"/ The Nation Award. He is the author of three collections of poetry—*Rise* (2001), *M-A-C-N-O-L-I-A* (2004), and *Quantum Lyrics* (2007). He has taught at the University of North Carolina, Greensboro; the University of Texas, Austin; and Warren Wilson College, where he served as the 1999–2000 and 2000–2001 Joan Beebe Graduate Teaching Fellow. He currently teaches in the English department at the University of Michigan.

Allison Joseph (b. 1967) was born in London to Caribbean parents and grew up in Toronto and the Bronx. She earned her B.A. from Kenyon College and her M.F.A. from Indiana University. She is the author of seven collections of poetry: *What Keeps Us Here* (winner of Ampersand Press's 1992 Women Poets Series Competition and the John C.

Zacharis First Book Award), *Soul Train* (1997), *In Every Seam* (1997), *Imitation of Life* (2003), *Worldly Pleasures* (2004), *Voice* (2009), and *My Father's Kites* (2010). Her poems are often attuned to the experiences of women and minorities. She is editor of the *Crab Orchard Review* and holds the Judge William Holmes Cook Endowed Professorship and directs the M.F.A. program in creative writing at Southern Illinois University, Carbondale.

John Keats (1795–1821) was born in London. His father, a worker at a livery stable who married his employer's daughter and inherited the business, was killed by a fall from a horse when Keats was eight. When his mother died of tuberculosis six years later, Keats and his siblings were entrusted to the care of a guardian, a practical-minded man who took Keats out of school at fifteen and apprenticed him to a doctor. As soon as he qualified for medical practice, in 1815, he abandoned medicine for poetry, which he had begun writing two years earlier. In 1818, the year he contracted tuberculosis, he also fell madly in love with a pretty, vivacious young woman named Fanny Brawne, whom he could not marry because of his poverty, illness, and devotion to poetry. In the midst of such stress and emotional turmoil, his masterpieces poured out between January and September 1819: the great odes, a number of sonnets, and several longer lyric poems. In February 1820, his health failed rapidly; he went to Italy in the autumn, in hopes that the warmer climate would improve his health, and died there on February 23, 1821. His poems are rich with sensuous, lyrical beauty and emotional resonance, reflecting his delight in life as well as his awareness of life's brevity and difficulty.

Jane Kenyon (1947–1995) was born in Ann Arbor, Michigan, and grew up in the Midwest. She earned her B.A. and M.A. from the University of Michigan. She was married to poet Donald Hall from 1972 until her death from leukemia in 1995. During her lifetime she published four books of poetry—*From Room to Room* (1978), *The Boat of Quiet Hours* (1986), *Let Evening Come* (1990), and *Constance* (1993)—and a book of translation, *Twenty Poems of Anna Akhmatova* (1985). Two additional volumes were published after her death: *Otherwise: New and Selected Poems* (1996) and *A Hundred White Daffodils: Essays, Interviews, the Akhmatova Translations, Newspaper Columns, and One Poem* (1999). At the time of her death, she was New Hampshire's poet laureate.

Galway Kinnell (b. 1927) was born in Providence, Rhode Island, and attended Princeton University and the University of Rochester. He served in the U.S. Navy and then went to Paris on a Fulbright Fellowship. Returning to the United States, he worked for the Congress on Racial Equality and then traveled widely in the Middle East and Europe. He has taught in France, Australia, and Iran as well as at numerous colleges and universities in the United States. He has published many books of poetry, including *Selected Poems* (1980), for which he received both the Pulitzer Prize and the National Book Award. He has also published translations of works by Yves Bonnefoy, Yvanne Goll, François Villon, and Rainer Maria Rilke. He was the Erich Maria Remarque Professor of Creative Writing at New York University. He is now retired and lives in Vermont.

Etheridge Knight (1933–1991) was born in Corinth, Mississippi. He dropped out of school at age sixteen and served in the U.S. Army in Korea from 1947 to 1951, returning home with a shrapnel wound that caused him to fall deeper into a drug addiction that had begun during his service. In 1960 he was arrested for robbery and sentenced to eight years in an Indiana state prison. During this time he began writing poetry. His first book, *Poems from Prison* (1968), was published one year before his release. The book was a success, and Knight joined other poets in what came to be called the Black Arts Movement, the aesthetic and spiritual sister of the Black Power concept. He went on to write several more books of poetry and to receive many prestigious honors and awards. In 1990 he earned a B.A. in American poetry and criminal justice from Martin Center University in Indianapolis.

Yusef Komunyakaa (b. 1947) was born and grew up in Bogalusa, Louisiana. He earned degrees at the University of Colorado, Colorado State University, and the University of California, Irvine. His numerous books of poems include *Neon Vernacular: New and Selected Poems, 1977–1989* (1994), for which he received the Pulitzer Prize and the Kingsley Tufts Poetry Award, and *Thieves of Paradise* (1998), which was a finalist for the National Book Critics Circle Award. Other publications include *Blues Notes: Essays, Interviews & Commentaries* (2000), *The Jazz Poetry Anthology* (coedited with J. A. Sascha Feinstein, 1991), and a translation (with Martha Collins) of *The Insomnia of Fire* by Nguyen Quang Thieu (1995). He has taught at the University of New Orleans, Indiana University, and Princeton University and is currently a professor in the creative writing program at New York University.

Ted Kooser (b. 1939) was born in Ames, Iowa. He received his B.A. from Iowa State University and his M.A. in English from the University of Nebraska, Lincoln. He is the author of twelve collections of poetry, including *Sure Signs* (1980), *One World at a Time* (1985), *Weather Central* (1994), *Winter Morning Walks: One Hundred Postcards to Jim Harrison* (2000, winner of the 2001 Nebraska Book Award for poetry), and *Delights & Shadows* (2004). His fiction and nonfiction books include *Local Wonders: Seasons in the Bohemian Alps* (2002, winner of the Nebraska Book Award for Nonfiction in 2003) and *Braided Creek: A Conversation in Poetry* (2003), written with fellow poet and longtime friend Jim Harrison. His honors include two National Endowment for the Arts fellowships in poetry, a Pushcart Prize, the Stanley Kunitz Prize, and a Merit Award from the Nebraska Arts Council. He served as the United States Poet Laureate Consultant in Poetry to the Library of Congress from 2004 to 2006. He lives on an acreage near the village of Garland, Nebraska and is Presidential Professor in the English department of the University of Nebraska, Lincoln.

Maxine Kumin (b. 1925) was born in Philadelphia and received her B.A. and M.A. at Radcliffe College. She has published eleven books of poetry, including *Up Country: Poems of New England* (1972), for which she received the Pulitzer Prize. Her most recent collection is *Where I Live: New and Selected Poems 1990–2010* (2010). She is also the author of a memoir, *Inside the Halo and Beyond: The Anatomy of a Recovery* (2000); five novels; a collection of short stories; more than twenty children's books; and four books of essays. She has taught at the University of Massa-

chusetts, Columbia University, Brandeis University, and Princeton University, and has served as Poet Laureate Consultant in Poetry to the Library of Congress and as poet laureate of New Hampshire, where she lives.

Stanley Kunitz (1905–2006) was among the most beloved of poets. His life in poetry spanned more than three-quarters of a century, during which time he was always at the center of the poetry world. Born in Worcester, Massachusetts, Kunitz earned his B.A. and M.A. at Harvard University. His work often explored the consequences of traumatic events on a person's life, many times his own. He was quoted as saying that poetry was for him the single most important thing one could do with one's life. His first two books garnered little attention, but after serving in World War II, he continued to write and received great recognition. His *Selected Poems, 1928–1958* won the Pulitzer Prize, and in 1995 he received the National Book Award for *Passing Through: The Later Poems, New and Selected* (1995). His work has often been called an extension of the vision of JOHN KEATS. In 2000, at age ninety-five, he was named Poet Laureate Consultant in Poetry to the Library of Congress. He taught for many years at Columbia University and divided his time between New York City and Provincetown, Massachusetts, where he tended his magnificent garden.

Philip Larkin (1922–1985) was born into a working-class family in Coventry, England. He received a scholarship to attend Oxford University. With his second volume of poetry, *The Less Deceived* (1955), Larkin became the preeminent poet of his generation and a leading voice of what came to be called

"The Movement," a group of young English writers who rejected the prevailing fashion for neo-Romantic writing exemplified by W. B. YEATS and DYLAN THOMAS. Like THOMAS HARDY, a major influence on his work, Larkin focused on intense personal emotion but strictly avoided sentimentality or self-pity. In addition to writing poetry, Larkin was a highly respected jazz critic. He worked as a librarian in the provincial city of Hull, where he died in 1985.

Li-Young Lee (b. 1957) was born in Jakarta, Indonesia, to Chinese parents. His father, who had been personal physician to Mao Tse-tung, relocated his family to Indonesia, where he helped found Gamaliel University. In 1959, the Lee family fled the country to escape anti-Chinese sentiment, and they settled in the United States in 1964. Lee studied at the University of Pittsburgh, the University of Arizona, and the Brockport campus of the State University of New York. He has taught at several universities, including Northwestern University and the University of Iowa. He is the author of four collections of poetry—*Rose* (1986), which won the Delmore Schwartz Memorial Poetry Award; *The City in Which I Love You* (1991), which was the 1990 Lamont Poetry selection; *Book of My Nights* (2001); and *Behind My Eyes* (2008)—and a memoir, *The Winged Seed: A Remembrance* (1995), which received an American Book Award from the Before Columbus Foundation. In his poems one often senses a profound sense of exile, the influence of his father's presence, and a rich spiritual sensuality.

Denise Levertov (1923–1997) was born in Ilford, Essex. Her mother was Welsh and her father was a Russian Jew who became an Anglican priest. She was educated at home and claimed to have decided to become a writer at the age of five. Her first book, *The Double Image* (1946), brought her recognition as one of a group of poets dubbed the "New Romantics"—her poems often blend the sense of an objective observer with the sensibility of a spiritual searcher. She moved to the United States after marrying the American writer Mitchell Goodman. There she turned to free-verse poetry, and with her first American book, *Here and Now* (1956), she became an important voice in the American avant-garde. In the 1960s, she became involved in the movement protesting the Vietnam War. Levertov went on to publish more than twenty collections of poetry, four books of prose, and three volumes of poetry in translation. From 1982 to 1993, she taught at Stanford University. She spent the last decade of her life in Seattle.

Philip Levine (b. 1928) was born in Detroit and received his degrees from Wayne State University and the University of Iowa. He is the author of twenty books of poetry, including *The Simple Truth* (1994), which won the Pulitzer Prize. He has also published a collection of essays, *The Bread of Time: Toward an Autobiography* (1994), edited *The Essential Keats* (1987), and coedited and translated books of poetry by Spanish poet Gloria Fuertes and Mexican poet Jamie Sabines. He served as the Poet Laureate Consultant in Poetry to the Library of Congress from 2011 to 2012. Levine divides his time between Fresno, California, and New York City, where he taught at New York University.

Larry Levis (1946–1996) grew up on a farm near Fresno, California. He earned his B.A. from Fresno State College (now California State University), an M.A.

from Syracuse University, and a Ph.D. from the University of Iowa. He published six collections of poetry—several of them receiving major awards—and a collection of short fiction. He taught at the University of Missouri, the University of Utah, and Virginia Commonwealth University. Levis died of a heart attack at the age of forty-nine. PHILIP LEVINE wrote that he had years earlier recognized Levis as "the most gifted and determined young poet I have ever had the good fortune to have in one of my classes."

Audre Lorde (1934–1992) was born in New York City to West Indian parents. She grew up in Manhattan and attended Roman Catholic schools. While she was still in high school, her first poem appeared in *Seventeen* magazine. She earned her B.A. from Hunter College in New York City and her M.A. in library science from Columbia University. In 1968 she left her job as head librarian at the University of New York to become a lecturer and creative writer. She accepted a poet-in-residence position at Tougaloo College in Mississippi, where she discovered a love of teaching; published her first volume of poetry, *The First Cities* (1968); and met her long-term partner, Frances Clayton. Many other volumes of poetry followed, several winning major awards. She also published four volumes of prose, among them *The Cancer Journals* (1980), which chronicled her struggles with cancer, and *A Burst of Light* (1988), which won a National Book Award. In the 1980s, Lorde and writer Barbara Smith founded Kitchen Table: Women of Color Press. She was also a founding member of Sisters in Support of Sisters in South Africa, an organization that worked to raise awareness about women under apartheid. She was

the poet laureate of New York from 1991 to 1992.

Robert Lowell (1917–1978) was born in Boston into a prominent New England family. He attended Harvard University and then Kenyon College, where he studied under JOHN CROWE RANSOM. At Louisiana State University he studied with Robert Penn Warren and Cleanth Brooks as well as Allen Tate. He was always politically active—a conscientious objector during World War II and a Vietnam protestor—and suffered from manic depression. Lowell's reputation was established early: His second book, *Lord Weary's Castle*, was awarded the Pulitzer Prize for Poetry in 1947. In the mid-1950s he began to write more directly from personal experience and loosened his adherence to traditional meter and form. The result was a watershed collection of the "confessional" school, *Life Studies* (1959), which changed the landscape of modern poetry, much as T. S. ELIOT's *The Waste Land* had done three decades earlier. He died suddenly from a heart attack at age sixty.

Randall Mann (b. 1972) is a writer and editor living in San Francisco. He was born in Provo, Utah, the son of Olympic track and field medalist Ralph Mann, and received his M.F.A. from the University of Florida. His poems, often set in the landscapes of Florida or California, are influenced by the work of ELIZABETH BISHOP, PHILIP LARKIN, and Donald Justice. He is the author of two collections of poems, *Complaint in the Garden* (2004), winner of the 2003 Kenyon Review Prize in Poetry, and *Breakfast with Thom Gunn* (2009). Mann often works in traditional forms. He has said, "Form helps me approach more comfortably the personal, helps me harden argument." Exploring subjects such as expectation and brutality, Mann's work has been called vulnerable, brave, and unflinching at the same time.

Christopher Marlowe (1564–1593) was born in Canterbury the same year as WILLIAM SHAKESPEARE. The son of a shoemaker, he needed the help of scholarships to attend King's School, Canterbury, and Corpus Christi College, Cambridge. He was involved in secret political missions for the government. He was one of the most brilliant writers of his generation in narrative poetry, lyric poetry, and drama (his best-known play is *Doctor Faustus*). He died after being stabbed in a bar fight, reportedly over his bill, at the age of twenty-nine. "The Passionate Shepherd to His Love" is among the most famous of Elizabethan songs.

Andrew Marvell (1621–1678) was born in Hull, Yorkshire, and educated at Trinity College, Cambridge. After traveling in Europe, he worked as a tutor and in a government office (as assistant to JOHN MILTON) and later became a member of Parliament for Hull. Marvell was known in his lifetime as a writer of rough satires in verse and prose. His "serious" poetry, like "To His Coy Mistress," was not published until after his death. It is a famous exploration of the **carpe diem** theme (see the glossary).

Heather McHugh (b. 1948) was born to Canadian parents in San Diego and grew up in Virginia. She is a graduate of Radcliffe College and the University of Denver. McHugh has published numerous books of poetry, including *Upgraded to Serious* (2009) and *Hinge & Sign: Poems 1968–1993* (1994), which won both the *Boston Book Review*'s

Bingham Poetry Prize and the Pollack-*Harvard Review* Prize, was a finalist for the National Book Award, and was named a "Notable Book of the Year" by the *New York Times Book Review*. She has also written a book of prose, *Broken English: Poetry and Partiality* (1993), and two books of translations. She was awarded a MacArthur Foundation grant in 2009. She teaches as a core faculty member in the M.F.A. Program for Writers at Warren Wilson College and as Milliman Writer in Residence at the University of Washington, Seattle.

Claude McKay (1890–1948), the son of poor farmworkers, was born in Sunny Ville, Jamaica. He was educated by his older brother, who possessed a library of English novels, poetry, and scientific texts. At age twenty, McKay published a book of verse called *Songs of Jamaica*, recording his impressions of black life in Jamaica in dialect. In 1912, he traveled to the United States to attend Tuskegee Institute. He soon left to study agriculture at Kansas State University. In 1914 he moved to Harlem and became an influential member of the Harlem Renaissance. After committing himself to communism and traveling to Moscow in 1922, he lived for some time in Europe and Morocco, writing fiction. McKay later repudiated communism, converted to Roman Catholicism, and returned to the United States. He published several books of poetry as well as an autobiography, *A Long Way from Home* (1937). He wrote a number of sonnets protesting the injustices of black life in the United States, "America" among them. They are of interest for the way they use the most Anglo of forms to contain and intensify what the poem's language is saying.

Erika Meitner (b. 1975) was born and raised in Queens and on Long Island, New York. Her father is from Haifa, Israel; her mother was born in Stuttgart, Germany, the city where her grandparents lived after surviving Auschwitz, Ravensbruck, and Mauthausen concentration camps. Meitner earned her A.B. in creative writing from Dartmouth, studied at Hebrew University in Jerusalem, and received her M.F.A. from the University of Virginia, where she studied with RITA DOVE. Her first book, *Inventory at the All-Night Drugstore* (2003), won the 2002 Anhinga Prize for Poetry. Her second collection, *Ideal Cities*, was a 2009 National Poetry Series winner. Her third collection, *Makeshift Instructions for Vigilant Girls*, was published in 2011. She has taught creative writing at the University of Virginia; the University of Wisconsin, Madison; and the University of California, Santa Cruz, and now teaches in the M.F.A. program at Virginia Tech while completing a doctorate in religious studies at the University of Virginia, where she is the Morgenstern Fellow in Jewish Studies. Meitner has worked as a member of a documentary film group, which has had an influence on her and her poetry. She has said that in many of her poems she is trying to write her way back home.

W. S. Merwin (b. 1927) was born in New York City and lived in New Jersey and Pennsylvania during his precollege years. He studied creative writing and foreign languages at Princeton University and became a translator, living mostly in England and France until 1968, when he returned to the United States. He is the author of more than twenty books of poetry, including *A Mask for Janus* (1952), which was selected by W. H. AUDEN for the Yale Series

of Younger Poets, and *Carrier of Ladders* (1970), which received the Pulitzer Prize. *Migration: New and Selected Poems* (2005) won the National Book Award for that year. His most recent collection, *The Shadow of Sirius* (2008), also won a Pulitzer Prize. He has also published many books of translation, including Dante's *Purgatorio* (2000); numerous plays; and four books of prose, including *The Lost Upland* (1992), his memoir of life in the south of France. He served as the Poet Laureate Consultant in Poetry to the Library of Congress from 2010 to 2011. He lives in Hawaii and is active in environmental movements.

Edna St. Vincent Millay (1892–1950) was born in Rockland, Maine, and was encouraged to write from an early age by her mother. In 1912, at her mother's urging, Millay entered her poem "Renascence" into a contest; she won fourth place, publication in *The Lyric Year*, and a scholarship to Vassar. She spent the Roaring Twenties in Greenwich Village acting, writing plays and prize-winning poetry, and living a bohemian lifestyle. In 1923 her book *The Harp Weaver* was awarded the Pulitzer Prize. Millay continued to write and take an active part in political affairs for several decades thereafter, despite a diminished literary reputation.

John Milton (1608–1674), son of a well-off London businessman, was educated at St. Paul's School and at home with private tutors. After graduating with an M.A. from Christ's College, Cambridge, he spent the next six years reading at home. Milton had written verse since his university days, but he broke off to write prose tracts in favor of Oliver Cromwell, in whose government he later headed a department. The strain of long hours of reading and writing for the revolutionary cause aggravated a genetic weakness and resulted in his total blindness around 1651. He wrote his most famous works, *Paradise Lost* (1667), *Paradise Regained* (1671), and *Samson Agonistes* (1671), by dictating them to his daughter and other amanuenses.

Marianne Moore (1887–1972) was born near St. Louis and grew up in Carlisle, Pennsylvania. After studying at Bryn Mawr College and Carlisle Commercial College, she taught at a government Indian school in Carlisle. She moved to Brooklyn, where she became an assistant at the New York Public Library. She loved baseball and spent a good deal of time watching her beloved Brooklyn Dodgers. She began to write **Imagist poetry** (see the glossary) and to contribute to the *Dial*, a prestigious literary magazine. She served as acting editor of the *Dial*, from 1925 to 1929, and later was editor for four years. Moore was widely recognized for her work, receiving among other honors the Bollingen Prize, the National Book Award, and the Pulitzer Prize.

Thylias Moss (b. 1954) was born in Cleveland, Ohio. She attended Syracuse University and received her B.A. from Oberlin College and M.F.A. from the University of New Hampshire. She is the author of numerous books of poetry, most recently *Tokyo Butter* (2006); a memoir, *Tale of a Sky-Blue Dress* (1998); two children's books; and two plays, *Talking to Myself* (1984) and *The Dolls in the Basement* (1984). Among her awards are a Guggenheim Fellowship and a MacArthur Foundation Fellowship. Her recent work has become more experimental: Her theory of interacting language systems, Limited Fork Poetics, combines genres, multiple fields of study, and computer technology. She lives in Ann Arbor, where she is a professor of English and a professor of art and design at the University of Michigan.

David Mura (b. 1952), a third-generation Japanese American, was born in Great Lakes, Illinois, and graduated from Grinnell College in Iowa; he did graduate work at the University of Minnesota and Vermont College. Mura is a poet, creative nonfiction writer, critic, playwright, and performance artist. He is the author of numerous books of poetry, including *After We Lost Our Way* (1989), which was selected by GERALD STERN as a National Poetry Series winner; two novels; and two memoirs, *Turning Japanese: Memoirs of a Sansei* (1991), which was a New York Times Notable Book of the Year, and *Where the Body Meets Memory: An Odyssey of Race, Sexuality & Identity* (1996).

Marilyn Nelson (b. 1946) was born in Cleveland, Ohio, and grew up on numerous military bases. Her father was a U.S. serviceman in the air force, one of the last Tuskegee Airmen, and her mother was a teacher. While still in elementary school, she started writing. She earned her B.A. from the University of California, Davis; her M.A. from the University of Pennsylvania; and her Ph.D. from the University of Minnesota. *The Homeplace* (1990), *The Fields of Praise: New and Selected Poems* (1997), and *Carver: A Life in Poems* (2001) were all finalists for the National Book Award. In addition to many collections of her own poetry for adults and for children, she has translated from the Danish Halfdan Rasmussen's *Hundreds of Hens and Other Poems.*

She is founder and director of Soul Mountain Retreat, a writers' colony that encourages and supports poets who belong to underrepresented racial or cultural groups. She is professor emerita of English at the University of Connecticut and was poet laureate of Connecticut from 2001 to 2006.

Lorine Niedecker (1903–1970) was born and died in Fort Atkinson, Wisconsin. She lived much of her life in a small cabin on Black Hawk Island on Lake Koshkonong. Though celebrated by many of the most acclaimed experimental, modernist, and objectivist writers of the twentieth century, among them WILLIAM CARLOS WILLIAMS and Louis Zukofsky, she chose to remain outside the poetry world, living an all but isolated life. Niedecker said that she spent her childhood outdoors and from that developed her keen eye and strong sense of place. In 1931 she discovered objectivist poetry, which called for sincerity and objectification, values that fit well with her own vision and influenced her poems from that time on. While living on Black Hawk Island, she worked in a local hospital cleaning the kitchen and scrubbing floors. Her books include *New Goose* (1946), *North Central* (1968), *My Life by Water* (published the year of her death), and *Blue Chicory* (published posthumously in 1976). Her book of selected poems, *The Granite Pail*, was not published until 1985.

John Frederick Nims (1913–1999) was born in Muskegon, Michigan, and studied at DePaul University, the University of Notre Dame, and the University of Chicago, where he received his Ph.D. in 1945. By that time, he had already distinguished himself as a poet and critic. He went on to teach at Harvard

University, the University of Florence, the University of Toronto, the Bread Loaf School of English, Williams College, and the University of Missouri, among others. He was editor of *Poetry* magazine from 1978 to 1984. He was the author of many books of poetry and many translations as well as several critical works and a widely used textbook, *Western Wind: An Introduction to Poetry* (1974).

Naomi Shihab Nye (b. 1952) was born in St. Louis of a Palestinian father and an American mother and grew up in both the United States and Jerusalem. She received her B.A. from Trinity University in San Antonio, Texas, where she still resides with her family. She is the author of many books of poems, most recently *You and Yours* (2005), which received the Isabella Gardner Poetry Award. She has also written short stories and books for children and has edited anthologies, several of which focus on the lives of children and represent work from around the world. She is a singer-songwriter and on several occasions has traveled to the Middle East and Asia for the U.S. Information Agency, promoting international goodwill through the arts. Nye's work often attests to a universal sense of exile, from place, home, love, and one's self and the way the human spirit confronts them.

Frank (Francis Russell) O'Hara (1926–1966) was born in Baltimore and grew up in Massachusetts. He studied piano at the New England Conservatory in Boston from 1941 to 1944 and served in the South Pacific and Japan during World War II. He majored in English at Harvard, then received his M.A. in English at the University of Michigan in 1951. He moved to New

York, where he worked at the Museum of Modern Art and began writing poetry seriously as well as composing essays and reviews on painting and sculpture. His first volume of poems, *A City in Winter*—thirteen poems together with two drawings by the artist Larry Rivers—was published in 1952. Other collaborations with artists followed. His first major collection of poetry was *Meditations in an Emergency* (1957). His poetry is often casual, relaxed in diction, and full of specific detail, seeking to convey the immediacy of life. He described his work as "I do this I do that" poetry because his poems often read like entries in a diary, as in the opening lines of "The Day Lady Died." He was killed at forty when he was struck by a sand buggy while vacationing on Fire Island, New York.

Sharon Olds (b. 1942) was born in San Francisco and educated at Stanford and Columbia Universities. She has written eleven books of poetry (most recently *Strike Sparks: Selected Poems, 1980–2002* [2004] and *One Secret Thing* [2008]) and received numerous important prizes and awards. In the words of Elizabeth Frank, "she and her work are about nothing less than the joy of making—of making love, making babies, making poems, making sense of love, memory, death, the feel—the actual bodily texture—of life." She held the position of New York State Poet from 1998 to 2000. She teaches poetry workshops at New York University's graduate creative writing program, along with workshops at Goldwater Hospital in New York, a public facility for people with physical disabilities.

Mary Oliver (b. 1935) was born in Cleveland and educated at Ohio State University and Vassar College. She is the author of over twenty volumes of poetry, including *American Primitive* (1983), for which she won the Pulitzer Prize, and four books of prose. Her most recent book is *Swan: Poems and Prose Poems* (2010). She held the Catharine Osgood Foster Chair for Distinguished Teaching at Bennington College until 2001 and now lives in Provincetown, Massachusetts. Oliver is one of the most respected of poets concerned for the natural world.

Charles Olson (1910–1970) was born and raised in Worcester, Massachusetts, but spent summers in Gloucester, Massachusetts, which later became the focus of his writing. He was a brilliant student at Classical High School and won a ten-week trip to Europe where he met WILLIAM BUTLER YEATS. He graduated and subsequently earned an M.A. in English from Wesleyan University. During World War II, he worked as assistant chief of the Foreign Languages Division of the Office of War Information, an agency responsible for monitoring and protecting minorities in the United States. Olson had a wide range of interests including mythology, anthropology, cultural history, languages, and science. He drew on his knowledge in his poetry and as a result challenged notions about both the form and content of a poem. In 1949, he published "The Kingfishers," a poem that renounces his European heritage and affirms native cultures. In 1950, he wrote his manifesto *Projective Verse*, in which he affirms that meter must be aligned with the breathing of the poet, that sound must take precedence over sense, and that the form of the poem should be a projection of the poet's mind onto the page, and in which he declares that the role of the poet is to regard the self as one object among all objects in nature.

In 1948, Olson joined the innovative arts school Black Mountain College, where he became the leader of the movement known as Black Mountain poetry. From the 1940s on, Olson worked on his epical work, *The Maximus Poems*, which deals with the origins of America. The first volume was not completed until 1960; the second appeared in 1968; and the third was published posthumously in 1975.

George Oppen (1908–1984) was born into a wealthy Jewish family. His father, George Oppenheimer, was a diamond merchant, who changed the family name to *Oppen* in 1927. When Oppen was four, his mother committed suicide. His father remarried in 1917, and Oppen had a difficult relationship with his stepmother, which troubled him the rest of his life. In 1926, he went to Oregon State University, where he met Mary Colby; both were expelled for staying out all night together. They hitchhiked across the country to New York, married, and turned away from the opulent life of his family. He met Louis Zukofsky and made himself a member of the objectivist movement, which emphasized simplicity and clarity and remaining faithful to facts. During the Great Depression and the rise of fascism, Oppen and his wife became politically active, eventually joining the Communist Party. Oppen stopped writing poetry and, in 1942, enlisted in the army to fight fascism. He was badly wounded and awarded the Purple Heart. Investigated by the House Un-American Activities Committee during the McCarthy era, the couple fled to Mexico City and Oppen worked as a carpenter. They returned to the United States and Oppen revived his poetic career on the basis of his core belief that "true seeing is an act of love." He

published several collections of poetry in the 1960s, including *Of Being Numerous* (1968), which won the Pulitzer Prize. The San Francisco Museum of Modern Art, in 1973, named him one of "Four Major American Poets," and later he received lifetime achievement awards from the American Academy and Institute of Arts and Letters and the National Endowment for the Arts.

Simon J. Ortiz (b. 1941) was born and raised in the Acoma Pueblo Community in Albuquerque, New Mexico. He received his early education from the Bureau of Indian Affairs school on the Acoma reservation, later attending the University of New Mexico and completing his M.F.A. at the University of Iowa, where he was a part of the International Writing Program. Unlike most Native American contemporary writers, Ortiz is a full-blooded Native American, and his first language was Keresan. By learning English, he found a way to communicate with those outside his immediate culture. His poetry explores the significance of individual origins and journeys, which he sees as forming a vital link in the continuity of life. His many writing accomplishments include poems, short stories, essays, and children's books. Ortiz has taught Native American literature and creative writing at San Diego State University, Navajo Community College, Marin College, the Institute for the Arts of the American Indian, the University of New Mexico, the University of Toronto, and most recently, Arizona State University.

Wilfred Owen (1893–1918) was born in Oswestry, Shropshire, and went to school at Birkenhead Institute and Shrewsbury Technical School. He studied at London University but was forced to withdraw for financial reasons. After that he went to Dunsden, Oxfordshire, as a vicar's assistant. At Dunsden, Owen grew disaffected with the church and left to teach in France. He enlisted in 1915 and six months later was hospitalized in Edinburgh, where he met Siegfried Sassoon, whose war poems had just been published. Owen was sent back to the front and was killed one week before the armistice. He is the most widely recognized of the "war poets," a group of World War I writers who brought the realism of war into poetry.

Linda Pastan (b. 1932) was born in New York City, graduated from Radcliffe College, and earned an M.A. from Brandeis University. She has published many books of poetry—most recently *Traveling Light* (2011)—and received numerous awards for them, including a Dylan Thomas Award. Her deeply emotional poetry often has grief at its center. She is known for writing short poems that address topics like family life, domesticity, motherhood, the female experience, aging, death, loss and the fear of loss, as well as the fragility of life and relationships. She served as poet laureate of Maryland from 1991 to 1994 and was a staff member at the Breadloaf Writers Conference for twenty years. She lives in Potomac, Maryland.

Marge Piercy (b. 1936) was born in working-class Detroit and studied at the University of Michigan and Northwestern University. She has published seventeen books of poetry, seventeen novels, a collection of essays on poetry, *Parti-Colored Blocks for a Quilt* (1982), and a memoir, *Sleeping with Cats* (2002). She has been deeply involved in many of the major progressive political battles of the past fifty years, including anti-Vietnam War activities, the women's movement, and most recently the resistance to the war in Iraq.

Wang Ping (b. 1957) received her B.A. from Beijing University and came to the United States in 1985. She earned a Ph.D. at New York University. She is the author of two short story collections, *American Visa* (1994) and *The Last Communist Virgin* (2007); a novel, *Foreign Devil* (1996); two poetry collections, *Of Flesh & Spirit* (1998) and *The Magic Whip* (2003); and a cultural study, *Aching for Beauty: Footbinding in China* (2000). She is also the editor and cotranslator of the anthology *New Generation: Poetry from China Today* (1999), and her writing has appeared in many journals and anthologies. She teaches English at Macalester College in St. Paul, Minnesota.

Robert Pinsky (b. 1940) was born in Long Branch, New Jersey. He is the author of many books of poetry, including *The Figured Wheel: New and Collected Poems, 1966–1996* (1996), which won the 1997 Lenore Marshall Poetry Prize and was a Pulitzer Prize nominee. He has also published several books of criticism, two books of translation, a biography—*The Life of David* (2005)—several books on reading poetry, and a computerized novel, *Mindwheel*. In 1999 he coedited with Maggie Dietz *Americans' Favorite Poems: The Favorite Poem Project Anthology*. He is currently poetry editor of the weekly Internet magazine *Slate* and teaches in the graduate writing program at Boston University. In 1997 he was named Poet Laureate Consultant in Poetry to the Library of Congress.

Sylvia Plath (1932–1963) grew up in a middle-class family in Boston and showed early promise as a writer, having stories and poems published in magazines such as *Seventeen* while she was in high school. As a student at Smith College, she was selected for an internship at *Mademoiselle* magazine and spent a month working in New York in the summer of 1953. Upon her return home, she suffered a serious breakdown and attempted suicide, was institutionalized, and then returned to Smith College for her senior year in 1954. She received a Fulbright Fellowship to study at Cambridge University in England, where she met the poet Ted Hughes. They were married in 1956. They lived in the United States as well as England, and Plath studied under ROBERT LOWELL at Boston University. Her marriage broke up in 1962, and from her letters and poems it appears that she was approaching another breakdown. On February 11, 1963, she committed suicide. Four books of poetry appeared during her lifetime, and her *Selected Poems* was published in 1985. The powerful, psychologically intense poetry for which she is best known (including "Daddy") was written after 1960, influenced by Lowell's "confessional" style (see **confessional poetry** in the glossary).

Edgar Allan Poe (1809–1849) was born in Boston. His parents were touring actors; both died before he was three years old, and he was taken into the home of John Allan, a prosperous merchant in Richmond, Virginia, and baptized Edgar Allan Poe. His childhood was uneventful, although he studied in England for five years (1815–1820). In 1826 he entered the University of Virginia but, because of gambling debts, stayed for only a year. He began to write and published a book of poems in 1827. He joined the army and gained an appointment to West Point, but was

dismissed after six months for disobeying orders. He turned to fiction writing and journalism to support himself. He began publishing stories and was appointed editor of the *Southern Literary Messenger* in Richmond, but his job was terminated after two years because of his drinking. He achieved success as an artist and editor in New York City (1837), then in Philadelphia (1838–1844), and again in New York (1844–1849), but failed to satisfy his employers and to secure a livelihood, and thus lived in or close to poverty his entire life. He is famous for his horror tales and is credited with inventing the detective story, as well as for writing poetry with a prominent use of **rhythms**, **alliteration**, and **assonance** (see the glossary) that gives it a strongly musical quality.

Alexander Pope (1688–1744) was born in London to a successful textile merchant and spent his childhood in the country, stunted by tuberculosis of the spine (his height never exceeded four and a half feet). Pope was also limited by his Catholicism: Laws prevented Catholics from attending a university, voting, or holding public office. He instead turned to writing and gained considerable fame for his satire *The Rape of the Lock* and his translations of Homer. Fame also brought ridicule and vehement attacks from critics holding different political views, and Pope struck back with nasty satires on his detractors. Later in his career, he wrote a good deal of ethical and philosophical verse.

Ezra Pound (1885–1972) was born in Idaho but grew up outside Philadelphia; he attended the University of Pennsylvania for two years and graduated from Hamilton College. He taught for two years at Wabash College, then left for Europe, living for the next few years in London, where he edited *Little Review* and founded several literary movements—including the **Imagists** (see the glossary) and the Vorticists. After moving to Italy, he began his major work, the *Cantos*, and became involved in fascist politics. During World War II he did radio broadcasts from Italy in support of Mussolini, for which he was indicted for treason in the United States. Judged mentally unfit for trial, he remained in an asylum in Washington, D.C., until 1958, when the charges were dropped. Pound spent his last years in Italy. He is generally considered the poet most responsible for defining and promoting a modernist aesthetic in poetry.

Dudley Randall (1914–2000) was born in Washington, D.C., and lived most of his life in Detroit. His first published poem appeared in the *Detroit Free Press* when he was thirteen. He worked for Ford Motor Company and then for the U.S. Postal Service and served in the South Pacific during World War II. He graduated from Wayne State University in 1949 and then from the library school at the University of Michigan. In 1965 Randall established the Broadside Press, one of the most important publishers of modern black poetry. "Ballad of Birmingham," written in response to the 1963 bombing of a church in which four girls were killed, has been set to music and recorded. It became an anthem for many in the civil rights movement.

John Crowe Ransom (1888–1974) was born in Pulaski, Tennessee, the son of a preacher. He studied at Vanderbilt University and then at Christ Church College, Oxford, on a Rhodes scholarship. After service in World War I, he taught first at Vanderbilt and later at Kenyon College, where he edited the *Kenyon Review*. He published three volumes of highly acclaimed poetry, but after 1927 principally devoted himself to critical writing. He was a guiding member of the Fugitives, a group of writers who sought to preserve a traditional aesthetic ideal that was firmly rooted in classical values and forms. As a critic, he promulgated the highly influential New Criticism, which focused attention on texts as self-sufficient entities, to be analyzed through rigorous methodologies intended to reveal their depth, subtleties, and intricacies of technique and theme.

Donald Revell (b. 1954) was born in the Bronx. He is a graduate of Harper College, with graduate degrees from the State University of New York at both Binghamton and Buffalo. His first book, *From the Abandoned Cities* (1983), was a National Poetry Series winner. He has published ten additional poetry collections, most recently *A Thief of Strings* (2007) and *The Bitter Withy* (2009). He has also published translation and criticism as well as books on creative writing and on the creative process and is poetry editor of the *Colorado Review*. He was the winner of the 2004 Lenore Marshall Award and two-time winner of the PEN Center USA Award in poetry. He is a professor of English and creative writing at the University of Nevada, Las Vegas.

Adrienne Rich (1929–2012) was born in Baltimore, the elder daughter of a forceful Jewish intellectual who encouraged and critiqued her writing. While she was at Radcliffe College in 1951, W. H. AUDEN selected her book *A Change of World* for the Yale Younger Poets Award. She became involved in radical politics, especially in the opposition to the Vietnam War, and taught inner-city minority youth. She had felt a tension as she modeled her early poetry on that of male writers, and in the 1970s Rich became a feminist, freeing herself from her old models and becoming an influential figure in contemporary American literature. She was the author of over twenty volumes of poetry—including *Diving into the Wreck* (1973), *Dark Fields of the Republic* (1995), and *The School Among the Ruins: Poems 2000–2004* (2004), which won the Book Critics Circle Award—and several books of nonfiction prose. She was awarded a MacArthur Foundation Fellowship in 1994 and in 1999 received the Lifetime Achievement Award from the Lannan Foundation. She was the 2006 recipient of the National Book Foundation's Medal for Distinguished Contribution to American Letters.

Atsuro Riley (b. 1960) grew up in South Carolina. His first book, *Romey's Order* (2010), received the Kate Tufts Discovery Award, *The Believer* Poetry Award, and a Witter Bynner Award from the Library of Congress. Riley's poetry has been called "percussive" because of its heavily stressed texture rich in consonants. The poems often focus on elemental images connected to living in a particular landscape, whether Vietnam during the war or the rural South. His works have been compared to those of GERARD MANLEY HOPKINS in their range of intensities and rich attention to often overlooked detail. Riley has received a Pushcart Prize and the J. Howard and M. J. Wood Prize from *Poetry* magazine.

Alberto Ríos (b. 1952) was born to a Guatemalan father and an English mother in Nogales, Arizona, on the Mexican border. He earned a B.A. in English and one in psychology and an M.F.A. at the University of Arizona. In addition to ten books of poetry, he has published three collections of short stories and a memoir, *Capirotada: A Nogales Memoir* (1999). His work often fuses realism, surrealism, and magical realism, as exemplified by "Nani" (p. 259). Since 1994 he has been Regents Professor of English at Arizona State University, where he has taught since 1982.

Edwin Arlington Robinson (1869–1935) was born in Head Tide, Maine, and grew up in the equally provincial Maine town of Gardiner, the setting for much of his poetry. He was forced to leave Harvard University after two years because of his family's financial difficulties. He published his first two books of poetry in 1896 and 1897 ("Richard Cory" appeared in the latter). For the next quarter-century Robinson chose to live in poverty and write his poetry, relying on temporary jobs and charity from friends. President Theodore Roosevelt, at the urging of his son Kermit, used his influence to get Robinson a sinecure job in the New York Custom House in 1905, giving him time to write. He published numerous books of mediocre poetry in the next decade. The tide turned for him with *The Man Against the Sky* (1916); the numerous volumes that followed received high praise and sold well. He was awarded three Pulitzer Prizes: for *Collected Poems* in 1921, *The Man Who Died Twice* in 1924, and *Tristram* in 1927. Robinson was the first major American poet of the twentieth century, unique in that he devoted his life to poetry and willingly paid the price in poverty and obscurity.

Theodore Roethke (1908–1963) was the son of a commercial greenhouse operator in Saginaw, Michigan. As a child, he spent much time in the greenhouse, and the impressions of nature he formed there later influenced the subjects and imagery of his verse. Roethke graduated from the University of Michigan and studied at Harvard University. Although he published only eight books of poetry, they were held in high regard by critics, some of whom considered him among the best poets of his generation. *The Waking* was awarded the Pulitzer Prize in 1954; *Words for the Wind* (1958) received the Bollingen Prize and the National Book Award. He taught at many colleges and universities and gained a reputation as an exceptional teacher of poetry writing, although his career was interrupted several times by serious mental breakdowns.

Christina Rossetti (1830–1894), born in London into a literary family (her brother Dante Gabriel Rossetti was one of the Pre-Raphaelite group), began writing poetry at an early age. Ill health saved her from a career as a governess; instead she nursed her ailing father and worked at the St. Mary Magdalen Home for Fallen Women. Rossetti had a strong Anglican religiosity that led her to give up theater and opera and turn down two offers of marriage. She wrote six collections of poetry as well as short stories, nursery rhymes, and religious essays.

Mary Ruefle (b. 1952) was born near Pittsburgh but spent her early life moving around the United States and Europe as the daughter of a military officer. She graduated from Bennington College with a literature major. She has published eleven books of poetry, including *Memling's Veil* (1982); *The Adamant* (1989), winner of the 1988 Iowa Poetry Prize; *A Little White Shadow* (2006); and *Selected Poems* (2010). She

published her first collection of short stories, *The Most of It*, in 2008. Among her awards are a Guggenheim Fellowship, an American Academy of Arts and Letters Award in Literature, and a Whiting Foundation Writer's Award. She lives in Vermont, where she is a professor in the Vermont College M.F.A. program.

Mary Jo Salter (b. 1954) was born in Grand Rapids, Michigan, and raised in Detroit, Michigan, and Baltimore, Maryland. She earned her B.A. from Harvard, where she studied under ELIZABETH BISHOP, and her M.A. from Cambridge University. She is the author of six collections of poetry, most recently *A Phone Call to the Future* (2008). She is often aligned with the New Formalists but has said that she is only interested in finding the appropriate way of saying something in a poem and that rhyme and meter please her and help her achieve that. Salter often connects domestic concerns to locales in this country and in Iceland, Italy, England, and France to reveal her confrontation with the ineffable. In addition to being a poet, Salter is an essayist, a playwright, and a lyricist. She worked as an editor at the *Atlantic Monthly* and the *New Republic* and is coeditor of *The Norton Anthology of Poetry*. She taught at Mount Holyoke College from 1985 to 2007 and currently is a professor in the writing seminars program at Johns Hopkins University. She served as vice president of the Poetry Society of America from 1995 to 2007.

Thom Satterlee (b. 1967) began writing at the age of seventeen, while he was an exchange student in Kolding, Denmark. He earned a B.A. in philosophy from Houghton College, an M.A. in English literature from SUNY Brockport, and an M.F.A. in literary translation from the University of Arkansas. He has taught at the University of Miami and Taylor University. Since the fall of 2011, he has pursued his dream of full-time writing. He is author of a collection of poems, *Burning Wyclif* (2006), and coeditor of *The Global Game: Writers on Soccer* (2008). He has also published translations of two noted Danish poets, Henrik Nordbrandt (*The Hangman's Lament*, 2003) and Per Aage Brandt (*These Hands*, 2011). He and his wife live in a hundred-year-old house across from farm fields in Marion, Indiana.

Anne Sexton (1928–1974) was born in Newton, Massachusetts, and dropped out of Garland Junior College to get married. After suffering nervous breakdowns following the births of her two children, she was encouraged to enroll in writing programs. Studying under ROBERT LOWELL at Boston University, she was a fellow student of SYLVIA PLATH. Like the work of other "confessional" poets, Sexton's poetry includes an intimate view of her life and emotions. She made the experience of being a woman a central issue in her poetry, bringing into it such subjects as menstruation, abortion, and drug addiction. She published at least a dozen books of poetry—*Live or Die* was awarded the Pulitzer Prize for Poetry in 1966—as well as four children's books coauthored with MAXINE KUMIN. Sexton's emotional problems continued, along with a growing addiction to alcohol and sedatives, and she committed suicide in 1974.

William Shakespeare (1564–1616) was born in Stratford-upon-Avon, England, where his father was a glovemaker and bailiff, and he presumably went to grammar school there. He married

Anne Hathaway in 1582, and sometime before 1592 he left for London to work as a playwright and actor. Shakespeare joined the Lord Chamberlain's Men (later the King's Men), an acting company for which he wrote thirty-five plays, before retiring to Stratford around 1612. In addition to being a skillful dramatist, he was perhaps the finest lyric poet of his day, as exemplified by songs scattered through his plays, two early nondramatic poems (*Venus and Adonis* and *The Rape of Lucrece*), and the sonnet sequence expected of all noteworthy writers in the Elizabethan Age. Shakespeare's sonnets were probably written in the 1590s, although they were not published until 1609.

Percy Bysshe Shelley (1792–1822) was born into a wealthy aristocratic family in Sussex County, England. He was educated at Eton and then went on to Oxford University but was expelled after six months for writing a defense of atheism, the first price he would pay for his nonconformity and radical (for his time) commitment to social justice. The following year he eloped with Harriet Westbrook, daughter of a tavern keeper, despite his belief that marriage was a tyrannical and degrading social institution (she was sixteen, he eighteen). He became a disciple of the radical social philosopher William Godwin, fell in love with Godwin's daughter, Mary Wollstonecroft Godwin (the author, later, of *Frankenstein*), and went to live with her in France. Two years later, after Harriet committed suicide, they married and moved to Italy, where they shifted about restlessly and Shelley was generally short on money and in poor health. In such trying circumstances, he wrote his greatest works. He died at age thirty, when the boat he was in was overturned by a sudden storm.

Sir Philip Sidney (1554–1586) was born into an important aristocratic family in Elizabethan England. He attended Shrewsbury School and Oxford University, although he left without a degree and completed his education through extended travel on the Continent. He was the epitome of the well-rounded courtier idealized in his era, excelling as a soldier, writer, literary patron, and diplomat. He was the author of an important work of prose fiction *(Arcadia)*, a landmark essay in literary criticism *(The Defense of Poesy)*, and an important sonnet cycle (*Astrophil and Stella,* which includes "Loving in truth, and fain in verse my love to show"). His poetry has been labeled "news from the heart."

Leslie Marmon Silko (b. 1948) was born in Albuquerque of mixed Pueblo, Mexican, and white ancestry and grew up on the Laguna Pueblo Reservation in New Mexico. She earned her B.A. (with honors) from the University of New Mexico. In a long and productive writing career (she was already writing stories in elementary school), she has published poetry, novels, short stories, essays, letters, and film scripts. The best known of her works is her 1977 novel, *Ceremony*. She taught creative writing first at the University of New Mexico and later at the University of Arizona. She has been named a Living Cultural Treasure by the New Mexico Humanities Council and has received the Native Writers' Circle of the Americas Lifetime Achievement Award. She was awarded a MacArthur Foundation grant in 1981. Her work is a graphic telling of the life of native peoples, maintaining its rich spiritual heritage while exposing the terrible consequences of European domination.

Charles Simic (b. 1938) was born in Belgrade, Yugoslavia. In 1953 he, his mother, and his brother joined his father in Chicago, where he lived until 1958. His first poems were published in 1959, when he was twenty-one. In 1961 he was drafted into the U.S. Army, and in 1966 he earned his B.A. from New York University. His first book of poems, *What the Grass Says*, was published in 1967. Since then he has published more than sixty books of poetry, translations, and essays, including *The World Doesn't End: Prose Poems* (1990), for which he received the Pulitzer Prize for Poetry. Simic is a professor of English at the University of New Hampshire. He served as Poet Laureate Consultant in Poetry to the Library of Congress from 2007 to 2008.

Edith Sitwell (1887–1964) was born into an aristocratic and literary family in late Victorian England. She both shocked and amused people by her writing, eccentric behavior, and dramatic Elizabethan dress. Influenced by Baudelaire and the symbolists, T. S. ELIOT's poetry, Stravinsky's music, and abstract art, Sitwell introduced verbal and rhythmic innovations that contrasted sharply with then-current verse.

Christopher Smart (1722–1771) was born in Shipbourne, Kent. He attended the Durham School and was later educated at Pembroke College, Cambridge, where he won prizes for his poetry. After college, Smart lived in London, editing and writing copy for periodicals and composing songs for the popular theater. In 1752 he published his first collection, *Poems on Several Occasions*. In the 1750s Smart developed a form of religious mania that compelled him to continuous prayer. From 1756 on, he was confined, with one brief intermission, in St. Luke's Hospital until 1763 and then in Mr. Potter's Madhouse in Bethnal Green. During his confinement, he wrote what many see as his most original and lasting works—*A Song to David* and *Jubilate Agno*, with its well-known homage to his cat, Jeoffry. Smart ranks as one of the most respected and influential religious poets in English literature.

Gary Snyder (b. 1930) was born in San Francisco and grew up in Oregon and Washington. He studied anthropology at Reed College and Oriental languages at the University of California, Berkeley, where he became associated with the Beat movement; however, his poetry often deals with nature rather than the urban interests more typical of Beat poetry. He has published twenty books of poetry and prose, including *Turtle Island* (1974), which won the Pulitzer Prize for Poetry. Snyder is active in the environmental movement and spent a number of years in Japan devoting extensive study to Zen Buddhism. He taught for many years at the University of California, Davis.

Cathy Song (b. 1955) was born in Hawaii and lived in the small town of Wahiawa on Oahu. She left Hawaii for the East Coast, earning a B.A. from Wellesley College and an M.A. in creative writing from Boston University. Her first book, *Picture Bride*, was chosen by Richard Hugo for the Yale Series of Younger Poets in 1982. Since then she has published four other books of poetry: *Frameless Windows, Squares of Light* (1988), *School Figures* (1994), *The Land of Bliss* (2001), and *Cloud Moving Hands* (2007).

Gary Soto (b. 1952) grew up in Fresno, California. He earned his B.A. from California State University, Fresno, and M.F.A. from the University of California, Irvine. At a young age, he began working in the fields of the San Joaquin Valley. Much of his poetry comes out of and reflects his working background, that of migrant workers and tenant farmers in the fields of southern California, and provides glimpses into the lives of families in the barrio. Soto's language comes from earthy, gritty, raw everyday American speech. His first book, *The Elements of San Joaquin*, won the 1976 United States Award from the International Poetry Forum. He has published thirteen collections of poetry, eight novels, four essay collections, numerous young adult and children's books, and a memoir, *Living Up the Street* (1985), which received the American Book Award.

Edmund Spenser (1552–1599), a contemporary of WILLIAM SHAKESPEARE, was the greatest English nondramatic poet of his time. Best known for his romantic and national epic *The Faerie Queene*, Spenser wrote poems of a number of other types as well and was important as an innovator in metrics and forms (as in his development of the special form of sonnet that bears his name—see **Spenserian sonnet** in the glossary). "One day I wrote her name upon the strand" is number 75 in *Amoretti*, a sequence of sonnets about a courtship addressed to a woman named Elizabeth, probably Elizabeth Boyle, who became his second wife.

William Stafford (1914–1995) was born in Hutchinson, Kansas, and studied at the University of Kansas and then at the University of Iowa Writers' Workshop.

In between, he was a conscientious objector during World War II and worked in labor camps. In 1948 Stafford moved to Oregon, where he taught at Lewis and Clark College until he retired in 1980. His first major collection of poems, *Traveling through the Dark*, was published when Stafford was forty-eight. It won the National Book Award in 1963. He went on to publish more than sixty-five volumes of poetry and prose and came to be known as a very influential teacher of poetry. From 1970 to 1971 he was Poet Laureate Consultant in Poetry to the Library of Congress.

A. E. Stallings (b. 1968) grew up in Decatur, Georgia, and studied classics at the University of Georgia and the University of Oxford. Since 1999 she has lived in Athens, Greece, where she is poetry program director at the Athens Centre. She was awarded a MacArthur Fellowship in 2011. Her first collection of poetry, *Archaic Smile* (1999), received the Richard Wilbur Award. She has published two more volumes of poetry— *Hapax* (2006) and *Olives* (2012)—and a verse translation of Lucretius's *De Rerum Natura—The Nature of Things* (2007). In 2010 she was awarded the Willis Barnstone Translation Prize. Stallings's poetry uses traditional forms, and she has been associated with the New Formalism, although her approach to formal verse is flexible and few of her poems are strictly regular metrically.

Gertrude Stein (1874–1946) was born in Allegheny, Pennsylvania. After attending Radcliffe College, Harvard University, and Johns Hopkins Medical School, she moved to France in 1903 and became a central figure in the Parisian art world. An advocate of the avant-garde, her salon became a gathering place for the "new moderns." What Henri Matisse and Pablo Picasso achieved in the visual arts, Stein attempted in her writing. Her first published book, *Three Lives* (1909), the stories of three working-class women, has been called a minor masterpiece. A number of other books followed, including *The Autobiography of Alice B. Toklas* (1933), actually Stein's own autobiography.

Gerald Stern (b. 1925) was born in Pittsburgh and studied at the University of Pittsburgh and Columbia University. Stern came late to poetry: He was forty-six when he published his first book. Since then he has published sixteen collections of poems, most recently *Save the Last Dance: Poems* (2008) and *Early Collected Poems, 1965–1992* (2010), and received many prestigious awards, including the 1998 National Book Award for Poetry for *This Time: New and Selected Poems*. Stern's work has often been compared to that of WALT WHITMAN and JOHN KEATS for its exploration of the self and the sometimes ecstatic exuberance of its verse. He taught at many universities, including Columbia University, New York University, Sarah Lawrence College, the University of Pittsburgh, and the University of Iowa Writers' Workshop, until his retirement in 1995.

Wallace Stevens (1879–1955) was born in Reading, Pennsylvania, and attended Harvard University for three years. He tried journalism and then attended New York University Law School, after which he worked as a legal consultant. He spent most of his life working as an executive for the Hartford Accident and Indemnity Company, spending his evenings writing some of the most imaginative and influential poetry of his time. Although now considered one of the major American poets of the twentieth century, he did not receive widespread recognition until the publication of his *Collected Poems* just a year before his death.

Ruth Stone (1915–2011) was born in Roanoke, Virginia. Her mother paid her a penny for every poem she could recite. Stone attended the University of Illinois at Urbana-Champaign and married fellow-poet Walter Stone. Her first book of poetry, *In an Iridescent Time*, was published in 1959, shortly before her husband committed suicide. The shock and grief of her husband's suicide marked her poetry for the rest of her life: She once called her works "love poems, all written to a dead man." She moved with her three daughters to a farmhouse in rural Vermont and took a series of short-term teaching positions before becoming a professor of English at SUNY Binghamton in 1990. She did not receive wide recognition for her poetry until 1999 when *Ordinary Words* won the National Book Critics Circle Award. In 2002, when she was eighty-seven, her collection *In the Next Galaxy* won the National Book Award, and in 2008 *What Love Comes To: New & Selected Poems* was a finalist for the Pulitzer Prize. Her lyrics are compact and known for their strangeness and way of at once attending to the domestic and the metaphysical. Stone called poetry "emotional opinion" and said that poetry coursed through her life. "I wrote it down. I can't take much credit for it."

Mark Strand (b. 1934) was born on Prince Edward Island, Canada, and studied at Antioch College, Yale University, the University of Florence, and the University of Iowa. He is the author of many collections of poetry, including *Reasons for Moving* (1968), *The*

Story of Our Lives (1973), *The Continuous Life* (1990), *Blizzard of One* (1998)—which won the Pulitzer Prize for Poetry—*New Selected Poems* (2007), and *Almost Invisible* (2012). He has also published several volumes of translation (of works by Rafael Alberti and Carlos Drummond de Andrade, among others), several monographs on contemporary artists, and many books for children. He served as Poet Laureate Consultant in Poetry to the Library of Congress from 1990 to 1991 and is a former chancellor of the Academy of American Poets. He teaches English and comparative literature at Columbia University in New York.

Virgil Suárez (b. 1962) was born in Havana, Cuba. Eight years later he left with his parents for Spain, where they lived until they came to the United States in 1974. He received his B.A. from California State University, Long Beach, and his M.F.A. from Louisiana State University. He is the author of eight collections of poetry, five novels, a collection of short fiction, and a memoir titled *Spared Angola: Memories from a Cuban-American Childhood* (1997). He is editor or coeditor of several important anthologies, including *Iguana Dreams: New Latino Fiction* (1993), which was the first anthology of Cuban American writers, and *Paper Dance: 55 Latino Poets* (2000), a collection of contemporary Latino poetry. His work has been included in hundreds of magazines, journals, and anthologies. He is professor of creative writing at Florida State University.

Sekou Sundiata (1948–2007) was born and raised in Harlem. His work is deeply influenced by the music, poetry, and oral traditions of African American culture. A self-proclaimed radical in the 1970s, for the past several decades he used poetry to comment on the life and times of our culture. His work, which encompasses print, performance, music, and theater, received praise for its fusion of soul, jazz, and hiphop grooves with political insight, humor, and rhythmic speech. He regularly recorded and performed on tour with artists such as Craig Harris and Vernon Reid.

Jonathan Swift (1667–1745) was born in Ireland of English parents and educated at Kilkenny College and Trinity College, Dublin. He worked in England for a decade as a private secretary and for four years as a political writer but spent the rest of his life in Ireland, as dean of St. Patrick's Cathedral in Dublin. Although he is best known for his satires in prose (such as *Gulliver's Travels* and "A Modest Proposal"), Swift's original ambition was to be a poet, and he wrote occasional verse throughout his life.

James Tate (b. 1943), a native of Kansas City, Missouri, studied at the University of Missouri and Kansas State College during his undergraduate years. He then earned his M.F.A. at the University of Iowa Writers' Workshop in 1967, the same year his first poetry collection, *The Lost Pilot*, was published (it was selected by Dudley Fitts for the Yale Series of Younger Poets). He is the author of numerous books of poetry, including *Selected Poems* (1991), which won the Pulitzer Prize and the William Carlos Williams Award, and *Worshipful Company of Fletchers* (1994), winner of the National Book Award for Poetry. Tate's poems often include highly unusual juxtapositions of imagery, tone, and context, as is evident in "The Wheelchair Butterfly." Tate has taught at the University of California, Berkeley, and Columbia University and now teaches at the University of Massachusetts, Amherst.

Edward Taylor (c. 1642–1729) was born in England and emigrated to the colonies, where he became a clergyman in Westfield, a frontier village in what is now Massachusetts. Taylor regarded his poems as sacramental acts of private devotion and asked that they never be published. When he died, his manuscripts were placed in the Yale University library, and two centuries passed before his work was discovered. The selection of his poems published in 1939 established him as a writer of genuine power, perhaps unsurpassed in America until William Cullen Bryant appeared a century and a half later.

Alfred, Lord Tennyson (1809–1892) was born in Somersby, Lincolnshire, and grew up there in the tense atmosphere of his unhappy father's rectory. He went to Trinity College, Cambridge, but was forced to leave because of family and financial problems, so he returned home to study and practice the craft of poetry. His early volumes, published in 1830 and 1832, received bad reviews, but his *In Memoriam* (1850), an elegy on his close friend Arthur Hallam, who died of a seizure, won acclaim. He was unquestionably the most popular poet of his time (the "poet of the people") and arguably the greatest of the Victorian poets. He succeeded WILLIAM WORDSWORTH as poet laureate, a position he held from 1850 until his death.

Dylan Thomas (1914–1953) was born in Swansea, Wales, and after grammar school became a journalist. He worked as a writer for the rest of his life. His first book of poetry, *Eighteen Poems*, appeared in 1934 and was followed by *Twenty-five Poems* (1936), *Deaths and Entrances* (1946), and *Collected Poems* (1952). His poems are often rich in textured rhythms and images. He also wrote prose, chiefly short stories collectively appearing as *Portrait of the Artist as a Young Dog* (1940), and a number of film scripts and radio plays. His most famous work, *Under Milk Wood*, written as a play for voices, was first performed in New York on May 14, 1953. Thomas's radio broadcasts and his lecture tours and poetry readings in the United States brought him fame and popularity. Alcoholism contributed to his early death in 1953.

Jean Toomer (1894–1967) was born in Washington, D.C., of mixed French, Dutch, Welsh, black, German, Jewish, and Native American blood (according to him). Although he passed for white during certain periods of his life, he was raised in a predominantly black community and attended black high schools. He began college at the University of Wisconsin but transferred to the College of the City of New York. He spent several years publishing poems and stories in small magazines. In 1921 he took a teaching job in Georgia and remained there four months; the experience inspired *Cane* (1923), a book of prose poetry describing the Georgian people and landscape that became a central work of the Harlem Renaissance. He later experimented in communal living and both studied and tried to promulgate the ideas of Quakerism and the Russian mystic George Gurdjieff. From 1950 on he published very little, writing mostly for himself.

Natasha Trethewey (b. 1966) was born in Gulfport, Mississippi. She has de-

grees from the University of Georgia, Hollins University, and the University of Massachusetts. She has won many awards for her poetry, including the inaugural Cave Canem Poetry Prize for her first collection, *Domestic Work* (2000). Her second collection, *Bellocq's Ophelia* (2002), received the 2003 Mississippi Institute of Arts and Letters Book Prize and was a finalist for both the Academy of American Poets' James Laughlin and Lenore Marshall prizes. In 2007 her collection *Native Guard* received the Pulitzer Prize. Her most recent collection is *Thrall* (2012). Her book of creative nonfiction, *Beyond Katrina: A Meditation on the Mississippi Gulf*, was published in 2010. She has taught at Auburn University, the University of North Carolina, and Duke University. In 2009–2010 she was the James Weldon Johnson Fellow in African American Studies at Yale University's Beinecke Rare Books and Manuscript Library. She presently teaches at Emory University, as holder of the Phillis Wheatley Distinguished Chair in Poetry. She was appointed Poet Laureate Consultant in Poetry to the Library of Congress in 2012.

Quincy Troupe (b. 1939) was born in New York City and grew up in St. Louis, Missouri. He is the author of sixteen books, including eight volumes of poetry, most recently *The Architecture of Language* (2006). He is recipient of two American Book Awards, for his collection of poetry *Snake-Back Solos* (1980) and his nonfiction book *Miles the Autobiography* (1989). In 1991 he received the prestigious Peabody Award for writing and coproducing the seven-part Miles Davis Radio Project aired on National Public Radio in 1990. *Transcircularities: New and Selected Poems* (2002) received the Milt Kessler Award for 2003 and was finalist for the Paterson Poetry Prize. Troupe has taught at numerous places, including the University of California, San Diego, where he is now professor emeritus of creative writing and American and Caribbean literature. He is the founding editorial director for *Code* magazine and former artistic director of "Arts on the Cutting Edge," a reading and performance series at the Museum of Contemporary Art, San Diego. He was the first official poet laureate of the State of California, appointed to the post in 2002 by Governor Gray Davis.

Catherine Tufariello (b. 1963) was born in Ithaca, New York, and grew up in Amherst, a suburb of Buffalo. She graduated from the University of Buffalo and earned her Ph.D. from Cornell. She has taught at Cornell, the College of Charleston, and the University of Maine, and now is the associate director of communications for the Project on Civic Reflection at Valparaiso University in Indiana. Her first full-length collection of poems, *Keeping My Name* (2004), was the winner of the 2006 Poets' Prize. Of her poetry, she has written, "I find the objective, 'impersonal' quality of form especially valuable because my subject matter is often deeply personal. I've never aspired to be a confessional poet, and form (I hope!) gives me the necessary aesthetic distance to avoid that."

Jean Valentine (b. 1934) was born in Chicago and raised in New York and Boston. She is a graduate of Radcliffe College. Her first book, *Dream Barker*, was selected for a Yale Younger Poets Award in 1965. Since then she has published ten books of poetry. *Door in the Mountain: New and Collected Poems 1965–2003* was the winner of the 2004

National Book Award for Poetry. Her most recent book, *Break the Glass* (2010), was a finalist for the 2011 Pulitzer Prize for Poetry. She was the New York State Poet from 2008 to 2010 and received the 2009 Wallace Stevens Award from the Academy of American Poets. She has taught at Sarah Lawrence College, New York University, and Columbia University and lives in New York City.

Ellen Bryant Voigt (b. 1943) was born in Danville, Virginia, and studied at Converse College, the University of South Carolina, and the University of Iowa, where she earned an M.F.A. in music and literature. She is a pianist as well as a writer; her highly tuned musical ear is evident in the rich textures of sound in her poetry. She is the author of six collections of poetry, most recently *Messenger: New and Selected Poems 1976–2006* (2007) and *The Flexible Lyric* (1999), a collection of craft essays. She has taught at Goddard College, where she founded the writing program, and at M.I.T. and now teaches at Warren Wilson College in North Carolina, where she is the founding director of the writing program. She lives in Cabot, Vermont, where she served as the Vermont State Poet from 1999 to 2003.

Derek Walcott (b. 1930), born on the eastern Caribbean island of St. Lucia, moves between the African heritage of his family and the English cultural heritage of his reading and education. Both of his parents were educators who immersed themselves in the arts. His early training was in painting, which like his poetry was influenced by his Methodist religious training. He attended St. Mary's College and the University of the West Indies in Jamaica. His first book, *Twenty-Five Poems* (1948), appeared when he was eighteen, and he has published prolifically since then: twenty books of poetry, more than twenty plays, and a book of nonfiction. His most recent collection of poetry, *White Egrets* (2010), received the T. S. Eliot Prize. His work, which explores both the isolation of the artist and regional identity, is known for blending Caribbean, English, and African traditions. He was awarded the Nobel Prize for Literature in 1992, the academy citing him for "a poetic oeuvre of great luminosity, sustained by a historical vision, the outcome of a multicultural achievement." He teaches creative writing at Boston University every fall and lives the rest of the year in St. Lucia.

Anne Waldman (b. 1945) was born in Millville, New Jersey, and grew up in Greenwich Village. She is associated with the bohemian poetics of the Lower East Side in New York and with "Beat poetics." She attended Bennington College, cofounded the literary magazine *Angel Hair*, and for ten years directed the St. Mark's Church Poetry Project in New York City. She became a Buddhist, guided by the Tibetan Chogyam Trungpa Rinpoche, who would also become ALLEN GINSBERG's guru. She and Ginsberg worked together to create the Jack Kerouac School of Disembodied Poetics, at Trungpa's Naropa Institute in Boulder, Colorado. Both an author and a performance artist, she has published more than forty books— most recently *The Iovis Trilogy* (2011)— and gives exuberant, highly physical readings of her own work.

James Welch (1940–2003) was born in Browning, Montana. His father was a member of the Blackfoot tribe, his mother of the Gros Ventre tribe. He attended schools on the Blackfoot and Fort Belknap reservations and earned a degree from the University of Montana, where he studied under Richard Hugo. Welch published many books of poetry, fiction, and nonfiction. His hard, spare poems often evoke the bleakest side of contemporary Native American life. He received a Lifetime Achievement Award for literature from the Native Writers' Circle in 1997.

Walt Whitman (1819–1892) was born in rural Long Island, the son of a farmer and carpenter. He attended grammar school in Brooklyn and took his first job as a printer's devil for the *Long Island Patriot*. Attending the opera, dabbling in politics, participating in street life, and gaining experience as student, printer, reporter, writer, carpenter, farmer, seashore observer, and teacher provided the bedrock for his future poetic vision of an ideal society based on the realization of self. Although Whitman liked to portray himself as uncultured, he read widely in the King James Bible, SHAKESPEARE, Homer, Dante, Aeschylus, and Sophocles. He worked for many years in the newspaper business and began writing poetry only in 1847. In 1855, at his own expense, Whitman published the first edition of *Leaves of Grass*, a thin volume of twelve long untitled poems. Written in a highly original and innovative **free verse**, influenced significantly by music, with a wide-ranging subject matter, the work seemed strange to most of the poet's contemporaries—but they did recognize its value: Ralph Waldo Emerson wrote to him shortly after Whitman sent him a copy, "I greet you at the beginning of a great career." He spent much of the remainder of his life revising and expanding this book. *Leaves of Grass* today is considered a masterpiece of world literature, marking the beginning of modern American poetry, and Whitman is widely regarded as America's national poet.

Richard Wilbur (b. 1921) was born in New York City and grew up in rural New Jersey. He attended Amherst College and began writing poetry during World War II, while fighting in Italy and France. Afterward, he studied at Harvard University and then taught there and at Wellesley College, Wesleyan University, and Smith College. He has published many books of poetry, including *Things of This World* (1956), for which he received the Pulitzer Prize for Poetry and the National Book Award, and *New and Collected Poems* (1988), which also won a Pulitzer Prize. He has always been respected as a master of formal constraints, comparing them to the genie in the bottle: The restraints stimulate the imagination to achieve results unlikely to be reached without them. He has also published numerous translations of French plays, two books for children, a collection of prose pieces, and editions of WILLIAM SHAKESPEARE and EDGAR ALLAN POE. In 1987 he was appointed Poet Laureate Consultant in Poetry to the Library of Congress. He now lives in Cummington, Massachusetts.

Nancy Willard (b. 1936) was raised in Ann Arbor, Michigan, and educated at the University of Michigan and Stanford University. She has published twelve books of poetry, including *Water Walker* (1989), which was nominated for the National Book Critics Circle Award, *Swimming Lessons: New and Selected Poems* (1996), and most recently *The Sea at Truro* (2012); two novels—*Things Invisible to See* (1984) and *Sister Water* (1993); and four books of stories and essays, including *The Left-Handed Story:*

Writing and the Writer's Life (2008). She has written dozens of children's books, including *A Visit to William Blake's Inn: Poems for Innocent and Experienced Travelers* (containing such delightfully titled poems as "The Wise Cow Enjoys a Cloud" and "The Marmalade Man Makes a Dance to Mend Us"), which was the first book of poetry to win the prestigious Newbery Medal. She lives in Poughkeepsie, New York, and teaches at Vassar College.

William Carlos Williams (1883–1963) was born in Rutherford, New Jersey; his father was an English emigrant and his mother was of mixed Basque descent from Puerto Rico. While in high school in New York City, he decided to be both a writer and a doctor. He graduated from the medical school at the University of Pennsylvania, where he was a friend of EZRA POUND's and HILDA DOOLITTLE's. After an internship in New York, writing poems between seeing patients, Williams practiced general medicine in Rutherford (he was ALLEN GINSBERG's pediatrician). His first book of poems was published in 1909, and he subsequently published poems, novels, short stories, plays, criticism, and essays. Initially one of the principal poets of the **Imagist** movement (see the glossary), Williams sought later to invent an entirely fresh—and distinctly American—poetic whose subject matter was centered on the everyday circumstances of life and the lives of common people. Williams, like WALLACE STEVENS, became one of the major poets of the twentieth century and exerted great influence on poets of his own and later generations.

William Wordsworth (1770–1850) was born and raised in the Lake District of England. Both his parents died by the time he was thirteen. He studied at Cambridge, toured Europe on foot, and lived in France for a year during the first part of the French Revolution. He returned to England, leaving behind a lover, Annette Vallon, and their daughter, Caroline, from whom he was soon cut off by war between England and France. He met SAMUEL TAYLOR COLERIDGE, and in 1798 they published *Lyrical Ballads*, the first great work of the English Romantic movement. He changed poetry forever by his decision to use common language in his poetry instead of heightened **poetic diction** (see the glossary). In 1799 he and his sister Dorothy moved to Grasmere, in the Lake District, where he married Mary Hutchinson, a childhood friend. His greatest works were produced between 1797 and 1808. He continued to write for the next forty years but never regained the heights of his early verse. In 1843 he was named poet laureate, a position he held until his death in 1850.

Charles Wright (b. 1935) was born in Pickwick Dam, Tennessee, and grew up in Tennessee and North Carolina. He studied at Davidson College, served a four-year stint in Italy as a captain in the U.S. Army Intelligence Corps, and then continued his education at the University of Iowa Writers' Workshop and at the University of Rome on a Fulbright Fellowship. He has published many books of poetry—including *Black Zodiac*, which won the Pulitzer Prize for Poetry in 1997—two volumes of criticism, and a translation of Eugenio Montale's poetry. His most recent collection, *Scar Tissue* (2007), was the international winner of the Griffin Poetry Prize. Wright's poems have been labeled impressionistic, combining images from the natural world, Catholicism, and the rural South. He taught at the University of California, Irvine, for almost twenty years and now is Souder Family Professor of English at the University of Virginia.

James Wright (1927–1980) grew up in Martin's Ferry, Ohio. He attended Kenyon College, where his study under JOHN CROWE RANSOM sent his early poetry in a formalist direction. After spending a year in Austria on a Fulbright Fellowship, he returned to the United States and earned an M.A. and a Ph.D. at the University of Washington, studying under THEODORE ROETHKE and STANLEY KUNITZ. He went on to teach at the University of Minnesota, Macalester College, and Hunter College. His working-class background and the poverty that he saw during the Depression stirred a sympathy for the poor and "outsiders" of various sorts that shaped the tone and content of his poetry. He published numerous books of poetry; his *Collected Poems* received the Pulitzer Prize in 1972.

Lady Mary Wroth (c. 1587–c. 1651), niece of SIR PHILIP SIDNEY and Mary Sidney Herbert, was one of the best and most prolific women writers of the English Renaissance and an important literary patron. Her husband's early death left her deeply in debt. She wrote *Pamphilia to Amphilanthus*, the only known English sonnet sequence on love themes by a woman of her time; seventy-four poems that appeared in *Urania* (the first full-length work of prose fiction by a woman); and several other pieces. BEN JONSON said that reading her sonnets had made him "a better lover and a much better poet."

Sir Thomas Wyatt (1503–1542) was born in Kent and educated at St. John's College, Cambridge. He spent most of his life as a courtier and diplomat, serving King Henry VIII as ambassador to Spain and as a member of several missions to Italy and France. These travels introduced Wyatt to Italian writers of the High Renaissance, whose work he translated, thus introducing the sonnet form into English. He was arrested twice and charged with treason, sent to the Tower of London, and acquitted in 1541. Aristocratic poets at the time rarely published their poems themselves: works circulated in manuscript and in published collections ("miscellanies") gathered by printers. The most important of these is a volume published by Richard Tottel in 1557 titled *Songs and Sonnets* but more commonly known as *Tottel's Miscellany*, which includes ninety-seven of Wyatt's sonnets and delightful lyrics.

William Butler Yeats (1865–1939) was born in Sandymount, Dublin, to an Anglo-Irish family. On leaving high school in 1883, he decided to be an artist, like his father, and attended art school, but soon gave it up to concentrate on poetry. His first poems were published in 1885 in the *Dublin University Review*. Religious by temperament but unable to accept orthodox Christianity, Yeats throughout his life explored esoteric philosophies in search of a tradition that would substitute for a lost religion. He became a member of the Theosophical Society and the Order of the Golden Dawn, two groups interested in Eastern occultism, and later developed a private system of symbols and mystical ideas. Through the influence of Lady Gregory, a writer and promoter of literature, he became interested in Irish nationalist art, helping to found the Irish National Theatre and the famous Abbey Theatre. He was actively involved in Irish politics, especially after the Easter Rising of 1916. He continued to write and to revise earlier poems, leaving behind at his death a body of verse that, in its variety and power, placed him among the greatest twentieth-century poets of the English language. He was awarded the Nobel Prize in Literature in 1923.

Al Young (b. 1939) was born in Ocean Springs, Mississippi, and lived for a decade in the South before moving to Detroit. He attended the University of Michigan and the University of California, Berkeley. He has been a professional guitarist and singer, a disk jockey, a medical photographer, and a warehouseman and has written eight books of poetry (most recently *Something about the Blues: An Unlikely Collection of Poetry* [2008]) and five novels as well as memoirs, essays, and film scripts. He has edited a number of books, including *Yardbird Lives!* (1978) and *African American Literature: A Brief Introduction and Anthology* (1995). In the 1970s and 1980s, Young cofounded the journals *Yardbird Reader* and *Quilt* with poet-novelist Ishmael Reed. He has taught literature and creative writing at numerous colleges and universities. He served as California Poet Laureate from 2005 to 2008.

Kevin Young (b. 1970) was born and raised in Lincoln, Nebraska. He received his B.A. from Harvard, where he took poetry workshops from SEAMUS HEANEY. After holding a Stegner Fellowship in Poetry at Stanford University, he earned an M.F.A. in creative writing from Brown University. Young has published seven volumes of poetry, among them *Jelly Roll* (2003), a finalist for the National Book Award, and *Ardency: A Chronicle of the Amistad Rebels* (2011). His most recent book is a collection of essays, *The Grey Album: On the Blackness of Blackness* (2012). He is also an editor of several anthologies, including *The Hungry Ear: Poems of Food and Drink* (2012). He has taught at the University of Georgia, Indiana University, and Emory University, where he is Atticus Haygood Professor of Creative Writing and English and Curator of Literary Collections at the Raymond Danowski Poetry Library. His poetry is often celebrated for the way it works with the story and music inherent in the oral tradition.

Ray A. Young Bear (b. 1950) was born and raised in the Mesquakie Tribal Settlement near Tama, Iowa. His poetry has been influenced by his maternal grandmother, Ada Kapayou Old Bear, and his wife, Stella L. Young Bear. He attended Pomona College in California as well as Grinnell College, the University of Iowa, Iowa State University, and Northern Iowa University. He has taught creative writing and Native American literature at the Institute of American Indian Art, Eastern Washington University, the University of Iowa, and Iowa State University. Young Bear and his wife cofounded the Woodland Song

and Dance Troupe of Arts Midwest in 1983. Young Bear's group has performed traditional Mesquakie music in the United States and the Netherlands. Author of four books of poetry, a collection of short stories, and a novel, he has contributed to contemporary Native American poetry and the study of it for over four decades.

Paul Zimmer (b. 1934) was born in Canton, Ohio, and educated at Kent State University. He is the author of fifteen poetry collections, including *The Great Bird of Love*, which was selected for the National Poetry Series in 1998, and *Crossing to Sunlight Revisited: New and Selected Poems* (2007). His latest collection, *The Importance of Being Zimmer* (2010), brings together a selection from his more than 130 poems in the voice of the persona "Zimmer," a tragicomic everyman. He has also published several collections of personal essays. Zimmer directed the university presses at the University of Pittsburgh, the University of Georgia, and the University of Iowa, where he was responsible for the discovery and first publication of many of the finest contemporary poets.

Groupings of Poems by Form and Type
[Poems Arranged Chronologically]

Accentual Meter

Elizabeth Bishop, "The Fish" (p. 150)

Allegory

George Herbert, "Redemption" (p. 21)
Edward Taylor, "Housewifery" (p. 25)

Ballad: Literary

John Keats, "La Belle Dame sans
  Merci" (p. 57)
Dudley Randall, "Ballad of
  Birmingham" (p. 157)

Ballad: Popular

Anonymous, "Lord Randal" (p. 7)

Ballad Stanza

Anonymous, "Western Wind" (p. 7)
John Keats, "La Belle Dame sans
  Merci" (p. 57)
W. H. Auden, "As I Walked Out One
  Evening" (p. 143)
Dudley Randall, "Ballad of
  Birmingham" (p. 157)

Blank Verse

William Wordsworth, "Lines Composed
  a Few Miles above Tintern Abbey"
  (p. 39)
Alfred, Lord Tennyson, "Ulysses"
  (p. 65)
William Butler Yeats, "The Second
  Coming" (p. 98)
Robert Frost, "The Death of the Hired
  Man" (p. 103)
Robert Frost, "'Out, Out—'" (p. 108)

Wallace Stevens, "Sunday Morning"
  (p. 112)
William Stafford, "Traveling through
  the Dark" (p. 158)

Canzone

Erika Meitner, "North Country
  Canzone" (p. 300)

Catalog Poetry

Christopher Smart, from *Jubilate Agno*
  (p. 34)
Walt Whitman, from *Song of Myself*
  (p. 69)
Walt Whitman, "When Lilacs Last in
  the Dooryard Bloom'd" (p. 82)
Langston Hughes, "The Negro Speaks
  of Rivers" (p. 137)
Joy Harjo, "She Had Some Horses"
  (p. 250)

Concrete Poetry

George Herbert, "Easter-wings" (p. 20)

Confessional Poetry

Robert Lowell, "Skunk Hour" (p. 163)
Sylvia Plath, "Daddy" (p. 195)

Couplets: Tetrameter

Andrew Marvell, "To His Coy Mistress"
  (p. 23)
A. E. Housman, "Loveliest of trees, the
  cherry now" (p. 97)

Couplets: Pentameter

Geoffrey Chaucer, from *The Canterbury
  Tales*: "The General Prologue" (p. 6)

Ben Jonson, "On My First Son" (p. 18)
Anne Bradstreet, "Before the Birth of
One of Her Children" (p. 22)
Robert Browning, "My Last Duchess"
(p. 68)

Couplets: Heroic

Ben Jonson, "On My First Son" (p. 18)
Anne Bradstreet, "Before the Birth of
One of Her Children" (p. 22)
Jonathan Swift, "A Description of a
City Shower" (p. 25)
Alexander Pope, from "An Essay on
Criticism" (p. 28)

Couplets: Other

Gerard Manley Hopkins, "Spring and
Fall" (p. 96)
Gwendolyn Brooks, "We Real Cool"
(p. 165)

Couplets: Unrhymed

Margaret Atwood, "True Stories"
(p. 217)
Wang Ping, "Syntax" (p. 282)
Virgil Suárez, "Tea Leaves, *Caracoles*,
Coffee Beans" (p. 286)
Vievee Francis, "1864, A Pocket Full of
Rye" (p. 287)
Kevin Young, "Song of Smoke" (p. 297)
Randall Mann, "The Heron" (p. 299)

Dramatic Monologue

Alfred, Lord Tennyson, "Ulysses"
(p. 65)
Robert Browning, "My Last Duchess"
(p. 68)
T. S. Eliot, "The Love Song of J. Alfred
Prufrock" (p. 125)

Elegy

Ben Jonson, "On My First Son" (p. 18)
Thomas Gray, "Elegy Written
in a Country Churchyard" (p. 30)
Walt Whitman, "When Lilacs Last in
the Dooryard Bloom'd" (p. 82)

John Crowe Ransom, "Bells for John
Whiteside's Daughter" (p. 124)
Theodore Roethke, "Elegy for Jane"
(p. 148)
Frank O'Hara, "The Day Lady Died"
(p. 175)
Geoffrey Hill, "In Memory of Jane
Fraser" (p. 194)

Epigram

Ezra Pound, "In a Station of the
Metro" (p. 119)

Haiku

Gary Snyder, "Hitch Haiku" (p. 190)

Imagist Poetry

William Carlos Williams, "The Red
Wheelbarrow" (p. 116)
William Carlos Williams, "This Is Just
to Say" (p. 118)
H. D. [Hilda Doolittle], "Garden"
(p. 119)
Lorine Niedecker, "My Life by Water"
(p. 141)

Language Poetry

Gertrude Stein, "Susie Asado" (p. 101)
Wang Ping, "Syntax" (p. 282)

Litany

Billy Collins, "Litany" (p. 221)
Joy Harjo, "She Had Some Horses"
(p. 250)

Narrative

Edgar Allan Poe, "The Raven" (p. 60)
Robert Frost, "The Death of the Hired
Man" (p. 103)
Robert Frost, "'Out, Out—'" (p. 108)
Langston Hughes, "Theme for English
B" (p. 138)
Elizabeth Bishop, "In the Waiting
Room" (p. 152)
William Stafford, "Traveling through
the Dark" (p. 158)

Rhyme Royal

Sir Thomas Wyatt, "They flee from me"
(p. 9)

Rondeau

Paul Laurence Dunbar, "We Wear the
Mask" (p. 100)

Satire

Jonathan Swift, "A Description of a
City Shower" (p. 25)
Denise Duhamel, "One Afternoon
when Barbie Wanted to Join the
Military" (p. 284)

Sestina

Julia Alvarez, "Bilingual Sestina"
(p. 247)

Sonnet, Curtal

Gerard Manley Hopkins, "Pied Beauty"
(p. 95)

Sonnet, English (Shakespearean)

Michael Drayton, "Since there's no help,
come let us kiss and part" (p. 11)
William Shakespeare, "Shall I compare
thee to a summer's day?" (p. 13)
William Shakespeare, "That time of
year thou mayst in me behold" (p. 13)
William Shakespeare, "Let me not to
the marriage of true minds" (p. 14)
William Shakespeare, "My mistress'
eyes are nothing like the sun" (p. 14)
John Keats, "When I have fears that I
may cease to be" (p. 57)
Claude McKay, "America" (p. 132)
Edna St. Vincent Millay, "Pity me not
because the light of day" (p. 133)
Seamus Heaney, "Glanmore Sonnets 4"
(p. 213)
Mary Jo Salter, "Half a Double Sonnet"
(p. 269)
Thom Satterlee, "Question 4: Whether,
Once Wounded by Love, One Ever
Heals Completely?" (p. 292)

Sonnet, Italian (Petrarchan)

John Donne, "Death, be not proud"
(p. 17)
John Milton, "When I consider how
my light is spent" (p. 21)
William Wordsworth, "The world is
too much with us" (p. 50)
Elizabeth Barrett Browning, "How do
I love thee? Let me count the ways"
(p. 60)
Gerard Manley Hopkins, "God's
Grandeur" (p. 95)

Sonnet, Spenserian

Edmund Spenser, "One day I wrote her
name upon the strand" (p. 10)

Sonnet, Other

Sir Philip Sidney, "Loving in truth, and
fain in verse my love to show" (p. 11)
Lady Mary Wroth, "Love like a juggler
comes to play his prize" (p. 18)
George Herbert, "Redemption" (p. 21)
Percy Bysshe Shelley, "Ozymandias"
(p. 53)
William Butler Yeats, "Leda and the
Swan" (p. 99)
E. E. Cummings, "'next to of course
god america i" (p. 135)
Anna Maria Hong, "The Frog-Prince"
(p. 292)

Surrealistic Poetry

Mark Strand, "Eating Poetry" (p. 201)
Nancy Willard, "Questions My Son
Asked Me, Answers I Never Gave
Him" (p. 206)
Charles Simic, "Begotten of the Spleen"
(p. 209)
James Tate, "The Wheelchair Butterfly"
(p. 231)
Joy Harjo, "She Had Some Horses"
(p. 250)

Syllabic Verse

Dylan Thomas, "Fern Hill" (p. 160)
Sylvia Plath, "Metaphors" (p. 194)

Groupings of Poems by Topic and Theme

(Arranged Alphabetically by Author's Name)

Aging

Gwendolyn Brooks, "The Bean Eaters" (p. 165)

T. S. Eliot, "The Love Song of J. Alfred Prufrock" (p. 125)

Queen Elizabeth I, "When I was fair and young" (p. 9)

Robert Frost, "After Apple-Picking" (p. 102)

Robert Frost, "The Death of the Hired Man" (p. 103)

Louise Glück, "The Wild Iris" (p. 230)

Seamus Heaney, "Glanmore Sonnets 4" (p. 213)

Gerard Manley Hopkins, "Spring and Fall" (p. 96)

A. E. Housman, "Loveliest of trees, the cherry now" (p. 97)

Philip Larkin, "High Windows" (p. 169)

John Milton, "When I consider how my light is spent" (p. 21)

Alberto Ríos, "Nani" (p. 259)

William Shakespeare, "That time of year thou mayst in me behold" (p. 13)

Alfred, Lord Tennyson, "Ulysses" (p. 65)

Dylan Thomas, "Fern Hill" (p. 160)

Jean Toomer, "Face" (p. 136)

William Wordsworth, "Lines Composed a Few Miles above Tintern Abbey" (p. 39)

William Wordsworth, "Ode: Intimations of Immortality" (p. 44)

Animals

Wendell Berry, "The Peace of Wild Things" (p. 202)

Elizabeth Bishop, "The Fish" (p. 150)

William Blake, "The Lamb" (p. 36)

William Blake, "The Tyger" (p. 37)

Philip Booth, "A Two Inch Wave" (p. 172)

Aracelis Girmay, "Snail, or, To a House" (p. 302)

Thomas Hardy, "The Darkling Thrush" (p. 94)

Joy Harjo, "She Had Some Horses" (p. 250)

Jane Hirshfield, "To Drink" (p. 264)

Linda Hogan, "Crow Law" (p. 239)

Anna Maria Hong, "The Frog-Prince" (p. 292)

Robinson Jeffers, "Hurt Hawks" (p. 120)

Richard Jones, "Cathedral" (p. 266)

Galway Kinnell, "The Bear" (p. 177)

Maxine Kumin, "The Sound of Night" (p. 171)

Robert Lowell, "Skunk Hour" (p. 163)

Randall Mann, "The Heron" (p. 299)

Erika Meitner, "North Country Canzone" (p. 300)

Lorine Niedecker, "My Life by Water" (p. 141)

Edgar Allan Poe, "The Raven" (p. 60)

Adrienne Rich, "Aunt Jennifer's Tigers" (p. 186)

Theodore Roethke, "Elegy for Jane" (p. 148)

Mary Ruefle, "Barbarians" (p. 260)

Christopher Smart, from *Jubilate Agno* (p. 34)

Gary Snyder, "Hitch Haiku" (p. 190)

William Stafford, "Traveling through the Dark" (p. 158)

Gerald Stern, "The Dog" (p. 170)

Wallace Stevens, "Thirteen Ways of Looking at a Blackbird" (p. 110)

Ruth Stone, "What We Have" (p. 162)
Ellen Bryant Voigt, "The Lotus
Flowers" (p. 228)
Walt Whitman, "A Noiseless Patient
Spider" (p. 89)
Walt Whitman, from *Song of Myself*
(p. 69)
James Wright, "A Blessing" (p. 181)

Art, Its Permanence

Adrienne Rich, "Aunt Jennifer's Tigers"
(p. 186)
William Shakespeare, "Shall I compare
thee to a summer's day? " (p. 13)
Percy Bysshe Shelley, "Ozymandias"
(p. 53)
Edmund Spenser, "One day I wrote her
name upon the strand" (p. 10)

Art, Poetry about

W. H. Auden, "Musée des Beaux Arts"
(p. 145)
Frank O'Hara, "Why I Am Not a
Painter" (p. 174)
Cathy Song, "Girl Powdering Her
Neck" (p. 272)
William Carlos Williams, "The Red
Wheelbarrow" (p. 116)
Paul Zimmer, "Zimmer Imagines
Heaven" (p. 203)

Battle of the Sexes

Denise Duhamel, "One Afternoon when
Barbie Wanted to Join the Military"
(p. 284)
Andrew Marvell, "To His Coy Mistress"
(p. 23)
Adrienne Rich, "Aunt Jennifer's Tigers"
(p. 186)
William Carlos Williams, "This Is Just
to Say" (p. 118)

Beauty

George Gordon, Lord Byron, "She
walks in beauty" (p. 53)

Stanley Kunitz, "The War against the
Trees" (p. 142)
Lorine Niedecker, "My Life by Water"
(p. 141)
Mary Oliver, "First Snow" (p. 204)
Richard Wilbur, "Love Calls Us to the
Things of This World" (p. 168)
Kevin Young, "Song of Smoke" (p. 297)

Birth

Sylvia Plath, "Morning Song" (p. 195)
Catherine Tufariello, "This Child"
(p. 288)

Blindness

Anita Endrezze, "The Girl Who Loved
the Sky" (p. 261)
John Milton, "When I consider how
my light is spent" (p. 21)

Borders

Julia Alvarez, "Bilingual Sestina"
(p. 247)
Jim Barnes, "Return to La Plata,
Missouri" (p. 199)
Philip Booth, "A Two Inch Wave"
(p. 172)
Sterling A. Brown, "Riverbank Blues"
(p. 136)
Lorna Dee Cervantes, "Freeway 280"
(p. 268)
Marilyn Chin, "How I Got That Name"
(p. 275)
Denise Duhamel, "One Afternoon when
Barbie Wanted to Join the Military"
(p. 284)
Marilyn Hacker, "Villanelle" (p. 228)
Honorée Fanonne Jeffers, "Unidentified
Female Student, Former Slave"
(p. 293)
Galway Kinnell, "The Bear" (p. 177)
Etheridge Knight, "Hard Rock Returns
to Prison from the Hospital for the
Criminal Insane" (p. 198)
Lorine Niedecker, "My Life by Water"
(p. 141)

Donald Revell, "Mignonette" (p. 270)
Adrienne Rich, "Diving into the Wreck"
(p. 187)
James Tate, "The Wheelchair Butterfly"
(p. 231)

Carpe Diem
Emily Dickinson, "Wild Nights—Wild
Nights!" (p. 91)
Queen Elizabeth I, "When I was fair
and young" (p. 9)
Robert Herrick, "To the Virgins, to
Make Much of Time" (p. 19)
A. E. Housman, "Loveliest of trees, the
cherry now" (p. 97)
Andrew Marvell, "To His Coy Mistress"
(p. 23)
Frank O'Hara, "The Day Lady Died"
(p. 175)
Linda Pastan, "love poem" (p. 193)
Edith Sitwell, "Lullaby" (p. 121)

Childhood and Innocence
Elizabeth Bishop, "In the Waiting
Room" (p. 152)
Rita Dove, "Fifth Grade Autobiography"
(p. 258)
Robert Frost, "'Out, Out—'" (p. 108)
Seamus Heaney, "Mid-Term Break"
(p. 212)
Li-Young Lee, "The Gift" (p. 280)
Theodore Roethke, "My Papa's Waltz"
(p. 147)
Mary Jo Salter, "Half a Double Sonnet"
(p. 269)
Gary Soto, "Moving Away" (p. 257)
Dylan Thomas, "Fern Hill" (p. 160)
Ellen Bryant Voigt, "The Lotus
Flowers" (p. 228)
Nancy Willard, "Questions My Son
Asked Me, Answers I Never Gave
Him" (p. 206)
William Wordsworth, "Lines Composed
a Few Miles above Tintern Abbey"
(p. 39)
William Wordsworth, "Ode:
Intimations of Immortality" (p. 44)

Children and Parents
Eavan Boland, "The Pomegranate"
(p. 232)
Anne Bradstreet, "Before the Birth of
One of Her Children" (p. 22)
Marilyn Chin, "How I Got That Name"
(p. 275)
Toi Derricotte, "A Note on My Son's
Face" (p. 222)
Kimiko Hahn, "Mother's Mother"
(p. 278)
Michael S. Harper, "Nightmare Begins
Responsibility" (p. 210)
Seamus Heaney, "Mid-Term Break"
(p. 212)
Langston Hughes, "Mother to Son"
(p. 138)
A. Van Jordan, "From" (p. 289)
Li-Young Lee, "Eating Alone"
(p. 280)
Li-Young Lee, "The Gift" (p. 280)
Sharon Olds, "I Go Back to May 1937"
(p. 227)
Sharon Olds, "The One Girl at the
Boys' Party" (p. 226)
Simon J. Ortiz, "Speaking" (p. 224)
Sylvia Plath, "Morning Song" (p. 195)
Atsuro Riley, "Drill" (p. 283)
Theodore Roethke, "My Papa's Waltz"
(p. 147)
Mary Jo Salter, "Half a Double Sonnet"
(p. 269)
Gary Soto, "Moving Away" (p. 257)
Virgil Suárez, "Tea Leaves, *Caracoles*,
Coffee Beans" (p. 286)
Catherine Tufariello, "This Child"
(p. 288)
Nancy Willard, "Questions My Son
Asked Me, Answers I Never Gave
Him" (p. 206)

Choices (and Lack Thereof)
Gwendolyn Brooks, "We Real Cool"
(p. 165)
Robert Frost, "'Out, Out—'" (p. 108)
Robert Frost, "The Road Not Taken"
(p. 107)

Aracelis Girmay, "Snail, or, To a House" (p. 302)

Terrance Hayes, "Talk" (p. 298)

Langston Hughes, "Theme for English B" (p. 138)

Galway Kinnell, "The Bear" (p. 177)

Stanley Kunitz, "The War against the Trees" (p. 142)

Frank O'Hara, "The Day Lady Died" (p. 175)

Frank O'Hara, "Why I Am Not a Painter" (p. 174)

Sharon Olds, "I Go Back to May 1937" (p. 227)

Adrienne Rich, "Aunt Jennifer's Tigers" (p. 186)

Adrienne Rich, "Diving into the Wreck" (p. 187)

William Stafford, "Traveling through the Dark" (p. 158)

Gerald Stern, "The Dog" (p. 170)

Alfred, Lord Tennyson, "Ulysses" (p. 65)

Richard Wilbur, "Love Calls Us to the Things of This World" (p. 168)

City Life

John Ashbery, "Mixed Feelings" (p. 180)

Gwendolyn Brooks, "The Bean Eaters" (p. 165)

Gwendolyn Brooks, "We Real Cool" (p. 165)

Lorna Dee Cervantes, "Freeway 280" (p. 268)

T. S. Eliot, "Preludes" (p. 129)

Allen Ginsberg, "A Supermarket in California" (p. 175)

Garrett Kaoru Hongo, "Yellow Light" (p. 252)

Langston Hughes, "Harlem" (p. 140)

Frank O'Hara, "The Day Lady Died" (p. 175)

George Oppen, "Myself I Sing" (p. 146)

Ezra Pound, "In a Station of the Metro" (p. 119)

Sekou Sundiata, "Blink Your Eyes" (p. 244)

Jonathan Swift, "A Description of a City Shower" (p. 25)

James Tate, "The Wheelchair Butterfly" (p. 231)

Classical Myth, Ancient Legend

W. H. Auden, "Musée des Beaux Arts" (p. 145)

Eavan Boland, "The Pomegranate" (p. 232)

Samuel Taylor Coleridge, "Kubla Khan" (p. 51)

Anna Maria Hong, "The Frog-Prince" (p. 292)

Randall Mann, "The Heron" (p. 299)

Ezra Pound, "The River-Merchant's Wife: A Letter" (p. 118)

Alfred, Lord Tennyson, "Ulysses" (p. 65)

Derek Walcott, "Sea Grapes" (p. 190)

William Wordsworth, "The world is too much with us" (p. 50)

William Butler Yeats, "Leda and the Swan" (p. 99)

William Butler Yeats, "The Second Coming" (p. 98)

Colors

Garrett Kaoru Hongo, "Yellow Light" (p. 252)

Yusef Komunyakaa, "Facing It" (p. 238)

Naomi Shihab Nye, "The Small Vases from Hebron" (p. 256)

Frank O'Hara, "Why I Am Not a Painter" (p. 174)

A. E. Stallings, "Olives" (p. 296)

Conflict, between Nations

Sherman Alexie, "Postcards to Columbus" (p. 291)

Carolyn Forché, "The Colonel" (p. 249)

Garrett Kaoru Hongo, "Yellow Light" (p. 252)

James Welch, "Christmas Comes to Moccasin Flat" (p. 218)

Ray A. Young Bear, "From the Spotted Night" (p. 249)

Conflict, between Parents and Children

Charles Bukowski, "my old man" (p. 166)

Sharon Olds, "I Go Back to May 1937" (p. 227)

Sylvia Plath, "Daddy" (p. 195)

Theodore Roethke, "My Papa's Waltz" (p. 147)

Gary Soto, "Moving Away" (p. 257)

Conflict of Values

John Ashbery, "Mixed Feelings" (p. 180)

Wendell Berry, "The Peace of Wild Things" (p. 202)

William Blake, "A Poison Tree" (p. 38)

Robert Browning, "My Last Duchess" (p. 68)

Lucille Clifton, "homage to my hips" (p. 207)

Stanley Kunitz, "The War against the Trees" (p. 142)

Thylias Moss, "The Lynching" (p. 267)

Charles Olson, "Maximus, to himself" (p. 148)

George Oppen, "Myself I Sing" (p. 146)

Conformity and Rebellion

Margaret Atwood, "True Stories" (p. 217)

Gwendolyn Brooks, "We Real Cool" (p. 165)

Marilyn Chin, "How I Got That Name" (p. 275)

Emily Dickinson, "Much Madness is divinest Sense" (p. 91)

Emily Dickinson, "Wild Nights—Wild Nights!" (p. 91)

Denise Duhamel, "One Afternoon when Barbie Wanted to Join the Military" (p. 284)

Allen Ginsberg, "A Supermarket in California" (p. 176)

Joy Harjo, "She Had Some Horses" (p. 250)

Etheridge Knight, "Hard Rock Returns to Prison from the Hospital for the Criminal Insane" (p. 198)

Heather McHugh, "What He Thought" (p. 242)

Claude McKay, "America" (p. 132)

Mark Strand, "Eating Poetry" (p. 201)

Anne Waldman, "Icy Rose" (p. 234)

Death

Anonymous, "Lord Randal" (p. 7)

John Berryman, "Certainty before Lunch" (p. 159)

Anne Bradstreet, "Before the Birth of One of Her Children" (p. 22)

Gwendolyn Brooks, "We Real Cool" (p. 165)

Judith Ortiz Cofer, "Cold as Heaven" (p. 254)

Victor Hernández Cruz, "Problems with Hurricanes" (p. 246)

E. E. Cummings, "'next to of course god america i" (p. 135)

Emily Dickinson, "Because I could not stop for Death" (p. 93)

Emily Dickinson, "I heard a Fly buzz— when I died" (p. 92)

Rita Dove, "Fifth Grade Autobiography" (p. 258)

T. S. Eliot, "Journey of the Magi" (p. 131)

Robert Frost, "The Death of the Hired Man" (p. 103)

Robert Frost, "'Out, Out—'" (p. 108)

Thomas Gray, "Elegy Written in a Country Churchyard" (p. 30)

Michael S. Harper, "Nightmare Begins Responsibility" (p. 210)

Seamus Heaney, "Mid-Term Break" (p. 212)

Bob Hicok, "In the loop" (p. 283)

Geoffrey Hill, "In Memory of Jane Fraser" (p. 194)

A. E. Housman, "To an Athlete Dying Young" (p. 97)

Randall Jarrell, "The Death of the Ball Turret Gunner" (p. 159)

Robinson Jeffers, "Hurt Hawks" (p. 120)

John Keats, "When I have fears that I may cease to be" (p. 57)

Li-Young Lee, "Eating Alone" (p. 280)

W. S. Merwin, "For the Anniversary of My Death" (p. 181)

Thylias Moss, "The Lynching" (p. 267)

Frank O'Hara, "The Day Lady Died" (p. 175)

Edgar Allan Poe, "Annabel Lee" (p. 63)

John Crowe Ransom, "Bells for John Whiteside's Daughter" (p. 124)

Donald Revell, "Mignonette" (p. 270)

Edwin Arlington Robinson, "Richard Cory" (p. 100)

Theodore Roethke, "Elegy for Jane" (p. 148)

Christina Rossetti, "Song" (p. 90)

Edith Sitwell, "Lullaby" (p. 121)

Gerald Stern, "The Dog" (p. 170)

Wallace Stevens, "The Emperor of Ice-Cream" (p. 112)

Virgil Suárez, "Tea Leaves, *Caracoles*, Coffee Beans" (p. 286)

Alfred, Lord Tennyson, "Crossing the Bar" (p. 67)

Dylan Thomas, "Do not go gentle into that good night" (p. 161)

Jean Toomer, "Face" (p. 136)

Jean Valentine, "December 21st" (p. 202)

Walt Whitman, "When Lilacs Last in the Dooryard Bloom'd" (p. 82)

Depression

John Berryman, "Certainty before Lunch" (p. 159)

Robert Lowell, "Skunk Hour" (p. 163)

Adrienne Rich, "Diving into the Wreck" (p. 187)

Edith Sitwell, "Lullaby" (p. 121)

Dreams

Agha Shahid Ali, "I Dream It Is Afternoon When I Return to Delhi" (p. 245)

Allen Ginsberg, "A Supermarket in California" (p. 176)

Michael S. Harper, "Nightmare Begins Responsibility" (p. 210)

Thylias Moss, "The Lynching" (p. 267)

Donald Revell, "Mignonette" (p. 270)

Paul Zimmer, "Zimmer Imagines Heaven" (p. 203)

Drugs and Alcohol

Gwendolyn Brooks, "We Real Cool" (p. 165)

Etheridge Knight, "Hard Rock Returns to Prison from the Hospital for the Criminal Insane" (p. 198)

Theodore Roethke, "My Papa's Waltz" (p. 147)

James Welch, "Christmas Comes to Moccasin Flat" (p. 218)

Duty

Robert Frost, "Stopping by Woods on a Snowy Evening" (p. 109)

Langston Hughes, "Theme for English B" (p. 138)

Mark Strand, "Eating Poetry" (p. 201)

Derek Walcott, "Sea Grapes" (p. 190)

Richard Wilbur, "Love Calls Us to the Things of This World" (p. 168)

Education/School

Gwendolyn Brooks, "We Real Cool" (p. 165)

Anita Endrezze, "The Girl Who Loved the Sky" (p. 261)

Honorée Fanonne Jeffers, "Unidentified Female Student, Former Slave" (p. 293)

Allison Joseph, "On Being Told I Don't Speak Like a Black Person" (p. 294)

Naomi Shihab Nye, "Kindness" (p. 255)

Adrienne Rich, "Diving into the Wreck"
(p. 187)
Nancy Willard, "Questions My Son
Asked Me, Answers I Never Gave
Him" (p. 206)

Environment

Wendell Berry, "The Peace of Wild
Things" (p. 202)
Philip Booth, "A Two Inch Wave"
(p. 172)
Gerard Manley Hopkins, "God's
Grandeur" (p. 95)
Galway Kinnell, "The Bear" (p. 177)
Stanley Kunitz, "The War against the
Trees" (p. 142)
Robert Lowell, "Skunk Hour" (p. 163)
Lorine Niedecker, "My Life by Water"
(p. 141)
Gary Snyder, "Hitch Haiku" (p. 190)
William Stafford, "Traveling through
the Dark" (p. 158)

Faith/Doubt

John Berryman, "Certainty before
Lunch" (p. 159)
T. S. Eliot, "Journey of the Magi"
(p. 131)
Robert Lowell, "Skunk Hour" (p. 163)
W. S. Merwin, "For the Anniversary of
My Death" (p. 181)
Thylias Moss, "The Lynching" (p. 267)
Mary Oliver, "First Snow" (p. 204)
Donald Revell, "Mignonette" (p. 270)
Wallace Stevens, "Sunday Morning"
(p. 112)
Virgil Suárez, "Tea Leaves, *Caracoles,*
Coffee Beans" (p. 286)
Jean Valentine, "December 21st"
(p. 202)
James Wright, "A Blessing" (p. 181)

Family

Jimmy Santiago Baca, "Family Ties"
(p. 253)
Marilyn Chin, "How I Got That Name"
(p. 275)

Rita Dove, "Fifth Grade Autobiography"
(p. 258)
Vievee Francis, "1864, A Pocket Full of
Rye" (p. 287)
Robert Frost, "'Out, Out—'" (p. 108)
Kimiko Hahn, "Mother's Mother"
(p. 278)
Michael S. Harper, "Nightmare Begins
Responsibility" (p. 210)
Seamus Heaney, "Mid-Term Break"
(p. 212)
A. Van Jordan, "From" (p. 289)
Ted Kooser, "Abandoned Farmhouse"
(p. 213)
Erika Meitner, "North Country
Canzone" (p. 300)
Sharon Olds, "I Go Back to May 1937"
(p. 227)
Atsuro Riley, "Drill" (p. 283)
Alberto Ríos, "Nani" (p. 259)
Theodore Roethke, "My Papa's Waltz"
(p. 147)
Gary Soto, "Moving Away" (p. 257)
Ruth Stone, "What We Have" (p. 162)
Virgil Suárez, "Tea Leaves, *Caracoles,*
Coffee Beans" (p. 286)

Fate

Victor Hernández Cruz, "Problems
with Hurricanes" (p. 246)
Thomas Hardy, "The Darkling Thrush"
(p. 94)
Dudley Randall, "Ballad of
Birmingham" (p. 157)

Fathers

Anonymous, "Lord Randal" (p. 7)
Charles Bukowski, "my old man"
(p. 166)
Michael S. Harper, "Nightmare Begins
Responsibility" (p. 210)
Robert Hayden, "Those Winter
Sundays" (p. 156)
Seamus Heaney, "Digging" (p. 211)
Li-Young Lee, "Eating Alone" (p. 280)
Li-Young Lee, "The Gift" (p. 280)
Thylias Moss, "The Lynching" (p. 267)

Sylvia Plath, "Daddy" (p. 195)
Theodore Roethke, "My Papa's Waltz" (p. 147)
Gary Soto, "Moving Away" (p. 257)
Dylan Thomas, "Do not go gentle into that good night" (p. 161)

Fear

Wendell Berry, "The Peace of Wild Things" (p. 202)
Eavan Boland, "The Pomegranate" (p. 232)
Michael S. Harper, "Nightmare Begins Responsibility" (p. 210)
Linda Hogan, "Crow Law" (p. 239)
Honorée Fanonne Jeffers, "Unidentified Female Student, Former Slave" (p. 293)
John Keats, "When I have fears that I may cease to be" (p. 57)
Sylvia Plath, "Daddy" (p. 195)
Adrienne Rich, "Aunt Jennifer's Tigers" (p. 186)

Feminist Concerns

Margaret Atwood, "True Stories" (p. 217)
Marilyn Chin, "How I Got That Name" (p. 275)
Lucille Clifton, "at the cemetery, walnut grove plantation, south carolina, 1989" (p. 208)
Lucille Clifton, "homage to my hips" (p. 207)
Denise Duhamel, "One Afternoon when Barbie Wanted to Join the Military" (p. 284)
Kimiko Hahn, "Mother's Mother" (p. 278)
Sharon Olds, "The One Girl at the Boys' Party" (p. 226)
Marge Piercy, "Barbie Doll" (p. 205)
Adrienne Rich, "Aunt Jennifer's Tigers" (p. 186)
Adrienne Rich, "Diving into the Wreck" (p. 187)
Anne Waldman, "Icy Rose" (p. 234)

Food

Gwendolyn Brooks, "The Bean Eaters" (p. 165)
Allen Ginsberg, "A Supermarket in California" (p. 176)
Ray Gonzáles, "Praise the Tortilla, Praise Menudo, Praise Chorizo" (p. 263)
Galway Kinnell, "The Bear" (p. 177)
Li-Young Lee, "Eating Alone" (p. 280)
Atsuro Riley, "Drill" (p. 283)
Alberto Ríos, "Nani" (p. 259)
A. E. Stallings, "Olives" (p. 296)
Wallace Stevens, "The Emperor of Ice-Cream" (p. 112)
Virgil Suárez, "Tea Leaves, *Caracoles*, Coffee Beans" (p. 286)
William Carlos Williams, "This Is Just to Say" (p. 118)

Grandparents

Judith Ortiz Cofer, "Cold as Heaven" (p. 254)
Rita Dove, "Fifth Grade Autobiography" (p. 258)
Kimiko Hahn, "Mother's Mother" (p. 278)
Seamus Heaney, "Digging" (p. 211)
Erika Meitner, "North Country Canzone" (p. 300)
David Mura, "Grandfather-in-Law" (p. 262)
Alberto Ríos, "Nani" (p. 259)
Virgil Suárez, "Tea Leaves, *Caracoles*, Coffee Beans" (p. 286)
Natasha Trethewey, "History Lesson" (p. 290)

Grief

Robert Frost, "'Out, Out—'" (p. 108)
Allen Ginsberg, "A Supermarket in California" (p. 176)
Aracelis Girmay, "Snail, or, To a House" (p. 302)
Michael S. Harper, "Nightmare Begins Responsibility" (p. 210)

Seamus Heaney, "Mid-Term Break"
(p. 212)
Ben Jonson, "On My First Son" (p. 18)
Li-Young Lee, "Eating Alone" (p. 280)
Edgar Allan Poe, "The Raven" (p. 60)
John Crowe Ransom, "Bells for John
Whiteside's Daughter" (p. 124)
Donald Revell, "Mignonette" (p. 270)
Theodore Roethke, "Elegy for Jane"
(p. 148)
Jean Toomer, "Face" (p. 136)

History

Sherman Alexie, "Postcards to
Columbus" (p. 291)
Margaret Atwood, "True Stories"
(p. 217)
Marilyn Chin, "How I Got That Name"
(p. 275)
Vievee Francis, "1864, A Pocket Full of
Rye" (p. 287)
Allen Ginsberg, "A Supermarket in
California" (p. 176)
Thomas Gray, "Elegy Written in a
Country Churchyard" (p. 30)
Langston Hughes, "Theme for
English B" (p. 138)
Honorée Fanonne Jeffers, "Unidentified
Female Student, Former Slave"
(p. 293)
Stanley Kunitz, "The War against the
Trees" (p. 142)
Thylias Moss, "The Lynching" (p. 267)
Adrienne Rich, "Diving into the Wreck"
(p. 187)
Natasha Trethewey, "History Lesson"
(p. 290)
Derek Walcott, "Sea Grapes" (p. 190)
William Butler Yeats, "Leda and the
Swan" (p. 99)
Ray A. Young Bear, "From the Spotted
Night" (p. 249)

Holocaust

Thylias Moss, "The Lynching"
(p. 267)
Sylvia Plath, "Daddy" (p. 195)

Charles Simic, "Begotten of the Spleen"
(p. 209)

Home, Memories of

Charles Bukowski, "my old man"
(p. 166)
Marilyn Chin, "How I Got That Name"
(p. 275)
Aracelis Girmay, "Snail, or, To a House"
(p. 302)
Robert Hayden, "Those Winter
Sundays" (p. 156)
Gary Soto, "Moving Away" (p. 257)
Ruth Stone, "What We Have" (p. 162)
Dylan Thomas, "Fern Hill" (p. 160)

Home, Returning to

Jim Barnes, "Return to La Plata,
Missouri" (p. 199)
Robert Frost, "The Death of the Hired
Man" (p. 103)
Seamus Heaney, "Mid-Term Break"
(p. 212)
Derek Walcott, "Sea Grapes" (p. 190)

Honor

Victor Hernández Cruz, "Problems
with Hurricanes" (p. 246)
Honorée Fanonne Jeffers, "Unidentified
Female Student, Former Slave"
(p. 293)
Heather McHugh, "What He Thought"
(p. 242)
Marilyn Nelson, "Minor Miracle"
(p. 236)

Humanity

Margaret Atwood, "True Stories"
(p. 217)
W. H. Auden, "As I Walked Out One
Evening" (p. 143)
Elizabeth Bishop, "In the Waiting
Room" (p. 152)
Marilyn Hacker, "Villanelle" (p. 228)
Marilyn Nelson, "Minor Miracle"
(p. 236)
Naomi Shihab Nye, "Kindness" (p. 255)

William Stafford, "Traveling through the Dark" (p. 158)

William Carlos Williams, "This Is Just to Say" (p. 118)

William Wordsworth, "Ode: Intimations of Immortality" (p. 44)

Humor

Billy Collins, "Litany" (p. 221)

Lucille Clifton, "homage to my hips" (p. 207)

Victor Hernández Cruz, "Problems with Hurricanes" (p. 246)

E. E. Cummings, "'next to of course god America i" (p. 135)

Denise Duhamel, "One Afternoon when Barbie Wanted to Join the Military" (p. 284)

Richard Garcia, "Why I Left the Church" (p. 225)

Allen Ginsberg, "A Supermarket in California" (p. 176)

Anna Maria Hong, "The Frog-Prince" (p. 292)

Frank O'Hara, "Why I Am Not a Painter" (p. 174)

Mary Jo Salter, "Half a Double Sonnet" (p. 264)

Anne Sexton, "Cinderella" (p. 183)

Mark Strand, "Eating Poetry" (p. 201)

Jonathan Swift, "A Description of a City Shower" (p. 25)

James Tate, "The Wheelchair Butterfly" (p. 231)

Nancy Willard, "Questions My Son Asked Me, Answers I Never Gave Him" (p. 206)

William Carlos Williams, "This Is Just to Say" (p. 118)

Paul Zimmer, "Zimmer Imagines Heaven" (p. 203)

Innocence and Experience

Elizabeth Bishop, "In the Waiting Room" (p. 152)

Denise Duhamel, "One Afternoon when Barbie Wanted to Join the Military" (p. 284)

Robert Frost, "'Out, Out—'" (p. 108)

Seamus Heaney, "Glanmore Sonnets 4" (p. 213)

Thylias Moss, "The Lynching" (p. 267)

Sharon Olds, "I Go Back to May 1937" (p. 227)

James Tate, "The Wheelchair Butterfly" (p. 231)

Dylan Thomas, "Fern Hill" (p. 160)

Ellen Bryant Voigt, "The Lotus Flowers" (p. 228)

Nancy Willard, "Questions My Son Asked Me, Answers I Never Gave Him" (p. 206)

Jazz

Gwendolyn Brooks, "We Real Cool" (p. 165)

Sterling A. Brown, "Riverbank Blues" (p. 136)

Frank O'Hara, "The Day Lady Died" (p. 175)

Anne Waldman, "Icy Rose" (p. 234)

Language (see also Words)

Julia Alvarez, "Bilingual Sestina" (p. 247)

Margaret Atwood, "True Stories" (p. 217)

Sterling A. Brown, "Riverbank Blues" (p. 136)

Marilyn Chin, "How I Got That Name" (p. 275)

Billy Collins, "Litany" (p. 221)

Marilyn Hacker, "Villanelle" (p. 228)

Kimiko Hahn, "Mother's Mother" (p. 278)

Terrance Hayes, "Talk" (p. 298)

Garrett Kaoru Hongo, "Yellow Light" (p. 252)

Langston Hughes, "Theme for English B" (p. 138)

A. Van Jordan, "From" (p. 289)

Allison Joseph, "On Being Told I Don't Speak Like a Black Person" (p. 294)

Marilyn Nelson, "Minor Miracle" (p. 236)

Wang Ping, "Syntax" (p. 282)

Alberto Ríos, "Nani" (p. 259)
Gertrude Stein, "Susie Asado" (p. 101)
Wallace Stevens, "The Emperor of
Ice-Cream" (p. 112)

Learning/Realization

Anonymous, "Lord Randall" (p. 7)
W. H. Auden, "As I Walked Out One
Evening" (p. 143)
John Berryman, "Certainty before
Lunch" (p. 159)
T. S. Eliot, "Journey of the Magi"
(p. 131)
T. S. Eliot, "The Love Song of J. Alfred
Prufrock" (p. 125)
Robert Hayden, "Those Winter
Sundays" (p. 156)
Denise Levertov, "The ache of
marriage" (p. 169)
Edna St. Vincent Millay, "Pity me not
because the light of day" (p. 133)
John Milton, "When I consider how
my light is spent" (p. 21)
Mary Oliver, "First Snow" (p. 204)
Charles Olson, "Maximus, to himself"
(p. 148)
Wilfred Owen, "Dulce et Decorum Est"
(p. 133)

Liberty

Julia Alvarez, "Bilingual Sestina"
(p. 247)
Sterling A. Brown, "Riverbank Blues"
(p. 136)
Lucille Clifton, "homage to my hips"
(p. 207)
E. E. Cummings, "'next to of course
god America i" (p. 135)
Honorée Fanonne Jeffers, "Unidentified
Female Student, Former Slave"
(p. 293)
Robinson Jeffers, "Hurt Hawks"
(p. 120)

Loneliness

Anonymous, "Western Wind" (p. 7)
Jim Barnes, "Return to La Plata,
Missouri" (p. 199)

Robert Bly, "Driving to Town Late to
Mail a Letter" (p. 177)
Sterling A. Brown, "Riverbank Blues"
(p. 136)
T. S. Eliot, "The Love Song of J. Alfred
Prufrock" (p. 125)
T. S. Eliot, "Preludes" (p. 129)
Vievee Francis, "1864, A Pocket Full of
Rye" (p. 287)
Allen Ginsberg, "A Supermarket in
California" (p. 176)
Etheridge Knight, "Hard Rock Returns
to Prison from the Hospital for the
Criminal Insane" (p. 198)
Ted Kooser, "Abandoned Farmhouse"
(p. 213)
Li-Young Lee, "Eating Alone" (p. 280)
Robert Lowell, "Skunk Hour" (p. 163)
George Oppen, "Myself I Sing" (p. 146)
Ezra Pound, "The River-Merchant's
Wife: A Letter" (p. 118)
Anne Waldman, "Icy Rose" (p. 234)
William Wordsworth, "I wandered
lonely as a cloud" (p. 43)

Love

Anonymous, "Western Wind" (p. 7)
Anne Bradstreet, "Before the Birth of
One of Her Children" (p. 22)
Elizabeth Barrett Browning, "How do
I love thee? Let me count the ways"
(p. 60)
Robert Burns, "A Red, Red Rose"
(p. 38)
Billy Collins, "Litany" (p. 221)
Emily Dickinson, "Wild Nights—Wild
Nights!" (p. 91)
John Donne, "The Flea" (p. 16)
John Donne, "A Valediction: Forbidding
Mourning" (p. 15)
Michael Drayton, "Since there's no
help, come let us kiss and part"
(p. 11)
Cornelius Eady, "My Mother, If She
Had Won Free Dance Lessons"
(p. 271)
Anita Endrezze, "The Girl Who Loved
the Sky" (p. 261)

Music

Sterling A. Brown, "Riverbank Blues" (p. 136)
Samuel Taylor Coleridge, "Kubla Khan" (p. 51)
T. S. Eliot, "Preludes" (p. 129)
Frank O'Hara, "The Day Lady Died" (p. 175)
Donald Revell, "Mignonette" (p. 270)
Walt Whitman, from *Song of Myself* (p. 69)
Al Young, "A Dance for Ma Rainey" (p. 214)
Paul Zimmer, "Zimmer Imagines Heaven" (p. 203)

Mutability

John Ashbery, "Mixed Feelings" (p. 180)
Jim Barnes, "Return to La Plata, Missouri" (p. 199)
John Berryman, "Certainty before Lunch" (p. 159)
Philip Booth, "A Two Inch Wave" (p. 172)
Seamus Heaney, "Mid-Term Break" (p. 212)
W. S. Merwin, "For the Anniversary of My Death" (p. 181)
Edna St. Vincent Millay, "Pity me not because the light of day" (p. 133)
Linda Pastan, "love poem" (p. 193)
A. E. Stallings, "Olives" (p. 296)
Charles Wright, "Reunion" (p. 204)

Names

Julia Alvarez, "Bilingual Sestina" (p. 247)
Marilyn Chin, "How I Got That Name" (p. 275)
Lucille Clifton, "at the cemetery, walnut grove plantation, south carolina, 1989" (p. 208)
Adrienne Rich, "Diving into the Wreck" (p. 187)
Atsuro Riley, "Drill" (p. 283)
Jean Valentine, "December 21st" (p. 202)

Nature

Wendell Berry, "The Peace of Wild Things" (p. 202)
Robert Bly, "Driving to Town Late to Mail a Letter" (p. 177)
Philip Booth, "A Two Inch Wave" (p. 172)
Geoffrey Chaucer, from *The Canterbury Tales*: "The General Prologue" (p. 6)
Victor Hernández Cruz, "Problems with Hurricanes" (p. 246)
Anita Endrezze, "The Girl Who Loved the Sky" (p. 261)
Robert Frost, "The Road Not Taken" (p. 107)
Robert Frost, "Stopping by Woods on a Snowy Evening" (p. 109)
Louise Glück, "The Wild Iris" (p. 230)
Linda Hogan, "Crow Law" (p. 239)
Gerard Manley Hopkins, "God's Grandeur" (p. 95)
Gerard Manley Hopkins, "Pied Beauty" (p. 95)
Gerard Manley Hopkins, "Spring and Fall" (p. 96)
A. E. Housman, "Loveliest of trees, the cherry now" (p. 97)
John Keats, "To Autumn" (p. 59)
Galway Kinnell, "The Bear" (p. 177)
Maxine Kumin, "The Sound of Night" (p. 171)
Stanley Kunitz, "The War against the Trees" (p. 142)
Robert Lowell, "Skunk Hour" (p. 163)
Randall Mann, "The Heron" (p. 299)
Erika Meitner, "North Country Canzone" (p. 300)
Lorine Niedecker, "My Life by Water" (p. 141)
Mary Oliver, "First Snow" (p. 204)
Charles Olson, "Maximus, to himself" (p. 148)
Theodore Roethke, "Elegy for Jane" (p. 148)
Mary Ruefle, "Barbarians" (p. 260)
Percy Bysshe Shelley, "Ode to the West Wind" (p. 54)

Gary Snyder, "Hitch Haiku" (p. 190)
William Stafford, "Traveling through the Dark" (p. 158)
Ruth Stone, "What We Have" (p. 162)
Dylan Thomas, "Fern Hill" (p. 160)
Ellen Bryant Voigt, "The Lotus Flowers" (p. 228)
Anne Waldman, "Icy Rose" (p. 234)
Walt Whitman, "A Noiseless Patient Spider" (p. 89)
Walt Whitman, from *Song of Myself* (p. 69)
Walt Whitman, "When Lilacs Last in the Dooryard Bloom'd" (p. 82)
William Wordsworth, "I wandered lonely as a cloud" (p. 43)
William Wordsworth, "Lines Composed a Few Miles above Tintern Abbey" (p. 39)
William Wordsworth, "Ode: Intimations of Immortality" (p. 44)
William Wordsworth, "The world is too much with us" (p. 50)
James Wright, "A Blessing" (p. 181)

Nonconformity

Marilyn Chin, "How I Got That Name" (p. 275)
Emily Dickinson, "Much Madness is divinest Sense" (p. 91)
Denise Duhamel, "One Afternoon when Barbie Wanted to Join the Military" (p. 284)
Allen Ginsberg, "A Supermarket in California" (p. 176)
Adrienne Rich, "Diving into the Wreck" (p. 187)
Mark Strand, "Eating Poetry" (p. 201)
Anne Waldman, "Icy Rose" (p. 234)

Patriotism

E. E. Cummings, "'next to of course god America i" (p. 135)
Allen Ginsberg, "A Supermarket in California" (p. 176)
Langston Hughes, "Mother to Son" (p. 138)

Heather McHugh, "What He Thought" (p. 242)
Claude McKay, "America" (p. 132)

Photography

John Ashbery, "Mixed Feelings" (p. 180)
Toi Derricotte, "A Note on My Son's Face" (p. 222)
Rita Dove, "Fifth Grade Autobiography" (p. 258)
Sharon Olds, "I Go Back to May 1937" (p. 227)
Natasha Trethewey, "History Lesson" (p. 290)
Charles Wright, "Reunion" (p. 204)

Play/Playfulness

Billy Collins, "Litany" (p. 221)
Victor Hernández Cruz, "Problems with Hurricanes" (p. 246)
E. E. Cummings, "in Just-" (p. 134)
Mark Doty, "Tiara" (p. 265)
Denise Duhamel, "One Afternoon when Barbie Wanted to Join the Military" (p. 284)
Marianne Moore, "Poetry" (p. 123)
Mary Jo Salter, "Half a Double Sonnet" (p. 269)
Mark Strand, "Eating Poetry" (p. 201)
Quincy Troupe, "A Poem for 'Magic'" (p. 215)
Nancy Willard, "Questions My Son Asked Me, Answers I Never Gave Him" (p. 206)
Al Young, "A Dance for Ma Rainey" (p. 214)
Paul Zimmer, "Zimmer Imagines Heaven" (p. 203)

Poetry

Galway Kinnell, "The Bear" (p. 177)
Larry Levis, "The Poem You Asked For" (p. 237)
Heather McHugh, "What He Thought" (p. 242)
Marianne Moore, "Poetry" (p. 123)

Michael S. Harper, "Nightmare Begins
Responsibility" (p. 210)
Terrance Hayes, "Talk" (p. 298)
Garrett Kaoru Hongo, "Yellow Light"
(p. 252)
Langston Hughes, "Harlem" (p. 140)
Langston Hughes, "Mother to Son"
(p. 138)
Langston Hughes, "The Negro Speaks
of Rivers" (p. 137)
Langston Hughes, "Theme for
English B" (p. 138)
Honorée Fanonne Jeffers, "Unidentified
Female Student, Former Slave"
(p. 293)
Allison Joseph, "On Being Told I
Don't Speak Like a Black Person"
(p. 294)
Etheridge Knight, "Hard Rock Returns
to Prison from the Hospital for the
Criminal Insane" (p. 198)
Audre Lorde, "Coal" (p. 200)
Claude McKay, "America" (p. 132)
Thylias Moss, "The Lynching" (p. 267)
Marilyn Nelson, "Minor Miracle"
(p. 236)
Dudley Randall, "Ballad of
Birmingham" (p. 157)
Sekou Sundiata, "Blink Your Eyes"
(p. 244)
Natasha Trethewey, "History Lesson"
(p. 290)
James Welch, "Christmas Comes to
Moccasin Flat" (p. 218)
Al Young, "A Dance for Ma Rainey"
(p. 214)
Ray A. Young Bear, "From the Spotted
Night" (p. 249)

Rebellion (see Conformity and
Rebellion, Nonconformity*)*

Religion
Matthew Arnold, "Dover Beach" (p. 89)
John Berryman, "Certainty before
Lunch" (p. 159)
William Blake, "The Lamb" (p. 36)
William Blake, "The Tyger" (p. 37)

Geoffrey Chaucer, from *The Canterbury
Tales*: "The General Prologue" (p. 6)
T. S. Eliot, "Journey of the Magi"
(p. 131)
Richard Garcia, "Why I Left the
Church" (p. 225)
George Herbert, "Easter-wings" (p. 20)
George Herbert, "Redemption" (p. 21)
Linda Hogan, "Crow Law" (p. 239)
Gerard Manley Hopkins, "God's
Grandeur" (p. 95)
Gerard Manley Hopkins, "Pied Beauty"
(p. 95)
Richard Jones, "Cathedral" (p. 266)
Philip Larkin, "High Windows" (p. 169)
John Milton, "When I consider how
my light is spent" (p. 21)
Thylias Moss, "The Lynching" (p. 267)
Donald Revell, "Mignonette" (p. 270)
Leslie Marmon Silko, "Prayer to the
Pacific" (p. 241)
Charles Simic, "Begotten of the Spleen"
(p. 209)
Christopher Smart, from *Jubilate Agno*
(p. 34)
Wallace Stevens, "Sunday Morning"
(p. 112)
Virgil Suárez, "Tea Leaves, *Caracoles*,
Coffee Beans" (p. 286)
Edward Taylor, "Housewifery" (p. 25)
Alfred, Lord Tennyson, "Crossing the
Bar" (p. 67)
Jean Valentine, "December 21st"
(p. 202)
Walt Whitman, from *Song of Myself*
(p. 69)
Charles Wright, "Reunion" (p. 204)
Paul Zimmer, "Zimmer Imagines
Heaven" (p. 203)

Rural Life
Jim Barnes, "Return to La Plata,
Missouri" (p. 199)
Vievee Francis, "1864, A Pocket Full of
Rye" (p. 287)
Robert Frost, "The Death of the Hired
Man" (p. 103)
Robert Frost, "'Out, Out—'" (p. 108)

Seamus Heaney, "Glanmore Sonnets 4" (p. 213)

Ted Kooser, "Abandoned Farmhouse" (p. 213)

Lorine Niedecker, "My Life by Water" (p. 141)

Atsuro Riley, "Drill" (p. 283)

Mary Ruefle, "Barbarians" (p. 260)

Gary Snyder, "Hitch Haiku" (p. 190)

William Stafford, "Traveling through the Dark" (p. 158)

Ellen Bryant Voigt, "The Lotus Flowers" (p. 228)

James Wright, "A Blessing" (p. 181)

Seasons

Judith Ortiz Cofer, "Cold as Heaven" (p. 254)

E. E. Cummings, "in Just-" (p. 134)

Robert Frost, "After Apple-Picking" (p. 102)

Robert Frost, "Stopping by Woods on a Snowy Evening" (p. 109)

Robert Hayden, "Those Winter Sundays" (p. 156)

Gerard Manley Hopkins, "Spring and Fall" (p. 96)

A. E. Housman, "Loveliest of trees, the cherry now" (p. 97)

John Keats, "To Autumn" (p. 59)

Lorine Niedecker, "My Life by Water" (p. 141)

Mary Oliver, "First Snow" (p. 204)

William Shakespeare, "Shall I compare thee to a summer's day?" (p. 13)

Percy Bysshe Shelley, "Ode to the West Wind" (p. 54)

Gary Snyder, "Hitch Haiku" (p. 190)

William Carlos Williams, "Spring and All" (p. 117)

Self

Julia Alvarez, "Bilingual Sestina" (p. 247)

A. Van Jordan, "From" (p. 289)

George Oppen, "Myself I Sing" (p. 146)

Walt Whitman, from *Song of Myself* (p. 69)

Sex

Lucille Clifton, "homage to my hips" (p. 207)

Emily Dickinson, "Wild Nights—Wild Nights!" (p. 91)

John Donne, "The Flea" (p. 16)

Denise Duhamel, "One Afternoon when Barbie Wanted to Join the Military" (p. 284)

Andrew Marvell, "To His Coy Mistress" (p. 23)

Sharon Olds, "The One Girl at the Boys' Party" (p. 226)

Donald Revell, "Mignonette" (p. 270)

Kevin Young, "Song of Smoke" (p. 297)

Soul and Body

Elizabeth Bishop, "In the Waiting Room" (p. 152)

Marilyn Hacker, "Villanelle" (p. 228)

Jane Hirshfield, "To Drink" (p. 264)

Linda Hogan, "Crow Law" (p. 239)

Galway Kinnell, "The Bear" (p. 177)

Jean Valentine, "December 21st" (p. 202)

Walt Whitman, from *Song of Myself* (p. 69)

Walt Whitman, "When Lilacs Last in the Dooryard Bloom'd" (p. 82)

Richard Wilbur, "Love Calls Us to the Things of This World" (p. 168)

William Wordsworth, "Ode: Intimations of Immortality" (p. 44)

Sports

Terrance Hayes, "Talk" (p. 298)

A. E. Housman, "To an Athlete Dying Young" (p. 97)

Quincy Troupe, "A Poem for 'Magic'" (p. 215)

Suffering

W. H. Auden, "Musée des Beaux Arts" (p. 145)

Elizabeth Bishop, "In the Waiting Room" (p. 152)

Victor Hernández Cruz, "Problems with Hurricanes" (p. 246)

Women's Issues (see also **Feminist Concerns***)*

Margaret Atwood, "True Stories" (p. 217)

Elizabeth Bishop, "In the Waiting Room" (p. 152)

Anne Bradstreet, "Before the Birth of One of Her Children" (p. 22)

Lucille Clifton, "at the cemetery, walnut grove plantation, south carolina, 1989" (p. 208)

Lucille Clifton, "homage to my hips" (p. 207)

Denise Duhamel, "One Afternoon when Barbie Wanted to Join the Military" (p. 284)

Kimiko Hahn, "Mother's Mother" (p. 278)

Langston Hughes, "Mother to Son" (p. 138)

Sharon Olds, "The One Girl at the Boys' Party" (p. 226)

Marge Piercy, "Barbie Doll" (p. 205)

Sylvia Plath, "Morning Song" (p. 195)

Adrienne Rich, "Aunt Jennifer's Tigers" (p. 186)

Adrienne Rich, "Diving into the Wreck" (p. 187)

Anne Waldman, "Icy Rose" (p. 234)

Words (see also **Language***)*

Julia Alvarez, "Bilingual Sestina" (p. 247)

Margaret Atwood, "True Stories" (p. 217)

Sterling A. Brown, "Riverbank Blues" (p. 136)

Kimiko Hahn, "Mother's Mother" (p. 278)

Terrance Hayes, "Talk" (p. 298)

Langston Hughes, "Theme for English B" (p. 138)

A. Van Jordan, "From" (p. 289)

Allison Joseph, "On Being Told I Don't Speak Like a Black Person" (p. 294)

Audrey Lorde, "Coal" (p. 200)

Erika Meitner, "North Country Canzone" (p. 300)

Marilyn Nelson, "Minor Miracle" (p. 236)

Frank O'Hara, "Why I Am Not a Painter" (p. 174)

Sharon Olds, "I Go Back to May 1937" (p. 227)

Alberto Ríos, "Nani" (p. 259)

Gertrude Stein, "Susie Asado" (p. 101)

Mark Strand, "Eating Poetry" (p. 201)

Work

Sterling A. Brown, "Riverbank Blues" (p. 136)

Lucille Clifton, "at the cemetery, walnut grove plantation, south carolina, 1989" (p. 208)

Vievee Francis, "1864, A Pocket Full of Rye" (p. 287)

Robert Frost, "The Death of the Hired Man" (p. 103)

Robert Frost, "'Out, Out—'" (p. 108)

Gerard Manley Hopkins, "Pied Beauty" (p. 95)

Ted Kooser, "Abandoned Farmhouse" (p. 213)

Philip Levine, "What Work Is" (p. 182)

Charles Olson, "Maximus, to himself" (p. 148)

Atsuro Riley, "Drill" (p. 283)

Gary Snyder, "Hitch Haiku" (p. 190)

Alfred, Lord Tennyson, "Ulysses" (p. 65)

Glossary of Poetic Terms

This selective glossary is intended to help readers who seek a better understanding of poetic terms and techniques. It often provides examples and explanations in addition to definitions, and it can be used as a reference, as needed, or it can be read straight through. Becoming more aware of the tools and techniques poets work with can help one experience a poem more richly and fully. We have drawn numerous illustrations from John Frederick Nims's "Love Poem" (p. 156) because it provides particularly clear and memorable examples of many figures of speech.

For a more complete, book-length guide to literary terminology, see Ross Murfin and Supryia Ray, *The Bedford Glossary of Critical and Literary Terms* (3rd ed., 2009); M. H. Abrams and Geoffrey Harpham, *A Glossary of Literary Terms* (10th ed., 2012); or William Harmon, *A Handbook to Literature* (12th ed., 2012), all excellent resources on which we have drawn frequently. The most authoritative work is the massive *New Princeton Encyclopedia of Poetry and Poetics*, ed. Roland Greene et al. (4th ed., 2012). Several glossaries of literary terms are available on the Internet.

Accent   The stress, or greater emphasis, given to some syllables of words relative to that received by adjacent syllables.

Accentual meter   A metrical system in which the number of accented, or stressed, syllables per line is regular (all lines having the same number, or the corresponding lines of different stanzas having the same number), while the number of unstressed syllables in lines varies randomly. Accentual meter with two accented syllables in each half-line, linked by a system of alliteration, was the principle of Old English poetry (up to the eleventh century), and some modern poets—e.g., W. H. Auden—have sought to revive it. Gerard Manley Hopkins developed a unique variety of accentual verse he called *sprung rhythm* (see pp. 95–96).

Accentual-syllabic verse   Verse whose meter takes into account both the number of syllables per line and the pattern of accented and unaccented syllables. The great majority of metrical poems in English are accentual-syllabic. Cf. **quantitative verse**.

Alexandrine   A poetic line with six iambic feet (iambic hexameter).

Allegory   A form or manner, usually narrative, in which objects, persons, and actions make coherent sense on a literal level but also are equated in a sustained and obvious way with (usually) abstract meanings that lie outside the story. A classic example in prose is John Bunyan's *The Pilgrim's Progress;* in narrative poetry, Edmund Spenser's *The Faerie Queene.* Edward Taylor's "Housewifery" (p. 25), though not narrative, is allegorical in approach. See also George Herbert's "Redemption" (p. 21).

Alliteration   The repetition of identical consonant sounds in the stressed syllables of words relatively near each other (in the same line or adjacent lines, usually). Alliteration is most common at the beginnings of words or syllables ("as the grass was green") but can involve consonants within words and syllables as well ("green and carefree, famous among the barns"). Alliteration applies to sounds, not spelling: "And honoured among foxes and pheasants" (examples from Dylan Thomas, "Fern Hill," p. 160). Cf. **consonance**.

Allusion   A figure of speech that echoes or makes brief reference to a literary or artistic work or a historical figure, event, or object; for example, the references to Lazarus and Hamlet in "The Love Song of J. Alfred Prufrock" (p. 125) are allusions. It is usually a way of placing one's poem within, or alongside, a whole other context that is evoked in a very economical fashion. See also **intertextuality**.

Ambiguity   (1) In expository prose, an undesirable doubtfulness or uncertainty of meaning or intention, resulting from imprecision in use of words or construction of sentences. (2) In poetry, the desirable condition of admitting more than one possible meaning, resulting from the capacity of language to function on levels other than the literal. Related terms sometimes employed are "ambivalence" and "polysemy."

Anapest   A metrical foot consisting of three syllables, with two unaccented syllables followed by an accented one (˘˘´). In "anapestic meter," anapests are the predominant foot in a line or poem. The following line from William Cowper's "The Poplar Field" (1784) is in anapestic meter: "Ănd thĕ whis | pĕrĭng soúnd | ŏf thĕ cóol | cŏlŏnnáde."

Anaphora   Repetition of the same word or words at the beginning of two or more lines, clauses, or sentences. For examples, see the portion of Christopher Smart's *Jubilate Agno* included in the anthology (p. 34); Walt Whitman employs it extensively in *Song of Myself* (p. 69) and "When Lilacs Last in the Dooryard Bloom'd" (p. 82).

Anticlimax   An arrangement of details such that one of lesser importance appears after one or ones of greater importance, where an even greater one is expected; for example, "Not louder shrieks to pitying heaven are cast, / When husbands or when lapdogs breathe their last" (Alexander Pope, "The Rape of the Lock" [1714]).

Antithesis   A figure of speech in which contrasting words, sentences, or ideas are expressed in balanced, parallel grammatical structures: for example, "She had some horses she loved. / She had some horses she hated" (Joy Harjo, "She Had Some Horses," p. 250) illustrates antithesis.

Apostrophe   A figure of speech in which an absent person, an abstract quality, or a nonhuman entity is addressed as though present. It is a particular type of personification. See, for example, Ben Jonson, "On My First Son" (p. 18).

Approximate rhyme   See **slant rhyme**.

Archetype   An image, a symbol, a character type, or a plot line that occurs frequently enough in literature, religion, myths, folktales, and fairy tales to be recognizable as an element of universal experience and thus to evoke a deep emotional response. In "Spring and Fall" (p. 96) Gerard Manley Hopkins develops the archetypes in his title, those of spring (archetype for birth and youth) and fall (archetype for old age and the approach of death).

Assonance   The repetition of identical or similar vowel sounds in words relatively near each other (usually within a line or in adjacent lines) whose consonant sounds differ. It can be initial ("*apple . . . and happy as*") or, more commonly, internal ("*green* and care*free*," "*Time* held *me green* and *dying*") (examples from Dylan Thomas, "Fern Hill," p. 160).

Aubade   A dawn song, ordinarily expressing the regret of two lovers that day has come to separate them.

Ballad   A poem that tells a story and was meant to be recited or sung; originally a folk art, transmitted orally from person to person and generation to generation. Many of the popular ballads were not written down and published until the eighteenth century, though their origins may have been centuries earlier. See "Lord Randal" (p. 7) for an example of a popular Scottish ballad.

Ballad stanza   A quatrain in iambic meter rhyming *abcb* with (usually) four feet in the first and third lines, three in the second and fourth. See, for example, Robert Burns, "A Red, Red Rose" (p. 38).

Blank verse   Lines of unrhymed iambic pentameter. It is the most widely used verse form of poetry in English because it is the closest to the natural rhythms of English speech. Shakespeare's plays as well as Milton's *Paradise Lost* and *Paradise Regained*, Wordsworth's *Prelude*, and countless other long poems were composed in blank verse because it is well suited to narrative, dialogue, and reflection. For a poem based on blank verse but using it freely, see Robert Frost's "The Death of the Hired Man" (p. 103).

Cacophony   A harsh or unpleasant combination of sounds. An example can be found in Alexander Pope's "An Essay on Criticism," lines 368–69: "But when loud surges lash the sounding shore, / The hoarse, rough verse should like the torrent roar" (p. 28). Cf. **euphony**.

Caesura   A pause or break within a line of verse, usually signaled by a mark of punctuation.

Canzone   A lyric poem of five or six equal length stanzas (ranging from seven to twenty lines) plus a shorter concluding stanza. See Erika Meitner, "North Country Canzone" (p. 300).

Carpe diem   "Seize the day," a Latin phrase from an ode by Horace. It is the label for a theme common in literature, especially sixteenth- and seventeenth-century English love poetry, that life is short and fleeting and that therefore we must make the most of present pleasures. See Robert Herrick, "To the Virgins, to Make Much of Time" (p. 19) and Andrew Marvell, "To His Coy Mistress" (p. 23).

Catalog   A list of items in a literary work that reveals a range of people, things, or attributes often in order to create texture, complexity, surprise, inclusiveness, or emphasis. For examples of poems made up entirely or in part as lists, see Christopher Smart, *Jubilate Agno* (p. 34), Walt Whitman, *Song of Myself* (p. 69), and Joy Harjo, "She Had Some Horses" (p. 250).

Chaucerian stanza   A seven-line iambic stanza rhyming *ababbcc*, sometimes having an alexandrine (hexameter) closing line. See, for example, Sir Thomas Wyatt, "They flee from me" (p. 9).

Closed form   Any structural pattern in a poem that employs repetition of meter, rhyme, or stanza. Cf. **open form**.

Compression   The dropping of a syllable to make a line fit the meter, sometimes marked with an apostrophe (e.g., William Shakespeare, Sonnet 73 [p. 13], line 13: "This thou perceiv'st"). One common device is elision, the dropping of a vowel at the beginning or end of a word (e.g., John Donne, "A Valediction: Forbidding Mourning" [p. 15], lines 7 and 28: " 'Twere profanation of our joys" and "To move, but doth, if th' other do").

Conceit   A figure of speech that establishes a striking or far-fetched analogy between seemingly very dissimilar things, either the exaggerated, unrealistic comparisons of love poems (such as those used in Shakespeare's Sonnet 18 [p. 13] and parodied in Sonnet 130 [p. 14]) or the complex analogies of metaphysical wit (as in John Donne's "The Flea," p. 16).

Concrete poem   A poem shaped in the form of the object the poem describes or discusses. See, for example, George Herbert's "Easter-wings" (p. 20).

Confessional poetry   Poetry about personal, private issues that usually speaks directly, without the use of a persona. See, for example, Robert Lowell, "Skunk Hour" (p. 163) and Sylvia Plath, "Daddy" (p. 195).

Connotation   The shared or communal range of emotional implications and associations a word may carry in addition to its dictionary definitions. Cf. **denotation**.

Consonance   The repetition of consonant sounds in words whose vowels are different. In perfect examples, all the consonants are alike—*live, love; chitter, chatter; reader, rider;* but words in which all the consonants following the main vowels are identical also are considered consonance—*dive, love; swatter, chitter; sound, bond; gate* and *mat, set, pit.*

Convention   A rule, method, practice, or characteristic established by usage; a customary feature.

Couplet   Two consecutive lines of poetry with the same end rhyme. English (Shakespearean) sonnets end with a couplet (see pp. 13–14); for an entire poem in tetrameter couplets, see Andrew Marvell, "To His Coy Mistress" (p. 23). See also **heroic couplets**.

Dactyl   A metrical foot consisting of three syllables, an accented one followed by two unaccented ones (˘˘˘). In "dactylic meter," dactyls are the predominant foot of a line or poem. The following lines from Thomas Hardy's "The Voice" (1914) are in dactylic meter: "Wómăn mŭch | mĭśśed, hŏw yŏu | cáll tŏ m̆e, | cáll tŏ m̆e, / Sáyĭng t̆hat | nów yŏu are | nót aš yŏu | wére."

Denotation   The basic meanings of a word; its dictionary definitions.

Diction   Choice of words; the kind of words, phrases, and figurative language used to make up a work of literature. See also **poetic diction**.

Dimeter   A line of verse consisting of two metrical feet.

Double rhyme   A rhyme in which the accented, rhyming syllable is followed by one or more identical, unstressed syllables: *thrilling* and *killing, marry* and *tarry.* Formerly known as "feminine rhyme."

Dramatic irony   A situation in which a reader or an audience knows more than the speakers or characters, either about the outcome of events or the discrepancy between a meaning intended by a speaker or character and that recognized by the reader or audience.

Dramatic monologue   A poem with only one speaker, overheard in a dramatic moment (usually addressing another character or characters who do not speak), whose words reveal what is going on in the scene and expose significant depths of the speaker's temperament, attitudes, and values. See Robert Browning, "My Last Duchess" (p. 68) and T. S. Eliot, "The Love Song of J. Alfred Prufrock" (p. 125).

Elegy   In Greek and Roman literature, a serious, meditative poem written in "elegiac meter" (alternating hexameter and pentameter lines); since the 1600s, a sustained and formal poem lamenting the death of a particular person, usually ending with a consolation, or setting forth meditations on death or another solemn theme. See Thomas Gray's "Elegy Written in a Country Churchyard" (p. 30) and Walt Whitman's "When Lilacs Last in the Dooryard Bloom'd" (p. 82). For a modern variant, see Theodore Roethke's "Elegy for Jane" (p. 148). The adjective "elegaic" is also used to describe a general tone of sadness or a worldview that emphasizes suffering and loss. It is most often applied to Anglo-Saxon poems like *Beowulf* or *The Seafarer* but can also be used for modern poems such as, for example, A. E. Housman's poems in *A Shropshire Lad* (1896).

Elision   See **compression**.

End rhyme   Rhyme at the ends of lines in a poem.

End-stopped line   A poetic line in which both the grammatical structure and the thought reach completion at the end. Cf. **run-on line**.

English sonnet   A sonnet consisting of three quatrains (four-line units, typically rhyming *abab cdcd efef*) and a couplet (two rhyming lines). Usually the subject is introduced in the first quatrain, expanded in the second, and expanded still further in the third; the couplet adds a logical, pithy conclusion or gives a surprising twist. Also called the **Shakespearean sonnet** (see examples on pp. 13–14). Cf. **Spenserian sonnet**.

Enjambment   See **run-on line**.

Epic   A long narrative poem that celebrates the achievements of great heroes and heroines, often determining the fate of a tribe or nation, in formal language and an elevated style. Examples include Homer's *Iliad* and *Odyssey*, Virgil's *Aeneid*, and John Milton's *Paradise Lost*.

Epigram   Originally an inscription, especially an epitaph; in modern usage a short poem, usually polished and witty with a surprising twist at the end. See, for example, Ezra Pound's "In a Station of the Metro" (p. 119). (Its other dictionary definition, "any terse, witty, pointed statement," generally does not apply in poetry.)

Epigraph   In literature, a quotation at the beginning of a poem or on the title page or the beginning of an essay or a chapter in a book. See the epigraph from Dante at the beginning of T. S. Eliot, "The Love Song of J. Alfred Prufrock" (p. 125).

Epiphany   An appearance or manifestation, especially of a divine being; in literature, since James Joyce adapted the term to secular use in 1944, a sudden sense of radiance and revelation one may feel while perceiving a commonplace object; a moment or event in which the essential nature of a person, a situation, or an object is suddenly perceived. The term is more common in narrative than in lyric poetry. William Wordsworth, in "Ode: Intimations of Immortality" (p. 44), writes about epiphanies, although the poem itself does not depict them; Robert Bly depicts one in "Driving to Town Late to Mail a Letter" (p. 177).

Euphony   Language that strikes the ear as smooth, musical, and agreeable. An example can be found in Alexander Pope, "An Essay on Criticism," lines 366–67: "Soft is the strain when Zephyr gently blows, / And the smooth stream in smoother numbers flows" (p. 29). Cf. **cacophony**.

Exact rhyme   Rhyme in which all sounds following the vowel sound are the same: *spite* and *night, art* and *heart, ache* and *fake, card* and *barred.*

Exaggeration   See **hyperbole**.

Explication   A literary approach involving close analysis of texts, clarifying how (for poetry) small units such as diction, images, figures of speech, symbols, sound, rhythm, form, and allusions, particularly textual ambiguities, complexities, and interrelationships, contribute toward shaping a work's meaning and effects.

Extension   Pronunciation that adds a syllable for the sake of the meter. See, for example, the second line of Edmund Spenser's sonnet "One day I wrote her name upon the strand" (p. 10): "But came the waves and washèd it away."

Falling meter   Meter using a foot (usually a trochee or a dactyl) in which the first syllable is accented, followed by unaccented syllables that give a sense of stepping down. Cf. **rising meter.**

Feminine rhyme   See **double rhyme.**

Figure of speech and **figurative language**   Uses of language that depart from standard or literal usage in order to achieve a special effect or meaning.

Fixed form   Poetry written in definite, repeating patterns of line, rhyme scheme, or stanza.

Foot   The basic unit in metrical verse, composed of (usually) one stressed and one or more unstressed syllables. See also **anapest, dactyl, iamb, spondee,** and **trochee.**

Form   (1) Genre or literary type (e.g., the lyric form); (2) patterns of meter, lines, and rhymes (stanzaic form); (3) the organization of the parts of a literary work in relation to its total effect (e.g., "The form [structure] of this poem is very effective").

Free verse   See **open form.**

Genre   A recurring type of literature; a literary form as defined by rules or conventions followed in it (e.g., tragedy, comedy, epic, lyric, pastoral, novel, short story, essay).

Haiku   A lyric form, originating in Japan, of seventeen syllables in three lines, the first and third having five syllables and the second seven, presenting an image of a natural object or scene that expresses a distinct emotion or spiritual insight. Gary Snyder incorporates haiku into "Hitch Haiku" (p. 190).

Half rhyme   See **slant rhyme.**

Heptameter   A poetic line with seven metrical feet.

Heroic couplets   Couplets in iambic pentameter, usually with a full stop at the end. See Jonathan Swift, "A Description of a City Shower" (p. 25). Also called "closed couplets."

Hexameter   A poetic line with six metrical feet. See also **alexandrine.**

Hyperbole   Exaggeration; a figure of speech in which something is stated more strongly than is logically warranted. Hyperbole is often used to make a point emphatically, as when Hamlet protests that he loved Ophelia much more than her brother did: "Forty thousand brothers / Could not with all their quantity of love / Make up my sum" (5.1.272–74). See also Robert Burns, "A Red, Red Rose" (p. 38).

Iamb   A metrical foot consisting of two syllables, an unaccented one followed by an accented one (˘´). In iambic meter (the most widely used of English metrical forms), iambs are the predominant foot in a line or poem. The following line from Thomas Gray's "Elegy Written in a Country Churchyard" (p. 30) is in iambic meter: "Thĕ cúr | fĕw tólls | thĕ knéll | ŏf párt | iňg dáy."

Image   (1) A word or group of words that refers to a sensory experience or to an object that can be known by one or more of the senses. "Imagery" signifies all such language in a poem or other literary work collectively and can include any of the senses; see, for example, the first two stanzas of T. S. Eliot's "Preludes" (p. 129). See also **synesthesia**. (2) A metaphor or other comparison. "Imagery" in this sense refers to the characteristic that several images in a poem have in common, for example, the Christian imagery in William Blake's "The Lamb" (p. 36).

Imagist poetry   Poetry that relies on sharp, concrete images, and is written in a highly concentrated style that is suggestive rather than discursive. See, for example, H. D.'s "Garden" (p. 119).

Implied metaphor   Metaphor in which the *to be* verb is omitted and one aspect of the comparison is implied, rather than stated directly. "A car thief is a dirty dog" is direct metaphor; "some dirty dog stole my car" contains an implied metaphor. Examples are "whose hands *shipwreck* vases," "A *wrench* in clocks and the solar system," "In *traffic* of wit expertly manoeuvre" in John Frederick Nims, "Love Poem" (p. 156).

Internal rhyme   Rhyme that occurs between words within a line, between words within lines near each other, or between a word within a line and one at the end of the same or a nearby line. Edgar Allan Poe's "Annabel Lee" (p. 64) offers many examples: "chilling / And killing," "Can ever dissever," "And the stars never rise but I see the bright eyes."

Intertextuality   The implied presence of previous texts within a literary work or as its context. Devices used to achieve this include allusion and choice of genre. An intertextual approach assumes that interpretation is incomplete until the relation of the new work to its predecessors—response, opposition, development— has been considered.

Irony   A feeling, tone, mood, or attitude arising from the awareness that what is (reality) is opposite from, and usually worse than, what seems (appearance). What a person *says* may be ironic (see **verbal irony**), or a discrepancy between what a character knows or means and what a reader or audience knows can be ironic (see **dramatic irony**), or, without centering on one person, a general situation can be seen as ironic (**situational irony**). Irony should not be confused with mere coincidence. See also **Socratic irony**.

Italian sonnet   A sonnet composed of an octave (an eight-line unit), rhyming *abbaabba*, and a sestet (a six-line unit), often rhyming *cdecde* or *cdcdcd*, although variations are frequent. The octave usually develops an idea, a question, or a problem; then the poem pauses, or "turns," and the sestet completes the idea, answers the question, or resolves the difficulty. Sometimes called a **Petrarchan sonnet. See** Gerard Manley Hopkins, "God's Grandeur" (p. 95).

Juxtaposition   Placement of things side by side or close together for comparison or contrast or to create something new from the union, without necessarily making them grammatically parallel. See, for example, Jimmy Santiago Baca, "Family Ties" (p. 253), lines 29–34: "My sons sleep in the back, / dream of the open clearing, / . . . / as I stare out the window / at no trespassing signs white flashing past."

Line   A sequence of words printed as a separate entity on a page; the basic structural unit in poetry (except prose poems).

Litany   The use in poetry of repetitions, incantations, or ceremonial recitations similar to those used in formal, liturgical prayers. See, for example, Billy Collins, "Litany" (p. 221), and Joy Harjo, "She Had Some Horses" (p. 250).

Literal   In accordance with the primary or strict meaning of a word or words; not figurative or metaphorical.

Litotes   See **understatement.**

Lyric   Originally, a poem sung to the accompaniment of a lyre; now a short poem expressing the personal emotion and ideas of a single speaker.

Masculine rhyme   See **single rhyme.**

Metaphor   A figure of speech in which two things usually thought to be dissimilar are treated as if they were alike and have characteristics in common. "Whose *palms are bulls* in china" (John Frederick Nims, "Love Poem," p. 156). See also **implied metaphor.**

Metaphysical poetry   The work of a number of seventeenth-century poets that was characterized by philosophical subtlety and intellectual rigor; subtle, often outrageous logic; imitation of actual speech, sometimes resulting in "rough" meter and style; and far-fetched analogies. John Donne, "A Valediction: Forbidding Mourning" and "The Flea" (pp. 15 and 16) exemplify the type. See also **conceit.**

Meter   A steady beat, or measured pulse, created by a repeating pattern of accents, syllables, or both.

Metonymy   A figure of speech in which the name of one thing is substituted for that of something closely associated with it, as in commonly used phrases such as "The *White House* announced today . . ." (the name of the building is substituted for the president or the staff members who issued the announcement), "He's got *a Constable* on his wall," "The *trains* are on strike," or "*Wall Street* is in a panic." In the last line of John Frederick Nims's "Love Poem" (p. 156), "All the toys of the world would break," *toys* is substituted for "things that give happiness" (as toys do to a child). See also **synecdoche.**

Mock epic   A literary form that imitates the grand style and conventions of the epic genre, such as the opening statement of a theme, an address to the muse, long formal speeches, and epic similes, but applies them to a subject unworthy of such exalted treatment. Alexander Pope's "The Rape of the Lock" (1712, 1714) is commonly regarded as the best example of the mock epic in English. Pope uses the form for comic effect and at the same time treats seriously the great epic themes concerning human destiny and mortality. Also called "mock heroic." See also **epic**.

Monometer   A poetic line with one metrical foot.

Narrative   A story in prose or verse; an account of events involving characters and a sequence of events, told by a storyteller (narrator).

Near rhyme   See **slant rhyme**.

Objectivist poetry   A movement that considers a literary work as being significant in and of itself, independent of its author's intentions, its effect on readers, or the world it reflects. Objectivist poets attempt to view their subject with total objectivity and to eliminate any subjectivity from the finished work. For examples of objectivist poetry, see Lorine Niedecker, "My Life by Water" (p. 141), and George Oppen, "Myself I Sing" (p. 146).

Octameter   A poetic line with eight metrical feet.

Octave   The first eight lines of an Italian sonnet.

Ode   A long lyric poem, serious (often intellectual) in tone, elevated and dignified in style, dealing with a single theme. The ode is generally more complicated in form than other lyric poems. Some odes retain a formal division into strophe, antistrophe, and epode, which reflects the ode's origins in the chorus of Greek tragedy. See William Wordsworth, "Ode: Intimations of Immortality" (p. 44), Percy Bysshe Shelley, "Ode to the West Wind" (p. 54), and John Keats, "To Autumn" (p. 59).

Onomatopoeia   The use of words whose sounds supposedly resemble the sounds they denote (such as *thump, rattle, growl, hiss*), or a group of words whose sounds help to convey what is being described; for example, Emily Dickinson's "I heard a Fly *buzz*—when I died" (p. 92).

Open form   A poetic form free of any predetermined metrical and stanzaic patterns. Cf. **closed form**.

Ottava rima   An eight-line stanza in iambic pentameter rhyming *abababcc*, originated by the Italian poet Giovanni Boccaccio (1313–1375) and used by English poets such as Spenser, Milton, Keats, and Byron. There are no examples of ottava rima in this book, but for a modern usage, see William Butler Yeats, "Among School Children" (1928).

Overstatement   See **hyperbole**.

Oxymoron   A figure of speech combining in one phrase (usually adjective-noun) two seemingly contradictory elements, such as "loving hate" or "feather of lead, bright smoke, cold fire, sick health" (Shakespeare, *Romeo and Juliet* 1.1.176–80). Oxymoron is a type of **paradox**.

Pantoum   A poem composed of quatrains rhyming *abab* in which the second and fourth lines of each stanza serve as the first and third lines of the next, this process continuing through the last stanza (it repeats the first and third lines of the first stanza in reverse order, so the poem ends with the same line with which it began).

Paradox   A figure of speech in which a statement initially seeming self-contradictory or absurd turns out, seen in another light, to make good sense. The closing line of John Donne's sonnet "Death, be not proud" (p. 17) contains a paradox: "Death, thou shalt die." See also **oxymoron**.

Parallelism   (1) A verbal arrangement in which elements of equal weight within phrases, sentences, or paragraphs are expressed in a similar grammatical order and structure. It can appear within a line or pair of lines ("And he was always quietly arrayed, / And he was always human when he talked"—Edwin Arlington Robinson, "Richard Cory" [p. 100]) or, more noticeably, as a series of parallel items, as in Langston Hughes's "Harlem" (p. 140). (2) A principle of poetic structure in which consecutive lines in open form are related by a line's repeating, expanding on, or contrasting with the idea of the line or lines before it, as in the poems of Walt Whitman (pp. 69–89).

Parody   Now, a humorous or satirical imitation of a serious piece of literature or writing. In the sixteenth and seventeenth centuries, poets such as George Herbert practiced "sacred parody" by adapting secular lyrics to devotional themes.

Partial rhyme   See **slant rhyme**.

Pastoral   A poem (also called an "eclogue," a "bucolic," or an "idyll") that expresses a city poet's nostalgic image of the simple, peaceful life of shepherds and other country folk in an idealized natural setting. Christopher Marlowe's "The Passionate Shepherd to His Love" (p. 12) uses some pastoral conventions, as do certain elegies (including Thomas Gray's "Elegy Written in a Country Churchyard," p. 30).

Pause   See **caesura**.

Pentameter   A poetic line with five metrical feet.

Persona   Literally, the mask through which actors spoke in Greek plays. In some critical approaches of recent decades, the "character" projected by the author, the "I" of a narrative poem or novel, or the speaker whose voice is heard in a lyric poem. In this view, the poem is an artificial construct distanced from the poet's autobiographical self. Cf. **voice**.

Personification   A figure of speech in which something nonhuman is treated as if it had human characteristics or performed human actions. Sometimes it involves abstractions, as in Thomas Gray's phrase "Fair Science frowned" ("Elegy Written in a Country Churchyard," p. 30); science cannot literally frown. In other cases concrete things are given human characteristics, as in the phrase "Wearing white for Eastertide" from A. E. Housman's "Loveliest of trees, the cherry now" (p. 97). Cherry trees do not actually wear clothes—they are being given, briefly, a human attribute. Difficulty can arise when personification is redefined (incorrectly) as treating something nonhuman in terms of anything alive rather than specifically human: "the mouth of time" in Nancy Willard's "Questions My Son Asked Me, Answers I Never Gave Him" (p. 206) is metaphor, not personification, since animals as well as humans have mouths. See also **apostrophe**.

Petrarchan sonnet   See **Italian sonnet**.

Poem   A term whose meaning exceeds all attempts at definition. Here is a slightly modified version of an attempt at definition by William Harmon and C. Hugh Holman in *A Handbook to Literature* (1996): A poem is a literary composition, written or oral, typically characterized by imagination, emotion, sense impressions, and concrete language that invites attention to its own physical features, such as sound or appearance on the page.

Poetic diction   In general, specialized language used in or considered appropriate to poetry. In the late seventeenth and the eighteenth centuries, a refined use of language that excluded "common" speech from poetry as indecorous—and substituted elevated circumlocutions, archaic synonyms, or such forms as *ope* and *e'er*.

Prose poem   A poem printed as prose, with lines wrapping at the right margin rather than being divided through predetermined line breaks. See Carolyn Forché, "The Colonel" (p. 249), and A. Van Jordan, "From" (p. 289).

Prosody   The principles of versification, especially of meter, rhythm, rhyme, and stanza forms.

Pun   A play on words based on similarity in sound between two words having very different meanings. Also called "paronomasia." See the puns on "heart" and "kindly" in Sir Thomas Wyatt's "They flee from me" (p. 9).

Quantitative verse   Verse whose meter is based on the length of syllables (phonetic length being a distinguishing feature of ancient Greek and Latin, whereas English is an accentual language). Classical poetry exhibits a great variety of meters, and some English poets in the late 1500s attempted to fashion English verse on this principle. In *Evangeline* Henry Wadsworth Longfellow used dactylic hexameter in imitation of Virgil's *Aeneid*, but defined it by accent, not quantity. Cf. **accentual-syllabic verse**.

Quatrain   A stanza of four lines or other four-line unit within a larger form, such as a sonnet.

Refrain   One or more identical or deliberately similar lines repeated throughout a poem, such as the final line of a stanza or a block of lines between stanzas or sections.

Rhyme   The repetition of the accented vowel sound of a word and all succeeding consonant sounds. See also **exact rhyme; slant rhyme.**

Rhyme Royal   A poetic form consisting of seven-line iambic pentameter stanzas rhyming *ababbcc*, called "Royal" because it was used by King James I of Scotland in his Chaucerian poem *The Kingis Quair*. See Sir Thomas Wyatt, "They flee from me" (p. 9).

Rhyme scheme   The pattern of end rhymes in a poem or stanza; the recurring sequence is usually described by assigning a letter to each word-sound, the same word-sounds having the same letter (e.g., a quatrain might be *abcb*).

Rhythm   The patterned "movement" of language created by the choice of words and their arrangement, usually described through such metaphors as fast or slow, smooth or halting, graceful or rough, deliberate or frenzied, syncopated or disjointed. Rhythm in poetry is affected, in addition to meter, by such factors as line length; line endings; pauses (or lack of them) within lines; spaces within, at the beginning or end of, or between lines; word choice; and combinations of sounds.

Rising meter   A foot (usually an iamb or an anapest) in which the final, accented syllable is preceded by one or two unaccented syllables, thus giving a sense of stepping up. Cf. **falling meter.**

Rondeau   A poetic form made up of fifteen lines, divided into three stanzas with the rhyme scheme *aabba aabc aabbac*; lines 1–8 and 10–14 (the *a* and *b* lines) have eight syllables; lines nine and fifteen (the *c* lines) have four syllables and serve as a refrain, repeating the opening words of the first line. See, for example, Paul Dunbar, "We Wear the Mask" (p. 100).

Run-on line   A line whose sense and grammatical structure continue to the next line. In the following lines by William Stafford ("Traveling through the Dark," p. 158), the first line is run-on, the second end-stopped: "Traveling through the dark I found a deer / dead on the edge of the Wilson River road." Also called "enjambment." Cf. **end-stopped line.**

Sarcasm   A harsh and cutting form of verbal irony, often involving apparent praise that is obviously not meant: "Oh, no, these are fine. I *prefer* my eggs thoroughly charred."

Satire   A work, or manner within a work, that combines a critical attitude with humor and wit with the intent of improving humanity or human institutions. See, for example, Jonathan Swift, "A Description of a City Shower" (p. 25).

Scansion   The division of metrical verse into feet in order to determine and label its meter. Scanning a poem involves marking its stressed syllables with an accent mark ['] and its unstressed syllables with a curved line [˘], using a vertical line to indicate the way it divides into feet, and then describing (or labeling) the type of foot used most often and the line length—that is, the number of feet in each line. See also **foot** and **line**.

Sestet   The last six lines of an Italian sonnet.

Sestina   A lyric poem consisting of six six-line stanzas and a three-line concluding stanza (or "envoy"). The six end-words of the first stanza must be used as the end-words of the other five stanzas, in a specified pattern (the first line ends with the end-word from the last line of the previous stanza, the second line with that of the first line of the previous stanza, the third line with that of the previous fifth line, the fourth line with that of the previous second line, the fifth line with that of the previous fourth line, the sixth line with that of the previous third line). The three lines of the envoy must use the end-words of lines five, three, and one from the first stanza, in that order, and must include the other three end-words within the lines. See Julia Alvarez, "Bilingual Sestina" (p. 247).

Shakespearean sonnet   See **English sonnet**.

Shaped poem   See **concrete poem**.

Simile   Expression of a direct similarity using such words as *like, as,* or *than* between two things usually regarded as dissimilar, as in "Shrinking from far *headlights pale as a dime*" (John Frederick Nims, "Love Poem," p. 156). It is important to distinguish *simile* from *comparison*, in which the two things joined by "like" or "as" are *not* dissimilar.

Single rhyme   A rhyme in which the stressed, rhyming syllable is the final syllable: *west* and *vest, away* and *today.* Formerly called "masculine rhyme."

Situational irony   The mood evoked when an action intended to have a certain effect turns out to have a different and more sinister effect.

Slant rhyme   Consonance at the ends of lines; for example, *Room* and *Storm, firm* and *Room,* and *be* and *Fly* in Emily Dickinson's "I heard a Fly buzz—when I died" (p. 92). It can also be internal, if repeated enough to form a discernible pattern.

Socratic irony   A pose of self-deprecation, or of belittling oneself, in order to tease the reader into deeper insight.

Sonnet   A fourteen-line poem usually written in iambic pentameter; originally lyrical love poems, sonnets came to be used also for meditations on religious themes, death, and nature and are now open to all subjects. Some variations in form have been tried: Sir Philip Sidney's "Loving in truth, and fain in verse my love to show" (p. 11) is in hexameters; George Meredith wrote sixteen-line sonnets; John Milton's "On the New Forcers of Conscience under the Long Parliament," written around 1646, is a "caudate" (tailed) sonnet with a six-line coda appended;

and Gerard Manley Hopkins designed "Pied Beauty" (p. 95) as a "curtal" (abbreviated) sonnet (six lines in place of the octave, then four lines, and a half-line ending in place of the sestet). See **English sonnet** and **Italian sonnet**.

Sonnet sequence   A group of sonnets so arranged as to imply a narrative progression in the speaker's experience or attitudes; used especially in the sixteenth century. Also called "sonnet cycle."

Spenserian sonnet   A variation of the English sonnet that employs the structure of three quatrains plus a couplet but joins the quatrains by linking rhymes: *abab bcbc cdcd ee*. For examples, see pages 10–11.

Spenserian stanza   A stanza of nine iambic lines, the first eight pentameter and the ninth hexameter, rhyming *ababbcbcc*. They are used in Edmund Spenser's *The Faerie Queene* (1590, 1596) and in such Romantic narrative poems as John Keats's *The Eve of St. Agnes* (1820) and Percy Bysshe Shelley's *Adonais* (1824).

Spondee   A metrical foot made up of two stressed syllables (´´), with no unstressed syllables. Spondees could not, of course, be the predominant foot in a poem; they are usually substituted for iambic or trochaic feet as a way of increasing emphasis, as in this line from John Donne's "Batter my heart, three-personed God" (1633): "Aš yét | bŭt kńock, | bréathe, shińe, | ańd séek | tŏ ménd."

Sprung rhythm   See **accentual meter**.

Stanza   A grouping of poetic lines into a section, either according to form—each section having the same number of lines and the same prosody (see Percy Bysshe Shelley's "Ode to the West Wind," p. 54)—or according to thought, creating irregular units comparable to paragraphs in prose (as in William Wordsworth's "Ode: Intimations of Immortality," p. 44).

Stress   See **accent**.

Structure   (1) The planned framework—the general plan or outline—of a literary work; (2) narrower patterns within the overall framework. Cf. **form**.

Substitution   The use of a different kind of foot in place of the one normally demanded by the predominant meter of a poem, as a way of adding variety, emphasizing the dominant foot by variation from it, speeding up or slowing down the pace, or signaling a switch in meaning.

Surrealism   An artistic movement that attempted to portray or interpret the workings of the unconscious mind, especially as realized in dreams, by an irrational, noncontextual choice and arrangement of images or objects. Now more often used to refer to anything defying the normal sense of reality.

Syllabic verse   A metrical pattern in which all lines in the poem have the same number of syllables (as in Sylvia Plath's "Metaphors," p. 194) or all first lines of stanzas have the same number, all second lines the same, and so on (see Dylan

Thomas's "Fern Hill," p. 160)—while the stressed syllables are random in number and placement.

Symbol   Something that is itself and also stands for something else; a literary symbol is a prominent or repeated image or action that is present in the poem (or story or play) and can be seen, touched, smelled, heard, tasted, or experienced imaginatively but also conveys a cluster of abstract meanings beyond itself. Most critics agree that the tiger in William Blake's "The Tyger" (p. 37) and the wrecked vessel in Adrienne Rich's "Diving into the Wreck" (p. 187), for example, carry symbolic meaning.

Synecdoche   A special kind of metonymy in which a part of a thing is substituted for the whole of which it is a part, as in the commonly used phrases "give me a hand," "lend me your ears," or "many mouths to feed." See, for example, "whose *hands* shipwreck vases" and "For should your *hands* drop white and empty" (John Frederick Nims, "Love Poem," p. 156).

Synesthesia   Description of one kind of sense experience in relation to another, such as attribution of color to sounds ("blue notes") and vice versa ("a loud tie") or of taste to sounds ("sweet music"). See, for example, "With Blue—uncertain stumbling Buzz—" (Emily Dickinson, "I heard a Fly buzz—when I died," p. 92).

Tercet   A stanza of three lines, each usually ending with the same rhyme; but see **terza rima**. Cf. **triplet**.

Terza rima   A poetic form consisting of three-line stanzas (tercets) with interlinked rhymes, *aba bcb cdc ded efe*, etc., made famous by Dante's use of it in *The Divine Comedy*. Terza rima is used in Percy Bysshe Shelley's "Ode to the West Wind" (p. 54).

Tetrameter   A poetic line with four metrical feet. Robert Frost's line "The woods are lovely, dark and deep" ("Stopping by Woods on a Snowy Evening," p. 109) is an example of iambic tetrameter.

Text   Traditionally, a piece of writing. In recent reader response criticism, "text" has come to mean the words with which the reader interacts; in this view, a poem is not an object, not a shape on the page or a spoken performance, but what is completed in the reader's mind.

Theme   The central idea embodied or explored in a literary work, for some idea-based approaches to literature; the general concept, explicit or implied, that the work incorporates and makes persuasive to the reader.

Title   The name attached to a work of literature. For poetry, a title in some cases is an integral part of a poem and needs to be considered in interpreting it; see, for example, George Herbert's "Redemption" (p. 21). In other cases the name has been added as a means of identifying the poem and is not integral to interpretation. Sometimes the poem is untitled and the first line is used as a convenient way of referring to it, but should not be thought of as a title and does not follow the capitalization rules for titles.

Tone   The attitude, or "stance," toward the subject and toward the reader or audience implied in a literary work; the "tone of voice" it seems to project (serious or playful; exaggerated or understated; formal or informal; ironic or straightforward; or a complex mixture of more than one of these).

Transferred epithet   A figure of speech in which a modifier that ought, strictly, to apply to one word is transferred to another word that it does not strictly fit. In "The drunk clambering on his undulant floor" (John Frederick Nims, "Love Poem," p. 156), the drunk's perception, not the floor, is undulating.

Trimeter   A poetic line with three metrical feet.

Triplet   A group of three consecutive lines with the same rhyme, often used for variation in a long sequence of couplets. Cf. **tercet**.

Trochee   A metrical foot consisting of two syllables, an accented one followed by an unaccented one (´ ˘). In trochaic meter, trochees are the predominant foot in a line or poem. The following lines from William Blake's introduction to *Songs of Innocence* (1789) are in trochaic meter (each line lacking the final unaccented syllable): "Pípĭng | dówn thĕ | válleўs | wíld, / Pípĭng | Sóngs ŏf | pléasănt | glée, / Ón ă | clóud Ĭ | sáw ă | chíld, / Ănd hé | laúghĭng | sáid tŏ | mé."

Understatement   A figure of speech expressing something in an unexpectedly restrained way. Paradoxically, to de-emphasize through understatement can be a way of emphasizing, of making people react with "there must be more to it than that." When Mercutio in Shakespeare's *Romeo and Juliet*, after being stabbed by Tybalt, calls his wound "a scratch, a scratch" (3.1.92), he is understating, for the wound is serious—he calls for a doctor in the next line, and he dies a few minutes later.

Verbal irony   A figure of speech in which what is said is nearly the opposite of what is meant (such as saying "Lovely day out" when the weather actually is miserable). See E. E. Cummings, " 'next to of course god america i" (p. 135).

Villanelle   A nineteen-line lyric poem divided into five tercets and a final four-line stanza, rhyming *aba aba aba aba aba abaa*. Line 1 is repeated to form lines 6, 12, and 18; line 3 is repeated to form lines 9, 15, and 19. See Elizabeth Bishop, "One Art" (p. 155), Dylan Thomas, "Do not go gentle into that good night" (p. 161), and Marilyn Hacker, "Villanelle" (p. 228).

Voice   The supposed authorial presence in poems that do not obviously employ persona as a distancing device.

Acknowledgments

Sherman Alexie. "Postcards to Columbus" from *Old Shirts and New Skins* (1999). Used by permission of Nancy Stauffer Associates.

Agha Shahid Ali. "I Dream It Is Afternoon When I Return to Delhi" from *The Half-Inch Himalayas*, copyright © 1987 by Agha Shahid Ali. Reprinted by permission of Wesleyan University Press.

Ai. "Why Can't I Leave You" from *Vice: New and Selected Poems*. Copyright © 1973 by Ai. Used by permission of the author and W. W. Norton & Company, Inc.

Julia Alvarez. "Bilingual Sestina" from *The Other Side/El Otro Lado*. Copyright © 1995 by Julia Alvarez. Published by Plume/Penguin, a division of Penguin Group (USA). By permission of Susan Bergholz Literary Services, New York, NY and Lamy, NM. All rights reserved.

John Ashbery. "Mixed Feelings," copyright © 1975 by John Ashbery, from *Self-Portrait in a Convex Mirror* by John Ashbery. Used by permission of Viking Penguin, a division of Penguin Group (USA) Inc.

Margaret Atwood. "True Stories" from *Selected Poems II: Poems Selected and New, 1976–1986* by Margaret Atwood. Copyright © 1987 by Margaret Atwood. Reprinted by permission of Houghton Mifflin Harcourt Publishing Company and Oxford University Press Canada. Canadian edition copyright © 1981 by Oxford University Press Canada. All rights reserved.

W. H. Auden. "As I Walked Out One Evening" and "Musée des Beaux Arts," copyright 1940 and renewed 1968 by W. H. Auden, from *Collected Poems of W. H. Auden*. Used by permission of Random House, Inc. Any third party use of this material outside of this publication, is prohibited. Interested parties must apply directly to Random House, Inc. for permission.

Jimmy Santiago Baca. "Family Ties" from *Black Mesa Poems*, copyright © 1989 by Jimmy Santiago Baca. Reprinted by permission of New Directions Publishing Corp.

Jim Barnes. "Return to La Plata, Missouri" from *American Book of the Death: Poems*, copyright © 1982 by Jim Barnes. Used with permission of the poet and the University of Illinois Press.

Wendell Berry. "The Peace of Wild Things" from *New Collected Poems*. Copyright © 2012 by Wendell Berry. Reprinted by permission of Counterpoint.

John Berryman. "Certainty before Lunch" from *Delusions, Etc*. Copyright © 1972 by the Estate of John Berryman. Reprinted by permission of Farrar, Straus and Giroux, LLC.

Elizabeth Bishop. "In the Waiting Room," "The Fish," and "One Art" from *The Complete Poems 1972–1979*. Copyright © 1979, 1983 by Alice Helen Methfessel. Reprinted by permission of Farrar, Straus and Giroux, LLC.

Robert Bly. "Driving to Town Late to Mail a Letter" from *Silence in the Snowy Fields* (Wesleyan Univ. Press, 1962). Copyright © 1962 by Robert Bly. Reprinted with permission of the author.

Eavan Boland. "The Pomegranate" from *In a Time of Violence*. Copyright © 1994 by Eavan Boland. Used by permission of the author and W. W. Norton & Company, Inc.

Philip Booth. "A Two Inch Wave" from *Lifelines: Selected Poems 1950–1999*, copyright © 1999 by Philip Booth. Used by permission of Viking Penguin, a division of Penguin Group (USA) Inc.

Gwendolyn Brooks. "We Real Cool" and "The Bean Eaters" are reprinted by consent of Brooks Permissions.

Sterling A. Brown. "Riverbank Blues" from *The Collected Poems of Sterling A. Brown*, selected by Michael S. Harper. Copyright © 1980 by Sterling A. Brown. Reprinted by permission of HarperCollins Publishers.

Charles Bukowski. "my old man" from *Love Is a Dog from Hell: Poems 1974–1977* by Charles Bukowski. Copyright © 1977 by Charles Bukowski. Reprinted by permission of HarperCollins Publishers.

Lorna Dee Cervantes. "Freeway 280" from *Latin American Literary Review*, Vol. V, No. 10 (1977). Reprinted with the permission of Latin American Literary Review Press.

Marilyn Chin. "How I Got That Name" from *The Phoenix Gone, the Terrace Empty* (Minneapolis: Milkweed Editions, 1994). Copyright © 1994 by Marilyn Chin. Reprinted with permission from Milkweed Editions. www.milkweed.org.

Lucille Clifton. "homage to my hips," copyright © 1980 by Lucille Clifton. First appeared in *two-headed woman* published by University of Massachusetts Press. Reprinted by permission of Curtis Brown, Ltd. Lucille Clifton, "at the cemetery, walnut grove plantation, south carolina, 1989" from *The Collected Poems of Lucille Clifton*. Copyright © 1991 by Lucille Clifton. Reprinted with the permission of The Permissions Company, Inc., on behalf of BOA Editions Ltd., www.boaeditions.org.

Judith Ortiz Cofer. "Cold as Heaven" from *Reaching for the Mainland and Selected New Poems*, reprinted by permission of the publisher and copyright holder Bilingual Press/Editorial Bilingue.

Billy Collins. "Litany," copyright © 2002 by Billy Collins, from *Nine Horses*. Used by permission of Random House, Inc. Any third party use of this material, outside of this publication, is prohibited. Interested parties must apply directly to Random House, Inc. for permission.

Victor Hernández Cruz. "Problems with Hurricanes" from *Red Beans*. Copyright © 1991 by Victor Hernández Cruz. Reprinted with the permission of The Permissions Company, Inc., on behalf of Coffee House Press, www.coffeehousepress.org.

Countee Cullen. "Incident" from *Color*, copyright © 1925 by Harper & Bros., New York, renewed 1952 by Ida M. Cullen. Copyrights held by Amistad Research Center, Tulane University, administered by Thompson & Thompson, Brooklyn, NY.

E. E. Cummings. "in Just-." Copyright 1923, 1951, © 1991 by the Trustees for the E. E. Cummings Trust. Copyright © 1976 by Georges James Firmage. "'next to of course god america i." Copyright 1926, 1954, © 1991 by the Trustees for the E. E. Cummings Trust. Copyright © 1985 by George James Firmage, from *Complete Poems: 1904–1962* by E. E. Cummings, edited by George J. Firmage. Used by permission of Liveright Publishing Corporation.

Toi Derricotte. "A Note on My Son's Face" from *Captivity*, copyright © 1989. Reprinted by permission of the University of Pittsburgh Press.

Emily Dickinson. Poems by Emily Dickinson are reprinted by permission of the publishers and the Trustees of Amherst College from *The Poems of Emily Dickinson*, Thomas H. Johnson, ed., Cambridge, Mass.: The Belknap Press of Harvard University Press. Copyright © 1951, 1955, 1979, 1983 by the President and Fellows of Harvard College.

Mark Doty. "Tiara" from *Bethlehem in Broad Daylight*. Reprinted by permission of Black Sparrow Books, an imprint of David R. Godine, Publisher, Inc. Copyright © 1991 by Mark Doty.

Rita Dove. "Fifth Grade Autobiography" from *Grace Notes*. Copyright © 1989 by Rita Dove. Used by permission of the author and W. W. Norton & Company, Inc.

Denise Duhamel. "One Afternoon when Barbie Wanted to Join the Military" from *Queen for a Day: Selected and New Poems*, copyright © 2001. Reprinted by permission of the University of Pittsburgh Press.

Cornelius Eady. "My Mother, If She Had Won Free Dance Lessons" from *Victims of the Latest Dance Craze* (Carnegie Mellon University Press, 1997). Copyright © 1985 by Cornelius Eady. Reprinted by permission of the author.

T. S. Eliot. "Journey of the Magi" from *Collected Poems 1909–1962* by T. S. Eliot, copyright 1936 by Harcourt, Inc. and renewed 1964 by T. S. Eliot, reprinted by permission of the publishers Houghton Mifflin Harcourt Publishing Company and Faber & Faber Ltd. All rights reserved. T. S. Eliot, "Preludes" and "The Love Song of J. Alfred Prufrock" from *The Collected Poems 1909–1962* is reprinted by permission of the publisher Faber & Faber Ltd.

Anita Endrezze. "The Girl Who Loved the Sky" from *at the helm of twilight* (Broken Moon Press, 1992). Copyright © 1992 by Anita Endrezze. Reprinted with the permission of the author.

Martín Espada. "The Saint Vincent de Paul Food Pantry Stomp" from *Rebellion Is the Circle of a Lover's Hand/Rebelion Es el Giro de Manos del Amante*. (Curbstone Press, 1990). Reprinted by permission of Northwestern University Press.

Carolyn Forché. "The Colonel" from *The Country Between Us*. Copyright © 1981 by Carolyn Forché. Originally appeared in "Women's International Resource Exchange." Reprinted by permission of HarperCollins Publishers.

Vievee Francis. "1864, A Pocket Full of Rye," from *Blue-Tail Fly*. Copyright © 2008 Wayne State University Press, with the permission of Wayne State University Press.

Robert Frost. "After Apple-Picking," "The Road Not Taken," "'Out, Out—'," "Stopping by Woods on a Snowy Evening," and "The Death of the Hired Man" from the book *The Poetry of Robert Frost*, edited by Edward Connery Lathem. Copyright © 1923, 1930, 1939, 1969 by Henry Holt and Company, copyright ©1936, 1944, 1951, 1958 by Robert Frost, copyright ©1964, 1967 by Lesley Frost Ballantine. Reprinted by permission of Henry Holt and Company, LLC.

Richard Garcia. "Why I Left the Church" from *The Flying Garcias*, copyright © 1993. Reprinted by permission of the University of Pittsburgh Press.

Allen Ginsberg. "A Supermarket in California" from *Collected Poems 1947–1980*. Copyright © 1955 by Allen Ginsberg. Reprinted by permission of HarperCollins Publishers.

Aracelis Girmay. "Snail, or, To a House" from *Teeth* (Curbstone Presss, 2007). Reprinted by permission of Northwestern University Press.

Louise Glück. "The Wild Iris" from *The Wild Iris*. Copyright © 1992 by Louise Glück. Reprinted by permission of HarperCollins Publishers.

Ray González. "Praise the Tortilla, Praise Menudo, Praise Chorizo" from *The Heat of Arrivals*. Copyright © 1996 by Ray González. Reprinted with the permission of The Permissions Company, Inc., on behalf of BOA Editions, Ltd., www.boaeditions.org.

H. D. "Garden" from *Collected Poems, 1912–1944*, copyright © 1982 by The Estate of Hilda Doolittle. Reprinted by permission of New Directions Publishing Corp.

Marilyn Hacker. "Villanelle." Copyright © 1974 by Marilyn Hacker from *Selected Poems: 1965–1990* by Marilyn Hacker. Used by permission of W. W. Norton & Company, Inc.

Kimiko Hahn. "Mother's Mother" from *Volatile*. Copyright © 1999 by Kimiko Hahn. Reprinted with the permission of Hanging Loose Press.

Joy Harjo. "She Had Some Horses" from *She Had Some Horses*. Copyright © 1983, 1997 by Thunder's Mouth Press. Reprinted with permission of the author.

Michael S. Harper. "Nightmare Begins Responsibility" from *Songlines in Michaeltree: New and Collected Poems*, copyright © 2000 by Michael S. Harper. Used with permission of the poet and the University of Illinois Press.

Robert Hayden. "Those Winter Sundays." Copyright © 1966 by Robert Hayden, from *Collected Poems of Robert Hayden*, ed. by Frederick Glaysher. Used by permission of Liveright Publishing Corporation.

Terrance Hayes. "Talk" from *Wind in a Box*, copyright © 2006 by Terrance Hayes. Used by permission of Penguin, a division of Penguin Group (USA) Inc.

Seamus Heaney. "Digging," Mid-Term Break," and "Glanmore Sonnets 4" from *Opened Ground: Selected Poems 1966–1996*. Copyright © 1998 by Seamus Heaney. Reprinted by permission of Farrar, Straus and Giroux, LLC and Faber & Faber Ltd.

Bob Hicok. "In the loop" from *Words for Empty and Words for Full*, copyright © 2010. Reprinted by permission of the University of Pittsburgh Press.

Geoffrey Hill. "In Memory of Jane Fraser" from *New and Collected Poems, 1952–1992*. Copyright © 1994 by Geoffrey Hill. Reprinted by permission of Houghton Mifflin Harcourt Publishing Company and Penguin Books Ltd. All rights reserved.

Jane Hirshfield. "To Drink" from *Of Gravity & Angels*, copyright © 1988 by Jane Hirshfield. Reprinted by permission of Wesleyan University Press.

Linda Hogan. "Crow Law" from *The Book of Medicines*. Copyright © 1993 by Linda Hogan. Reprinted with the permission of The Permissions Company, Inc., on behalf of Coffee House Press, www.coffeehousepress.org.

Anna Maria Hong. "The Frog-Prince" was first published in the *Harvard Gazette*. Reprinted by permission of Anna Maria Hong.

Garrett Kaoru Hongo. "Yellow Light" from *Yellow Light*, copyright © 1982 by Garrett Kaoru Hongo. Reprinted by permission of Wesleyan University Press.

Langston Hughes. "The Negro Speaks of Rivers," "Mother to Son," "Theme for English B," and "Harlem (2)" from *The Collected Poems of Langston Hughes*, edited by Arnold Rampersad with David Roessel, Associate Editor, copyright © 1994 by the Estate of Langston Hughes. Used by permission of Alfred A. Knopf, a division of Random House, Inc. Any third party use of this material, outside of this publication, is prohibited. Interested parties must apply directly to Random House, Inc. for permission.

Randall Jarrell. "The Death of the Ball Turret Gunner" from *The Complete Poems*. Copyright © 1969, renewed 1997 by Mary von S. Jarrell. Reprinted by permission of Farrar, Straus and Giroux, LLC.

Honorée Fanonne Jeffers. "Unidentified Female Student, Former Slave (Talladega College, circa 1885)" from *Outlandish Blues*, copyright © 2003 by Honorée Fanonne Jeffers. Reprinted by permission of Wesleyan University Press.

Robinson Jeffers. "Hurt Hawks," copyright 1928 and renewed 1956 by Robinson Jeffers, from *Selected Poetry of Robinson Jeffers*. Used by permission of Random House, Inc. Any third party use of this material, outside of this publication, is prohibited. Interested parties must apply directly to Random House, Inc. for permission.

Richard Jones. "Cathedral" from *The Blessing: New and Selected Poems*. Copyright © 2000 by Richard Jones. Reprinted with the permission of The Permissions Company, Inc. on behalf of Copper Canyon Press, www.coppercanyonpress.org.

Allison Joseph. "On Being Told I Don't Speak Like a Black Person" from *Imitation of Life*, published by Carnegie Mellon Univ. Press, 2003. Reprinted by permission of the author.

Jane Kenyon. "Let Evening Come" from *Collected Poems*. Copyright © 2005 by The Estate of Jane Kenyon. Reprinted with the permission of The Permissions Company, Inc., on behalf of Graywolf Press, Minneapolis, MN, www.graywolfpress.org.

Galway Kinnell. "The Bear" from *Body Rags*. Copyright © 1965, 1966, 1967 by Galway Kinnell. Reprinted by permission of Houghton Mifflin Harcourt Publishing Company. All rights reserved.

Etheridge Knight. "Hard Rock Returns to Prison from the Hospital For The Criminal Insane" from *The Essential Etheridge Knight*, copyright © 1986. Reprinted by permission of the University of Pittsburgh Press.

Yusef Komunyakaa. "Facing It" from *Neon Vernacular: New and Selected Poems*, copyright © 1993 by Yusef Komunyakaa. Reprinted by permission of Wesleyan University Press.

Ted Kooser. "Abandoned Farmhouse" from *Sure Signs: New and Selected Poems*, copyright © 1980. Reprinted by permission of the University of Pittsburgh Press.

Maxine Kumin. "The Sound of Night" from *Halfway* by Maxine Kumin. Reprinted by permission of The Anderson Literary Agency Inc.

Stanley Kunitz. "The War against the Trees." Copyright © 1957 by Stanley Kunitz from *The Collected Poems* by Stanley Kunitz. Used by permission of the author and W. W. Norton & Company, Inc.

Philip Larkin. "High Windows" from *Collected Poems*. Copyright © 1998, 2003 by the Estate of Philip Larkin. Reprinted by permission of Farrar, Straus and Giroux, LLC and Faber & Faber Ltd.

Li-Young Lee. "The Gift" and "Eating Alone" from *Rose*. Copyright © 1986 by Li-Young Lee. Reprinted with the permission of The Permissions Company, Inc., on behalf of BOA Editions, Ltd., www.boaeditions.org.

Denise Levertov. "The ache of marriage" from *Poems 1960–1967*, copyright © 1964 by Denise Levertov. Reprinted by permission of New Directions Publishing Corp.

Philip Levine. "What Work Is," copyright © 1992 by Philip Levine from *What Work Is*. Used by permission of Alfred A. Knopf, a division of Random House, Inc. Any third party use of this material, outside of this publication, is prohibited. Interested parties must apply directly to Random House, Inc. for permission.

Larry Levis. "The Poem You Asked For" from *Wrecking Crew* by Larry Levis, copyright © 1972. Reprinted by permission of the University of Pittsburgh Press.

Audre Lorde. "Coal." Copyright © 1973, 1970, 1968 by Audre Lorde from *Undersong: Chosen Poems Old and New*. Used by permission of the author and W. W. Norton & Company, Inc.

Robert Lowell. "Skunk Hour" from *Collected Poems*. Copyright © 2003 by Harriet Lowell and Sheridan Lowell. Reprinted by permission of Farrar, Straus and Giroux, LLC.

Randall Mann. "The Heron" from *Complaint in the Garden* (Zoo Press, 2004). Copyright © 2004 by Randall Mann. Reprinted by permission of the author.

Heather McHugh. "What He Thought" from *Hinge & Sign: Poems, 1968–1993*, copyright © 1994 by Heather McHugh. Reprinted by permission of Wesleyan University Press.

Erika Meitner. "North Country Canzone" from *Ideal Cities: Poems*. Copyright © 2010 by Erika Meitner. Reprinted by permission of HarperCollins Publishers.

W. S. Merwin. "For the Anniversary of My Death," copyright © 1992 by W. S. Merwin. Used by permission of The Wylie Agency LLC.

Edna St. Vincent Millay. "Pity me not because the light of day" from *Collected Poems*. Copyright 1923, 1951 by Edna St. Vincent Millay and Norma Millay Ellis. Reprinted with the permission of The Permissions Company, Inc., on behalf of Holly Peppe, Literary Executor, The Millay Society. www.millay.org.

Marianne Moore. "Poetry" (1921 version) is reprinted with the permission of Scribner, a division of Simon & Schuster, Inc. from *The Collected Poems of Marianne Moore*. Copyright 1921 by Marianne Moore, renewed 1949 by Marianne Moore and T. S. Eliot. All rights reserved.

Thylias Moss. "The Lynching" from *Rainbow Remnants in Rock Bottom Ghetto Sky*. Copyright © 1991 by Thylias Moss. Reprinted by permission of Persea Books, Inc., New York. All rights reserved.

David Mura. "Grandfather-in-Law" from *After We Lost Our Way* (E. P. Dutton, 1989). Copyright © 1989 by David Mura. Reprinted with the permission of the author.

Marilyn Nelson. "Minor Miracle" from *The Fields of Praise*. Reprinted by permission of Louisiana State University Press.

Lorine Niedecker. "My Life by Water" from *Collected Works*, ed. by Jenny Lynn Penberthy. Reproduced with permission of University of California Press via Copyright Clearance Center.

John Frederick Nims. "Love Poem" from *Selected Poems*. Copyright © 1982 by the University of Chicago. Reprinted with the permission of the publisher.

Naomi Shihab Nye. "Kindness" from *Words Under the Words: Selected Poems* by Naomi Shihab Nye, copyright © 1995. Reprinted with the permission of Far Corner Books, Portland, Oregon. "The Small Vases from Hebron" from *Fuel*. Copyright © 1998 by Naomi Shihab Nye. Reprinted with the permission of The Permissions Company, Inc., on behalf of BOA Editions, Ltd., www.boaeditions.org.

Frank O'Hara. "Why I Am Not a Painter," copyright © 1971 by Maureen Granville-Smith, Administratrix of the Estate of Frank O'Hara, from *The Collected Poems of Frank O'Hara*, edited by Donald Allen. Used by permission of Alfred A. Knopf, a division of Random House, Inc. Any third party use of this material, outside of this publication, is prohibited. Interested parties must apply directly to Random House, Inc. for permission. "The Day Lady Died" from *Lunch Poems*. Copyright © by Frank O'Hara. Reprinted by permission of City Lights Books.

Sharon Olds. "The One Girl at the Boys' Party" from *Strike Sparks: Selected Poems 1980–2002*, copyright © 2004 by Sharon Olds. "I Go Back to May 1937" from *The Gold Cell*, copyright © 1987 by Sharon Olds. Used by permission of Alfred A. Knopf, a division of Random House, Inc. Any third party use of this material, outside of this publication, is prohibited. Interested parties must apply directly to Random House, Inc. for permission.

Mary Oliver. "First Snow" from *American Primitive*. Copyright © 1978, 1979, 1980, 1981, 1982, 1983 by Mary Oliver. By permission of Little, Brown and Company. All rights reserved.

Charles Olson. "Maximus, to himself" from *The Maximus Poems* by Charles Olson, ed. by George F. Butterick. Copyright © 1983. Reproduced with permission of the University of California Press via Copyright Clearance Center.

George Oppen. "Myself I Sing" from *New Collected Poems*, copyright © 1962 by George Oppen. Reprinted by permission of New Directions Publishing Corp.

Simon J. Ortiz. "Speaking" from *Woven Stone*. Copyright © 1992. Reprinted with the permission of the author.

Linda Pastan. "love poem" from *The Imperfect Paradise*. Copyright © 1988 by Linda Pastan. Used by permission of the author and W. W. Norton & Company, Inc.

Marge Piercy. "Barbie Doll" from *Circles on the Water*, copyright © 1982 by Middlemarsh, Inc. Used by permission of Alfred A. Knopf, a division of Random House, Inc. Any third party use of this material, outside of this publication, is prohibited. Interested parties must apply directly to Random House, Inc. for permission.

Wang Ping. "Syntax" from *Of Flesh & Spirit*. Copyright © 1998 by Wang Ping. Reprinted with the permission of The Permissions Company, Inc., on behalf of Coffee House Press, www.coffeehousepress.org.

Robert Pinsky. "Shirt" from *The Want Bone*. Copyright © 1990 by Robert Pinsky. Reprinted by permission of HarperCollins Publishers.

Sylvia Plath. "Metaphors" from *Crossing the Water*. Copyright © 1960 by Ted Hughes. "Morning Song" from *Ariel*. Copyright © 1961 by Ted Hughes. Sylvia Plath, "Daddy" from *Ariel*. Copyright © 1963 by Ted Hughes. Reprinted by permission of HarperCollins Publishers and Faber & Faber Ltd.

Ezra Pound. "The River-Merchant's Wife: A Letter," original by Rihaku, and "In a Station of the Metro" from *Personae*, copyright © 1926 by Ezra Pound. Reprinted by permission of New Directions Publishing Corp.

Dudley Randall. "Ballad of Birmingham" from *Roses and Revolutions* (2009) is reprinted by permission of the Dudley Randall Literary Estate.

John Crowe Ransom. "Bells for John Whiteside's Daughter" from *Selected Poems* by John Crowe Ransom, copyright 1924 by Alfred A. Knopf, a division of Random House, Inc. and renewed 1952 by John Crowe Ransom. Used by permission of Alfred A. Knopf, a division of Random House, Inc. Any third party use of this material, outside of this publication, is prohibited. Interested parties must apply directly to Random House, Inc. for permission.

Donald Revell. "Mignonette" from *From the Abandoned Cities*. Copyright © 1983 by Donald Revell. Reprinted by permission of HarperCollins Publishers.

Adrienne Rich. "Aunt Jennifer's Tigers." Copyright © 2002, 1951 by Adrienne Rich. "Diving into the Wreck." Copyright © 1973 by Adrienne Rich. From *The Fact of a Doorframe: Selected Poems 1950–2001* by Adrienne Rich. Used by permission of W. W. Norton & Company, Inc.

Atsuro Riley. "Drill" from *Romey's Order*, copyright © 2010 by The University of Chicago. Reprinted by permission of the University of Chicago Press.

Alberto Ríos. "Nani" from *Whispering to Fool the Wind* (1982). Reprinted by permission of the Sheep Meadow Press.

Theodore Roethke. "My Papa's Waltz," copyright © 1942 by Hearst Magazines, Inc., and "Elegy for Jane," copyright © 1950 by Theodore Roethke from *Collected Poems of Theodore Roethke*. Used by permission of Doubleday, a division of Random House, Inc. Any third party use of this material, outside of this publication, is prohibited. Interested parties must apply directly to Random House, Inc. for permission.

Mary Ruefle. "Barbarians" from *Life Without Speaking* (University of Alabama Press, 1987) is reprinted by permission of the author.

Mary Jo Salter. "Half a Double Sonnet" from *Sunday Skaters*, copyright © 1994 by Mary Jo Salter. Used by permission of Alfred A. Knopf, a division of Random House, Inc. Any third party use of this material, outside of this publication, is prohibited. Interested parties must apply directly to Random House, Inc. for permission.

Thom Satterlee. "Question 4: Whether, Once Wounded by Love, One Ever Heals Completely?" from *Burning Wyclif*, copyright © 2006 by Thom Satterlee. Used by permission of Texas Tech University Press, www.ttupress.org.

Anne Sexton. "Cinderella," copyright © 1971 by Anne Sexton, renewed 1999 by Linda G. Sexton. Reprinted by permission of Houghton Mifflin Harcourt Publishing Company. All rights reserved.

Leslie Marmon Silko. "Prayer to the Pacific" from *Storyteller*, copyright © 1981 by Leslie Marmon Silko. Used by permission of Viking Penguin, a division of Penguin Group (USA) Inc.

Charles Simic. "Begotten of the Spleen" from *Selected Early Poems* by Charles Simic. Copyright © 1999 by Charles Simic. Reprinted by permission of George Braziller, Inc., New York. All rights reserved.

Edith Sitwell. "Lullaby" from *Collected Poems* is reprinted by permission of Peters Fraser & Dunlop, www.petersfraserdunlop.com, on behalf of the Estate of Edith Sitwell.

Gary Snyder. "Hitch Haiku" from *The Back Country*, copyright © 1968 by Gary Snyder. Reprinted by permission of New Directions Publishing Corp.

Cathy Song. "Girl Powdering Her Neck" from *Picture Bride*. Copyright © 1982 by Yale University Press. Reprinted with the permission of Yale University Press.

Gary Soto. "Moving Away" from *New and Selected Poems*, copyright © 1995 by Gary Soto. Used with permission of Chronicle Books LLC, San Francisco. Visit ChronicleBooks.com.

William Stafford. "Traveling through the Dark" from *The Way It Is: New and Selected Poems*. Copyright © 1962, 1998 by William Stafford and the Estate of William Stafford. Reprinted with the permission of The Permissions Company, Inc. on behalf of Graywolf Press, Minneapolis, Minnesota, www.graywolfpress .org.

A. E. Stallings. "Olives" from *Olives: Poems* (TriQuarterly Books) is reprinted by permission of the publisher Northwestern University Press.

Gerald Stern. "The Dog." Copyright © 1987 by Gerald Stern, from *This Time: New and Selected Poems*. Used by permission of the author and W. W. Norton & Company, Inc.

Wallace Stevens. "The Emperor of Ice-Cream," "Thirteen Ways of Looking at a Blackbird," and "Sunday Morning" from *The Collected Poems of Wallace Stevens*, copyright 1954 by Wallace Stevens and renewed 1982 by Holly Stevens. Used by permission of Alfred A. Knopf, a division of Random House, Inc. Any third party use of this material, outside of this publication, is prohibited. Interested parties must apply directly to Random House, Inc. for permission.

Ruth Stone. "What We Have" from *In the Next Galaxy*. Copyright © 2002 by Ruth Stone. Reprinted with the permission of The Permissions Company, Inc. on behalf of Copper Canyon Press, www.coppercanyonpress.org.

Mark Strand. "Eating Poetry" from *Reasons for Moving; Darker; The Sargentville Notebook*, copyright © 1973 by Mark Strand. Used by permission of Alfred A. Knopf, a division of Random House, Inc. Any third party use of this material, outside of this publication is prohibited. Interested parties must apply directly to Random House, Inc. for permission.

Virgil Suárez. "Tea Leaves, *Caracoles*, Coffee Beans" from *90 Miles: Selected and New Poems*, by Virgil Suárez, copyright © 2005. Reprinted by permission of the University of Pittsburgh Press.

Sekou Sundiata. "Blink Your Eyes." Reprinted with the permission of the Estate of Robert F. Feaster.

James Tate. "The Wheelchair Butterfly" from *Selected Poems*, copyright © 1991 by James Tate. Reprinted by permission of Wesleyan University Press.

Dylan Thomas. "Fern Hill" from *The Poems of Dylan Thomas*, copyright © 1945 by The Trustees for the Copyrights of Dylan Thomas. "Do not go gentle into that good night," copyright © 1952 by Dylan Thomas. Reprinted by permission of New Directions Publishing Corp.

Jean Toomer. "Face" from *Cane*. Copyright © 1923 by Boni & Liveright, renewed 1951 by Jean Toomer. Used by permission of Liveright Publishing Corporation.

Natasha Trethewey. "History Lesson" from *Domestic Work*. Copyright © 2009 by Natasha Trethewey. Reprinted with the permission of The Permissions Company, Inc., on behalf of Graywolf Press, Minneapolis, MN, www.graywolfpress .org.

Quincy Troupe. "A Poem for "'Magic'" from *Avalanche*. Copyright © 1996 by Quincy Troupe. Reprinted with the permission of The Permissions Company, Inc., on behalf of Coffee House Press, www.coffeehousepress.com.

Catherine Tufariello. "This Child" by Catherine Tufariello from *Keeping My Name*, copyright © 2004 by Catherine Tufariello. By permission of Texas Tech University Press, www.ttupress.org.

Jean Valentine. "Dec. 21st" from *Door in the Mountain: New and Collected Poems, 1965–2003*. Copyright © 2004 by Jean Valentine. Reprinted by permission of Wesleyan University Press.

A. Van Jordan. "From," from *M-A-C-N-O-L-I-A: Poems* by A. Van Jordan. Copyright © 2004 by A. Van Jordan. Used by permission of the author and W. W. Norton & Company, Inc.

Ellen Bryant Voigt. "The Lotus Flowers" from *The Lotus Flowers*. Copyright © 1987 by Ellen Bryant Voigt. Used by permission of the author and W. W. Norton & Company, Inc.

Derek Walcott. "Sea Grapes" from *Collected Poems 1948–1984* by Derek Walcott. Copyright ©1986 by Derek Walcott. Reprinted by permission of Farrar, Straus and Giroux, LLC.

Anne Waldman. "Icy Rose" from *Life Notes*. Copyright © 1973 by Amy Waldman. Reprinted with the permission of the author.

James Welch. "Christmas Comes to Moccasin Flat" from *Riding the Earthboy 40* by James Welch, copyright © 1971, 1976, 1990 by James Welch. Used by permission of Penguin, a division of Penguin Group (USA) Inc.

Richard Wilbur. "Love Calls Us to the Things of This World" from *Things of This World*, copyright © 1956 and renewed 1984 by Richard Wilbur, reprinted by permission of Houghton Mifflin Harcourt Publishing Company. All rights reserved.

Nancy Willard. "Questions My Son Asked Me, Answers I Never Gave Him" from *Household Tales of Moon and Water*, copyright © 1978 by Nancy Willard, reprinted by permission of Houghton Mifflin Harcourt Publishing Company. All rights reserved.

William Carlos Williams. "The Red Wheelbarrow," "This Is Just to Say," and "Spring and All, Section 1" from *The Collected Poems: Volume 1, 1909–1939*, copyright © 1938 by New Directions Publishing Corp. Reprinted by permission of New Directions Publishing Corp.

Charles Wright. "Reunion" from *Country Music: Selected Early Poems*, copyright © 1991 by Charles Wright. Reprinted by permission of Wesleyan University Press.

James Wright. "A Blessing" from *The Branch Will Not Break*, copyright © 1963 by James Wright. Reprinted by permission of Wesleyan University Press.

William Butler Yeats. "Leda and the Swan" is reprinted with the permission of Scribner, a Division of Simon & Schuster, Inc. from *The Collected Works of W. B. Yeats, Volume One: The Poems*, rev. by W. B. Yeats, ed. by Richard J. Finneran. Copyright 1928 by The Macmillan Company, renewed 1956 by Georgie Yeats. All rights reserved.

Al Young. "A Dance for Ma Rainey" from *Heaven: Collected Poems 1956–1990* (Creative Arts Book Company, 1992). Copyright © 1992, 2007 by Al Young. Reprinted with permission of the author.

Kevin Young. "Song of Smoke," copyright © 2003 by Kevin Young. Used by permission of Alfred A. Knopf, a division of Random House, Inc. Any third party

Art

Index of Authors, Titles, and First Lines

When I was fair and young, and favor
graced me, 9
*When Lilacs Last in the Dooryard
Bloom'd*, 82
When snow like sheep lay in the fold,
194
Which reminds me of another knock-
on-wood, 236
While my hair was still cut straight
across my forehead, 118
WHITMAN, WALT, 69, 82, 89, 363
Whose woods these are I think I
know, 109
Why Can't I Leave You?, 240
Why I Am Not a Painter, 174
Why I Left the Church, 225
WILBUR, RICHARD, 168, 364
Wild Iris, The, 230
Wild Nights—Wild Nights!, 91
WILLARD, NANCY, 206, 364
WILLIAMS, WILLIAM CARLOS, 116,
117, 118, 364
WORDSWORTH, WILLIAM, 39, 43,
44, 50, 364
World is too much with us, The, 50

Would she have been a person, 271
WRIGHT, CHARLES, 204, 365
WRIGHT, JAMES, 181, 365
WROTH, LADY MARY, 18, 365
WYATT, SIR THOMAS, 9, 365

YEATS, WILLIAM BUTLER, 98, 99,
366
Yellow Light, 252
You always read about it, 183
You are clear, 119
You are the bread and the knife, 221
You do not do, you do not do, 195
You might have heard a story like this
one well, 293
YOUNG, AL, 214, 366
YOUNG, KEVIN, 297, 366
YOUNG BEAR, RAY A., 249, 367
You're just like every toad I've ever
met, 292
You stand behind the old black mare,
240

ZIMMER, PAUL, 203, 367
Zimmer Imagines Heaven, 203